Land Warfare: Brassey
Weapons Systems and T

Volume 7

FIGHTING VEHICLES

Land Warfare:
Brassey's New Battlefield Weapons Systems and Technology Series

---

The success of the first series on Battlefield Weapons Systems and Technology and the pace of advances in military technology have prompted Brassey's to produce a new Land Warfare series. This series updates subjects covered in the original series and also covers completely new areas. The books are written for military personnel who wish to advance their professional knowledge. In addition, they are intended to aid anyone who is interested in the design, development and production of military equipment.

Volume 1 Guided Weapons—R G Lee *et al.*

Volume 2 Explosives, Propellants and Pyrotechnics—A Bailey and S G Murray

Volume 3 Noise in the Military Environment—R F Powell and M R Forrest

Volume 4 Ammunition for the Land Battle—P R Courtney-Green

Volume 5 Communications and Information Systems for Battlefield Command and Control—M A Rice and A J Sammes

Volume 6 Military Helicopters—E J Everett-Heath, G M Moss, A W Mowat and K E Reid

Volume 9 Radar—P S Hall, T K Garland-Collins, R S Picton and R G Lee

For full details of titles in this series, please contact your local Brassey's office.

FIGHTING

VEHICLES

T. W. TERRY

S. R. JACKSON

C. E. S. RYLEY

B. E. JONES

P. J. H. WORMELL

BRASSEY'S (UK)

A Member of the Maxwell Macmillan Group

LONDON · OXFORD · WASHINGTON · NEW YORK

UK (Editorial)	Brassey's (UK) Ltd., 50 Fetter Lane, London EC4A 1AA, England
(Orders, all except North America)	Brassey's (UK) Ltd., Headington Hill Hall, Oxford OX3 0BW, England
USA (Editorial)	Brassey's (US) Inc., 8000 Westpark Drive, Fourth Floor, McLean, Virginia 22102, USA
(Orders, North America)	Brassey's (US) Inc., Front and Brown Streets, Riverside, New Jersey 08075, USA Tel (toll free): 800 257 5755

First edition 1991

Library of Congress Cataloging in Publication Data

Fighting vehicles/T. W. Terry . . . [et al.]. — 1st ed.
p. cm. — (Land warfare, Brasseys new battlefield weapons systems & technology series: no 7)
Includes index.
1. Armored vehicles, Military. 2. Tanks (Military science)
I. Terry, T. W. II. Title. III. Series.
UG446.5.F54 1990 358′.18—dc20 90-44579

British Library Cataloguing in Publication Data

Fighting vehicles.
1. Military vehicles, history
I. Terry, T. W.
623.747

ISBN 0-08-036705-4 Hard cover
ISBN 0-08-036704-6 Flexi cover

Front cover photo: M1A1 Abrams MBT (*courtesy General Dynamics Land Systems*)
Frontispiece photos: Vickers Valkyr (*courtesy Vickers Defence Systems*)

Printed in Great Britain by BPCC Wheatons Ltd., Exeter

Preface

This Series
This series of books is written for those who wish to improve their knowledge of military weapons and equipment. It is equally relevant to professional soldiers, those involved in developing or producing military weapons or indeed anyone interested in the art of modern warfare.

All the texts are written in a way which assumes no mathematical knowledge and no more technical depth than would be gleaned by any person who keeps himself or herself informed of developments in the modern world. It is intended that the books should be of particular interest to officers in the Armed Services wishing to further their professional knowledge as well as anyone involved in research, development, production, testing and maintenance of defence equipments.

The principal authors of the books are all members of the staff of the Royal Military College of Science, Shrivenham, which is composed of a unique blend of academic and military experts. They are not only leaders in the technology of their subjects, but are aware of what the military practitioner needs to know. It is difficult to imagine any group of persons more fitted to write about the application of technology to the battlefield.

This Volume
Fighting Vehicles provides an understanding of the military vehicles required by an army and explains which type is best suited to the operational requirement, the terrain and the battlefield conditions. It examines the principles of design of a whole range of armoured vehicles, both wheeled and tracked, in such a way which does not demand a detailed technical education: an understanding of general mechanical and electrical principles would be an asset but essentially an interest in armoured vehicles is all that is required.

To save constant explanation of the many technical terms which are an inescapable part of the study of this subject, a full Glossary has been included at the back of the book.

December 1990
Shrivenham

Geoffrey Lee

Acknowledgements

The authors wish to thank all those who have helped in their many and various ways with advice and assistance. This includes a number of Ministry of Defence (Army Department) branches, Research and Development Establishments and the various Academic Departments of the Royal Military College of Science, Shrivenham and the Library at the Royal Armoured Corps Centre. Their co-operation and kindness has been unstinting and has been a major factor in the production of this Volume.

Crown Copyright photographs reproduced by kind permission of The Controller of H.M.S.O.

St. Christopher House
December 1990

T.W.T.
B.E.J.
P.J.H.W.
C.E.S.R.
S.R.J.

Contents

List of Illustrations and Tables

Chapter 3 The Weapon System

Chapter 11 Running Gear—Wheels

1

The Evolution of the Tank

Origins

The concept of an 'armoured' fighting vehicle does not, as many people think, start with the introduction of the tank during the Great War. The earliest ancestor of the tank was probably the war chariot, as used by the Assyrians, Syrians and the Egyptians in Biblical times. The warrior was armed with bow and arrow; javelin for long range attack and sword and shield for close quarter engagement. The chariot gave good service for many generations and in many wars. Its weakness lay in the absence of protection for the horse, the chariot's sole means of propulsion, as any additional armoured protection had to be balanced by an increase in the power requirements—a dilemma encountered today in the design of the chariot's modern counterpart, the tank. Nevertheless, the chariot was the first vehicle that enabled armies to exploit mobility and shock action. In all contests the more agile and mobile of opponents have always had the advantage of seizing and maintaining the initiative—factors so obviously lacking in the conduct of the First World War until the advent of the modern tank enabled commanders to break away from the stagnation of trench warfare.

The next development of the 'armoured warrior' idea was the knight of the Middle Ages. Encased in mail or plate, he was impervious to the missiles of the time but his total weight demanded strong but inevitably slow horses and the special mounting methods, usually steps or some type of crane, rendered him virtually useless should he become dismounted. For a thousand years he ruled the battlefields of Europe. No infantryman could stand up to him in an open fight and the battles resolved themselves into duels between groups of these protected figures in which victory was determined by superiority of discipline and tactics rather than armament or skill at arms. The weakness of this prototype of the tank was that as he was a shock action warrior only and could not hit at a distance: walls, ramparts or even simple natural obstacles such as ditches could provide almost complete protection against him. Improved missiles enabled suitably armed but more mobile infantrymen to keep the knight at arms' length where he could not use his sword or lance and his attempts to regain his invincibility by means of thicker and therefore heavier armour merely reduced his mobility even further. Finally, it became clear that complete protection could not be provided without making both the rider and horse so ponderous and clumsy that their capability for shock action was all but eliminated. The uncontested supremacy of the mailed horseman on the battlefield was at an end.

Meanwhile an interesting variation of the basic idea of the armoured knight had developed. Designs for some sort of a battle car which would enable soldiers to fire on the move appeared from all sources. Leonardo da Vinci, for instance, told a friend in 1482: 'I am building secure and covered chariots which are invulnerable, and when they advance with their guns into the midst of their foe, even the largest enemy masses must retreat and behind them the infantry can follow in safety without opposition'—indicating an understanding of the need for infantry-tank co-operation some four centuries before Cambrai and forgotten on numerous occasions since.

There were many other designs for battle cars before and after Leonardo's time. Some of them actually appeared on the battlefield but all were incapable of much movement once the fighting had begun. Therein lay the main problem of the battle car—its motive power—as until the invention of the steam engine the only possible sources of motive power were man or horse. In the last third of the 18th century, when the steam age may be said to have begun, the idea of a mobile, protected machine was revived. In France, as early as 1769, a Monsieur Cugnot produced a steam propelled wagon designed for war purposes. Its first and only public outing was disastrous and landed the inventor in gaol as he was unable to pay the bill for a wall demolished by the machine. Nevertheless, the steam engine demonstrated that it could provide a mobile power source and was utilised with success by the railways. Its application to road movement however, was to prove less successful, mainly due to the relatively heavy weight of the engine itself, the need to carry a large volume of coal and water for the boiler and the difficulty of keeping a suitable head of steam while in motion. The resultant heavy weight favoured rail as a means of achieving a form of strategic mobility rather than the tactical or battlefield mobility sought by the tank designers.

It was not long before cross country movement became possible thanks to the various devices designed to replace the heavily-laden wheels and thus to distribute the weight of the vehicle more evenly. The most efficient of these took the form of a series of short planks attached to the wheels which came down to the ground in succession as the wheels revolved and so formed a sort of endless 'track' for them to rest on. The tracks of all military tanks from their first appearance in 1916 to the present time as still designed on this principle.

By 1890, a form of track had been developed which was, in effect, an endless chain encircling the wheels of the vehicle. The track was (and still is) laid in the path of the vehicle and picked up as the machine moved forward or backwards, this process being facilitated by the use of toothed wheels (or sprockets) at either the front or rear of the wheel system. However, important though this inovation was, the problem of finding a satisfactory means of propulsion remained. Though powerful, steam engines were bulky, conspicuous and, worst of all, unreliable. Not until the advent of the internal combustion engine at the end of the 19th century was a solution in sight.

The Need for a Tank

Initially, the internal combustion engine was regarded as only suitable to replace the horse where hard surfaced roads existed. Indeed, the early vehicles were so unreliable that they invited rejection by the military authorities with their instinctive distrust of any form of innovation.

Between the years 1900 and 1914, many designs were put forward and many experimental vehicles constructed from which a satisfactory tank might well have evolved. Indeed, more than one was, in fact, evolved; the designs and specifications were submitted to the then War Office in London and duly pigeon-holed, only to be rediscovered after the First World War had ended. Fortunately, the matter was not left exclusively in the hands of the General Staff, for if it had, it is possible that the tank would have yet to be conceived.

At the outbreak of the First World War all those concerned—save a few hundred unheeded voices—expected it to be bloody but certainly brisk and brief: all save the few hundred were completely wrong. After some initial swaying to and fro in the winter of 1914, the armies found themselves facing each other from Belgium to the Swiss border. Both sides set to work to dig and put up wire and fortify and along the whole front there developed a state of siege on a scale unprecedented in history. Impassable jungles of barbed wire appeared, backed by machine guns and massed artillery and, for the first time, surveyed and directed from the air by man in aircraft rather than the balloon.

The most obvious way to break the stalemate was to take a leaf from the book of siege warfare and blow a breach in the enemy defences by a combination of the use of massed guns and mines. The earliest attempts to employ this strategy were successful enough, despite the heavy casualties, to encourage further attempts. But this road turned out to be a dead end as the enemy garrison only superficially resembled a siege fortress. There was no wall to be breached but a series of barbed wire entanglements and as each was cut so the next was revealed beyond. Often, too, the rear lines were out of range of the artillery as they have been sited for the first state of the assault and no further support could be provided until the guns had been moved forward, giving more time for the enemy to prepare for the next assault. The commanders believed they knew the answer—more men, more guns and more ammunition woud guarantee victory if only the nations would provide them in sufficient quantity. But the more men that were supplied, the more the losses mounted and the more untrained were their replacements; the more intense were the artillery barrages, the more impassable became the ground over which the infantry and the supporting guns had to advance. So strong was the conviction in generals and statesmen alike that victory would inevitably result that even the idea of a tank seemed sufficiently doubtful to justify the search for any alternative to the current stalemate.

Early Development

The requirement for some device to traverse the mud and shell-cratered battlefield, break through the wire fortifications and overcome the trenches became paramount; and in 1915 all efforts were devoted to producing such a machine. Off-road vehicles had not received the same intensive development in Britain as they had in the United States where the need to travel across vast tracts of undeveloped land had inspired several versions of track laying vehicles. Early attempts were directed towards a 'big wheeled' machine but it soon became apparent that the sheer size of the wheel required to surmount the likely obstacles and to cross trenches would lead to a vehicle of immense size and weight and very doubtful mobility.

Attention then focused on some form of track-laying device. The 'footed' wheel was heavy and gave little advantage over the conventional farm tractor wheel but track-laying tractors were now being built embodying some of the earlier pioneer work of Hornsby who had sold the patents to the American tractor firm of Holt's in 1912. The War Office pursued several lines of inquiry but the most likely contenders were the entirely British 'Pedrail' together with the Killen-Strait and Bullock tractors, the latter of American origin. All these machines demonstrated, to a greater or lesser extent, a capability to meet the mobility requirements. The problem now was to develop what was basically a farm tractor into a machine of war. The firm of Foster & Co, an engineering company in Lincoln, had successfully

FIG. 1.1 Killen-Strait tractor.

utilised the Holt track system to produce a cross-country tractor capable of pulling several trailers over broken ground and minor obstacles. Producing a modified vehicle capable of crossing an 8-foot wide trench would be a severe test of their engineering skills, but as they seemed to be the firm most likely to succeed, the contract was awarded to them. The original design was a failure but the next prototype using an improved pressed steel track showed great promise and came to be called 'Little Willie'. As is usually the case with any worthwhile invention several different people appear to have thought of the tank at about the same time and indeed an official committee after the War had considerable difficulty in coming to a decision and having it accepted by all the claimants. But it is safe to say that had it not been for Colonel E. W. Swinton of the Royal Engineers, an

FIG. 1.2 Little Willie.

official correspondent with the British Expeditionary Force in France and later Secretary of the Government War Committee, the tank would never come into being at all in time to prove itself in the later stage of the First World War. Although Swinton's brilliant and visionary ideas failed to gain acceptance either in the War Office or General Headquarters in France, all was not lost. An equally far sighted and vigorous thinker, Mr Winston Churchill, then First Lord of the Admiralty, had come to realise the pressing need for action and set up a Landship Committee, under the Director of Naval Construction, Mr Eustace Tennyson D'Eyncourt, and an experimental body to study and develop the landship idea. Although Swinton's memorandum had fallen on stony ground in the Army, the basic principles of design that it contained and the tactical concepts he outlined for the employment of a fighting machine were to prove thoroughly sound and, in the end, came to fruition—but not before much time, money and blood had been wasted—as was the vital element of surprise upon which the initial success of any new weapon system must to some extent rely. Thus it is fair to say that it was, in reality, Swinton who was the real founder of the tank idea and who was responsible for raising, training and inspiring the early tank units, providing them with the basic principles upon which their handling of the new arm in battle was to rest but that it was Churchill who broke down the barriers of reaction and made the whole thing possible. Happily, both were supported by some brilliant subordinates. After a difficult birth, the new arm was ready to step forward but its teething troubles would prove formidable and it was to be many months before it was able to prove beyond any doubt that Swinton and Churchill were right and that a new era in warfare had begun.

At this time there were two remarkable men at Fosters in Lincoln. They were

William Tritton, the Managing Director and Major Walter Wilson who was attached on special duty from the War Office. Together they were responsible for the successful translation of the military requirements into hardware. They realised that although the demonstration of 'Little Willie' had been successful, it could not meet Swinton's demands for a 2.4 metre (8 feet) trench crossing capability, a speed of 6.5 kph (4 mph) and an ability to climb 1.8 metre (5 feet) parapets. The paramount requirement to cross the 2.4 metre gap and to breach the barbed wire entanglements inevitably led to a reassessment and from this came the classical rhomboid shape of the British First World War tanks. There was an obvious need for secrecy and after much deliberation a cover story was evolved to explain these strange shapes to the mainly women workers at Fosters. They were told that they were manufacturing tracked vehicles for use in Mesopotamia to carry water to the drought areas—an unusual and highly implausible cover story which would involve the diversion of valuable resources at a time when the remainder of the nation was fully employed on armament production. The women decided that 'water tanks' or simple 'tanks' was easier to say than 'water carriers for Mesopotamia' and a new word entered the English language.

It would be fair to say that the story of tank design and production revolved round three men, Tritton, Wilson and Albert Stern, a banker who was impressed into the Navy to be Secretary of the Landship Committee and then became a soldier—in charge first of the Tank Supply Department and later Director General of the Department of Mechanical War Supply (as a Lieutenant Colonel!). Tritton and Wilson were the creators of the hardware but it was Stern who had to fight the Whitehall battle and persuade a reluctant War Office and Treasury to authorise the production of tanks on the scale which was essential if success in battle was to be assured.

Early Solutions

Although there was a process of continued development during the War, the basic configuration of the British tanks remained unchanged. The early Mark 1 tanks had two 6-pounder guns, one mounted in each sponson on either side of the hull. These 'long' 6-pounders were naval guns adapted for military use and although they were fairly accurate, the length of the barrel made them heavy and cumbersome to operate. Later marks of the 'Male' tank, as the 6-pounder version became known, were fitted with the short barrel version seen in Figure 1.3 below. The 'Female' tanks were armed only with Lewis machine guns but as the main task of both types of tank was to break through the enemy trenches and wire entanglements this could be accomplished as easily by a tank armed with machine guns as with one mounting 6-pounders. Later, as we shall be concerned with the various factors which affect the design of the modern tank, it is worth examining some of the main characteristics of the 1916 design. The most obvious feature is the rhomboid shape with a high front idler, over two metres from the ground. This very high (by modern standards) idler height was required in order to give the tank an exceptionally good step-climbing ability on the battlefield. However, it meant that the track had to be carried along the top of the hull and it became impossible to mount a rotating gun turret on top without increasing yet further the tank's

FIG. 1.3 British Mk V 'Male' tank fitted with the short barrel version of the Naval 6-pounder gun.

overall height, raising the centre of gravity and making the vehicle top heavy. No suspension system was fitted and though the maximum speed was only 8 kph (5 mph) the crew inevitably had a very rough ride. They had also to contend with the heat, noise and fumes from the 150 hp engine mounted in the centre of the vehicle. An added danger was bullet splash as the armour was only boiler plate riveted on to a metal framework, leaving many small cracks for hot bullet fragments to find their way inside. To combat this, the crew had to wear protective masks and helmets, made of chain mail and leather, which added to their discomfort.

As can be seen, the Mark I tank was a very rudimentary vehicle. Its mechanical reliability was poor and it had a very limited radius of action. To help overcome the difficulties of steering, a pair of heavy wheels was attached to the tail of the machine on the earliest models. For all its failings, to have got the tank into service and into battle in seven months from the date of the Hatfield Park demonstration was a near miracle of organisation and training, bringing great credit to all concerned, from Fosters' shop floor to the crews of the vehicles.

The propulsion train ran from the centrally mounted engine through a clutch to a primary gearbox, a differential and out to the steering gearboxes, one for each track. The power was then transmitted to the sprockets by chains. The vehicle was steered, as in all track-laying vehicles, by achieving some speed differential between the two tracks, either by braking or gearing. In these early marks of tanks this was accomplished by giving the two gearsmen signals to change gears in either the left or right hand track gearbox according to the direction which the commander wished to go. In his book *Tanks in the Great War*, J. F. C. Fuller (who was the senior staff officer at Tank Corps Headquarters in France until the end of the war and became one of the great 'prophets' of armoured warfare) writes that the system was 'exceedingly clumsy and often involved much loss of temper'. The task of general coordination fell to the driver who controlled the engine speed and would signal to the gearsmen (either by gesture or by blows with a hammer on the hull) when he wanted to change direction. This situation persisted until the introduction of the Mark V in 1918. Fitted with Wilson's epicyclic gearbox, this machine gave the driver full control of the vehicle. This leap forward in design also enabled the commander to concentrate much more upon his principal task instead of having to keep an eye on the driver and the two gearsmen. For the first time, too, the tank had a specially designed engine—the 6-cylinder 150 horsepower Ricardo. Fuller describes the improvements by saying 'great progress was made in the all-round speed, ease of manoeuvre, radius of action, simplicity of control and feasibility of observation'—all characteristics we look for in a modern battle tank.

It was in the role of machine gun destroyer and barbed wire crusher that the first British tanks went into action on 15 September 1916 in the Somme. Instead of being held back in secrecy until they could be used *en masse* in one large combined operation, they were sent forward in driblets on a wide front. The ground for their attack, instead of being specially chosen to comply with their known limitation, was totally unsuitable. The time allowed for reconnaissance, the marking of routes through our own trench systems and other necessary preparations was totally inadequate. The artillery had not had time to prepare and to organise themselves to support the new weapon and the infantry did not have the faintest idea how to exploit the situation should the tanks achieve a breakthrough. Such success as was achieved was due mainly to the effectiveness of the armoured protection which enabled the tanks to disregard the machine gun fire, giving rise to the view that armoured protection was the principle characteristic of the tank. From this inauspicious beginning came the many erroneous conclusions amongst which was the suggestion that the tank was finished whenever the enemy produced a new anti-armour weapon.

The new Tank Corps had only one more battle day on the Somme, at the end of November, when the foul weather conditions and mud made its action ineffective. Then the winter pause set in and the great secret had been given away to no purpose whatever.

By now, the Mark IV had become the workhorse of the Tank Corps. With greatly improved reliability, better quality armour and redesigned gun sponsons, which swung inwards to ease the problems of travel by rail. It was to give yeoman service until well beyond the arrival of the first Mark Vs.

During the winter of 1917 the Tank Corps and indeed the tank itself were under a cloud and much time was devoted to questions of tactics and training. The War Office and General Headquarters could not make up their minds whether they wanted a new and more formidable type of tank or whether the existing Mark IV machines, slightly modified, would serve for the next year's battles. Their hesitation was disastrous for before they had finished their discussions, the matter had been decided for them and it was too late to re-arm the Tank Corps. This was a serious blunder as the Mark V had been designed and could have been produced in large numbers by the spring of 1917. The tanks were sent into action again in a desultory and haphazard fashion in the early part of 1917—at Arras in April—where they faced the armour-piercing ammunition recently developed by the Germans and later at Messines and at Passchendaele. A fiasco occurred at Bullecourt where the Australians refused to have anything to do with the 'infernal machines' and it was a year before they agreed to work with them again. The opinion of other formations that summer of the usefulness of the tank was not all that different from the Australians more forcefully expressed view; and the experiences of our other Allies also did little to counteract the unfavourable verdict of the new weapon system.

The battle of Cambrai, which took place in the last week of November 1917, formed a landmark in the history of war. Even then it was not fought as the Tank Corps staff had planned. The battle was important because it proved conclusively the value of the tank as a new weapon which, within a year, was to furnish the Allies with victory and the general, though belated, realisation of the tank's role in the new age of mechanised warfare. Not to be outdone, the other participants in this combat had been forced into hasty development of some form of 'tank'. The Germans had produced a curious shaped vehicle on tracks which suffered from severe mobility difficulties, most notably in its inability to cross trenches (see Figure 1.4) The French produced a similar shaped vehicle but this also have several shortcomings and it was left to Colonel Etienne to prompt Renault to design the successful Mark 17 light tank (see Figure 1.5). This design was also adopted by the Americans in 1917 although few ever went into action in Europe. The Americans also became involved in an Anglo-American project for the 38-ton Mark VII which was really the last of the rhomboid shaped tanks.

FIG. 1.4 The German A7V tank.

FIG. 1.5 The French Renault M17 tank.

Development Between the Wars

British Developments

When the Great War ended in November 1918 the British Tank Corps was the best equipped and most efficient in the world. But peace brought many changes, most notably the demobilisation of practically the whole Tank Corps and, more seriously, the personnel involved in vehicle design. The result was that all research work stopped and the Corps was left to do the best it could with old tanks and new, inexperienced men. Things remained in this state of suspended animation for five years. These were years of much theoretical discussion and debate but as far as any practical progress was concerned, the British Army had lost its lead in tank design.

Nevertheless, Vickers, the makers of the successful Mark V tank, saw the commercial possibilities and their ideas led to the Vickers Medium Mark II (Figure 1.6), produced in 1923. As a vehicle it was well in advance of anything produced by any other country. It had a maximum speed of about 32 kph (20 mph), a fully rotating turret, a rudimentary suspension system and a reasonable radius of action. As a fighting machine however, it left a lot to be desired. The first models were so thinly armoured that they could be penetrated by ordinary bullets at close range; the later versions did have better protection but the extra weight reduced their speed very considerably and the increased wear on engine and tracks made the tank less reliable.

FIG. 1.6 Vickers Medium Mk II, 16 tons.

The 1920s and 1930s led to various extremes in design, some never getting beyond the drawing board and even fewer beyond the prototype stage. Tank development in the 20 years after the Great War resulted in the then British Royal Tank Corps being armed with the three categories of tanks summarised below:

A light tank of between 2 to 8 tons with a crew of 2 or 3 and armed with either 1 or 2 machine guns.

A medium tank of about 18 tons with a maximum speed of 48 kph (30 mph), a crew of 5 or 6 men and armed with a light gun and machine guns, either mounted coaxially with the main armament in the turret or, additionally, in the hull.

A close support tank for work with the infantry weighing up to 30 tons, a speed of under 25 kph (15 mph), much thicker armour and armed with a light gun in the main turret and machine guns in smaller turrets.

Although these vehicles never fired a round in anger they undoubtedly provided the means to test the various tactics that formed the basis of the armoured battles to come. Because everything was subordinated to protection, their firepower suffered to the extent that they were virtually impotent against anything except the lightest opposition. The ultimate example of this unbalanced evolution was the British Churchill tank of 1941 with 10 cm (4 inch) thick armoured protection but only mounting a 40 mm gun (see Figure 1.7).

FIG. 1.7 The A22 Infantry Mk IV 'Churchill' (Mark I), 38.7 tons.

United States Development

The United States was not able to produce any home built tanks before the end of the War and those used by their Tank Corps were all French light Renaults or British mediums and heavies. Up to some fifteen years after the Armistice, though a large number of experimental models of all types were produced, the main United States tank armament continued to be of wartime pattern and, for the most part, were of wartime construction. Finally, a light tank, closely resembling the Vickers, was selected as the standard vehicle. Meanwhile, an inventive genius names Walter Christie put forward a series of ideas that were to have a profound and lasting effect on tank design. Christie was initially concerned with producing a vehicle that could run either on its tracks or wheels, thus avoiding the inherent unreliability that was the bane of all tracked vehicles of those days. After several revolutionary experimental vehicles, including the 8.6 ton, 40 kph (26 mph) wheeled and tracked tank, Christie concentrated on producing a fast, reliable tracked vehicle capable of maintaining high average speeds cross country.

The culmination of his designs was the M 1931 which incorporated his ideas of high power-to-weight ratio and large suspension travel achieved by springing each wheel independently through a bell crank arrangement coupled with a coil spring. Although the Americans purchased some of these vehicles, they never really took the design seriously and it was the Russians who, after purchasing two examples, developed it into a very fine tank the T34, which, on its first appearance in battle against the Germans gave new meaning to the phrase 'tactical mobility'.

FIG. 1.8 Experimental Christie tank M1928, 40 kph (26 mph) on tracks and 80 kph (50 mph) on wheels.

Tactical Development

It had been apparent, even as early as 1917, that armoured warfare would always be unable to realise its full potential unless the problems of communications could be solved. Semaphore helped with inter-vehicle communication and pigeons provided an unreliable and slow means of sending information back to headquarters but there was no means whereby the commander could send his orders forward once battle had been joined. By 1931, crystal controlled radios were available giving the commander an ability to contact a large number of widely spread vehicles by voice radio. The age of mobile armoured formations, able to react to plans while on the move, had dawned.

Despite the spirit of lethargy and the general revulsion for war which pervaded Britain in the 1920s and early 1930s, a small group of enthusiasts pushed relentlessly on to preserve and develop the 'tank idea'. J. F. C. Fuller (still a serving colonel and Military Assistant to the Chief of the Imperial General Staff—General Sir George Milne) and Basil Liddell Hart (military correspondent of the *Daily Telegraph*) blazed the trail through their lectures and writing and by making full use of their personal contacts at the higher levels in the War Office. In addition, Colonel Charles Broad, who was responsible for army organisation in the Directorate of Staff Duties, was writing speeches and lectures for Milne on the need for mechanisation. In 1929, Broad wrote that historic pamphlet on armoured warfare *Mechanised and Armoured Formations*, soon to be dubbed by the Army as 'the Purple Primer' and to prove a foundation stone for tactical policy on mechanised operations and formations and a source document for much of the thinking that was going on in both Germany and Russia as each built up their tank forces and developed their own philosophies.

It is one of the tragedies of British military history that, despite its lead in tactical thought and practical experience of the use of tanks, the Army became the victim of a combination of inter-arm prejudice, political indifference and cheese-paring parsimony of which the most pernicious aspect was a self-perpetuating political ordinance known as 'the ten year rule'. This 'rule' assumed that there would be no war in Europe within the next ten years and was responsible for a virtual stranglehold on funds for defence, particularly for new equipment. It was inevitable that such a situation should breed fierce competition for such funds as were available and would lead to the fuelling of the conservatism of those reactionaries who were determined to preserve the place of the horse on the battlefield at all costs—a prime cost was the development of the tank and the spirit of mechanisation, as we have already seen.

Inevitably there was a deep seated distrust and reluctance to accept the need for change, particularly amongst the cavalry. The feeling was probably strongest in the British Army but it was also present in the American, French and other European armies. Another factor which delayed the acceptance of a mobile armoured doctrine was what appeared to the generals to be the extremely high cost of the equipment itself, leading inevitably to an increasingly high proportion of the army's equipment budget being used solely to finance this new arm.

In 1927, General Milne set up what was known as the Experimental Mechanised Force at Tidworth under a Colonel Collins, an infantryman with no previous armoured experience. This mixed brigade-sized formation consisted of a tank battalion, some armoured cars, lorryborne infantry and mechanised artillery and engineers. Command had been offered to Fuller who, for reasons which need not concern us, turned it down. The force was short-lived and although it had a rather chequered career, some useful pointers for the future emerged—pointers which, once again, were not lost upon other armies. It was after this experiment that Broad wrote the 'Purple Primer' described above.

By 1934 a British tank brigade had been formed using a mixture of Vickers medium and light tanks. This brigade, together with the 7th Infantry Brigade and the mechanised 9th Field Brigade RA, took part in a major exercise on Salisbury Plain in September that year. The intention was to demonstrate the effectiveness of integrated mechanised formations and to learn from it so that the organisations and tactics for future armoured formations could be evolved. Unfortunately other factors, considered pertinent at the time, led the exercise controllers to place unrealistic constraints on the armoured formations with the result that the War Office adjudged the formation and modernisation of mobile armoured forces to be of a lower priority than the renovation of infantry divisions.

Other nations had been watching developments very closely, none more so than the Germans, who quickly realised the potential for such a force. Although the Germans did not form a tank battalion until 1934, by the end of 1935 they had three tank brigades and by 1939 had six armoured divisions while the British Army had but two incomplete divisions. An examination of some of the tactics employed by Guderian in 1940 and Patton in 1944 show a marked resemblance to the manner in which Hobart had deployed his forces in those exercises in 1934 on Salisbury Plain.

By 1936 it was apparent to even the most optimistic that Hitler's re-armament programme was a serious and deadly threat. Tank development in Britain was in the doldrums, hindered by the lack of money to explore new avenues and by rigid thinking which would not accept that mechanised warfare would be anything more than an extension of the tactics used in 1918.

The picture was very black indeed. The A6 or Vickers 16 ton tank which had been offered to the British Army in 1928 had been dropped as too expensive but it was a very fine tank indeed for its time and if the normal process of development had continued and it had entered service, doubtless we would have been in a far better position in 1939.

Lessons from the Second World War

Tank Characteristics

By the middle of the Second World War it was apparent that neither the light tanks nor the infantry tanks had any place on the battlefield. Additionally, the medium tank's main role of exploitation was being called into question as it was found that these tanks had to fight and win the battle before they could be used for any exploitation and their armament was simply not up to the task. With the ever-present problem of limited resources, it was neither possible nor prudent to expect to hold these tanks in reserve until a suitable exploitation role presented itself.

We now see how the tactics of the armoured formations were influencing the design of fighting vehicles. Each country was searching for a design which provided the optimum balance between firepower, mobility and protection—and all at an acceptable cost. Those, of course, are not the only characteristics of an armoured fighting vehicle but they are the most important and the secret of a successful design lies in the tank designer's ability to amalgamate aspects of all those characteristics without any one predominating and unbalancing the overall design. Other aspects which have to be considered to a greater or lesser extent are:

Availability, which includes Reliability and Maintainability
Communications
Surveillance
Endurance
Silence

Priorities of the Characteristics

The role of any combat vehicle is to carry a payload whether it be men, combat supplies or a gun and will determine the priority accorded to that characteristic in the overall vehicle design. For example, a reconnaissance vehicle requires high mobility and agility and low thermal and other signatures. This in turn demands small overall size and weight. On the other hand, since the Second World War all tank producing nations have acknowledged the pre-eminence of firepower but have given different emphasis to the relative merits of mobility and protection.

Throughout the greater part of the Second World War the tank was always vulnerable to an anti-tank defence system based on a large calibre high velocity gun, often towed but occasionally mounted on some sort of self-propelled chassis. The sheer size of these guns made it impossible to mount them on a conventional tank chassis of the early war years with their relatively small diameter turret ring. The Germans managed it at a later stage when they mounted the 88 mm anti-aircraft gun in their Tiger tanks which, in spite of some mechanical limitations and rather limited mobility, both of which sprang from their 56 tons weight, were to become a most menacing feature of the European battlefields. In Russia, where the vast plains and marshlands created tactical problems of their own, the Tiger was less effective.

One of the better designs to come out of the War was the British Centurion. Design work commenced in 1943 and a few prototypes were sent over to Europe in 1945 but were never used in action. This design was the culmination of all the lessons learned so expensively in the Western Desert and elsewhere. At last the Allies had a tank with a high velocity gun that was the match for any other tank on the battlefield and yet the design was sufficiently well balanced to provide good protection and, by the standards of time, good mobility. It was to be Britain's first Main Battle Tank.

The first Centurion mounted a 76.2 mm gun and a 20 mm Polson cannon but by 1948 the Mark III was fitted with a 84 mm high velocity gun and was a very efficient fighting machine incorporating the world's first gun stabilisation system. The basic concept for this tank, fitted with the ubiquitous Royal Ordnance 105 mm gun at a later date, remained unchanged throughout its long and distinguished career. Indeed, it was developed up to Mark XIII for the British Army, is still in service in many parts of the world today and has been fitted with a wide variety of diesel engines in place of its original Meteor petrol engine. In one installation, a microprocessor is used to control the layshaft gearbox, an idea that shows great promise for the control of a compact, low loss tank gearbox of the future. In many ways the later marks of Centurion could be used as a yardstick against which to measure the performance of any tank right up to and including the American M60.

Postwar Development

The Concept of the Main Battle Tank

Thus, the idea of the 'universal' main battle tank gained ground. The line of development was set for the next 40 years or so with the majority of countries pursuing the same basic concept of a balanced design, tempered by their past experience and national concepts of operations. Since most tanks are fielded to destroy enemy armour, one can imagine that all these tanks need is adequate firepower and protection with mobility as a secondary requirement. For a long time the UK's, and to an extent the USA's, operational requirements moved in parallel whereas the West German, and notably the French, adopted the high mobility approach. These two staunch supporters of the need for high mobility felt that the tank had to be capable of moving fast at short notice to concentrate firepower where needed on the battlefield.

It is interesting to note that in 1956 the Germans, the French and the Italians started collaborating in their tank development and the agreement reached through FINABEL, an important NATO co-ordinating committee, aimed at producing a NATO standard main battle tank. They all expressed a desire to keep as close to 30 tons as possible but difficulties arose over the interpretation of these requirements as each country gave different priorities and emphasis to vehicle characteristics. Eventually, when it became apparent that it would not be possible to produce a common tank, each country began its own separate development programme with Germany producing the Leopard 1 and France the AMX 30. They are very different tanks, the former mounting the UK 105 mm gun and weighing about 40 tons whilst the latter weighed about 34 tons, had limited protection and mounted a medium velocity gun firing Chemical Energy (CE) rounds only; yet both tanks stemmed from the same initial requirement.

A brief examination of the various main battle tanks recently in production show how national doctrine influences the priority accorded to vehicle characteristics. These have been modified over time to cater for changes in the threat posed by the Warsaw Pact tanks and other sophisticated modern anti-armour weapons.

Soviet Priorities

It came as a considerable shock to the Germans when they invaded Russia in 1941 and, after their initial swift advance, ran into the Russian T-34 76 mm armed tank (later to become T-34/85 when up-gunned and given a new turret). So seriously did they regard the T-34 menace that Hitler ordered the immediate production of a German tank on similar lines—an order which ultimately led to the Panther (like the Churchill, this rushed design gave a lot of trouble until perfected over a longish period).

Whilst their experience in 1941–45 has obviously influenced Soviet armoured philosophy, its roots are still to be detected in the 'Deep Battle' theory of Marshal Tukhachevskii, the brilliant young Chief of Staff of the Red Army who was 'purged' by Stalin in 1938 and whose writing was suppressed until 1942 and first allowed to influence Soviet operational policy in 1943. Tukhachevskii's Field Service Regulations 1936 show that he was light years ahead of any other contemporary soldier at that time in his thinking and they repay study to this day.

The Soviet concept is the supremacy of the offensive; of massive thrusts on a wide front; of reinforcing success not failure and the practice of passing new formations through spent ones. They also place great emphasis on speed and depth of penetration, bypassing opposition if necessary and setting formidable rates of advance. Of course they have massive resources to call upon and as long as they are prepared to devote the current high proportion of the Gross National Product (GNP) to arms production they will be in a position to apply the doctrine of attack en masse. For some time Western experts were unable to state with confidence whether or not Soviet tanks had an advanced, relatively light weight armour giving them superior ballistic protection without the penalty of an increase in weight. The T80 which represents classic Soviet tank design expertise appears to supply the answer; there are no unknown armour developments in the Soviet Union. An increase in armoured protection without a commensurate increase in weight can only be achieved at the expense of some other characteristics such as the substitution of one member of the crew by an autoloader or sacrificing gun depression. Much to the relief of Western designers, the laws of physics are the same in the Soviet Union as in the West; only the solutions are different because the operational concepts and vehicle design priorities are different.

The principle of the primacy of the offensive has two other important consequences. As their tanks will be used only occasionally in defensive positions, the severe operational penalty of limited gun depression, currently about 90 mils (5 degrees), is accepted whereas it would not be in NATO tanks. The requirement for a large amount of gun depression inevitably increases the roof height of the turret and therefore the overall height of the tank. The inter-relationship of the various tank design parameters is explained in more detail in Chapter 3.

The second effect is that the Russians have a different interpretation of the requirements for survivability, accepting that ammunition will have to be stowed above the turret ring, a better position to give protection against mine attack but more vulnerable to the full range of anti-tank weapons. Furthermore, the stowage of diesel fuel in external tanks, a procedure universally rejected by all NATO tank designers as a fire risk, is readily accepted by the Soviets.

Finally, with a conscript army drawn from a vast populace the Soviets can be selective in their choice of tank crews, choosing men of smaller stature, permitting the tank designer to make the crew stations more compact. The Western Allies, on the other hand, are restricted by the necessity to accommodate the '95 percentile man', dimensions which encompass 95% of the adult male population.

Israeli Priorities

Israeli has one of the few Armoured Corps in the world with recent experience of using tanks on a large scale, employing shock action with high ammunition expenditure rates and against modern anti-tank weapons, particularly guided weapons. These operations demand armoured vehicles with a high degree of mobility but the Israelis also recognise that they have to survive the initial onslaught, win the breakthrough battle and then still have enough tanks available to achieve success. This has led them into making survivability, notably fire suppression, the highest priority in the design of their 56 tonne Merkava (Chariot) tank. So successful was the design that the Israelis claim that not one Merkava tank crewman suffered burn injuries in their campaigns in the Golan Heights and in Lebanon.

Swedish Priorities

The Swedes have tended to have an unconventional if not a revolutionary approach to tank design. The Bofors S-tank is perhaps the best example of this. With its rigid, hull mounted 105 mm gun with autoloader, both diesel and turbine engines, hydraulically operated suspension used also for traversing and elevating, a three man crew but operable by one man in an emergency, the tank was a radical departure from anything else in service at the time. It is interesting to note that as early as 1953—54, the British experimented with a similar vehicle with hydro-pneumatic suspensions as a means of both traversing and elevating the gun. The reasons for not continuing the development however, were that the ability to track a target and lay-on the main armament were not nearly as good as with the conventional turret. Firing on the move was an impossibility. Furthermore, reliance upon the running gear, engine, suspension and just about every other component in the tank for engagement with the main weapon is most unwise. The

Swedes more recent flirtation with a tank, the UDES XX (see Figure 1.9), articulated like the Haaglund over-snow vehicle with gun and crew in the front half and engine in the rear half, has been discontinued in view of the horrendous complexity and spiralling costs.

FIG. 1.9 The Bofors experimental UDES XX articulated tank.

Western Nations' Priorities

After their experience in the Second World War in which they were out-gunned by German tanks to the very end, the British have laid great emphasis on the need for exceptionally good firepower. They developed what is arguably the best tank gun of all time, the Royal Ordnance 105 mm, and were the first in the West to field the 120 mm gun, initially in the Conqueror and later in the Chieftain and Challenger tanks. While predominance is still given to firepower, it is also apparent that near equal priority weighting is given to protection. This is due not only to the evaluation of the immediate threat but also to build in some stretch potential to meet the future threat over the 20 years or more that most tanks are now likely to remain in front line operational service. The apparent low priority accorded to mobility should be seen in context with the mobility offered by Leopard 1 and AMX 30 achieved at the expense of protection. The Chieftain represents a continuous increase in British mobility levels since 1945 and met the levels required by the Army when it came into service in 1964. The Challenger tank continued the UK design philosophy of giving priority to protection though it broke new ground in that at 62 tonnes, it exceeded the agreed NATO Military Load

Classification 60 (MLC 60) maximum of 55 tonnes. The increase in the threat posed by the new generation of sophisticated anti-tank weapons, notably top attack, may dictate an increase in the all-up weight beyond MLC 60 or a reduction in the size of the crew to three, following Soviet practice.

Against a concept of massive armoured thrusts supported by helicopters, the traditional main battle tank philosphy of the West is undergoing gradual modification. To begin with, anti-helicopter ammunition will have to be developed or a separate anti-helicopter weapon system on the lines of the FRG anti-aircraft Gepard or the quick-firing Italian OTO-Melara 76 mm naval gun mounted on a standard OF-40 tank chassis, will be required. Both are very expensive solutions to the problem but their time may come sooner than expected. Certainly the tank commander cannot afford to ignore the new and increasing threat from the anti-tank helicopter despite the extension of his duties to encompass both ground and now air launched anti-tank guided weapon systems.

Both the Germans and the French have been down the road of high mobility at the expense of protection. However, in later versions of Leopard 2 the Germans have shifted towards greater levels of protection and there is some evidence to suggest that the adherence to the MLC 60 (55 tonne) limit may be a political rather than purely operational or logistic imperative.

A more recent development is the French third generation main battle tank, the Leclerc. It has a three man crew, autoloader for the GIAT 120 mm gun, 1500 hp hyperbar diesel engine, sophisticated integated day/night panoramic sights and a fire control system using 'Digibus' digital data transmission. It will have an exceptional power-to-weight ratio of around 30 hp per tonne and the hydrogas suspension will permit it to use its mobility to the full when moving cross country. Its silhouette is both lower and shorter than all other NATO main battle tanks and the application of 'stealth' technology to defeat detection by battlefield radar and the homing systems of 'smart' weapons and the redistribution of armour protection within the 55 tonnes permitted under the MLC 60 limit could make the tank one of the best protected in NATO. Unlike the Americans and Germans, the French were not given the secret of the British Chobham armour (a laminated 'sandwich' of armoured plate and ceramics which gave much improved protection against most forms of attack without any significant weight penalty). However, they claim to have developed their own.

An examination of US doctrine discloses several different factors. The first is that as a superpower isolated from the European land mass with worldwide defence commitments the importance of the tank as a weapon of war and as an accoutrement to the exercise of power is overshadowed by the requirement for naval and air power. The acceptance of advanced technology has nowhere been greater than in the United States. This has often made them believe that a quantum jump in any particular field is just around the corner and has also led them down several very expensive and unconventional paths, usually with disappointing results. After the successful M60 series the Americans flirted with advanced technology with the MBT 70 (a revolutionary design project, costing many millions of dollars, in which the Germans were also involved) but it proved to be too expensive and far too complex. The Sheridan, firing the gun-launched Shillelagh guided missile, was perhaps the classic example of trying to extract a quart from a pint pot or in tank terminology, trying to give a light vehicle a heavyweight punch. In a final attempt to justify the very considerable development money spent on the Sheridan, the US fitted the Shillelagh missile system in a modified M60 turret, classifying the vehicle as the M60 A1E2. After about 4 or 5 unhappy years trying to find a suitable role for this specialised tank in their European Army, all the M60 A1E2s were withdrawn to mainland USA.

When the US decided to replace the M60 series the vast resources available in the United States and the potential size of the final order allowed the Americans the luxury of placing a contract with both Chrysler and General Motors to make one prototype each for validation trials. Both tanks were conventional in that they had a fully rotating turret and a four man crew but the former had a hydraulic gun control system and was powered by a 1120 kM (1500 hp) gas turbine engine whereas the latter had a conventional diesel engine and an electrically powered turret. In 1976 the Chrysler turbine tank was selected and entered service as the M1 General Abrams. The first 1,000 or so examples were fitted with the American version of the ubiquitous Royal Ordnance 105 mm rifled gun but subsequently has been fitted with the Rheinmetall (FRG) 120 mm smooth bore gun, turning the tank into the M1A1.

Similarities and Differences

This brief survey has traced the development of the tank from the early beginnings to the present day. A great deal of similarity can be detected in many features of current tank design. Decades of experience has confirmed aspects of successful design and has pointed up the unconventional forays where they have met with little success. The lessons of experience are well known by all nations and have been distilled over the years into a set of design principles that find a remarkable level of agreement. In the final analysis, it is national defence priorities and military interpretations of that requirement which ultimately decide the design of the tank.

One factor above all others has bedevilled post-war NATO tank development, added considerably to costs and must have reduced NATO operational flexibility, is the failure to agree on a standard tank gun. Much has been written chronicling collaborative attempts to build a common tank, all of which have ended in failure after varying lengths of time. Perhaps if the aim had been more modest to agree common standards for gun and ammunition rather than a complete tank, on the lines of Quadripartite Memorandum of Understanding (UK, USA, FRG and France) for the 155 mm howitzer ammunition, more might have been achieved in the long run. The Royal Ordnance 105 mm gun became the *de facto* NATO standard tank gun in the 1960s and 1970s because of its outstanding performance. Perhaps now it is the turn of the Rheinmetall 120 mm smooth bore gun to become the NATO standard ordnance by virtue of its commonality as, by the late 1990s, it could have been fitted to upwards of 12,000 American, German, Dutch, Belgian, Swiss and possibly other country's tanks. Whatever the merits of the UK's rival 120 mm rifled bore gun, even if fitted to the full UK fleet, it will never equal the deployed totals of the 120 mm smooth bore gun.

2

Tank Firepower

Once the initial idea of using a mechanical device to cross ditches and barbed wire entanglements had proved feasible, the potential of such a machine as a weapon platform quickly became apparent and by the end of The First World War the most common calibre was 57 mm with only a few tanks mounting a larger gun. These guns would be classed as low to medium velocity by today's standards and their battlefield effectiveness was strictly limited. As tanks began to use thicker armour for their own protection, the parallel development of higher velocity guns to penetrate this armour was put in hand.

The increase in muzzle velocity obtained tended to satisfy the requirement at the time and calibres remained relatively small. Thus the Crusader tank of 1941 mounted only a 40 mm gun but this was a high velocity armour-defeating weapon. It was not until the superiority of the German tank guns became so marked as to dominate the battlefield that the Allies began seriously to consider mounting heavier, more powerful weapons.

Roles

A fighting vehicle is a versatile carrier and can be fitted with a wide range of weapon systems. The weapon and its carrier are interdependent, the carrier serving to increase mobility and the weapon, the battle-winning effectiveness of the system as a whole. This complex, reciprocal relationship involves vehicle characteristics, weapon installation and integration of the fire control system to achieve a compromise within the prescribed design limits.

The tank's most important role is Shock Action but a corollary might be the disablement and destruction of enemy armoured vehicles of a similar weight class, preferably at ranges greater than the effective range of the enemy's armament. Other roles will be the destruction of lightly armoured or unarmoured vehicles, men in the open and protected pinpoint targets such as emplacements or fortified positions. In the past, the requirement to take on a miscellany of alternative roles demanded the carriage of smoke shells and illuminants. However, the advent of infra-red and image intensification night viewing equipment has all but eliminated the requirement for the latter and the ability of thermal imagers to operate through conventional smoke screens and, of course, at night has reduced the need for both types of shells. Instead though, the advent of the battlefield helicopter, which can engage tanks out to 4000 m and possibly longer ranges, demands that the tank itself be capable of destroying this new threat by the use of a purpose-made anti-helicopter round.

Night Fighting

Ideally, a tank should be able to fight equally effectively by day and night and in all weathers but the problems of firing accurately in these conditions have only recently been overcome, albeit very expensively, by the introduction of the Thermal Imager (TI). Though some tanks still field the earlier, less effective Image Intensifying (II) or even infra-red equipment, the superiority of TI is such as to make it the only passive system likely to be considered for any tank in the future. As far as training for the 24-hour, all-weather battle is concerned, the two prime considerations are to have an identical sight graticule pattern and gunnery techniques for both the optical daylight and the all-weather sight. This keeps the number of fire control orders and operations as few as possible, thus reducing recruit training time and making continuation training in service easier and simpler. Having the identical graticule pattern and firing techniques in all sights ensures that the transition from day to night and from prime to auxiliary sight does not require the eye to adjust to another sight picture, again leading to identical firing techniques and reduced training complexity. Since TI equipment is frequently used in daylight to identify heat sources such as tank engines or gun barrels, the need for identical day and night techniques is a paramount operational requirements. This will reduce engagement times since the well trained gunner will be changing from TI to daylight sight depending on the circumstances.

Further details of night fighting aids are discussed later in this Chapter and in Volume 8 of this series, entitled Surveillance and Target Acquisition.

Target Characteristics

Before the main armament can be selected, it is necessary to decide what the target will be. The most likely, and the most difficult to defeat will be enemy tanks. The size of target presented to an observer depends not only on its physical dimensions but also on the way it is being used tactically. Tanks in the open usually present a full sized target but as they are likely to be moving, they will be more difficult to hit. In other circumstances, tanks present much smaller targets. If, for example, the enemy is merely observing then he will probably adopt a turret down position. If he intends to fire then he will have to move into a hull down position (see Figure 2.1). In this position the hull and running gear are concealed but the turret above the gun trunnions, usually the best protected aspect of the tank, is exposed. Gun depression, as described in Chapter 1, is important here. If the enemy's tank has depression limited to about 90 mils (5 degrees) it will have to expose more of itself to engage targets from a fire position. Having decided on the types of target to be engaged, the choice then lies between a versatile system capable of engaging a wide variety of targets or a more specialised one in which the vehicle has only one role. In the latter case, a light vehicle like a wheeled or tracked guided weapon carrier is capable of destroying tanks but is not capable of taking on other tasks. If, on the other hand, a more versatile vehicle is required not only to destroy tanks but also to carry out a wide variety of secondary tasks, then the current choice is the high velocity gun. The weights and dimensions of some typical weapons are shown in Figure 2.2. It is noticeable that there is a considerable size and weight penalty to pay in moving from 76 mm to 105 mm.

FIG. 2.1 Hull and turret down position.

Weapon	Length (m)	Weapon weight (kg)	Weight of Ammunition (kg) AP	HESH/HE	HEAT
12.5 mm	1.65	37	0.2		
20 mm	2.56	75	0.33	0.33	
30 mm	3.5	84–136	0.9	0.9	
76 mm	2.16	200	—	9	
105 mm	5.8	1260	19	22	22
120 mm	6.2	1800	17	21	29

FIG. 2.2 Weight and princpal dimensions of typical weapons.

The size of a target can be expressed as the angle it presents at the gun. This angle is called target subtense. It is a useful way of describing the size of a target because it takes into account not only the targets's physical dimensions but also the range at which it is being engaged. The further away the target is, the smaller the error in the gun system has to be if the target is to be hit. To give some idea of the difficulty of hitting a tank, at 4 kms range the apparent size (subtense) is the same as a man's head at 1 km or a pinhead on the far wall of a large living room. The width of a target is normally greater than its height and it is in the vertical plane that weapon system errors are greater, so normally the target subtense refers to height. It can be calculated as in this example below:

$$\text{Subtense (mils)} = \frac{\text{height (or width) in metres} \times 1{,}000}{\text{range (m)}}$$

The dimensions of a tank turret will vary but generally they are of the order of 1 m high and 1.5 m–2 m wide. Thus a hull down tank at 100 m has a vertical subtense of 1 mil.

The range of 100 m is convenient for calculation of target subtenses, but the actual range at which targets will appear will depend on a variety of factors of which inter-visibility has the single greatest influence. In desert conditions targets may well appear at 6,000 m or more and engagement ranges of 3,000 m are common. However, in North West Europe the contours of the ground, the forests, buildings and other obstacles to vision are so distributed that 75% of all targets appear at ranges of 2,000 m or less and very few ground targets indeed are even seen over 4,000 m.

It is always difficult to be specific about the ranges that should be considered 'short' or 'long' but, as a rough guide, for tank engagements, 0–1000 m is defined as short range, 1000–2000 m as medium range and 2000–4000 m as long range.

Apart from the small size of the target, the next most difficult problem is the short time the target is exposed. If the enemy tank or armoured vehicle is being commanded correctly, then it will offer only a fleeting target as it moves from one fire position to another. This will probably be the only time a complete, full-sized vehicle is seen by the tank carrying out the engagement as, on most other occasions, it is likely that only the turret will be exposed. Exposure times will vary greatly with the nature of the cover available on the battlefield, the difficulty of the ground the tank has to negotiate and the power-to-weight ratio or agility of the vehicle itself. As a general guide, maximum exposure times at maximum ranges might be of the order of one minute but as the range decreases so will exposure time and at battle ranges it will rarely be more than about 15–25 seconds. From this it can be seen that for any armour-defeating weapon the main characteristics must be:

Accuracy

- The target will be very small, even at relatively short range and the first shot must hit.

Lethality

- The target must be defeated, with a high degree of overmatch, ideally by the first shot and through the thickest armour (the worst case).

Short time of engagement

- The target will only present itself for short periods. In that time the commander or gunner must detect the target, identify it, acquire it and then carry out the full engagement sequence.

With the introduction of complex armours, it is no longer appropriate to define lethality of a weapon system solely in terms of the penetration of Rolled Homogeneous Armour (RHA). The chance of defeating a tank depends not only on the chance of hitting it but of penetrating the armour. By multiplying accuracy and penetration together, a figure called Single Shot Kill Probability (SSKP) is obtained which more accurately conveys the performance of the whole weapon system than a penetration figure alone. For example, if a gun system has a probability of achieving a hit with a single shot of 0.5 and the shell, given a hit, has a lethality of 0.6, then the SSKP is:

$$0.5 \times 0.6 = 0.3 \text{ or } 30\%$$

Damage Criteria

Choice of Weapon

The choice of weapon has already been discussed in general terms and though there is unanimity in the selection of the kinetic energy round as the primary tank-defeating ammunition, there is disagreement about both the calibre of the gun and whether it should be rifled or smooth bore.

The Russians, the Germans (Leopard 2) and the French (Leclerc) have all chosen smooth bore guns. The Americans, while initially fitting the Royal Ordnance designed rifled 105 mm gun to the first 1,000 or so M1 Abrams tank, now fit their version of the German Rheinmetall 120 mm smooth bore gun. Both the German and the American 120 mm guns, while not being directly inter-changeable, can at least fire each other's ammunition.

The tank has already been described as essentially an offensive weapon system but the full meaning only becomes apparent when considering lethality and the damage criteria. In order to eliminate an attacking tank and its crew, the tank must be damaged beyond repair or the crew disabled. A hit must put at least one major sub-system out of action, perhaps disabling at least two members of the crew at the same time. The high degree of protection afforded by modern spaced armour, possibly assisted by Explosive Reactive Armour (ERA) is such that, in practice, we may have to settle for less than total destruction of the tank. Knocking out a tank calls for a high degree of overmatch of the armour—marginal penetration is not enough. There are several ways of rendering a tank ineffective on the battlefield much in the same way that it is possible either to 'neutralise' or 'destroy' any target.

Mobility or 'M' Kill

If a tank is incapable of exercising controlled movement on the battlefield, then the type of kill is classified as a Mobility or 'M' Kill. This could be caused by crew injury, damage to the engine or final drives or perhaps the most likely cause, by an anti-tank mine damaging a track or the suspension. By not fully destroying the tank, there is the possibility that it might still be able to use its gun but since it can see to fire it also can be seen and without the ability to move to cover, it is unlikely to survive for very long.

Firepower or 'F' Kill

The second partial damage criterion is the Firepower or 'F' Kill. This definition covers the occasion when the main armament cannot be operated either because it is damaged or because the crew are no longer capable of operating it.

Knocked out or 'K' Kill

The term 'knocked out' is used to describe a tank which is no longer functional in any respect. The ideal is to achieve a K Kill with a single round.

Passenger or 'P' Kill

The three previous definitions can be fairly widely applied or adapted to all types of armoured fighting vehicles although there is an additional criterion of a Passenger or 'P' Kill which applies to armoured personnel carriers when at least 40% of the personnel inside have been rendered incapable of performing their role.

Penetration and Lethality

Although the types of kill are easily understood and defined, it is not always so easy to achieve the desired degree of lethality. Penetration itself may not be enough to produce any one of the types of kill. There are several well-documented instances in the Yom Kippur War when tanks were hit and penetrated a number of times by anti-tank guided weapons without the crews being aware of the damage until much later. This introduces the vexed question of lethality which is usually described as the percentage chance of a particular projectile producing an M, F or K kill against the target with a single shot. It is a vexed question because if a kinetic energy projectile penetrates with sufficient residual energy it will normally produce a K kill, whereas the lethality of attack by a hollow charge round is highly dependent on the direction of attack, the point of impact and the degree of over-match (diameter of the exit hole on the inside of the armour plate) as described later in this chapter. Trials against modern armours have shown that it is not sufficient to achieve marginal penetration by kinetic energy rounds. Although 105 mm can still achieve effective penetration at all reasonable battle ranges against most in-service Soviet tanks, at longer ranges against the best protected aspects, 105 mm and even 120 mm calibres may not achieve a K kill with the first shot. Thus, the development of larger calibre guns continues as Soviet tank armour improves and vice versa.

Warhead effects

Kinetic Energy Attack

In order to prevent an armoured fighting vehicle taking any further part in the battle, the vehicle must be incapacitated in one of the ways described. Whatever type of incapacitation is effected, it can only be achieved by expending a considerable amount of energy at the target. Nuclear weapon effects apart, this 'energy' package can be delivered to the target in one of two ways. Kinetic Energy (KE) consists of applying sufficient energy at the point of attack to overmatch the capability and strength of the target material to resist penetration. Quite simply, it is the application of brute force but in a highly specialised manner. KE penetration

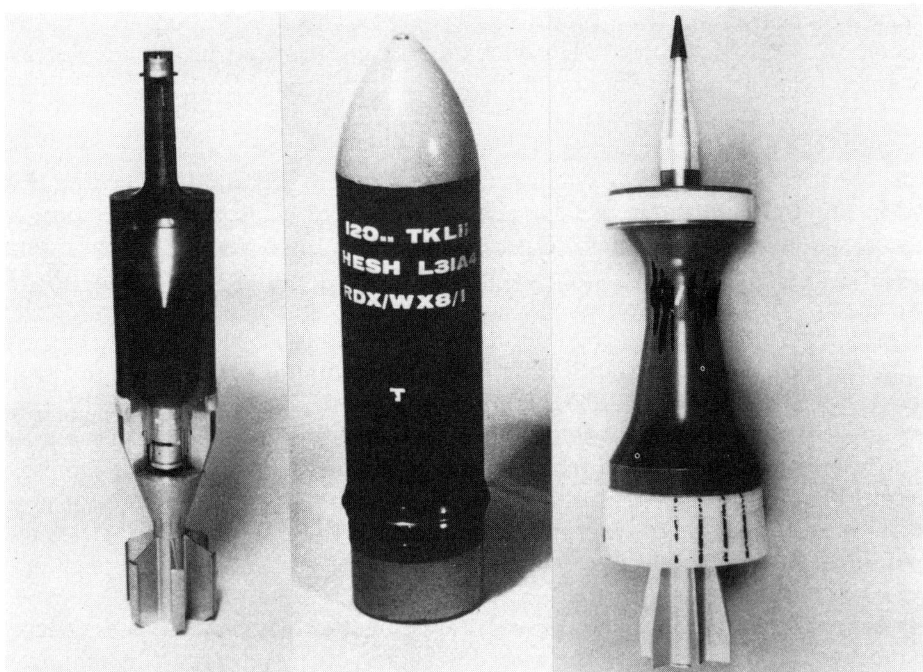

FIG. 2.3 HEAT, HESH and fin stabilised projectiles.

is achieved by the transfer of the residual energy in the projectile to the target at the point of impact according to the following formula:

$$KE = \frac{1}{2} MV^2$$

The above formula shows that since KE varies as the unit power of the Mass (*M*) but the square of the velocity (*V*), the use of very high muzzle velocities, of the order of 1600 m/second, show greater dividends in increasing total KE than an increase in Mass alone. If the diameter of the shot fills the whole gun barrel, then it can easily be made very heavy but it then becomes difficult to accelerate to the required velocity within the length of the barrel. Additionally, a large diameter solid shot will expend more energy penetrating a given thickness of armour compared to a projectile of the same mass but smaller diameter—it is easier to push a small diameter needle through material rather than a large one. Consequently, the larger shot is not only less effective at the target but it is difficult to give it the necessary velocity in the first place.

Early attempts to overcome this problem included the use of the ‘squeeze bore’ principle whereby the outer casing of the shot was squeezed down to a smaller calibre by a device at the end of the barrel. Although quite effective in the smaller calibres of anti-tank guns in service in the early days of the Second World War, it has distinct limitations and now can only be considered as a historical curiosity.

Another method employed for a time used a core of dense material surrounded by a lighter jacket or case. When the projectile hit the target, the outer, lighter material was stripped off leaving the inner core to penetrate inside the tank.

Although more efficient than the full calibre shot, this type suffers from ballistic inefficiency. Air resistance on the relatively large frontal area causes excessive drag and a large drop in velocity which seriously degrades the penetrative power of the shot at anything more than very short ranges.

Towards the end of the Second World War, the first really effective solution to the problem was developed in the form of the Armour Piercing Discarding Sabot (APDS) round. A penetrator of a dense material (in the early days before tungsten was used it was high grade steel) is surrounded by a light-weight 'pot' or circular support, the object of which is to present the largest possible base area within the barrel, over which the propellant gas can exert pressure. The projectile is accelerated very quickly up the barrel and once it exits from the muzzle the air resistance causes the 'pot' to fall off allowing the smaller diameter penetrator to continue towards the target. The penetrator normally has a ballistically shaped outer shell or cap to make it more aerodynamic in flight. This ballistic casing normally shatters on contact with the armour, leaving the solid core to penetrate. Although simple in conception, it is difficult to manufacture rounds to give a consistent performance and as protection levels of the tank increase, the mass of the solid penetrator must also increase, so we return to the same problem of velocity versus mass.

Depth of penetration at the target will depend not only on the residual energy of the shot but also on its shape and size. The shape of the curve at the head of the penetrator (the ogive) is most important as it must not only be able to pierce the armour but must 'turn into' it to reduce the advantage of sloped armour and not ricochet. Ideally, the penetrator must not break up, should pass through taking as much armour material with it as possible and should break up inside the tank and not exit on the far side, expending all its energy within the vehicle. If, for a given mass, the diameter of the penetrator is reduced and its length is increased, then for the same residual velocity, it will penetrate a greater thickness of armour as it will be expending its energy over a smaller cross-sectional area. The ratio of the length-to-diameter is called the 'slenderness' ratio or length/diameter (L/D) ratio and although a projectile with a ratio in excess of 7:1 cannot be spin stabilised it is not until they reach a ratio of approximately 20:1 that they can be called 'long rods'. The long rod penetrator has been the most significant advance in KE ammunition for many years though the idea itself is far from new. Perhaps the most famous application of the principal of the long rod penetrator was the arrow used by the English longbowman to defeat the armoured knight.

Hollow Charge Warhead

The first method of attacking armour which is not velocity dependent uses the chemical energy available from the detonation of high explosive. This type of warhead can be fired from a gun, delivered by a guided weapon or by an air-launched projectile. There are three main types of Chemical Energy (CE) munitions but by far the most important and common of which is the High Explosive Anti-Tank (HEAT).

The detonation of the limited amount of high explosive contained within a shell fired from a tank gun is unlikely to do lethal damage to a tank and therefore a means must be found to focus the energy of the detonation into some form of high-energy jet. The most effective and widely used method is to shape the detonation wave so that the total energy available is directed onto a small cross-sectional area of the target. This is achieved by manufacturing the explosive charge into the shape of an inverted, rearward-facing cone and lining it with copper or some other low melting point, ductile metal. When the charge is detonated by the fuze mounted in the nose, a jet of high-energy gas and vaporised metal from the cone is projected axially forward (the Munroe effect). This jet, travelling at a speed of around 6,000 m per second, burns its way through the armour like a cutting torch. The effectiveness and penetration of the jet depends on the diameter of the cone and hence the calibre of the gun, the type of metal liner and the 'stand-off' distance from the target at which the charge is detonated. The need for manportable anti-tank weapons has increased the demand for greater penetration at smaller calibres and at lower overall weight. The use of 'charge shapers', usually inert plastic material placed at particular points around the metal cone, assist in focusing the jet and increasing penetration and lethality.

The penetration of a HEAT round is severely degraded if the charge is spun, so the projectile must be fin stabilised (even at 400 rpm penetration is reduced by about 25%). If the hollow charge is to be fired from a rifled barrel, then some means such as slipping driving bands must be used to limit, or preferably eliminate, the spin. Although a relatively small cone diameter can produce a very impressive depth of penetration (typically 5–6 times cone diameter), lethality is low unless it over-matches the target by at least 33%. However, if an exit hole in excess of 24 mm in diameter is produced, the terminal effect inside the vehicle is likely to be considerable as the jet continues into the target with considerable residual energy bringing with it 'spall' or splinters torn off the armour plate. Thus, the performance and effect of the hollow charge round is largely dependent on cone diameter. On the basis of extensive tests, the Americans established a minimum diameter of 152 mm for the HEAT round for their Shillelagh missile fired from the Sheridan M551 reconnaissance tank. There are many HEAT rounds of smaller cone diameter, though their lethality with a single shot must be questionable, particularly against ERA armour.

HEAT attack is ideally suited to Anti-Tank Guided Weapons (ATGW) where the projectile is unspun and is travelling at relatively low speed. If the projectile strikes a target at very high velocity the fuze will not be able to initiate the charge at the correct stand-off distance, greatly reducing penetration and behind armour effects. Hence, if the HEAT round is to be fired from a gun, not only must its spin be limited but so must its velocity, reducing the chance of a hit.

The effectiveness of modern spaced armour, optimised against HEAT attack, may well eliminate this round as the general purpose nature carried in a tank. At present the largest calibre tank gun in service is the Soviet 125 mm smooth bore and even this is well below the 152 mm minimum the Americans found was necessary for an effective HEAT over-match. However, its effectiveness as a guided weapon warhead is not in doubt, partly as there is no alternative at present and partly because guided missiles usually permit a cone diameter in excess of 120 mm. A number of technical improvements are currently in development and should improve even further the HEAT warhead's ability to defeat ERA.

High Explosive Squash Head (HESH)

High Explosive Squash Head (HESH), for which the American term is High Explosive Plastic or HEP, is the second form of chemical energy attack which is not velocity dependent. In this form of attack the explosive is contained in a thin-walled projectile which collapses on striking the target, allowing the plastic explosive to spread. A base fuze then denotes the explosive which sends strong shock waves through the armour. Reflection from the internal armour surface causes an overmatch of the armour which then fails, causing a large 'scab' to form and fragments to fly off inside the vehicle. The success of HESH against armour depends on the explosive forming a suitably shaped 'pat' on the outside of the armour plate before it is detonated (the British term 'squash-head' describes the process very well). This poses several problems, because if the projectile hits the target at a very acute angle, the explosive will not form a cohesive mass and consequently its effectiveness will be greatly reduced. Similarly, if the projectile arrives at the target with very high residual velocity ie. if the target is at very close range, the explosive will be dispersed on impact, before the fuze has time to function. The latter problem is easily resolved by keeping the muzzle velocity low but the result is a lower chance of a hit because of the higher trajectory. HESH can be defeated relatively easily by having a discontinuity (spaced armour) in the path of the shock wave though the outer plate will almost certainly be destroyed.

The major advantage of HESH lies in its usefulness as a multipurpose round. It is approximately 90% as effective as a conventional High Explosive (HE) round against unarmoured targets and considerably better than HE against bunkers and buildings. It has a devastating effect against lightly armoured targets and even if a kill is not obtained against a more heavily armoured target, the secondary effects will damage all the optics, antennae and any equipment mounted externally. In common with HEAT, it gives a realistic anti-tank capability to a medium velocity gun but, unlike HEAT, is a genuine dual purpose round.

Miznay Schardin Effect

The third form of chemical energy attack uses the Miznay Schardin effect: it is a method of arranging the charge to project a self-forming fragment at the target. It is not particularly well suited for use in guns but the technique has been used in mines and more recently in an American programme to develop an aerially delivered sub-munition to attack tanks from above.

Comparison of Kinetic Energy and Chemical Energy Attack

However good the target effects of chemical energy attack may be, it must be delivered at a lower velocity than a kinetic energy shot and therefore will suffer from relative inaccuracy and longer time of flight. The former is especially important today as firing on the move at a moving target is a prime operational requirement and is feasible with modern digital fire control systems. Kinetic energy ammunition is universally regarded as the prime tank-killing round although there is a place for chemical energy as a secondary form of attack and, of course as the prime anti-tank guided missile warhead. Some attempts have been made to make a lightweight MBT relying on a lower velocity CE round as the main anti-tank round. More recently 'low recoil' mechanisms and more efficient muzzle brakes have enabled 105 mm guns firing KE ammunition to be fitted to medium weight armoured vehicles. Oto-Melara have recently produced the B-1 Centauro, a 6.6 tonne, 6-wheeled armoured vehicle mounting a 52 calibre, 105 mm gun firing fin stabilised ammunition. It is fitted with a high efficiency muzzle brake and the long recoil length of 750 mm limits the recoil force to 12 tonnes.

A summary of the warhead options for defeating tanks at all aspects of attack is in Figure 2.4.

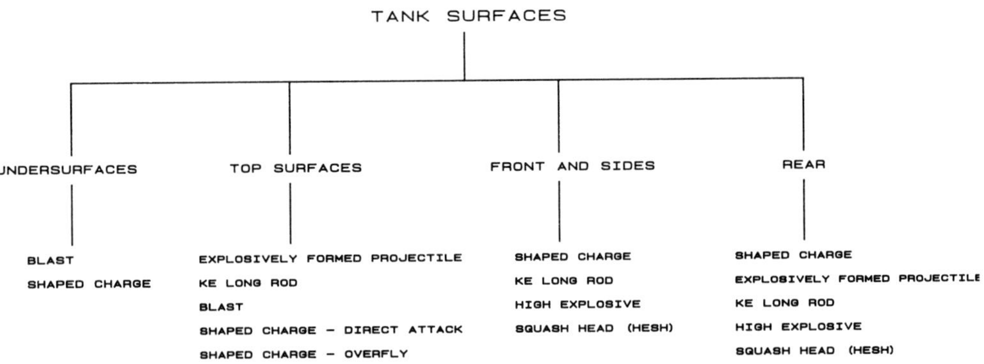

FIG. 2.4 Warhead options.

Choice of Launcher

Like everything else, long rod penetrators are not without their disadvantages. Spin stabilised projectiles must have a low slenderness ratio: the length divided by the diameter (L/D ratio) must not exceed 4.5. This is impossible with a long rod where L/D ratios commonly used are around 14–20:1 so it must remain unspun and be fin stabilised. Once it has been decided that all rounds to be fired can be unspun and fin stabilised, then the next logical step is to utilise a smooth bore gun. Initially, significantly lower rates of barrel wear were claimed by smooth bore manufacturers because they were able to chrome plate the interior of the barrel. The chrome surface plating has a very good resistance to high temperatures, allowing higher energy, hotter, propellant to be used. While chrome plating the interior surface of the smooth bore barrel is relatively straightforward, it has proved to be far more difficult to plate the grooves and the lands (the rifling) in a rifled bore barrel. Recently however, plating techniques have been improved to the extent that chrome plate retention in rifled bores is now as good as in the smooth bore barrel. Chrome plated barrels, by significantly increasing barrel life and maintaining gun accuracy, could be a decisive battle-winning factor.

It is possible to use slipping driving bands in a rifled bore gun and fire fin stabilised projectiles but there must be some doubt concerning their effectiveness as muzzle velocities increase over the current limits of about 1600 m/second. However, a rifled barrel permits the use of a variety of ammunition, allowing the vehicle to fulfil the more classic role as a multi-purpose battle tank rather than solely as an anti-tank weapon. This requirement to retain the multi-purpose capabilities of MBTs is more apparent in armies with smaller tank fleets. As was indicated in Chapter 1, Soviet doctrine has no doubts concerning the offensive rather than the defensive capabilities it requires from its tanks and their designs over the years have made few concessions to the multi-purpose role.

Both Armour Piercing Fin Stabilised Discarding Sabot (APFSDS) and HEAT can be satisfactorily fired from both smooth and rifled bore guns but because of the weight of explosive and the metal shell case, the HESH round can only be fired from a rifled bore gun. To make a HESH round fin stabilised would require it to have a very long tail and it would be impossible to fit into the chamber of a gun let alone to stow it inside the tank.

Readers who wish to know more about the attack of armour are encouraged to read Volume 4 in this series, Ammunition for the Land Battle.

Secondary Weapon Systems

Tanks have been armed with a variety of secondary weapons. The possibilities are virtually unlimited, the choice being driven by the battle role envisaged for the tank. If it is required to engage large numbers of infantry in the open and soft targets such as buildings and bunkers, then a weapon mix that allows for a good HE capability will be provided. In some early Second World War tanks this was achieved by mounting a large calibre low-velocity gun with limited traverse. If it is expected that a high proportion of the secondary targets will be lightly armoured vehicles such as APCs or reconnaissance vehicles, then it is worth considering installing a 20–30 mm cannon as fitted on the Mark 1 Centurion and the French AMX 32. All these solutions have advantages but they all suffer from the same problem of integrating a large secondary weapon and its ammunition into the limited space in the turret.

Machine-Gun

A medium machine-gun of approximately 7.62 mm calibre offers the most effective and economical way of disabling men at short and medium ranges. This is normally mounted co-axially with the main gun because it allows the same sighting system to be used for both primary and secondary weapon systems. Most turret machine-guns are gas or recoil operated and in an attempt to keep costs to a minimum, have been developed from weapons used by the infantry. In many cases they have proved to be manifestly unsuitable for their specialised role of producing a high rate of sustained fire from within the confines of a tank turret. The Hughes chain gun however, has been specifically designed to operate in an AFV turret. Though belt fed, the gun is powered by an electric motor and does not rely on gas or recoil energy to cock the mechanism and is thus the ideal weapon for remote mounting in an external gun tank. The Hughes chain gun ejects the empty cases forward, that is outside the tank, virtually eliminating the problem of carbon monoxide toxicity associated with gas or recoil operated weapons.

It is normal for a second machine-gun to be mounted on the top of the turret, usually operated by the commander. This gun should have sufficient elevation to provide anti-aircraft fire though its effectiveness in that role must be open to question. Recently, in an attempt to rationalise and reduce some of the non-essential tasks carried out by the tank commander, the machine-gun has been relocated and the job of operating it given to the loader.

Future Developments

Improved Kinetic Energy Ammunition

Despite the adoption of the 120 mm gun by the Germans, the United States and the French, the rifled 105 mm is still the most widely used tank gun with the exception of those manufactured by the Soviet Union. There are well over 12,000 105 mm guns in service world wide and most of them owe their origins to the British L7 rifled design although the majority are now made under licence. The 105 mm gun was initially designed to up-gun the British Centurion from the 20 pounder and since then has been fitted to the M60 and its successor the M1, to Leopard 1, the Swedish S tank and the tanks made by Japan, South Korea, India, Israel and Brazil. It has also been retro-fitted to T55 tanks used by Saudi Arabia although the breech was rotated 180 degrees to enable the gun to be loaded with the left hand as Soviet four man tanks have the loader on the right hand side of the turret.

The British, the first NATO country to field a 120 mm gun, have continued development of the rifled concept and intend to replace the current gun with a high pressure version in the early 1990s. The Germans will continue with the 120 mm smooth bore in Leopard 2 and the Americans will mount their version in the remaining examples of M1, redesignating it M1A1, and in M1A2.

Over the next decade there will be a steady improvement in the accuracy and penetrative powers of APFSDS since KE ammunition is the most difficult to defeat. There are at least four ways of increasing the penetration performance of any tank gun without changing to a larger calibre or a new concept such as liquid propellant or the electro-magnetic gun:

Increasing the Energy of the Propellant

The total energy of a given weight and volume of propellant can be increased either by packing the propellant more tightly into the case or by altering the chemical composition of the propellant itself to make it react more energetically. The former course of action is difficult if not impossible to achieve if an increase in chamber size is required as guns are seldom manufactured with sufficient 'stretch potential' to permit the chamber to be enlarged. However, the second option, increasing the energy of the propellant, could be achieved as the gun may withstand operating at slightly higher chamber pressures. However, if a large increase in chamber pressure is required, a new gun will almost certainly be needed. There will be penalties with almost any course of action. Propellants are a highly efficient way to store energy and very considerable precautions are taken by all tank designers to protect the crew from the effects of ammunition fires. If the propellant is ignited, no fire prevention system can prevent burning as it contains its own oxygen; and if a substantial amount of the propellant catches fire at the same time, the near instantaneous generation of a large volume of hot gas will almost certainly kill the crew and could blow the turret off the tank. The many pictures of Soviet tanks alongside their upturned turrets gives evidence that their designers may not have paid sufficient attention to internal ammunition protection and overall survivability.

Increasing the Length of the Barrel

The propellant 'all burnt' position in high pressure guns is usually after shot exit. Thus, if the barrel were to be made longer, more energy could be imparted to the shot as it would have spent longer in the barrel. Unfortunately a longer barrel causes a number of static and dynamic problems, most of which are mutually conflicting and usually lead to greater system inaccuracy. A longer barrel will be heavier and therefore will take a greater amount of power to stabilise leading to greater inaccuracy when firing on the move. The barrel will suffer more from droop unless it is made thicker or of stronger but lighter steel. This would result in a barrel that is either heavier or more costly or both.

Improve the Material or Increase the L/D Ratio of the Penetrator

These two improvements are usually tackled together since an improvement in the metallurgy of the penetrator will usually permit a higher L/D ratio to be used. Reducing the cross-sectional area of the penetrator, while keeping the weight the same or even increasing it, increases the kinetic energy, reduces the air resistance and thus increases the total energy delivered to the target. However, there are problems with ultra-long rod penetrators. Unless the metallurgy of the penetrator is improved at the same time, it will have less longitudinal strength which could result in the long rod breaking up on impact with the target. The higher the L/D ratio, the more difficult it will be to stow inside the tank. Also the problems of maintaining in-flight stability are significantly greater.

Anti-Helicopter Ammunition

As Figure 5.2 indicates, in the future about 25% of the threat to the tank will come from the anti-tank helicopter. Though most anti-aircraft weapons can be used against both fixed wing and helicopters, the tank must be able to take some effective action itself and not rely on other weapons always being available to protect it. Modern fire control systems have good control and speed of response but it is doubtful if the gunner will be able to achieve the necessary hand and eye coordination and dexterity to track an agile anti-tank helicopter successfully. However, his task will be made far easier by the introduction of Automatic Target Detection and Tracking (ATDT) as discussed later in this chapter. Fin stabilised ammunition could be used and even though the time of flight is short (2.5 seconds to 4,000 m), the latest Russian helicopter could move 35–40 m in that time; and with this non-explosive ammunition, even a near miss is as good as a mile.

At present most tanks, with the exception of the United Kingdom which uses HESH, carry HEAT as a dual-purpose secondary ammunition nature. This round could be adapted to serve as a primary anti-helicopter round while retaining a good capability against medium and light armoured vehicles. The round will require a dual-purpose fuze, impact for anti-armour and proximity for anti-helicopter. It will also need a higher muzzle velocity than currently used in order to keep the time of flight to a minimum.

Protection

Parallel developments in armoured protection will ensure that neither the attacker nor the defender gains any overwhelming advantage. Though it is rare for a breakthrough in both areas to occur at the same time, a development increasing penetration usually redoubles efforts in the search for a counter in armoured protection. Protection is discussed in Chapter 5.

Fire Control Systems

Probably the most significant developments will come in the fire control area where the possibilities of using digital data techniques seem limitless. Future developments in fire control systems are covered in greater detail in Chapter 3. Technology is advancing so fast in this field that it is more a matter of deciding how much to invest in the system rather than whether it is technically feasible.

Optronics and fire control equipment account for an ever-increasing proportion of the total capital costs of modern battle tanks. As improvements increase the chance of a hit nearer the theoretical maximum, the cost of such sophisticated equipment will come under more and more detailed scrutiny.

Just as in the 1970s and 1980s the fire control computer added a new dimension to tank gun accuracy, so in the 1990s will the introduction of Automatic Target Detection and Tracking (ATDT). With more than sufficient storage capacity available in modern computers and the thermal imager sensors already installed, it is just a matter of time and money to develop the pattern recognition algorithms. Fire control systems will be able to lock on to even the most agile target, thus eliminating the gunner's tracking error, usually the largest single source of error when firing at a moving target. It will then be possible to fire accurately on the move at a moving target, the most difficult engagement of all and with a very good chance to do the same to the much higher speed anti-tank helicopter. Despite the increased threat, especially from the ATGW helicopter, the long term future of the tank is reasonably assured; or as assured now as it has ever been in the tank's history.

Advances in Gun Technology

The gun systems in use today employ the same fundamental principles of operation as the ancient cannon of 600 years ago. The materials have all been progressively improved but the underlying principles of operation represent a limitation on performance. In recent years, there have also been major changes in armour technology and the new advanced armours are becoming more and more difficult to defeat. This has prompted renewed research into new methods of weapon propulsion which offer real advantages in performance.

The Electromagnetic Gun

One line of research is being directed to develop the Electromagnetic (EM) gun. By definition this is any mechanism in which the projectile is propelled by an electromagnetic interaction between itself and the launcher. Several attempts to use this concept for weapon propulsion have been made over the last century but each failed because of the inability to handle the huge amounts of energy required. However, research continued and if solutions to the problems could be found, then EM technology would offer some significant advances over conventional guns:

The potential to achieve higher velocities, giving higher hit probabilities, especially against fast-moving and agile targets as well as the potential for increased terminal effects. Speeds up to 8 kms per second have been achieved in research demonstrations with velocities of 10–15 kms per second a real possibility.

A very considerable reduction in the vulnerability due to the absence of any high explosive propellant in the tank. The potential to achieve very rapid firing rates due to the absence of individually loaded propellant charges and the need to seal the chamber.

A reduction of the flash and blast caused in a conventional gun by propellant gases expanding and burning in the atmosphere at shot exit.

A reduction in the overall cost of ammunition due primarily to the replacement of the high explosive propellant charges by a normal hydrocarbon fuel to drive the electrical generator.

Principle of Operation

Whatever the type of EM gun, the fundamental principle of operation is the same and is described by Fleming's Left Hand Rule. The simplest embodiment of this rule in EM guns is widely termed the Railgun and is the configuration used in the early Australian research and which is receiving most development effort. The Railgun (see Figure 2.5) comprises two parallel rails, normally copper or a copper alloy, which are rigidly secure and electrically insulated. The bore thus formed can be square, rectangular or circular in section. The projectile is attached to a conductor which rides between the rails and acts as an armature. A power source is applied across the ends of the pair of rails and this causes the current to flow along the rail, through the armature and back down the second rail. The current produces a magnetic field around the rails which combine to generate a perpendicular field between the rails. Where the current passes across the armature the field and

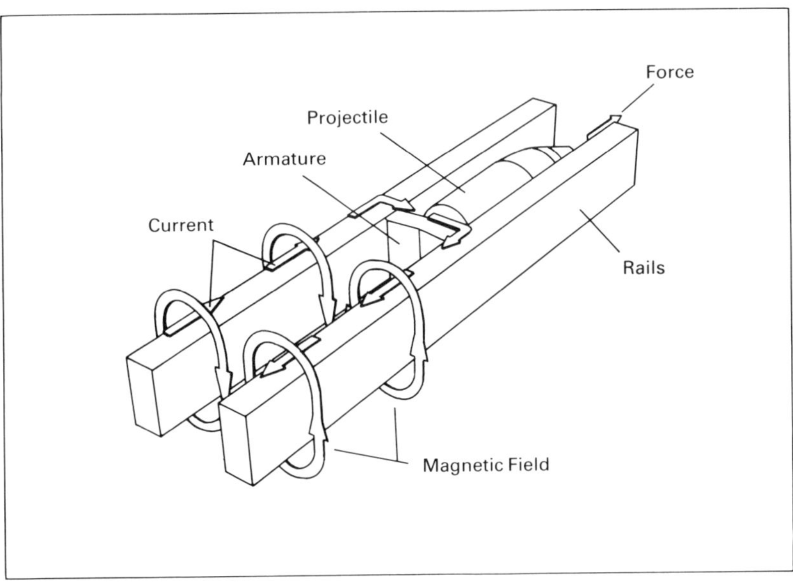

FIG. 2.5 The basic railgun concept.

current are mutually perpendicular and produce a force in the third axis, that is along the gun bore. The Railgun is clearly very simple in construction and requires the minimum of power switching but is relatively inefficient and does have the inherent problems associated with passing very high currents, of the order of 3 mega amps, through armatures travelling at high velocities. One way round the problem is to do away with metal contact altogether and employ a plasma—that is a gas at high temperature which is able to conduct electricity—to fulfill the function of the armature. This however, does present additional problems as the plasma operates at temperatures of around 20,000 degrees Kelvin.

Several different devices can be used to power a Railgun such as capacitors, batteries, or rotating energy storage systems like the compulsator or homopolar generator, the latter being essentially a metal disc or drum rotating in a magnetic field. The rotor of the homopolar generator can be made with sufficient mass to act as a flywheel so that it can be charged with mechanical energy over a relatively long period and then discharged as electrical energy over a very much shorter period, generating the high currents required.

In summary, a number of countries are carrying out research into EM systems and significant advances have been made in the last 10 years. There are still many engineering problems to be overcome and design options to be investigated. However, when they have been successfully developed, EM guns offer the potential radically to change the land battle in ways that have not yet been fully realised.

Liquid Propellant Gun

Initial work on liquid propellants was derived in 1940 in the USA from a catapult for launching aircraft from carriers. The advantages offered by Liquid Propellant

(LP) guns over conventional solid propellant guns can be substantial. For example, LP guns achieve an increase in muzzle velocity for a given weight of projectile as peak chamber pressures are lower and there is a more sustained, less violent acceleration of the projectile up the bore, as shown by the figures for acceleration in Figure 2.6. LP offers the prospect of a lower peak pressure for the

Optimised characteristic	Conventional gun	Liquid propellant
Velocity (m/sec)	1550	1710
Shot acceleration (g)	57,000	35,000
Propellant mass (kg)	8.3	21.7

FIG. 2.6 Characteristics of LP and conventional gun.

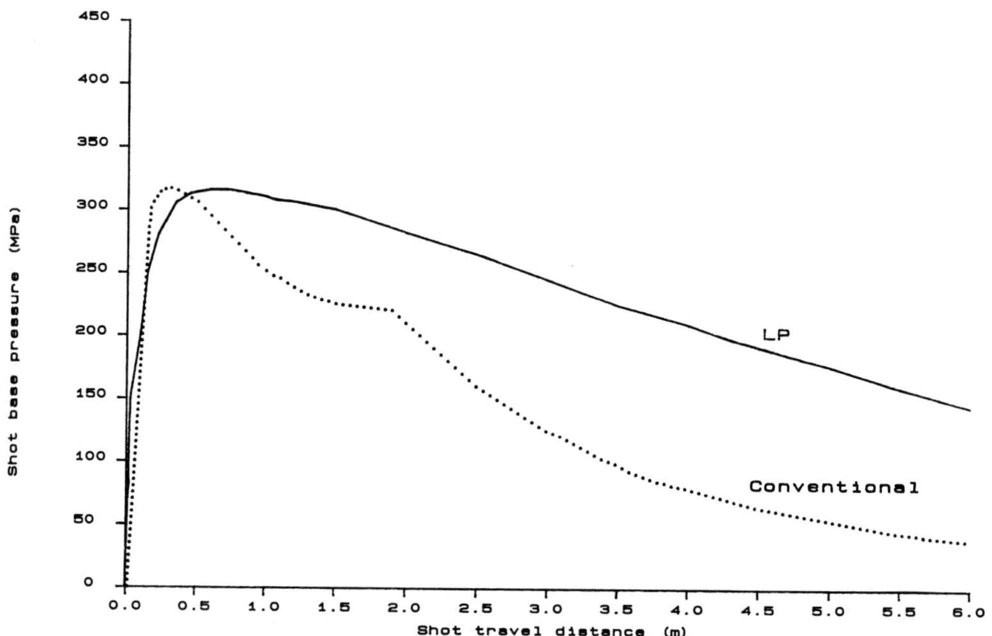

FIG. 2.7 Comparison of shot pressure of liquid propellant and conventional powder gun.

same muzzle velocity (see Figure 2.7) with longer sustained pressure until shot exit, a lower operating temperature, reduced chamber and bore wear and simplified stowage arrangements for the liquid propellant inside the tank. A reduction in peak pressure also reduces barrel wear and increases fatigue life, permits a reduction in the parasitic weight of the sabot and thus a similar increase in the weight of the penetrator. In addition, the manufacturing costs of LP are considerably less than the costs of solid propellant. Of particular significance to field artillery guns is the LP gun's ability to cover from minimum to maximum range (zoning) without the need for a variety of charges. This markedly reduces costs and waste, simplifies and reduces the volume of logistic support, reduces the demands on crew and enhances response time, particularly the gun's ability to lay down the initial burst quickly.

Principles of Operation

Three methods of combusting the liquid propellants in guns have been developed. The two main methods are bulk and regenerative loading and work in the United States on the third, the travelling charge system, continues. Potentially, this system offers significant improvements in performance but details are scarce at present.

Monopropellant

There are three main types of propellant, hypergolic bipropellant (ignites spontaneously when mixed) or non-hypergolic mono or bipropellants. As with a conventional powder propellant, a liquid monopropellant contains its own oxygen and is therefore capable of sustaining the chemical reaction once it has been ignited. Examples of monopropellants are nitromethane, HTP (High Test Peroxide and water) and hydrazine all of which were originally developed for torpedo propulsion.

Bipropellant

A bipropellant consists of a fuel and an oxidiser which are injected into the gun chamber and ignited. A commonly used oxidiser such as liquid oxygen in combination with either kerosene or liquid hydrogen as the fuel requires a separate igniter, usually some form of pyrotechnic. Other oxidisers such as nitric acid when used with fuels such as hydrazine are hypergolic.

Choice of Propellant

The choice of a liquid propellant, either mono or bipropellant, for a particular application is a compromise of several factors:

Performance
Safety
Handling properties

Although high performance is always sought, the safety and handling properties, both in the vehicle itself and in the logistic chain, are major considerations. Cryogenic liquids such as oxygen would be impractical because of the problems of storage but also because of the difficulty of pre-cooling the transfer lines and breech to prevent boil-off during the loading of a shot. For in-service use, 'packageable' propellants have to be chosen with sufficient chemical stability to withstand long term sealed storage, even at relatively high temperatures combined with low enough freezing point for operation at low temperatures.

Choice of Gun

Bulk Loaded LP Gun

The bulk loaded method may be used for either monopropellants and non-hypergolic bipropellants and is shown schematically at Figure 2.8. Ignition of the propellant is usually achieved either using a pyrotechnic or spark. The shot must be rammed home in the gun to form the seal at the bore end of the chamber. After

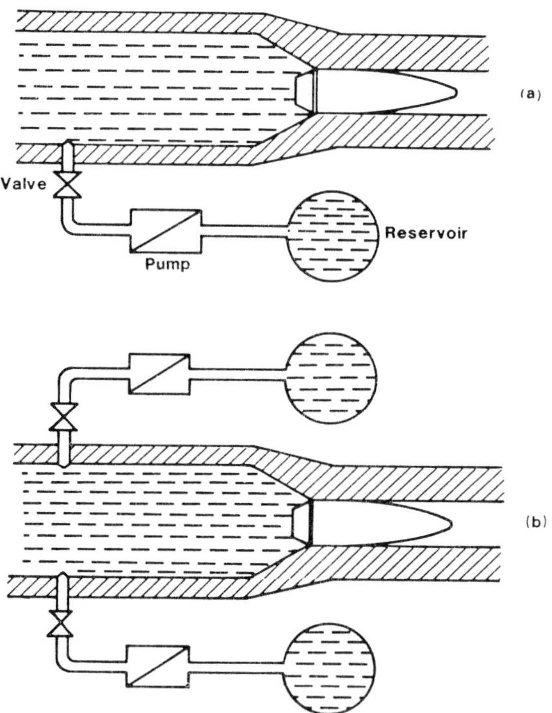

FIG. 2.8 Schematic diagram of bulk loaded liquid propellant gun (a) Mono-propellant hyperbolic, (b) Non-hyopergolic bipropellant.

the breech is closed, propellant is pumped into the chamber but in order to prevent the formation of a myriad of bubbles in the liquid, the air should be evacuated either by a venting valve or preferably by vacuum line as bubbles can have a catastrophic effect on the subsequent combustion. Probably because of its apparent simplicity, many studies have claimed that a bulk loaded LP gun is virtually ready for installation in a tank. But the practical difficulties of accurate metering of the liquid propellant and particularly the reproducibility of the ballistics are greater than those for a solid propellant gun and many of the technical demonstrators have not demonstrated its best features.

Regenerative Injection LP Gun

Regenerative injection can be used to combust both monopropellants and hypergolic and non-hypergolic bipropellants and a system is shown schematically in Figure 2.9. Ignition may be achieved spontaneously, catalytically or by

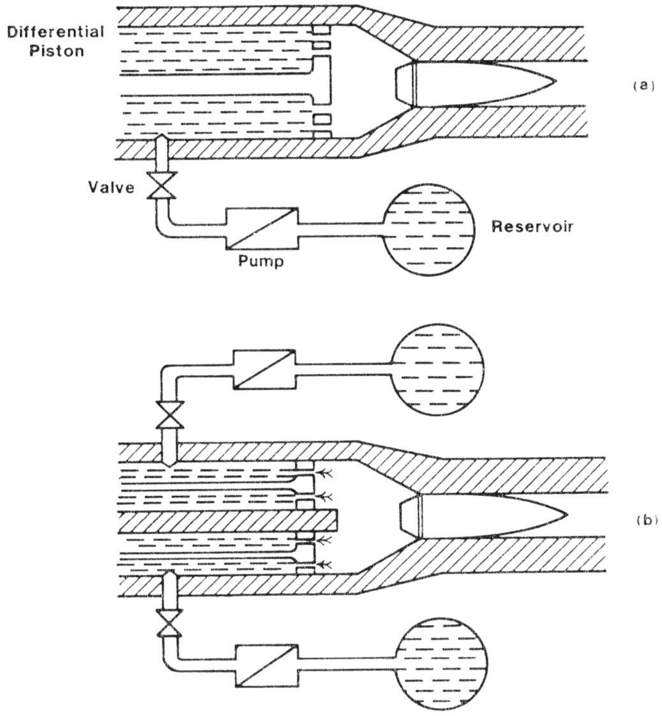

FIG. 2.9 Schematic diagram of regenerative injection liquid propellant gun (a) Monopropellant, (b) Bipropellant.

pyrotechnic or spark methods depending on the nature of the propellant. In this type of gun the igniter must not only provide the combustion stimulus but also the initial pressure to activate the propellant injection process. These two activities may be difficult to achieve harmoniously, have yet to be entirely solved and have added to the complexity of the overall system. Hypergolic bipropellants offer simplified ignition but still require the initial pressure stimulus.

The principle of operation is that the pressure generated by the combustion process acts on a piston which has a number of injectors. The area on the liquid side of the piston is less than that on the gas side and this causes the injection and atomisation of the liquid propellant into the combustion chamber. The mechanical arrangement of the injectors creates some weight and size penalties. An axially (or in line) injector makes loading the projectile more difficult and complex as the mechanism must be so constructed as to allow easy access. To overcome this difficulty, radially opposed injectors were developed but this led to a large gun breech which made installation difficult in the confines of a tank turret. A similar concept developed in the United Kingdom used four pistons parallel to the gun axis with a standard split block breech. This is shown in Figure 2.10. However, the

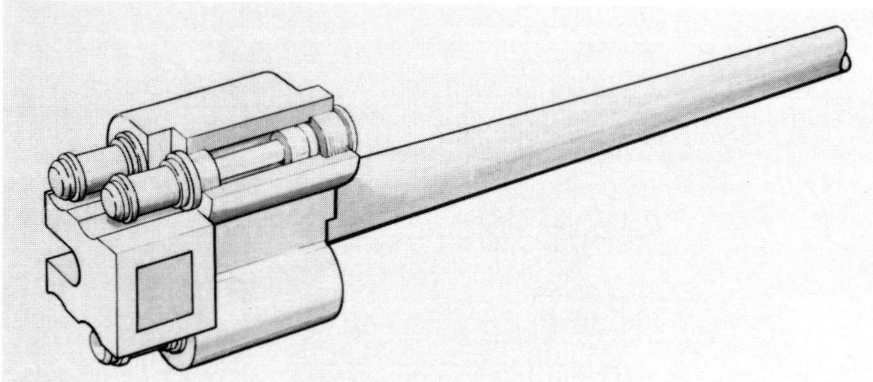

FIG. 2.10 Diagram of a regenerative liquid propellant tank gun with radially opposed injectors.

mounting of a LP gun into a tank turret entails a far less radical transformation than would be the case with electromagnetic weapons. In any case larger calibre powder guns cannot be accommodated without substantial redesign. An artist's impression of a liquid propellant gun installed in a tank is at Figure 2.11. Other

FIG. 2.11 A concept of a future MBT with a liquid propellant gun.

advantages of LP over the conventional powder gun include more efficient use of the internal volume of the vehicle; a saving in the manufacturing costs of propellant once the set-up costs have been paid; reduced storage space and much simplified logistic transport arrangements in the operational theatre. For a given number of rounds, in volume terms, liquid propellant occupies less space than the equivalent number of solid charges, so less internal space needs to be devoted to ammunition stowage. The designer has more options in deciding the most favourable location within the vehicle for stowing the liquid propellant than with the more bulky solid charges. A summary of the advantages and disadvantages of liquid propellant and a 'standard' conventional high energy powder propellant is at Figure 2.12.

Characteristic	***Liquid propellant***	***Remarks***
Force	135%	10%
Wear	Similar	Flame temperature lower but local high spots occur
Shock sensitivity	Better	
Toxicity	Varies	Some types better, some worse
Corrosiveness	Varies	As above
Temperature limitation	Similar	Good low temperature performance
Penetration	Up to 25% improvement	
Range	Potentially greater	
Zoning	Much better	Saving between 30–60% in weight of propellant
Loading density	Better	More charges stowed on board but larger breech
Propellant costs	Much cheaper	About 10% of powder propellant
Flash/smoke	Much better	
Blast overpressure	Much worse	Hearing and blast damage
Gun weight	Similar	

FIG. 2.12 Comparison of the advantages and disadvantages of liquid propellant with a typical high energy solid propellant.

Autoloaders

The development of the plethora of modern anti-tank weapons have given urgent need to reduce the signatures (thermal, radar, acoustic etc) of the next generation of main battle tank. Most of all, though, there is a need to reduce the size of the tank because of the many additional benefits that result (descending the Weight Spiral, see Fig. 4.12). The most significant advantage of reduced size is that a smaller target is more difficult to acquire and more difficult to hit.

The idea of reducing the number of the crew is not new but the ability first, to decide which member should be eliminated and secondly, how his duties should be carried out has lead to more heated discussion between armoured corps soldiers than any other factor. As is so often the case when radical design changes are required, the Soviets have lead the way. The T-64 and every tank entering service since the early 1970s have had a three man crew and an autoloader. The Russians realised long ago that their infrastructure, both civil and military, would not be able to cope with a 60 tonne tank but the threat from the wide variety of NATO anti-tank weapons would require them to have a well protected tank. The only way this could be achieved was to reduce the size; certainly, a shortage of manpower was not a consideration. The only Western tank with a three man crew is the new French tank, Leclerc, which was fitted with a bustle autoloader though most NATO nations have carried out studies and initiated technical demonstration programmes.

In a tank with a conventional rotating turret, the most obvious crewman to be eliminated is the loader, replacing him by an autoloader. Autoloaders have been used in warships for some considerable time and their selection for the tank was both an obvious and technically simple decision. The conventional wisdom, therefore, was that the only crewman who could be automated was the loader, since no mechanical or other system was available to replace either the commander or the driver. However, the advent of the wide variety of technical aids—thermal imaging, map display, automatic target detection and tracking, and inter-vehicle digital communication should cause one to consider whether the loader is necessarily the most suitable crewman to be replaced. In view of the mechanical complexity of an autoloader, a more practical and robust alternative might be to retain the man as the loader and combine the tasks of the gunner and commander. Most modern tanks have virtually identical facilities for both commander and gunner, the only significant difference being that the commander retains an override capability as befits his command function.

Types of Autoloader

There are two main types of autoloader, the bustle and the carousel. Both have advantages and disadvantages and both can be either electric or hydraulic or a combination of the two. The use of some form of electronic control system for ammunition selection, for example, would be in keeping with the other systems in the tank, although the Soviets did not use electronics in their original autoloaders. Needless to say, the requirement for reliability is paramount, since no control system yet devised has anything like the ability of the crewman to circumvent minor faults or battle damage and to cater for the unexpected. The two different types are described below.

Bustle Autoloader

A schematic diagram of a bustle autoloader is shown in Figure 2.13. Of the two types, the bustle is the only one which could be fitted to in-service tanks during a retrofit programme. Most current tanks, even the British Chieftain and Challenger, stow some part of their ammunition above the turret ring and even though a major restowage exercise would be required, it could be achieved, see Figure 2.14.

The number of rounds carried would depend on the length and the calibre but a figure of around 24 would be usual. Current tanks carry about 40–50 rounds so either the tank fitted with the bustle autoloader would have to be replenished more often or more rounds would have to be carried in the hull. The rounds are stowed in

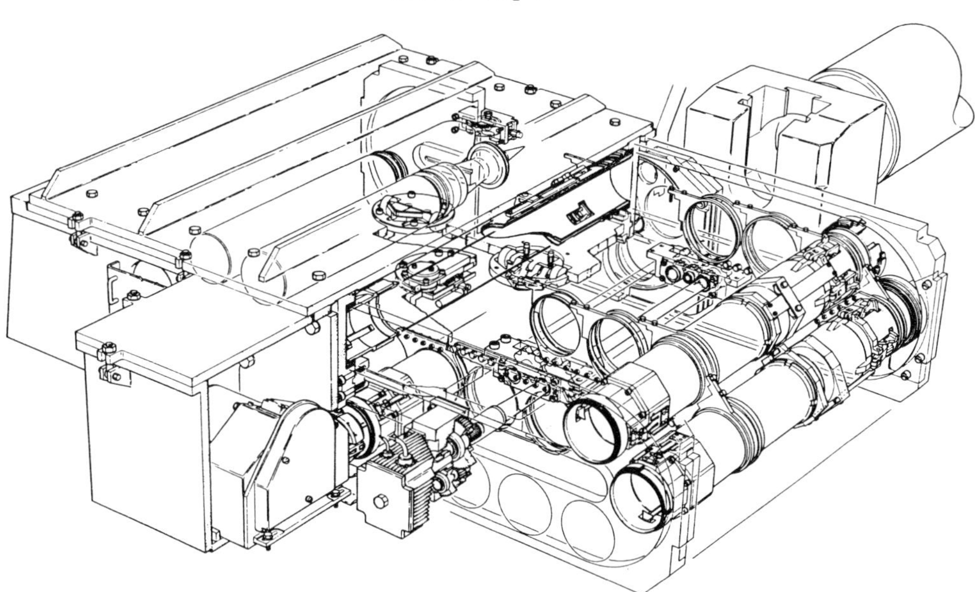

FIG. 2.13 Schematic diagram of a bustle autoloader.

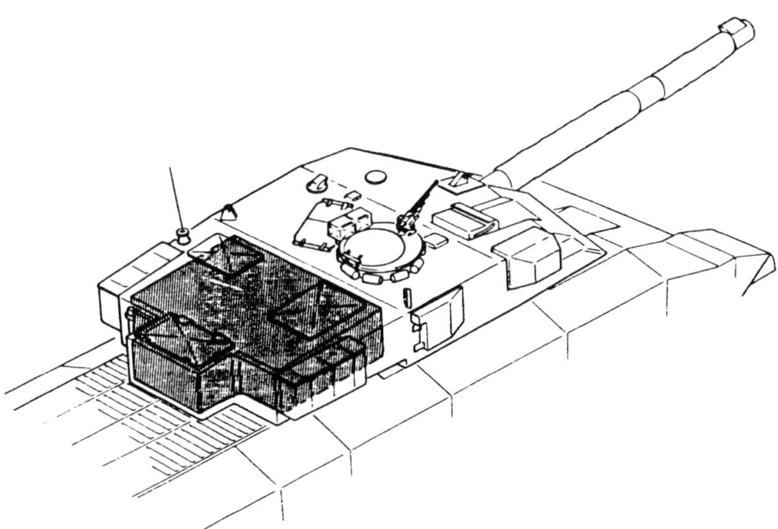

FIG. 2.14 The bustle autoloader shown mounted at the rear of a tank turret.

tubes on an endless belt within the autoloader. Mechanical or optical devices detect which type of round (fin stabilised or HEAT) has been loaded so the gunner only has to initiate the loading sequence for the control system to move the correct type of round to the ramming position.

A typical loading sequence would run along the following lines:

The gun breech is opened on gun recoil and the gun returns to an index position.
The rammer rams the next round of the type selected by the gunner.
The breech closes, the gun returns to the last point of aim.
The autoloader control system automatically selects a round of the same type and moves it to the ramming position.

Carousel Autoloader

A schematic diagram of a carousel autoloader is shown in Figure 2.15. As can be seen, the main difference is that the ammunition is stowed in a circular, rotating structure on the turret floor. Ammunition is two-piece, the projectile and propellant stowed one above the other, each complete round called a cassette. A loading sequence would run along the following lines:

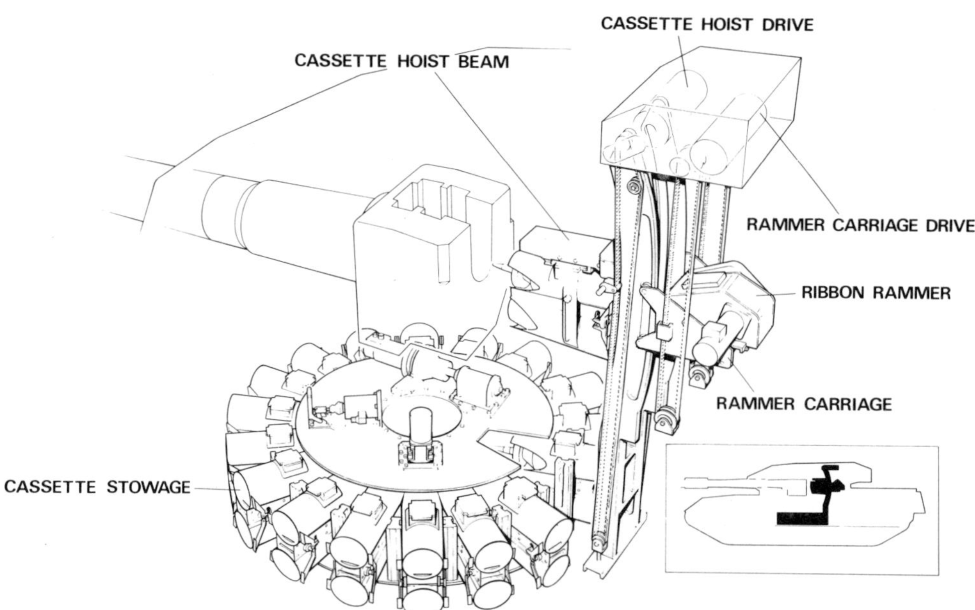

FIG. 2.15 Schematic diagram of a carousel autoloader.

The gun breech is opened on gun recoil and the gun returns to an index position.
A cassette of the selected type of ammunition is rotated to the lower end of the hoist and locked in position.
The belt-driven vertical hoist lifts the cassette first to align the projectile opposite the breech for ramming and then the charge which is rammed in a two-part operation.

The cassette is then lowered by the hoist ready to load the next round of the same type if required.

As in the bustle autoloader, a microprocessor with the capability to recognise types of ammunition, controls the whole operation. Because of the two separate ramming operations, the process takes a little longer than the bustle autoloader. Again, high reliability levels are demanded of the system.

3

The Weapon System

The principal purpose of the Weapon System in any fighting vehicle is to enable the crew to acquire a target and bring the gun to bear as quickly and accurately as possible, in order to engage that target. For the purposes of this chapter, therefore, the 'Weapon System' encompasses the equipment which:

> Provides the crew members with the means of observing and acquiring targets,
> Determines the range to the target, and measures those other parameters which effect engagement accuracy,
> Calculates the correct gun position for a first round hit,
> Drives the gun in azimuth and elevation to the fire position.

This list deliberately excludes the gun and ammunition, which are covered in detail in Chapter 2.

In order to describe the Weapon System, it is convenient to divide it into its various sub-systems and consider them individually. Therefore, this chapter will describe each of the elements which go to make up the weapon system, consider the integration of these elements into armoured fighting vehicles and then assess their impact on overall performance. However, if a Weapon System is to function successfully, it must be considered as an entity. Like a chain, the system is only as strong as its weakest link, so it is essential that the capabilities of each element be matched to produce a balanced whole.

Target Observation and Acquisition

Introduction

When the first tanks went into action in the First World War, they were provided with the most rudimentary vision devices—small apertures or peep holes, sometimes equipped with thin glass prisms. Peering through these slits, their eyes blinded by exhaust gases and gun fumes, the crews found it very difficult to spot targets, maintain course and keep station with accompanying vehicles. Nevertheless, for the slow-moving vehicles of the time, operating in an infantry-support role against relative short-range targets, these crude vision devices were sufficient.

In order to exploit the key features of the tank—its mobility, firepower and protection—it was essential that improved vision devices should be provided. With these the tank could detect targets and (as firepower improved) engage and destroy them at longer ranges. Furthermore, better observation enhanced the shock effect of tanks, by enabling them to move quickly *en masse* and to fight closed down. At the same time, it was essential that any improvements to the vision devices should not degrade the integrity of the armour.

Despite massive improvements in technology, as optical sights have been joined by various opto-electronic vision devices, these fundamental requirements remain.

Optical Vision Devices

Introduction

Optical vision devices still play an important role in modern AFVs because, compared with electronic units, they are generally cheaper, simpler, more reliable and relatively easy to maintain. The modern optical sight provides a full colour image with good resolution and it can operate quite successfully in less than optimum light conditions. Users feel comfortable with optical sights, because the image presented is akin to what is seen in everyday life.

On the other hand, optical sights are practically useless during the hours of darkness, unless artificial illumination is provided, and are of limited value in smoke and mist. The daylight sight requires a relatively large hole to be cut in the armour of the tank, which degrades the protection, and it must be positioned close to the crewman, thus limiting the choice of location for the unit. The glass in optical sights will be permanently darkened by the radiation from nuclear explosions. This effect can be offset by choosing glass which is nuclear hard, but at the expense of a permanent reduction in light transmission. For example, a sight with non nuclear-hard glass might have a light transmission of 65% reduced to 10–15% by nuclear radiation. The same sight with nuclear-hard glass would have an initial light transmission of perhaps 35%, but this would only drop to about 30% following a nuclear event. Finally, as the threat of laser weapons increases, so does the need for sight protection. Whether these protection measures are mechanical, optical or electronic they are likely to increase the cost and complexity of the sights and reduce or limit their performance.

Vision Blocks

The simplest optical device is the unity magnification (×1) periscope vision block, which can be used in a number of locations in the tank. The commander's station is usually provided with a number of these to give an instantaneous 'all round' vision facility when closed own. They are particularly useful for:

Observing a broad sector,
Map reading,
Keeping station with accompanying vehicles while on the move,
Guarding against attacks by infantry armed with short range anti-tank missiles.

To maximise their usefulness, the commander's unity vision blocks should be positioned so that their Fields of View (FOV) overlap and leave the minimum of 'dead' ground close in to the tank. The external face of the vision block should be

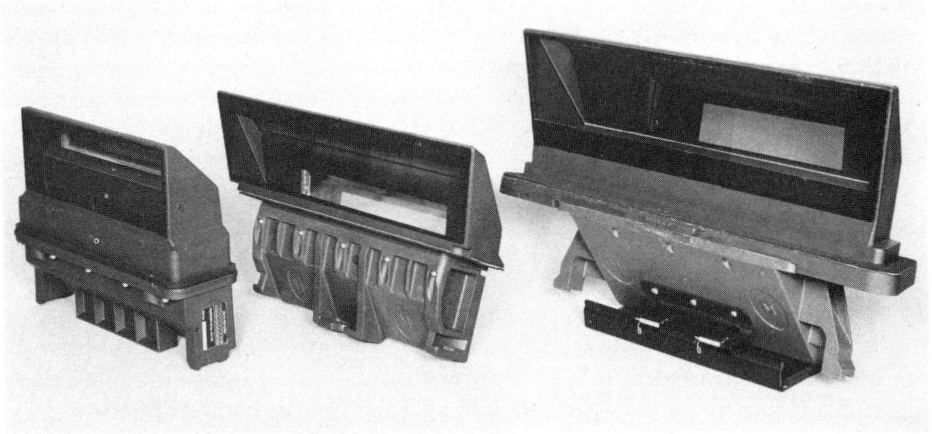

FIG. 3.1 Unity Vision Periscope.

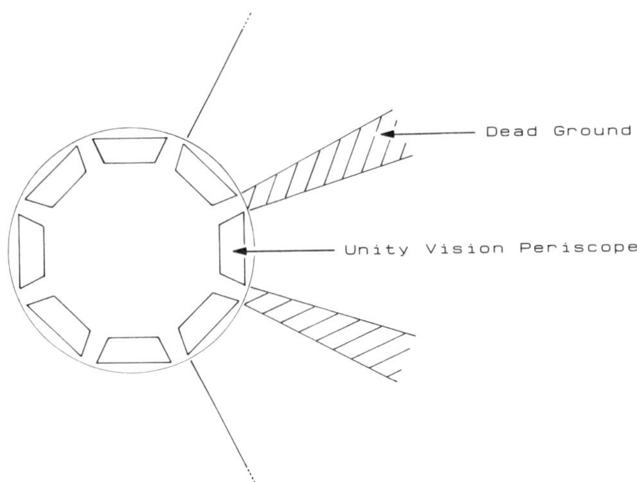

FIG. 3.2 Schematic diagram illustrating 'dead' ground.

angled away from the vertical, to prevent it's acting as a reflector for laser weapons, or sunlight early and late in the day. The driver, normally located low down in the tank, requires good forward and peripheral vision if he is to manoeuvre the vehicle successfully in close country or built-up areas. To do this he will have either one unity vision block with a wide azimuth FOV or two or three, positioned with their FOVs overlapping. For the loader, a rotatable unity vision block provides a 'window on the world', which is important psychologically when operating in a closed-down vehicle and which also allows him to play an active role in the observation task.

For the future, the day of the simple vision block may be numbered as far as the most modern tanks are concerned. Although they are simple and inexpensive, they do require apertures in the tank's armour close to the crew stations and crewmen using them are vulnerable to attack by laser weapons. A simple system using a low cost television camera would provide a relatively cheap and flexible alternative, since it could easily be integrated with existing viewers, such as those currently used for thermal imager displays.

High Magnification Sights

The definition of 'high magnification' varies, but ×10 (approximately) is a typical current value. Sights with higher magnifications (up to ×15) have been used, but they tend to suffer from picture vibration and heat shimmer, reduced light transmission and a very limited field of view. The high magnification channel is used principally for target engagements and, to assist the operator in his observation and acquisition task, a separate low magnification channel is usually included in the sight. For the latter, magnification values in the range ×1 to ×3 are typical.

Zoom lenses, capable of changing continuously from low to high magnification, have not found significant application in tank sights. This stems from a number of factors, but particularly:

Such lens systems are more complex and hence more expensive,
Their moving parts are vulnerable to mechanical failure in the hostile environment of the tank,
The need to operate over a range of magnifications means that optimum performance at any one magnification is difficult to achieve,
Maintaining graticule alignment with moving optical components is complicated.

Nevertheless, if these problems can be overcome, the zoom lens could offer an elegant solution to the dual magnification requirement.

For a number of years now there have been significant improvements in optical sight design, leading to better performance in a number of areas. Advances in optical coating technology and the use of computers as design tools, have helped to create sights with fewer optical components, distortion-free images and higher light transmission figures—60 to 70% now being achievable in the less complicated sights. These high transmission figures enable such sights to be used to advantage during the dusk and dawn period, when ambient light conditions are less than ideal.

Sight Eyepieces

The eyepieces of most modern high magnification sights are either monocular or biocular. Monocular sights, in which the scene is presented to one eye, are the simplest and produce the minimum light loss, although they can cause eye strain and other physiological problems, especially when used for long periods. Also, since each eye is connected to one side of the brain, the monocular system does not make full use of the operators cognitive facilities.

With binocular eyepieces, the light enters the sight via a single objective lens and is divided by a beam splitter, with the same image being presented to both eyes. Although the beam splitter causes some light loss, the overall effect is beneficial. Apart from the reduction in eye strain, there is evidence that operator performance is improved by some 10% to 15% when both eyes are used.

From the performance point of view, the optimum system is the binocular, in which each eye has a totally independent channel. However, binocular systems are rarely used because they have a number of disadvantages. In particular, they need a larger aperture in the turret, the increased number of components makes them more expensive and they require careful setting up and maintenance to keep the two channels optically aligned.

The conventional main battle tank, with a turret and a four man crew, usually has two high magnification daylight optical sights, one each at both the gunner's and commander's stations. For convenience, they can be divided into two types:

Periscopic sights, which are mounted on the roof of the turret, and
Direct sights, or telescopes, which require an aperture in the front of the turret.

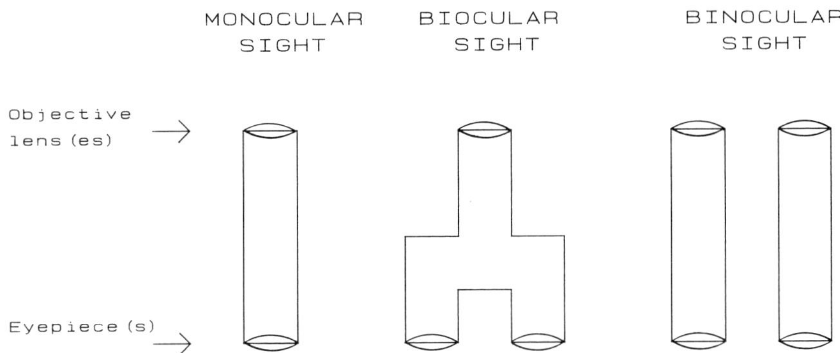

FIG. 3.3 Monocular, Biocular and Binocular Eyepieces.

Periscopic Sights

Until the advent of Overhead Top Attack (OTA), the periscopic sight had a distinct advantage from the protection point of view, as it preserved the integrity of the turret frontal armour. However, to maintain the alignment of the periscopic sight with the gun, it is necessary to elevate and depress the Line of Sight (LOS), either by moving the sight itself or its top mirror, using a mechanical parallelogram linkage or sensors. The offset between the gun and the sight produces a parallax error, but this can be compensated for by means of the fire control computer. When a parallelogram linkage is used, the accuracy of the system can be degraded if the vehicle is subjected to large changes in temperature.

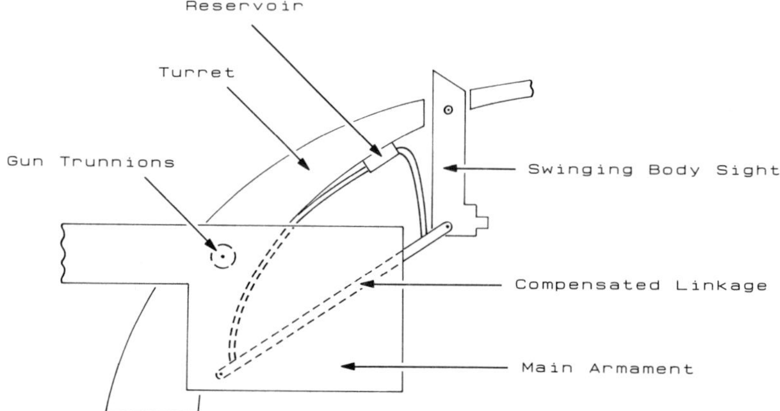

FIG. 3.4 Parallelogram Linkage with Temperature Compensation.

In these circumstances, the turret shell (which forms one side of the parallelogram) will expand or contract and affect the geometry of the parallelogram. To overcome this problem, a compensated linkage can be used. Water is pumped through the linkage from a reservoir adjacent to the outer skin of the turret, equalising the turret and linkage temperatures. Thus, expansion or contraction is also equalised and system accuracy is maintained.

The fixed link is still present in some of today's tanks as it is simple, robust and reasonably reliable. Nevertheless, it does have a number of limitations, as follows:

It occupies valuable space in the turret and requires careful adjustment to maintain accuracy,
The turret and gun must be moved in order to move the LOS,
The speed of movement of the LOS is restricted to the speed at which the turret can be traversed and the gun can be elevated or depressed,
The stabilisation of the LOS cannot be better than that of the gun and turret to which it is linked, assuming that they are stabilised.

Stabilised Sights

These restrictions make it very difficult for the tank to engage moving targets and fight on the move, something it must be able to do if it is to survive on today's battlefield. For these reasons, stabilised periscopic sights are now taking the place of 'fixed link' sights in modern MBTs. In these sights the sight body inside the vehicle is fixed while the top mirror in the sight head is gyro stabilised, usually in both the elevation and traverse axes. Being independent of the gun and turret, the very light top mirror (typically a few kilogrammes) can easily be steered by the operator in azimuth and elevation, enabling him to lay quickly and accurately onto targets and track them smoothly. Although these improvements in performance are most marked when either the firing tank or its target are moving, there are also benefits in speed and accuracy when firing static versus static engagements. However, whatever the benefits of an independent stabilised sight,

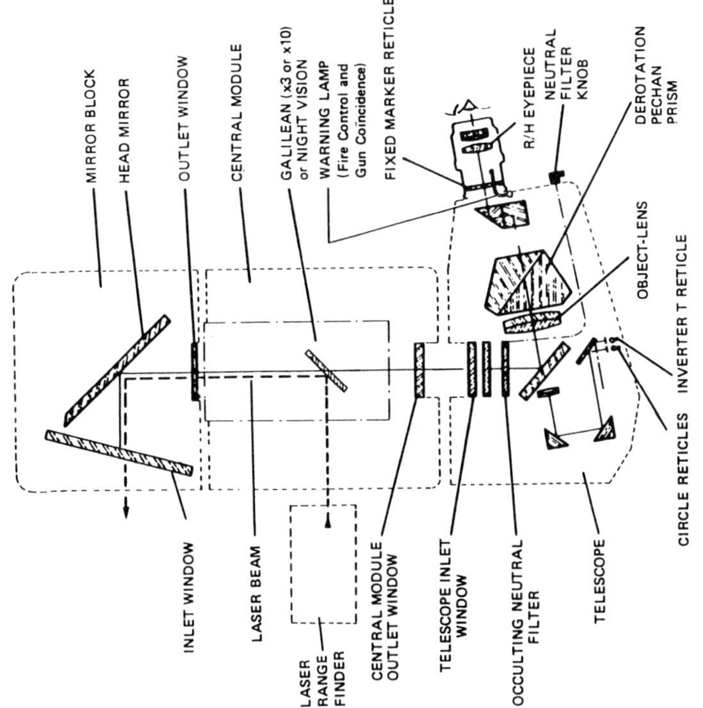

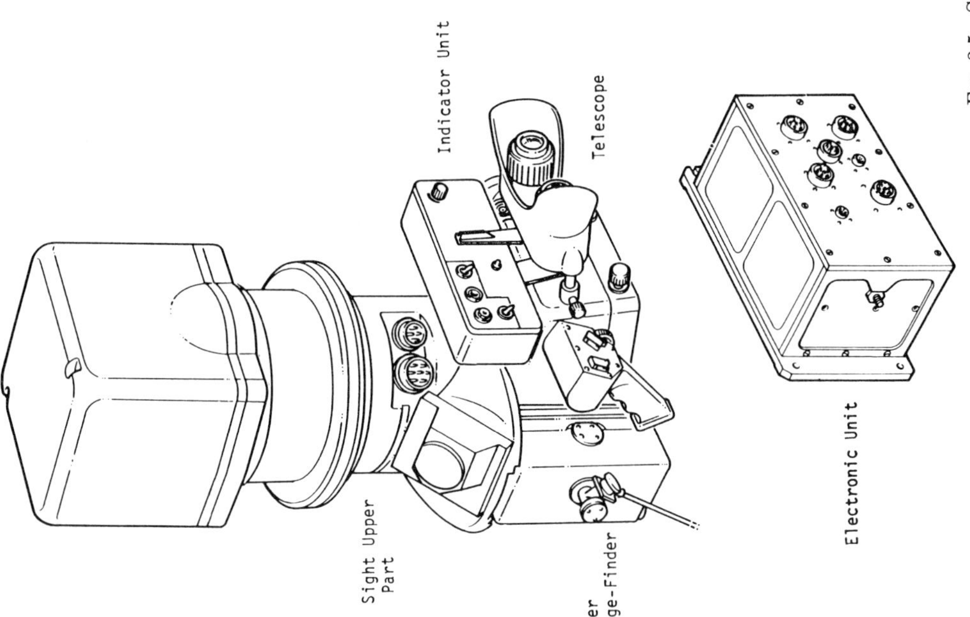

FIG. 3.5 Stabilised Panoramic Sight.

they are at their most potent when integrated with a computerised fire control system, as detailed in a later section of this chapter.

Panoramic Sights

A commander's stabilised sight would normally be positioned at the highest point of the turret, enabling him to rotate his LOS through 6400 mils (360 degrees) in azimuth—a panoramic sight. However, to prevent the image from being inverted after 3200 mils (180 degrees) of rotation, the sights must be fitted with de-rotation optics. These additional elements make panoramic optical sights more complicated, and hence more expensive, and also reduce the light transmission.

Stabilised sights at the gunner's station normally have a limited degree of movement in azimuth, since the gunner's sight head is often sunk slightly into the roof armour and consequently has only a restricted forward view. In these circumstances, the gunner's stabilised sight has no need to be panoramic and will often omit the de-rotation optics, in order to reduce the cost and complexity of the sight and achieve the maximum light transmission. One drawback is that the image in the sight tips over slightly from the vertical when the LOS is traversed left or right, but this is not significant enough to disorient the gunner and prevent him from using the sight.

In general, stabilised and panoramic sights, with their gyro systems and de-rotation optics, are expensive and, being more complicated than the fixed link sights, they can be less reliable and require more maintenance. Nevertheless, such sights are essential equipment in a modern battle tank if it is to acquire and engage moving targets while itself being in motion. Quite simply, without this capability, a tank is likely to find itself outclassed.

Direct Sights or Telescopes

In the direct sight, the objective lens is normally positioned alongside the gun barrel and moves with it. Although this eliminates the need for any kind of linkage and overcomes the parallax problem, it does result in an aperture in the turret frontal armour, albeit a small one. Compared to the stabilised panoramic sight, the direct sight is cheap, reliable and relatively simple, apart from the flexible optical elbow between the objective lens (which moves with the gun) and the eyepiece (which must remain fixed, close to the operators eye). Where a tank has a periscopic gunners sight, a direct sight is often fitted as an auxiliary or emergency sight. The direct sight normally has one high magnification channel only, in order to minimise the aperture in the frontal armour. As with the mechanically linked periscopic sight, the turret and gun must be moved in order to lay onto and track targets and, similarly, the stabilisation performance is limited to what can be achieved with the gun and turret.

Graticules

The high magnification sight is normally equipped with a graticule (or reticule). The graticule, which overlays the field of view, is a pattern of marks which can be

FIG. 3.6 Stabilised Sight Head Mirror.

used for alignment and gunnery purposes. For each particular set of conditions (such as charge temperature, air pressure and target speed) a different set of graticule markings would be required, but such an approach is impractical since it would clutter the field of view and render the sight unusable. Therefore, most graticules define the correct gun position for a number of target ranges but they are only accurate for one particular set of circumstances. A typical graticule is shown in Figure 3.7. The Muzzle Bore Sight (MBS) mark in the graticule acts as a reference for aligning the sight with the main armament, and an integral laser range finder, if fitted, would also be collimated with this MBS mark. Thus, the MBS mark defines the line of sight to the target. The gunnery ranging marks in the example cover two types of ammunition—a high velocity KE round (which requires relatively small gun offsets in elevation) and a lower velocity HE round.

Conventional graticules are etched on to glass and either positioned in the optical path or injected via a half-silvered mirror. If too much information is included on the graticule, the operator's field of view can become cluttered. To overcome this problem, it is possible to have graticules which can be switched in and out or partially masked, although great care must be taken to maintain alignment accuracy. As an alternative, graticules may be generated electronically and these can easily be switched off or masked when not required. As both etched and electronic graticules physically exist, they can provide a reflector for the radiation from a Laser Sensor Damage Weapon. In the future, therefore, it is likely

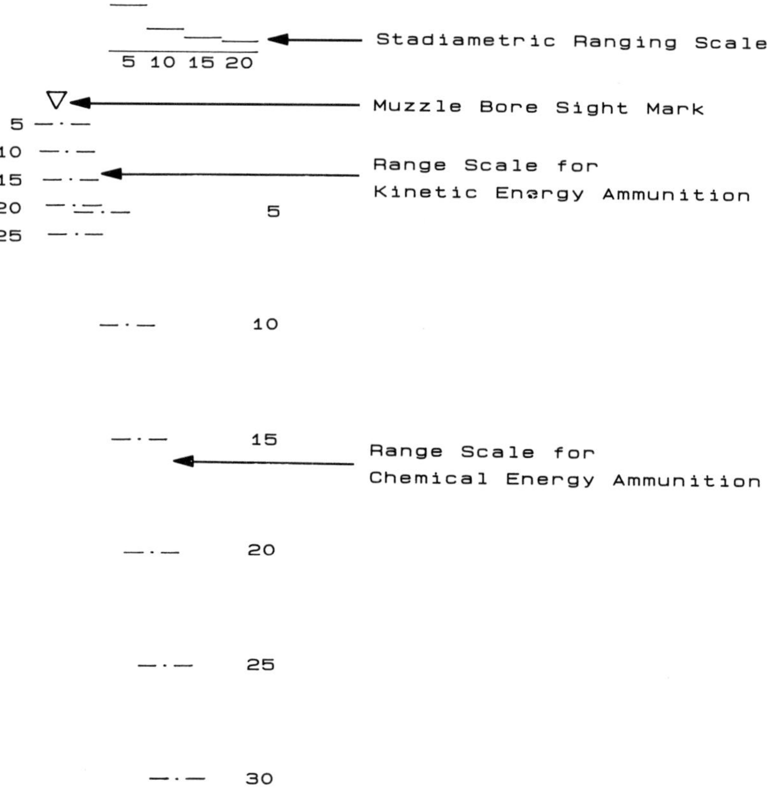

FIG. 3.7 Typical Sight Graticule.

that sight graticules will be generated by holograms, which present no reflector for laser light.

Sight Installation and Alignment

Initial Alignment

When a sight is used for target acquisition and engagement, its physical relationship to the main armament must be known and, preferably, should remain consistent. Fundamental alignment is achieved during turret manufacture, with shims being used to eliminate initial machining errors or permanent distortions. The objective is to ensure that the axis of the gun trunnions is parallel to the axis of rotation of the sight or sight head. Unless this is achieved, the alignment of the gun and sight will not be maintained when they are moved away from their initial setting position.

Muzzle Bore Sight

While the vehicle is in service, it is necessary to have a method of adjusting the gun-to-sight alignment, to cater for distortions of the turret, gun or sighting

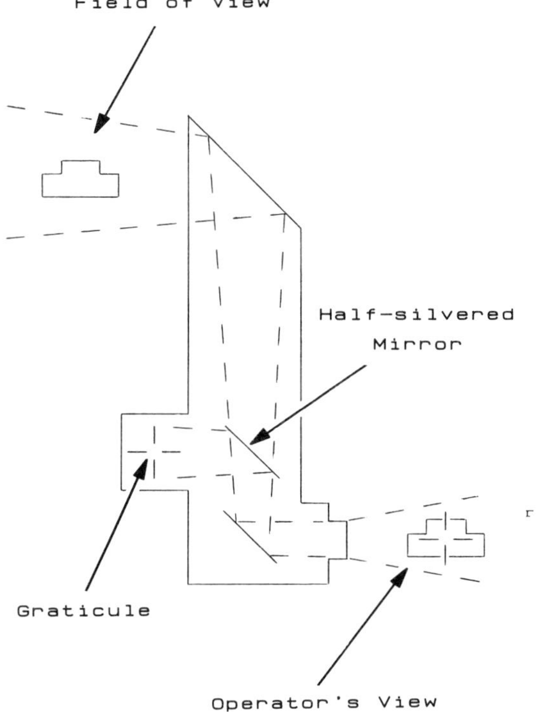

FIG. 3.8 Graticule Injection via a Half-silvered Mirror.

system. This is achieved by using a Muzzle Bore Sight, a highly accurate optical instrument which can be inserted into the muzzle of the gun barrel, where its optical axis aligns precisely with the bore of the barrel. Using this sight, a crewman standing at the muzzle instructs the gunner to lay the barrel bore onto a target at a predetermined range, typically about 1000 metres. The graticule in the sight is then adjusted to align with the same target.

Muzzle Reference System

Once a tank is in action, the use of the Muzzle Bore Sight becomes impractical. However, the initial alignment of the gun and sight can be degraded as the barrel warms up and distorts, albeit minutely. To overcome this misalignment, modern tanks use a Muzzle Reference System (MRS). A basic MRS consists of a light source on the turret, a mirror at the muzzle end of the barrel (protected by a cowling from mud and rain) and a reference mark in the sight graticule, to be used for checking the alignment. Figure 3.9 illustrates how adjustment in azimuth is achieved, but the same principle applies in elevation. Once the gun bore and the sight graticule have been aligned, using the Muzzle Bore Sight, the light source (L) is switched on and then adjusted, so that is virtual image ($V1$) is aligned to the reference mark in the sight (S). Assuming that the gun is then fired and the muzzle moves through a small angle (θ), the virtual image will move through an angle 2θ to

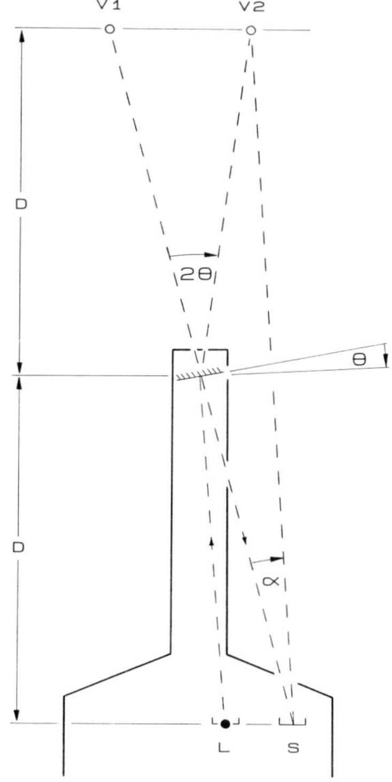

FIG. 3.9 The Principle of Operation of a Muzzle Reference System.

a new position ($V2$). Since the angles involved are small, the distance $V1$ to $V2$ (=x) can be defined as follows:

$$\frac{\mathrm{x}}{\mathrm{D}} = 2\theta \therefore \mathrm{x} = 2\theta . D$$

If the sight (S) is now realigned with the new virtual image ($V2$) it must be moved through an angle α. However, provided the light source is the same distance (D) from the mirror as the sight, the virtual image will be $2D$ distant from the sight and then the angle α can be defined as:

$$\alpha \frac{x}{S \rightarrow V2} = \frac{2\theta . D}{2D} = \theta$$

Thus, the sight is moved through the same angle as the muzzle and alignment is maintained.

The original MRS was first introduced by the United Kingdom in the 1970s and fitted on Chieftain MBTs. The system was manually initiated and, with the light source and receiving sight head being turret roof mounted, could only work at one angle of gun elevation. The latter limitation can be overcome by mounting the light source on the gun mantlet and having the reference mark in a direct sight, also mounted in the mantlet. Thus, all the elements move together and alignment checking is possible at all angles of gun elevation.

Automatic Muzzle Reference System

For the future, an Automatic Muzzle Reference System (AMRS) is likely to replace the current manual or semi-automatic equipment. A light-sensitive detector such as a photodiode is positioned to receive the reflected light, effectively replacing the sight and the gunners eye in Figure 3.9. On initial alignment, the electrical signal produced in the detector becomes a system null. Any subsequent deflection of the MRS mirror causes the reflected light to move across the detector, producing an electrical change which can be used to reposition sight graticules automatically. With an automatic system, it may be possible to correct for gun distortion while the vehicle is on the move, provided that the dynamic effects of vehicle vibrations can be overcome. Operation of an AMRS would probably be initiated after each firing of the gun of following the operation of the laser rangefinder, but the choice lies entirely with the system designer.

Electronic Vision Devices

When visibility is poor and during the hours of darkness, optical vision devices have a very limited capability. In misty or smoky conditions, there is little that can be done to improve observation. At night they can only be employed if the battlefield goes 'white'—ie: if searchlights or flares are used. However, this is far from satisfactory and has a number of serious drawbacks:

A searchlight gives away the attacker's position,
Flares give the target warning of impending attack,
The use of any illumination destroys the dark adaption of the operators eye.

In these circumstances, the growing family of electronic vision devices comes into its own.

Infra-red (IR) Sights

The earliest of these systems appeared towards the end of the Second World War, when the Germans deployed infra-red sensitive sights. A searchlight illuminated the target with invisible near infra-red light and the sight image convertor was able to detect a proportion of the reflected light energy. For a number of years, infra-red was the only form of night vision available but it did not prove particularly satisfactory. The picture definition and range were poor, the IR searchlight required a substantial amount of power and, as an 'active' system, it was easily detected by an infra-red sensor. So a better solution had to be found.

Image Intensifier (II) Sights

The first 'passive' night vision sight to be developed and deployed successfully in MBTs was the image intensifier. In this system, ambient visible and near infra-red radiation which reaches the sight is electronically amplified through an image intensifier tube to produce an image. The basic II tube consists of a semitransparent multi-alkali photocathode upon which the photons of ambient light fall, producing electrons inside the tube. These are accelerated by an electric field and hit an aluminised phosphor screen at high speed, producing a photon image which is transmitted through the output window to appear as a directly viewable image on the intensifier screen. A single-stage electrostatically focused 'first generation' II tube would have a typical luminance gain of 1000, sufficient to produce a good image of a moonlit scene. The process can be repeated through a second and a third stage to produce a 'cascade' tube, with luminance gains of greater than 50,000. A typical three-stage First Generation tube is shown in Figure 3.10.

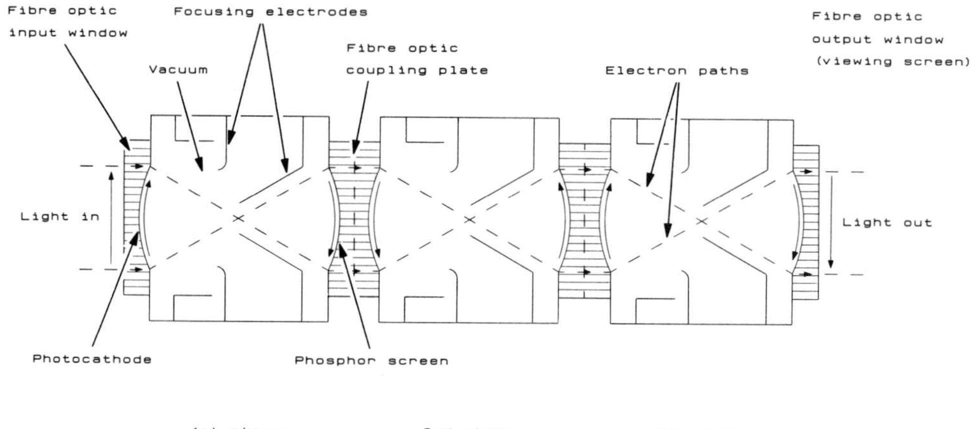

FIG. 3.10 A Three-stage First Generation Image Intensifier Tube.

Direct sunlight	100,000
Bright daylight	10,000
Overcast day	1,000
Very dark day	100
Twilight	10
Deep twilight	1
Full moon	0.1
Quarter moon	0.01
Starlight	0.001
Overcast starlight	0.0001

FIG. 3.11 Range of Scene Illuminance (measured in Lux).

Although they are reliable and produce a good output at low light levels, three-stage II tubes are bulky, a significant disadvantage when sights need to be as compact as possible. This problem has been overcome in the Second Generation II tube, in which the second and third stages of the cascade system are replaced by a microchannel plate. This contains millions of minute parallel channels (10 to 15 microns in diameter), running from the front of the plate to the back and each coated with an emissive substance. Electrons entering the channels are accelerated by a high electrical potential and strike the emissive coating, which acts as an electron multiplier to produce the required luminance gain. Further improvements in performance are obtained in the Third Generation tube, which uses the microchannel plate but with a Galium Arsenide photocathode. First and Second Generation II tubes can be combined, as shown in Figure 3.13. Apart from

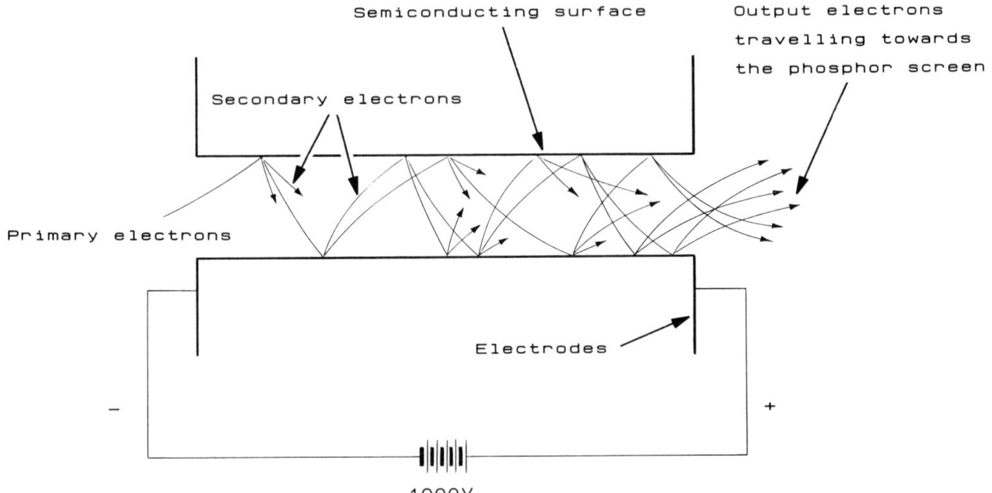

FIG. 3.12 Electron Multiplication through a Microchannel Plate.

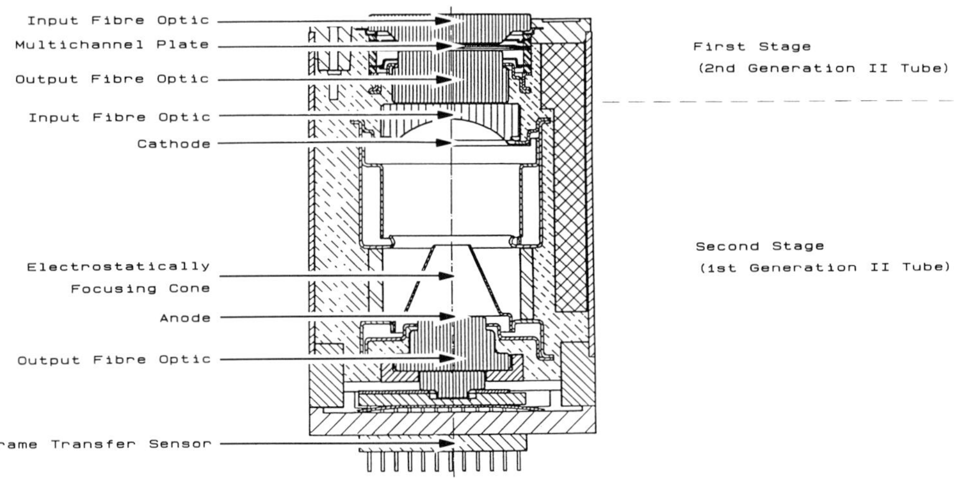

FIG. 3.13 Combined First and Second Generation Image Intensifier Tube.

the degree of amplification provided by its tube, the other major factor governing the performance of the II sight is the size of the objective lens. Larger lenses are able to gather more of the ambient light and provide a bigger input to the amplification stages. However, the size of the objective lens cannot be made too large, otherwise the sight head will be vulnerable to damage from small arms, shell fragments and branches of trees.

The basic II sight is a relatively simple device with minimal associated electronics and, as it operates in the visual waveband, it has no requirement for special optical materials or cooling. The picture is produced directly on the image screen and cannot be transmitted around the tank unless the II sight is linked with a television camera (See the section on Low Light Television Systems on page 77.). Hence basic II sights have the same installation drawbacks as optical daylight sights, in that they require an aperture in the turret armour and must be located adjacent to the operator. One additional problem peculiar to the II sight is the need to protect the tube from damage caused by intense bursts of light, usually from the tank's own gun flash. In the past, II sights have been fitted with mechanical shutters which were linked into the gun firing circuits, but modern tubes now have light sensors which automatically shut them down.

In a sense, the basic II sight can be regarded as a direct electronic substitute for the optical daylight sight and, in many cases, a II system has been integrated with an optical system to create a combined day/night sight. In these combined sights, elements such as the top mirror and the eyepiece assembly serve both channels. A simple switch enables the operator to change from the daylight chanel to the II channel and back again. These combined sights have some significant advantages as follows:

The crewman does not have physically to exchange sights, thus reducing the workload and maintaining vehicle NBC sealing,

As light levels change at dawn and dusk, it is easy to flick back and forth between the day and II channels,

Stowage space is not required for a second sight,

The cost of a combined sight is likely to be less than that of two single channel sights.

II sights and combined sights are likely to continue in use for the forseeable future because they offer a relatively simple and effective night vision capability at a reasonable cost. In particular, they are suitable for smaller vehicles, where weight and space is at a premium, and in the retrofit market, where simplicity of installation and minimum cost are important factors. They are also ideal for the driver's station, where a compact and relatively short range device will usually satisfy the night driving requirements. Continuing improvements in II tube technology and optical design and coatings can be anticipated but startling advances in performance are unlikely.

Thermal Imaging (TI) Systems

The most recent night vision system to be deployed in MBTs is the Thermal Imager. It is a passive system which detects infra-red (IR) radiation emitted by the target and converts this into an electrical signal which can be used to create a visual image. Unlike the Image Intensifier, which requires some ambient visible radiation—however faint, the Thermal Imager will function in complete darkness.

Thermal Radiation

All bodies above absolute zero (= −273 degrees Centigrade) produce radiation and as the temperature increases, the wavelength of the radiation shortens. Figure 3.14 shows the radiation (black body) curves for ideal objects at different

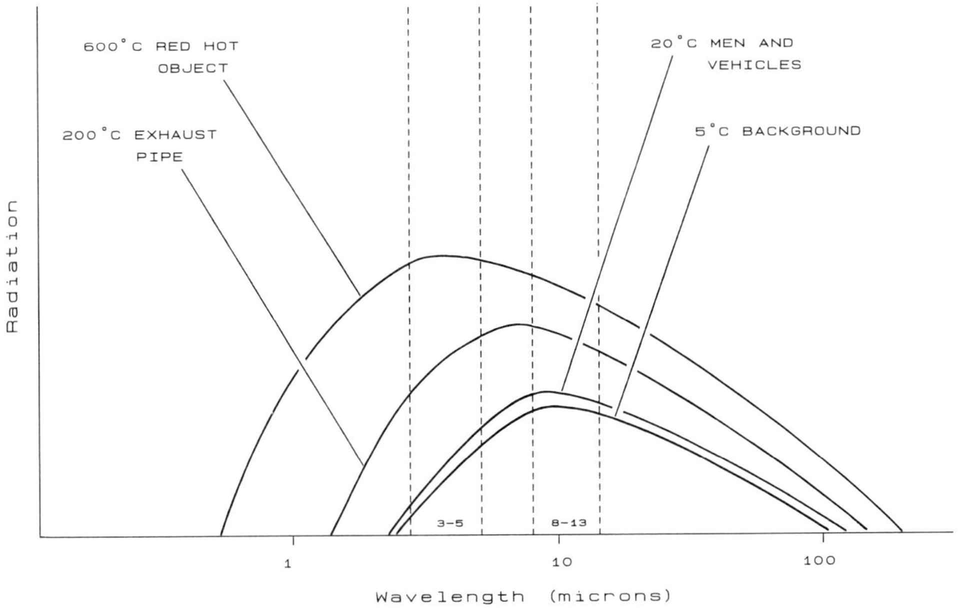

FIG. 3.14 Black Body Radiation.

temperatures. Note that radiation is emitted across a range of wavelengths, but there is one wavelength where output is at a maximum. The hotter the body, the more energy it radiates, but there is little difference between the energy radiated by a body at say 20 degrees Centigrade against a background at say 5 degrees Centigrade.

Eventually, of course, if a body becomes hot enough it will emit radiation in the visual waveband, to which the retina in the eye is sensitive. The Thermal Imager, however, uses a detector material which is sensitive to the longer IR wavelengths that are invisible to the human eye. Just as visible light can be attenuated by atmospheric conditions, such as mist, so infra-red radiation can be absorbed by gases and vapours in the atmosphere. However, there are two parts of the infra-red spectrum where transmission values above 80% occur and these are the 3–5 and 8–13 micron wavebands (See Figure 3.15). On the battlefield, target temperatures

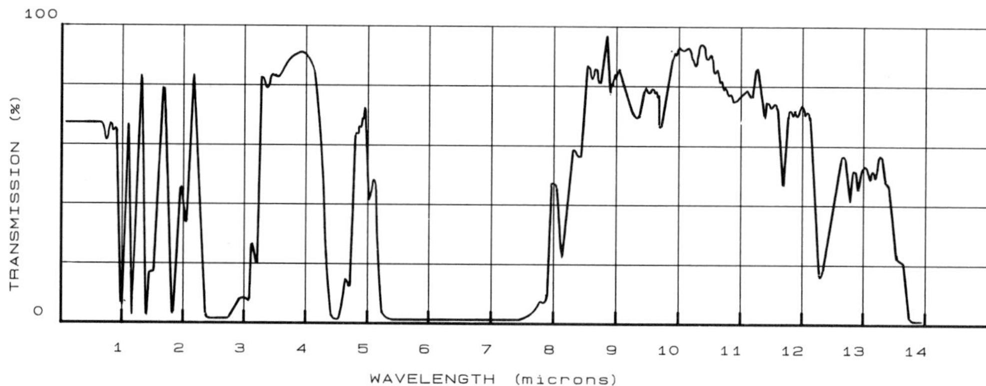

FIG. 3.15 Atmospheric Transmission 'Windows'.

in the region of 800 degrees Centigrade can occur but lower values below 100 degrees Centigrade are also much in evidence. From Figure 3.14 it can be seen that the peak radiation level from cooler objects occurs at the longer of these wavelengths. For this reason, TIs operating in the 8–13 micron waveband are preferred for ground system use.

There are a number of materials which produce an electrical signal when exposed to IR radiation, but the most commonly used is Cadmium Mercury Telluride (CMT). This semiconductor material, with suitable doping, produces usable outputs in both the 3–5 and the 8–13 micron wavebands. With the CMT cooled to about −200 degrees Centigrade, particularly high sensitivity is achieved in the 8–13 micron waveband. Thus, when good picture quality is required, 8–13 microns has proved to be first choice for scanning TI systems, in which the detector is only briefly exposed at each picture point. Detectors operating in the 3–5 micron waveband will produce usable images at about −60 degrees Centigrade. Other materials, such as Indium Antimonide are also used in the 3–5 micron waveband.

As noted at the beginning of this section, all matter above absolute zero emits electro-magnetic energy and this applies equally to the material forming the detector. The signals generated in the detector by the incident thermal energy from the target are very small and, at ambient temperatures, would be swamped by the signals which occur naturally. Hence, it is necessary to cool the detector to cryogenic temperatures. This suppresses the naturally occurring noise to give a better signal to noise ratio.

Implementation

In the early days, only single element detectors were available and the systems produced were necessarily simple, being essentially thermal pointers. Using these, it was possible to identify a 'hot spot', but with only one detector element it was not feasible to scan the whole scene and produce a full picture. Thus the 'hot spot' would have to be identified using either an optical or an II sight. However, the technology of Thermal Imaging developed very rapidly and thermal pointers were never deployed in operational tanks.

With the advance of technology, it has become possible to produce detector arrays containing multiple detector elements. Using opto-mechanical means, the field of view can now be scanned by the detector array to build up an image of the scene. The electrical outputs from the detectors are then processed and fed to a viewer, where a picture is built up using the television raster scan technique.

Compared with Image Intensifiers, the first generation Thermal Imagers now in operational service are relatively complicated. There are four areas in particular where much development has been required—namely infra-red materials, scanning, detector technology and cooling.

Infra-red Materials

Radiation at the 8–13 micron wavelength is barely transmitted by optical glass and, therefore, alternative materials must be employed. The most widely used is germanium, a 10 mm thick slab of which has a transmission value of between 45% and 35% in the 8–13 micron waveband. Being a metal, germanium demands sophisticated manufacturing techniques to produce lenses with the required high standards of form and 'optical' quality. Of course, germanium is opaque as far as the human eye is concerned, so combined optical and TI sights using common optical components cannot be constructed using germanium.

Thermal Imager sight heads which are open to the atmosphere must be capable of being kept clean, especially when used in the ground role where mud and dust is a constant problem. Thus, much development has been carried out to produce coatings for these infra-red glasses. These coatings must be able to resist the abrasion of wash/wipe systems, while maintaining the transmission properties of the glass.

Scanning

To produce a TV-compatible image using a detector array it is necessary to scan the field of view a number of times. Different methods are used, but a typical system is shown in Figure 3.17. Here, vertical scanning is achieved using a mirror, which nods at the TV frame repetition rate, while horizontal scanning is produced by a rotating disc with a number of optically flat faces machined on it. Together, these sweep the detector image across the field of view in a raster scan to produce an output which can easily be converted into a standard CCIR video format. To produce an undistorted image, it is essential that the vertical and horizontal scanning mechanisms are made to a very high precision and accurately synchronised with one another. Such mechanisms are expensive and, if they are to function reliably in an AFV, they must be of rugged construction.

Detector Technology

Detector arrays were originally made up of a number of single CMT elements, arranged in parallel rows. Each element required its own pre-amplifier and delay and summation circuit to produce a serial output signal, resulting in an unreliable system with a less than optimum performance. The current state-of-the-art detector for scanning systems is the SPRITE (Signal Processing In The Element) in

FIG. 3.16 A Thermal Imaging Sight.

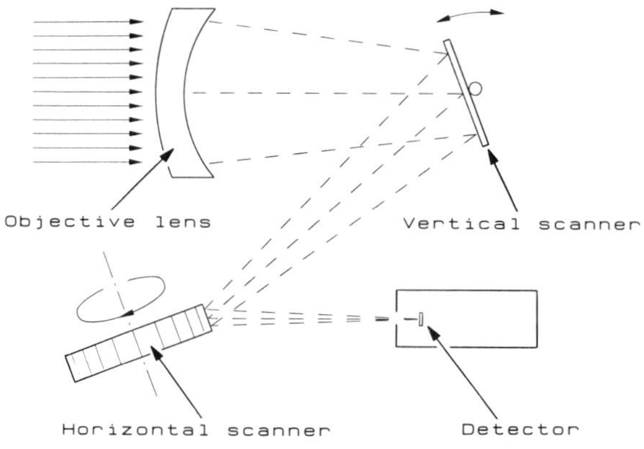

FIG. 3.17 A Thermal Imaging Scanning Mechanism.

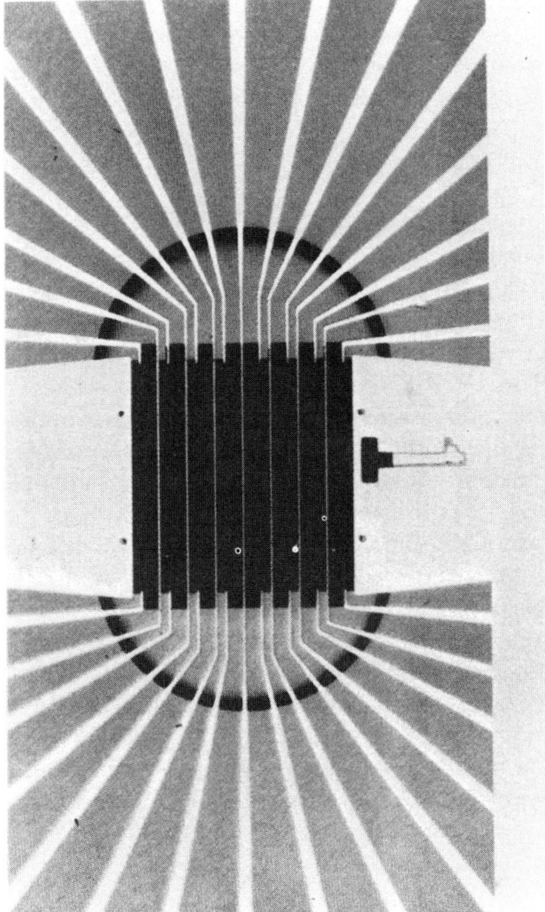

FIG. 3.18 An Eight-element SPRITE Detector.

which each parallel row of detectors is replaced by one filament of CMT. As the IR radiation scan along the CMT detector it produce current carriers in the material and these are driven along the filament by a bias current, at a rate equal to the scan rate. Arriving at the end of the filament, the signals then pass serially through the pre-amplifier to the processing circuits. Thus, the SPRITE requires only one pre-amplifier per detector filament and eliminates the need for delay and summation circuits, resulting in a more reliable system with a better performance. In current thermal imagers the detector array consists of a number of SPRITE filaments. Thus a system with an eight-filament detector would cover eight picture lines during each scan of the scene.

Detector Cooling

Current high performance TI systems, operating in the 8–13 micron waveband, have their detectors cooled to about −200 degrees Centigrade. At this temperature, the IR-induced signal is clearly distinguishable from the naturally occurring 'noise', enabling target temperature differences of less than 1 degree Centigrade to be detected. The two most commonly used methods of cooling the detector are the Reverse Stirling Cycle engine and the Joule-Thompson minicooler.

Reverse Stirling Cycle Cooler

The Reverse Stirling Cycle engine is in effect a closed-cycle refrigerator, in which a gas is compressed by a piston and then allowed to expand through a nozzle, the resulting drop in pressure producing a drop in temperature. The cold gas is then recycled through the compressor unitl the required temperature is achieved.

The Reverse Stirling Cycle cooler offers a number of advantages, being reasonably small and light and having a small input power requirement. As a closed cycle system, it does not require an external gas supply from a compressor or bottles and this makes it simple from the operator's point of view. The small size of the Stirling Cycle cooler and the fact that it is a self contained unit are also attractive features for tank designers, since units can be built into sighting systems without the need for high pressure piping in the fighting compartment.

On the other hand, the system does have two major drawbacks. First, the compressor motor can produce excessive noise in the crew compartment and generate vibrations at the detector, leading to a degradation of the thermal picture. However, these problems are being minimised by the use of linear electric motors (with no rotating parts) and by having the cold finger separated from the compressor by a narrow bore pipe, which isolates the detector from the vibration source. The second and most important problem is the long cool-down time of the Stirling Cycle cooler, which can be of the order of ten minutes. This can be an important factor if a crew needs to come to action at very short notice.

Joule-Thompson Minicooler

The Joule-Thompson (JT) minicooler also uses the rapid expansion of a high pressure gas to produce a temperature reduction, but in this case the gas is externally supplied, either from bottles or a compressor (or both). The incoming high pressure gas is fed through a heat exchanger to a nozzle, where it expands and cools. The gas is then exhausted to atmosphere, passing back over the heat exchanger as it does so and thus cooling both the detector and the incoming high pressure gas. Once a continuous flow has been established, the temperature falls rapidly to a point where the gas emanating from the nozzle becomes a liquid. At this point, the change of state can be detected and the flow of gas automatically reduced, to give a stable temperature with minimal gas consumption. The JT minicooler itself is a simple device with few moving parts and is, therefore, fairly reliable and silent in operation. From the operational point of view, its ability to reach operating temperature rapidly—cool down times of less than one minute being achievable—is a decisive factor in its favour.

The main problem associated with this device is the need for a continuous supply of pure high pressure gas, a requirement which imposes significant design, maintenance and logistic penalties. The gas must be kept clean of impurities if it is

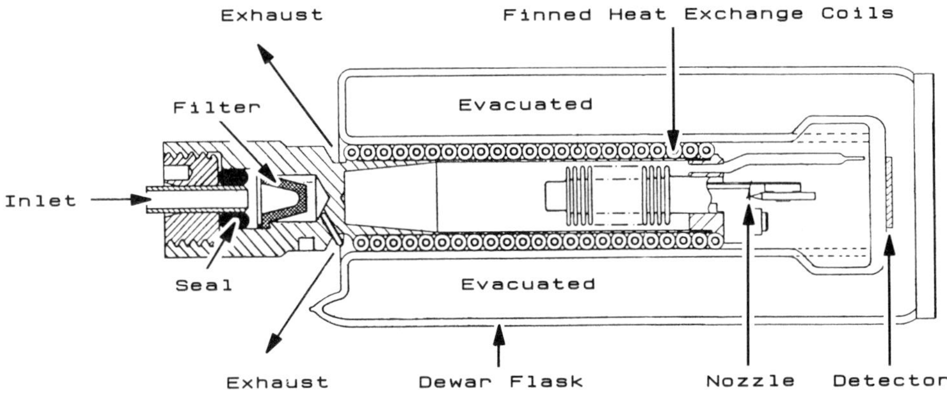

FIG. 3.19 A Joule-Thompson Minicooler.

not to become an explosive mixture and this process can require filters and adsorbant chemicals. With operating pressures of up to 4000 psi, the pipework and valves must be carefully designed and maintained if they are to operate reliably and safely. Finally, the supply of fresh filters, chemical adsorbants and replenishment gas bottles imposes a considerable logistic load. Nevertheless, the JT minicooler is still the preferred system where speed into action is a priority requirement.

Figure 3.20 shows the cooling pack for the Thermal Observation and Gunnery System (TOGS) on British Army Main Battle Tanks. The pack consists of a compressor to charge the bottles, and the high pressure bottles themselves. The latter provide initial rapid cool down and enable the system to function when the vehicle is on silent watch, with no power sources operating.

Other Cooling Methods

There are two further methods of cryogenic cooling which have been examined for thermal imagers.

Liquid nitrogen was considered in the late 1960s but the anticipated difficulties of handling this material under field conditions led to its not being pursued.

Thermo Electric coolers based on the Peltier Effect do not require a gas or a liquid. In these, two dissimilar conductive materials are connected to form two junctions. When an electric current is passed through the circuit, the temperature of one junction rises while the other falls. By connecting devices in series, with the hot junction of one adjacent to the cold face of its neighbour, a cumulative effect can be produced. Unfortunately, these systems have a low heat load capacity and can only achieve temperatures of around -120°C, which is insufficient for high performance thermal imaging.

Future Developments in Thermal Imaging

For the future, there are numerous areas of thermal imaging where current developments will bring significant gains. Considerable work is underway to

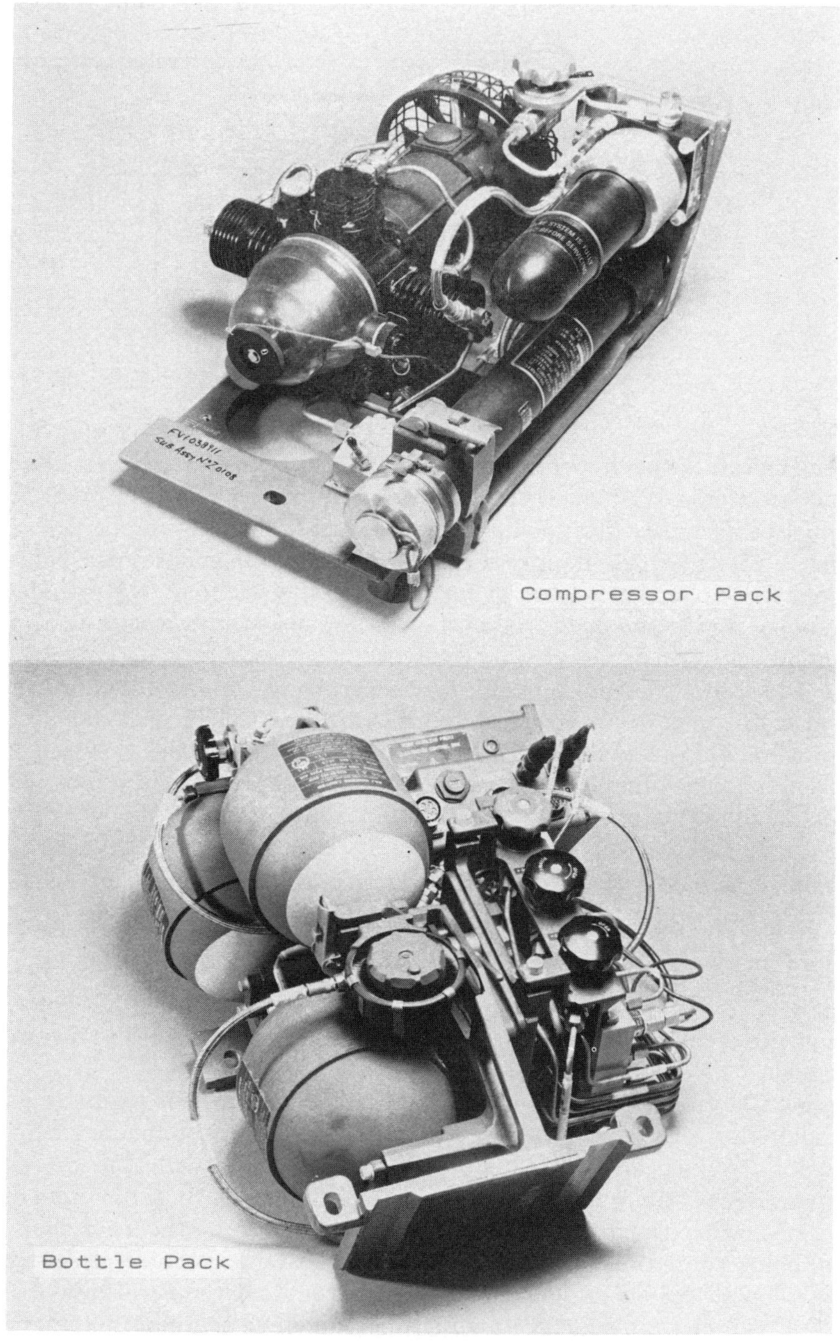

FIG. 3.20 The TOGS Cooling Pack.

develop materials such as Zinc Sulphide and Zinc Selenide, both of which transmit in the optical and the 8–13 micron wavebands. At present, components made from these materials do have a yellow cast and less than outstanding optical transmission properties, and they are also expensive. Nevertheless, provided that the drawbacks can be overcome, materials such as Zinc Sulphide and Zinc Selenide offer the possibility of combined day/TI sights with common optical facilities, able to operate in the 8–13 micron waveband.

The problems associated with scanning will be eliminated by the introduction of the staring array, a matrix made up of a large number of individual detectors. Figure 3.21 shows an array with 128 × 128 elements, contained on a 4 mm square

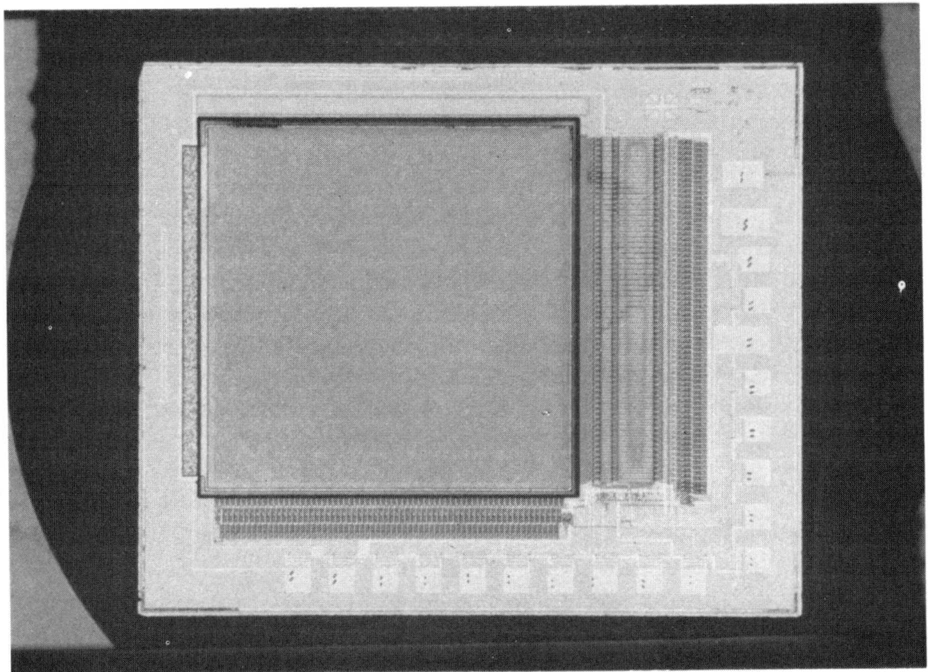

FIG. 3.21 A 128 × 128 Element Staring Array.

surface. The array is pointed at the scene to be observed and each detector 'stares' at a point in space, so that all the elements of the scene are created simultaneously. Using electronics to access the output of each detector, a serial signal is produced for use as a normal video output. The quality of the output can be improved by 'shimmering' the array by half the width of a detector. In this way, the space between detectors can be observed, which effectively doubles the system resolution in each axis.

With staring arrays, the detector exposure time is greatly increased, and in these circumstances CMT operating at the 3–5 micron wavelength has a very high sensitivity. Radiation at this wavelength will also pass through glass which transmits visible light. Hence, using a staring array which operates at the 3–5 micron wavelength, combined day/TI sights with common optical components can be constructed. Such a sight, developed by Marconi Command & Control Systems and based on the Sfim VS580 panoramic sight, is shown in Figure 3.22. Apart from eliminating scanning and enabling the development of combined day/TI sights, the staring array also has other advantages. If a detector element in a **scanning** array fails, a number of lines are lost from the image. With a **staring** array only one picture point is lost. Staring arrays require less processing time, enabling the image to be refreshed quicker and enhancing the dynamic performance of the TI system. To date, the main problem has been the cost and difficulty of manufacturing large arrays. However, these problems are being overcome and with increased output will come a reduction in price.

Advances in detector technology could bring about improvements in a number of areas. Enhanced sensitivity will enable systems to differentiate smaller temperature differences and, hence, produce better images. However, if such detectors are to be fully exploited they must be linked with high definition viewers capable of displaying the available information. As with II sights, the performance of a TI system is dependent on the size of the objective lens. A larger lens captures more of the target radiation, but is also more vulnerable to damage and more difficult to clean. Using a higher sensitivity detector, systems could be designed to give good performance with smaller and less vulnerable apertures.

Detectors which operate at higher temperatures will require much less cooling power. This will be of particular benefit in AFVs, since the cryogenic cooling system occupies valuable space and, inevitably, degrades the overall reliability of the vehicle. Furthermore, cooling systems impose an additional maintenance and logistic burden, which can be particularly onerous under combat conditions.

Television Systems

To date, basic television systems which operate in the visible waveband have been little used in AFVs. Based on charge-coupled devices (CCDs), such systems can give good performance at light levels down to about 1 lux (= deep twilight), but this slight advantage over optical sights does not compensate for the inferior picture quality and the added cost and complexity. However, a number of factors have emerged which could lead to a greater role for television systems.

First, modern tanks equipped with Thermal Imagers already have television-compatible viewers and these could easily be linked to a CCD camera, to produce a full TV system at an economical cost. Secondly, by using television systems in place of optical sights, the need for optical paths to pass through the armour is eliminated. Lastly, with a TV system the operator's eye is protected from direct attack by laser damage weapons—a growing danger on the modern battlefield.

Low Light Television Systems

The low light capability of television systems can be transformed by combining a II tube with a CCD camera. This produce a Low Light Television (LLTV) sensor, which can be connected to a standard television display. Like the basic II sight, LLTV can produce usable images under starlight conditions, but it has added

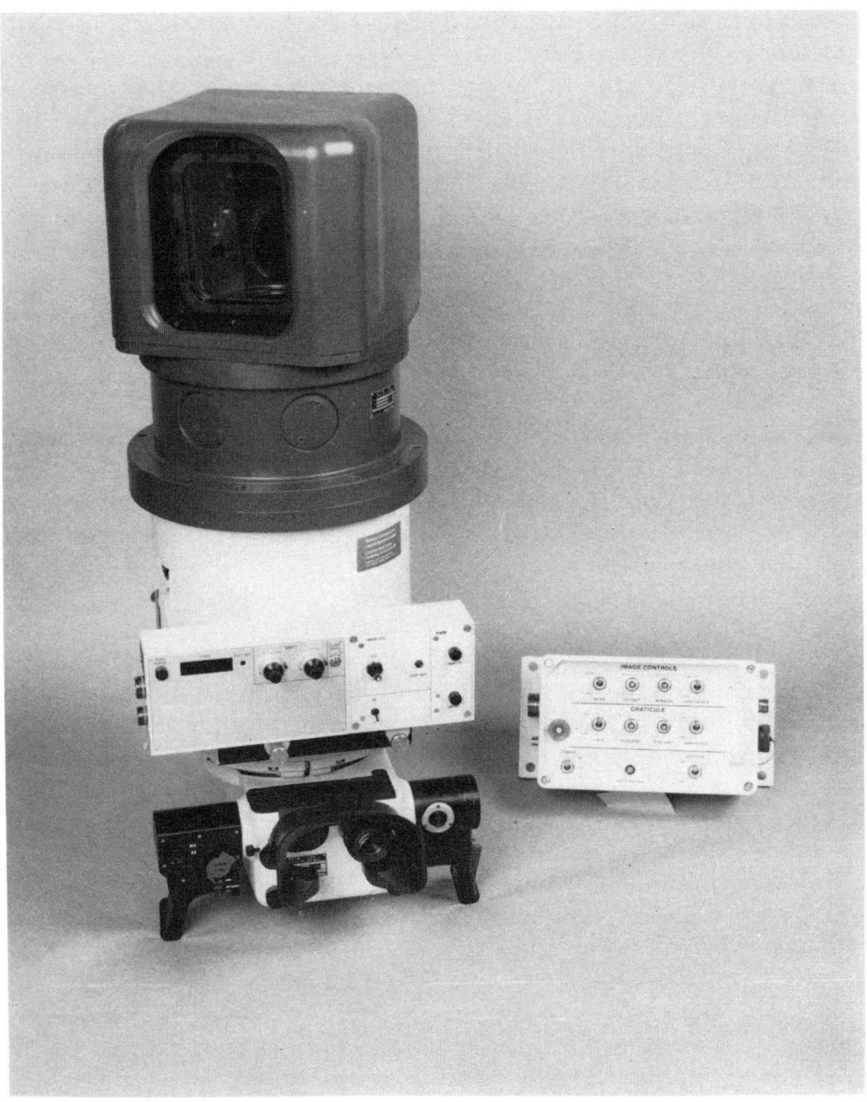

FIG. 3.22 COSMIC Combined Day/TI Sight.

advantages, in that the sensor head need not be adjacent to the operator, only tiny holes are required in the armour and the image can be displayed at any crew station with a viewer.

Future Developments in Television Systems

Current TV systems are based mainly on existing commercial units, which produce a picture of 625 horizontally scanned lines. Although this picture is adequate, it does not provide good enough resolution for acquiring and engaging small or distant targets. To overcome this drawback, high definition systems having 1000+ lines are already under development for commercial use and these have obvious potential in AFVs.

Using a computer to process the TV image, the picture quality can be further enhanced. The processing can heighten the contrast between shades of grey and sharpen the edges of indistinct objects in the field of view. Image enhancement, however, must be carried out with care to ensure that the computer is not 'creating' its own objects from shadows or image defects. Picture enhancements can be applied to any television image, whether they are generated by a CCD or a Thermal Imager.

The overall performance of a CCD camera can be improved by cooling the CCD chip and reading out the image at less than the conventional TV frame rate. Cooling the chip reduces the 'dark current', the thermally induced noise which occurs naturally in the silicon of the CCD chip. This is analogous to the cooling applied to TI detectors. However, the cooled CCD will not be sensitive to radiation in the infra-red waveband and it is debatable whether the enhanced performance would be worth the complications which cooling bring. Equally, a slower output rate may not be acceptable when the sight is being used to observe a fast changing scene, e.g. one containing a moving target.

Target Ranging

In order to achieve the highest hit probability from a tank weapon system, account must be taken of the factors which affect accuracy. Some random factors cannot be compensated for and others are too small to warrant any consideration. However, of those many factors which are worthy of attention, the most important is the target range. In static engagement it is paramount, while in moving target or moving-own-vehicle engagements it ranks equal with the measurement of the target's relative motion. The following section details the various methods used to establish target range and describes the means of compensating for other sources of system inaccuracy.

Range Estimation and Fall of Shot Correction

Relying mainly on his skill and experience, a gunner can visually estimate the distance to a target. With training, his performance can be improved but typically his error will be plus or minus a quarter of the actual range. The range estimation technique can be improved by using information from neighbouring tanks or a map to create a range card, listing the distances to all the key features where a target may appear. This is very useful when a tank is operating from a static fire position, but impracticable for a battle of movement.

One method of compensating for range estimating errors is to fire a round at the target and then make a correction, based on the distance between the target and the fall of shot. This system compensates for a considerable number of factors, such as barrel wear, charge temperature, vehicle attitude, gun to sight misalignment and atmospheric conditions, but it does depend on accurate observation of the fall of shot. In larger calibre weapons, the obscuration caused by gun blast can prevent this accurate observation. In general, the Fall of Shot method is far from satisfactory because it is wasteful of ammunition, lengthens the overall engagement time and gives away the firing tank's position.

Ranging Machine Gun

Until well into the 1970s, the Ranging Machine Gun (RMG) was a popular means of determining the distance to the target. As in the preceding paragraph, this method uses fall of shot as a means of correcting for errors in range estimation (and other factors). Mounted adjacent to and coaxial with the main armament, the RMG fires a sub-calibre round (typically 0.5″/12.7 mm) which is ballistically matched as far as possible to the main round, usually out to about 2,000 metres. The gunner fires bursts of 2 or 3 rounds until a central target strike is observed and then uses the range information to lay the main armament. To enable fall of shot to be observed, the sub-calibre round must be tracer ammunition and it must contain a pyrophoric compound in order to give a clear indication of a target strike.

The RMG is simple to use, relatively inexpensive and it does compensate automatically for some errors such as vehicle attitude, down range wind and gun-to-sight misalignment. It can also be a useful secondary armament against soft skinned vehicles and personnel. However, the method does have numerous drawbacks. It is relatively slow, limited in range and not very practicable when firing on the move or at moving targets. Like any machine gun, the RMG can jam and space must be found to store the ammunition.

Optical Rangefinders

Prior to the invention of the tank, optical rangefinders based on the principal of triangulation were is use for many years, especially in warships. In this system, the target is observed from two positions and the angle between the two lines of sight ($=\theta$) can be measured. Knowing the base distance D between the two viewing positions, the range can be deduced by simple geometry. For a fixed base distance, changes in θ get less as the range increases. Hence, the longer the range, the less accurate the system and, with optical rangefinders, the error is typically proportional to the square of the true range.

To achieve the best performance, D should be as wide as possible to give the largest value of θ, which means that the system has to use the full width of the turret and, in order to have a clear field of view, it needs to be in the upper part of the turret. Both of these requirements impose significant design constraints on turret layout.

Optical rangefinders based on triangulation normally use either the stereoscopic or split field methods. In the former, each of the gunner's eyes receives one of the images and by adjusting their position he can bring them into coincidence. However, tests show that less than 50% of people possess the innate ability to use stereoscopic systems and this is a serious drawback. In the split field system, the target image is divided horizontally, with the top half coming from one side of the rangefinder and the lower half from the other side. When the upper and lower halves are aligned, the rangefinder is set.

Optical rangefinders are passive and, in skilled hands, can be reasonably

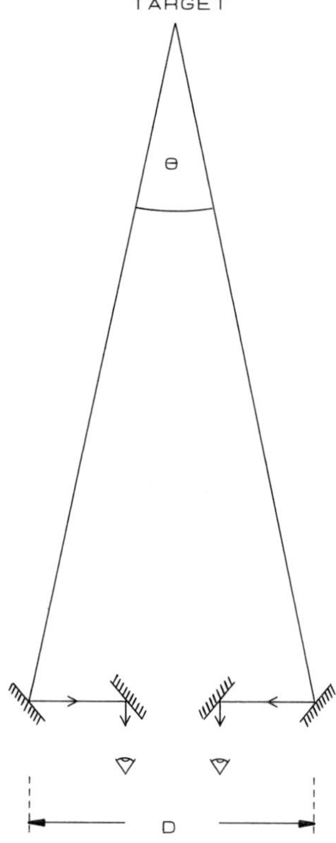

FIG. 3.23 Rangefinding using Triangulation.

accurate. However, apart from their diminishing accuracy at longer range and the design constraints they impose, they are also subject to wear, relatively slow in operation and, like any optical system, not particularly effective in poor visibility or during the hours of darkness.

Stadiametric Rangefinding

An alternative, but much less accurate, method of optical rangefinding uses the stadiametric technique. If a standard value is assumed for a key target dimension (e.g. target tank height = 2.5 metres), graticule marks can be set in the gunner's field of view which correspond to that dimension at different ranges. The operator determines which marks just bracket the target and reads off the appropriate range. This is a relatively quick, simple and inexpensive technique but it is not particularly accurate, because the true target dimension must be close to the pre-determined value, the relevant target dimension must be clearly visible and the gunner must be skilled in judging when the marks are bracketing the target.

In general, stadiametric marks are a useful secondary method of rangefinding, being relatively simple to implement in existing sights, both optical and electronic.

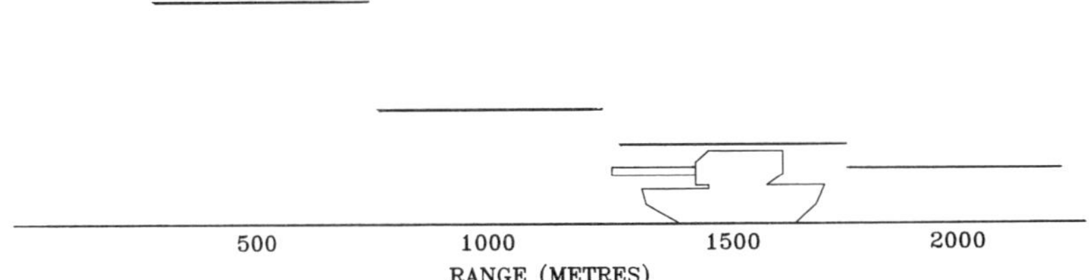

FIG. 3.24 Stadiametric Rangefinding.

Laser Rangefinding

The principal drawbacks of all the ranging systems previously described are the slow speed of operation, the rapid decrease in accuracy with increasing range and the skill needed to operate them effectively. Thus, these systems are not used in modern MBTs and they are rapidly being replaced in older tanks which remain in service. The technological breakthrough required for simple and accurate target ranging came in 1960 with the invention of the laser, which is an acronym for Light Amplification by Stimulated Emission of Radiation.

The Principle of the Laser and its Capabilities

In the laser, a flash tube is used to pump photons of light into an active material, which is the source of the laser light. The active material can be either a solid, in the form of a rod, or a gas, contained in a glass or quartz tube. By pumping in energy quickly, atoms in the laser material are raised to a higher energy state, creating a temporary 'population inversion'. As the unstable high energy atoms fall back to their stable state, they emit photons of light, which strike other excited atoms and create further photons. Thus the strength of the light beam will quickly build up and eventually it emerges as a very narrow laser beam of great intensity and lasting a few nanoseconds.

Apart from being narrow and intense, the important features of the laser beam are that all its photons have the same wavelength and are travelling in phase. Thus it is easily distinguishable from normal sources of light, be they natural or artificial. On striking a target, some of the light is reflected back towards the source where, because of its peculiar properties, it can be detected by a receiver. By timing the interval between 'transmit' and 'receive' and knowing the speed of light, the range to the target can be accurately calculated. The resolution of the rangefinder depends on the clock rate of the timer, but plus or minus 10 metres is usually sufficient for good basic weapon system accuracy.

The maximum range of the laser depends on the type, the power output and the sensitivity of the detector. For land-based weapon systems such as tanks, 10 kilometres is a typical maximum range. This covers all likely ground targets and gives the tank a useful capability against helicopters firing stand-off missiles.

Even with its narrow beam, it cannot be guaranteed that the laser will strike the target only. Thus, multiple returns can occur and it would be possible to display all the measured ranges to the operator and allow him to select what appeared to be the best. However, this is not a sensible approach as it would cause delay at a crucial point in the engagement sequence. Instead, the laser can be switched to display either the first (closest) or last (furthest) return received, the operators choice being dictated by the target's nearness to other objects and the presence or otherwise of obscurants such as battlefield smoke.

Types of Laser Rangefinder

The original 1960 laser was based on a Ruby crystal and the first operational Tank Laser Sight went into service in the mid 1970s with this type of laser. The Ruby laser has good atmospheric penetration and ranges out to 10 kilometres are readily achieved. However, generating laser light from a Ruby crystal is a very inefficient process and to achieve the range performance, a lot of power must be put in and extensive cooling is required to dissipate the waste heat. This propensity for overheating means that the Ruby laser's rate of fire or 'repetition rate' must be kept fairly low.

Ruby laser light has a wavelength of 0.6943 microns, which lies in the visible spectrum and to which the retina of the eye is, of course, highly sensitive. With Ruby lasers, therefore, there is always the danger of eye damage and this severely restricts their use in training. Furthermore, just as visible light cannot pass through mist and smoke, so the capability of the Ruby laser is severely restricted under these conditions. Modern Tank Laser Rangefinders use Neodymium Yttrium Aluminium Garnet (Nd YAG) as the laser material. This type of laser can also achieve ranges of 10 kilometres and is more efficient than the Ruby. Hence, it requires much less cooling and is capable of higher repetition rates. The Nd YAG wavelength is 1.06 microns, which is slightly outside the visible spectrum, but within the eye damage threshold of 1.4 microns. Therefore, the Nd YAG does constitute an eye hazard and, as with the Ruby laser, it is subject to training restrictions. Its performance is also severely degraded by mist and battlefield smoke. Operating as they do in or close to the visible waveband, both the Ruby and Nd YAG lasers function with normal optical glass and this make their integration into optical sights very straightforward. 'Add-on' Nd Yag laser modules are readily available and can be used to upgrade existing daylight sights to give them a range-finding capability.

The third type of system which has found application in the rangefinding role is the Carbon Dioxide (CO2) laser, which uses a tube of the gas as its active material. The early CO2 lasers only produced an output power of about 0.5 megawatts (compared to approximately 2 megawatts for a Ruby and 5 megawatts for an Nd YAG laser). As a result, their range capability was limited to about 4 or 5 kilometres. However, by adding catalyts to the CO2 gas, the output power is being raised towards 1 megawatt, with corresponding increases in range.

The CO2 laser produces a beam with a wavelength of 10.6 microns, which is in the far infra-red part of the spectrum and well outside the visible range. Thus, for all practical purposes, the CO2 laser is eye-safe and can be used for field training with unprotected troops. At 10.6 microns, the CO2 is fully compatible with thermal imagers operating in the 8–13 micron waveband and it shares the TI's ability to penetrate mist and battlefield smoke. To get the full benefit from a TI system it should be linked with a CO2 laser, so that what can be seen can be lased. The main disadvantages of the CO2 laser are the need to cool the detector (to achieve

FIG. 3.25 A Neodymium YAG Tank Laser Sight.

sufficient sensitivity) and the requirement for optical components which transmit at the 10.6 micron wavelength. However, if fitted as part of a TI system, the CO_2 laser would be able to share the optical components, detector and cooling system, thus reducing overall volume and cost.

Potential Future Developments

Since their introduction into service with AFVs, lasers have been used almost exclusively for target ranging. However, they do have the potential for a considerable number of other uses. For example, the missile-armed helicopter poses a very dangerous threat to the tank and is very difficult to hit because of its

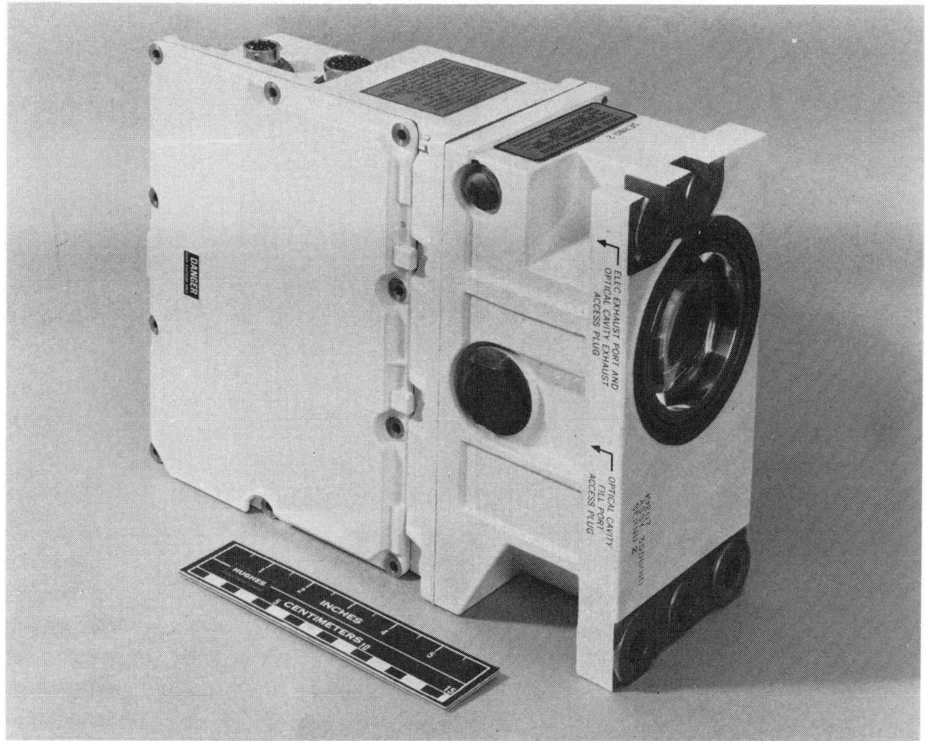

FIG. 3.26 An 'add-on' Nd YAG Laser Module.

small size, high speed and manoeuvrability. If a high explosive round with a laser sensitive fuse in the base were to be developed, this could be command detonated by the tank's own laser at the appropriate range. As part of the guidance system of an unmanned autonomous vehicle, short range lasers can be used to locate obstacles and monitor terrain features on the vehicle's route.

Gas lasers (such as the CO2) can be operated efficiently as continuous wave (CW) devices without overheating. In this CW mode, the laser has a number of potential applications over and above simple target ranging. For example:

CW lasers can directly measure target velocity towards the lasing tank,
By modulating the signal, the CW laser can be used to transmit radio signals as part of a highly directional secure communication link,
Classification and recognition of targets can be achieved by monitoring the effect of their vibrating or rotating components on the return signal,
Direct-fire-weapon-effect-simulation can be implemented using the tanks on-board operational laser.

All the above features would complicate the basic laser and require additional computing power. However, the latter factor cannot be considered a major drawback, given the rapid growth of computer-based AFV fire control systems.

Other Factors Affecting Engagement Accuracy

As stated in the section on target ranging, there are many factors which affect weapon system accuracy. For convenience they can be grouped into the following categories:

Constant factors which can be permanently accounted for during vehicle design, including:
- Sight Offset
- Drift
- Mean Jump and Throw-off

Slowly varying factors which can be measured at regular intervals and for which adjustments can be made, including:
- Basic Gun to Sight Alignment
- Other Mechanical and Electrical Alignment Errors
- Jump and Throw-off Specific to the Barrel

Rapidly varying factors which can change at any time and which need to be measured at the instant of firing, including:
- Target Range
- Target Rate and Direction of Movement
- Barrel Wear
- Barrel Bend
- Trunnion Tilt and Angle of Gun
- Charge Temperature
- Air Density
- Wind Effects

Randomly variable or residual factors which cannot easily be compensated for or eliminated, including:
- Gunner's Laying Error
- Ballistic Dispersion of the Round
- Propellant Variation
- Gusts of Wind
- Bending of the Optical Path
- Jitter
- Computer Rounding Error

Target ranging has already been discussed in some depth in the previous paragraphs. The other factors are detailed below and, where a method of compensation exists, this is also described.

Sight Offset

In many tanks, the main sights are located above and to one side of the gun. The gun bore and the line of sight must be aligned with one another and the method of achieving this is explained in the earlier section entitled 'Muzzle Bore Sight'. However, at anything other than the setting up range, there will be misalignment, and a correction must be made. Since the gun bore-to-sight line offsets are permanent, it is relatively simple to include an equation in the fire control programme, which will calculate an angular correction for the measured target range. Similarly, the offset can be taken into account when designing sight graticules.

Drift

Ammunition which is spun for stability will be subject to forces, which causes the round to drift laterally. Knowing the rate of spin of the round and its velocity, the magnitude of this drift can be calculated and an allowance made in the computer fire control equations and the graticules.

Mean Jump and Throw-off

The launch angle of the round is determined by the position of the last few calibres of the barrel at the instant the shot leaves the muzzle. All barrels exhibit small positional inconsistencies when the gun is fired and many factors contribute to these errors, such as gun vibration, the presence of non-symmetrical masses (e.g., an MRS mirror), residual manufacturing stresses and barrel droop. For convenience, the errors are aggregated as 'jump' for the vertical axis and as 'throw-off' in azimuth. From Range and Accuracy firing trials, mean values can be derived for jump and throw-off and they can thus be compensated for in graticule design and in the fire control software. However, it must be noted that each barrel is subtly different and will exhibit variations on the mean value. The method of accommodating these variations is given in a later paragraph.

Basic Gun to Sight Alignment

During the life of a vehicle, the alignment of the gun and sight will be subject to variation, either as a result of gradual wear and settling of the system or whenever major components are changed. This alignment must be checked regularly and re-established, using the Muzzle Bore Sight described in an earlier section.

Other Mechanical and Electrical Alignment Errors

Over a period of time, the sighting system will be subject to gradual variations, as mechanical items wear and electrical components suffer drift and small changes in their physical structure. Normally, these are eliminated by carrying out calibration checks at appropriate intervals. However, because there must be some clearances to allow linkage systems to operate, it is not possible to eliminate all mechanical errors. Changes in linkage accuracy arising from differential expansion are covered by the temperature-compensated linkage described in an earlier section.

Jump and Throw-off Specific to the Barrel

As described above, mean values of jump and throw-off can be determined by trials and then included in the fire control software and the sight graticules. However, all barrels will vary slightly, for example as a result of manufacturing tolerances and heat treatment stresses, so each will exhibit its own value of jump and throw-off. The magnitude of these variations can be judged by the crew during operations and an adjustment fed into the fire control computer. Should this adjustment to the Mean Point of Impact (MPI) prove inaccurate or vary with time, the crew can readily change it. However, crews must be dissuaded from making changes every few rounds, since other factors, such as round to round ballistic dispersion, can give a false impression of a permanent shift in MPI.

Target Rate and Direction of Movement

When engaging moving targets, it is essential to know their speed and direction of movement. With this data and the measured range, the position of the target at the end of the round's time of flight can be calculated by the fire control computer. This 'lead angle' is taken into account when moving the gun to its fire position. Rate and direction of target movement is normally derived as the gunner tracks the target, either by measuring the rate of traverse of the turret on the hull or by monitoring the outputs from the gyros in a stabilised sight head.

Barrel Wear

As barrels wear, some of the propellant gases will escape past the round, leading to a decrease in the muzzle velocity and, hence, a lower trajectory. The mean rate of wear for each type of ammunition can be determined from trials and stored in the fire control software. Then, once the initial wear state has been physically measured and an input made into the system, it is a simple matter for the fire control computer to update it each time a round is fired and make the necessary correction.

Barrel Bend

During operations, the barrel of the gun can be distorted by uneven heating, arising from irregular dissipation of the heat from firing, rain on the upper surface or a side wind. Such effects can be greatly reduced by covering the barrel with an insulating or thermal sleeve, but there is still the possibility of some distortion. This can be compensated for by using a Muzzle Reference System as detailed in an earlier paragraph (see page 61).

Trunnion Tilt and Angle of Gun

If a vehicle is operating on a side slope during an engagement, the gun will not elevate vertically. As shown in Figure 3.27, it will move along the line A to C, resulting in a reduced angle of Tangent Elevation (TE). At the same time, the gun

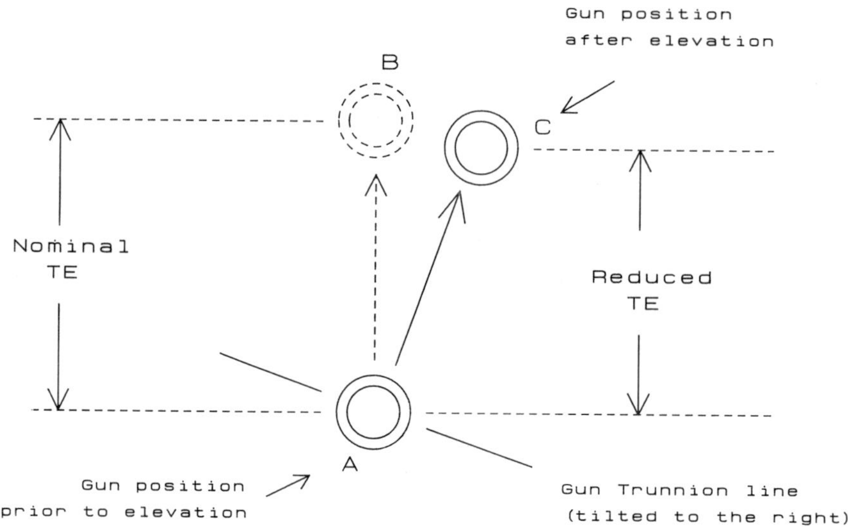

FIG. 3.27 Trunnion Tilt.

will be displaced to one side (in this case the right) and the end result will be a round which falls short and to one side of the target. The greater the gun angle, the greater the errors, so trunnion tilt is most important at longer ranges and when using low-velocity rounds. For most engagements, the firing tank and the target are at approximately the same level and gravity can be considered to act normally to the mean line of flight of the round. However, if the target is at a different height to the firing tank, the round will have to travel 'uphill' or 'downhill' and, in these circumstances, the effect of gravity will change the ballistic path of the round.

Trunnion tilt and gun angle can be measured using a hydraulically or magnetically damped pendulum mounted on the gun. The correction obtained is usually used for static vehicle engagements only, since it is difficult to obtain a usable signal from a moving vehicle, and other errors tend to swamp the effects of trunnion tilt and gun angle.

Charge Temperature

Variations in charge temperature effect the energy produced by the propellant and, hence, the muzzle velocity. The fire control software can readily make corrections for this effect but it is not a simple or convenient matter to obtain a meaningful charge temperature, either in the chamber or in the charge stowage bin. If the actual charge temperature were measured by means of a probe, it would need to be disconnected before the charge could be loaded, a cumbersome and unsatisfactory arrangement. Once loaded, the charge temperature could be altered by the heat of the chamber, but it is not a simple matter to find a sensor able to survive in this hostile environment. As a compromise, most systems have provision for a manual input, which will cater for the heat of summer or the cold of winter.

Air Density

As air density increases, the drag on the round will also increase, causing it to decelerate more quickly and thus fall short. Density is a function of air temperature and pressure and these factors can easily be measured at the tank by a sensor and fed directly into the fire control computer.

Wind Effects

Both cross winds and head/tail winds can affect accuracy, especially with the slower flying CE rounds which have a longer time of flight. A sensor mounted on the turret roof can be used to measure the wind speed in both the lateral and the fore and aft axes, as an input for a computerised fire control system. Ideally, the sensor should be as high as possible, to ensure that the speed and direction of the air flow is not disturbed by equipment on the turret roof but practical considerations mean that a height of approximately one metre is the maximum that can be accommodated.

The error in the lateral axis is an order of magnitude greater than the fore and aft error and, therefore, vehicles often have only a cross wind sensor, for reasons of economy. Because wind speed and direction can vary between the tank and its target, the tank-mounted sensor is necessarily a compromise. However, in general a sensor of this kind does improve the chances of a first round hit with CE rounds.

Gunner's Laying Error

This can take a number of forms, but essentially it arises from his failure to lay the sight consistently on target, resulting in a random dispersion of shots about the chosen point of aim. These errors are greater for the more difficult types of engagement (i.e.: against moving targets and when operating from a moving vehicle) and the situation is further worsened when the gunner is tired or subjected to the stress of battle. To minimise the errors, gunners should be tested for good hand and eye coordination, they must be provided with realistic training aids and their working environment must be ergonomically optimised to make laying of the sight a quick and simple operation.

Ballistic Dispersion of the Round

Like any man-made item, ammunition is subject to machining tolerances and, when handled, it can suffer minor damage. Both of these factors can affect the ballistic performance of the round when it is fired. These additional errors can be reduced by careful manufacturing and transportation, but good basic design is the most important factor in achieving minimal ballistic dispersion.

Propellant Variation

Minor differences in the weight and chemical composition of the charges will result in a variation in the energy released when they are initiated. Such variations will in turn produce inconsistent muzzle velocities, which add to ballistic dispersion. Again, care in the manufacturing process is the way to minimise such errors.

Wind Gusts, Bending of the Optical Path and Jitter

Gusty conditions will affect the accuracy of the rounds, particularly the slow flying CE projectiles and mainly in the traverse axis. Bending of the optical path (refraction) is caused by atmospheric conditions and results in the gunner seeing a misplaced image of the target. This error occurs in the elevation axis. Jitter is the apparent target vibration caused by localised heating and the resultant air density gradients. This tends to produce errors in both axes and, as with wind gusts and optical refraction, there is no method of compensating for the loss of accuracy.

Computer Rounding

When a computer is used as part of the weapon control system, random errors will occur due to numerical approximations and rounding errors. These can be minimised by careful design of the computer, its input sensors and the system software.

The Error Budget

Combining all the errors produces an error budget (Figure 3.28), which defines the overall weapon system accuracy. Each error is assumed to have a normal distribution, so that its magnitude can be defined by its Standard Deviation (SD). Squaring each error, summing the squares and taking the square root of this sum produces the SD for the overall weapon system. The following theoretical error budget is typical of the figures that might be obtained when firing a high velocity KE round in a static versus static engagement, using a computerised fire control system with the sensors described in the preceding paragraphs. The errors are 1 SD values, measured in mils and grouped according to their source.

Assuming a Mean Point of Impact (MPI) on the point of aim (i.e. the centre of the target), a system with the above dispersions would have the following hit probabilities at 2000 m against static targets:

NATO Standard Head-on (2.3 m square) = 65.0%
NATO Standard Side-on (4.6 m long × 2.1 m high) = 75.3%

Against a moving target, the Operator errors could be expected to change as follows:

	Elevation axis	Traverse axis
Operator		
Gun Laying	0.22	0.30
Tracking/Lead Angle Prediction	0.25	0.50

With these values in the error budget, the elevation and traverse dispersions

Error source	Elevation axis	Traverse axis
Ammunition		
Ballistic Dispersion	0.30	0.30
Propellant Variation	0.03	0.00
Weapon		
Barrel Wear	0.01	0.00
Barrel Jump/Throw off	0.15	0.15
Barrel Band	0.10	0.10
Fire Control System		
Range	0.03	0.00
Trunnion Tilt	0.01	0.01
Angle of Gun	0.05	0.05
Computer Rounding	0.05	0.05
Sight to Weapon Harmonisation		
Gun/Sight Alignment	0.15	0.15
Other Mechanical/Electrical Errors	0.15	0.15
Operator		
Gun Laying	0.15	0.15
Tracking/Lead Angle Prediction	0.00	0.00
Environment		
Charge Temperature	0.06	0.00
Air Density	0.01	0.00
Cross Wind at Tank	0.00	0.10
Head Wind at Tank	0.01	0.00
Down Range Gusts	0.00	0.04
Optical Refraction	0.06	0.00
Jitter	0.06	0.06
Overall System Error	0.456	0.445

FIG. 3.28 The Error Budget.

become 0.523 and 0.711 mils respectively and the hit probability against the moving NATO side-on target at 2000 m reduces to 62.4%.

It is clear from the method of summing the individual errors, that the biggest improvement in system accuracy is gained by reducing the more substantial errors. Attempting to eliminate all the errors by fitting every conceivable sensor can prove to be very expensive—and far from cost-effective.

Computer Based Fire Control Systems

Introduction

Fire control is one of the areas of tank technology which has seen the most significant advances in recent years, coinciding with rapid developments in electronics and computers. Prior to and during the Second World War, electro-mechanical gun-aiming computers were fitted in ships, but these analogue systems were relatively cumbersome and slow and, hence, ill-suited to AFVs. Lacking any such system, the tank gunner had to rely on his sight graticule—and his skill and expertise—with all the drawbacks noted in the previous paragraphs. However, as electrical, electronic and computing components became more compact, reliable and affordable, the installation of fire control systems in AFVs became a viable proposition. At the same time, computers offered the only realistic means of achieving the speed and accuracy of engagement essential for survival on the battlefield.

Thus, modern MBTs are equipped with computer based fire control systems, for the following principal purposes:

To maximise the chance of hit in basic static engagements,
To give the MBT a good chance of a hit against moving targets and during moving-own-vehicle engagements,
To reduce engagement times,
To simplify crew tasks and reduce the skill levels required,
To provide additional capabilities for the crew, such as on-board training facilities, system health checks and first line diagnostic testing.

System Operation

The computer based system receives data automatically from the vehicle sensors and this is combined with information fed in manually by the operator. Figure 3.29. illustrates schematically the relationship between the computer and the other elements of the system.

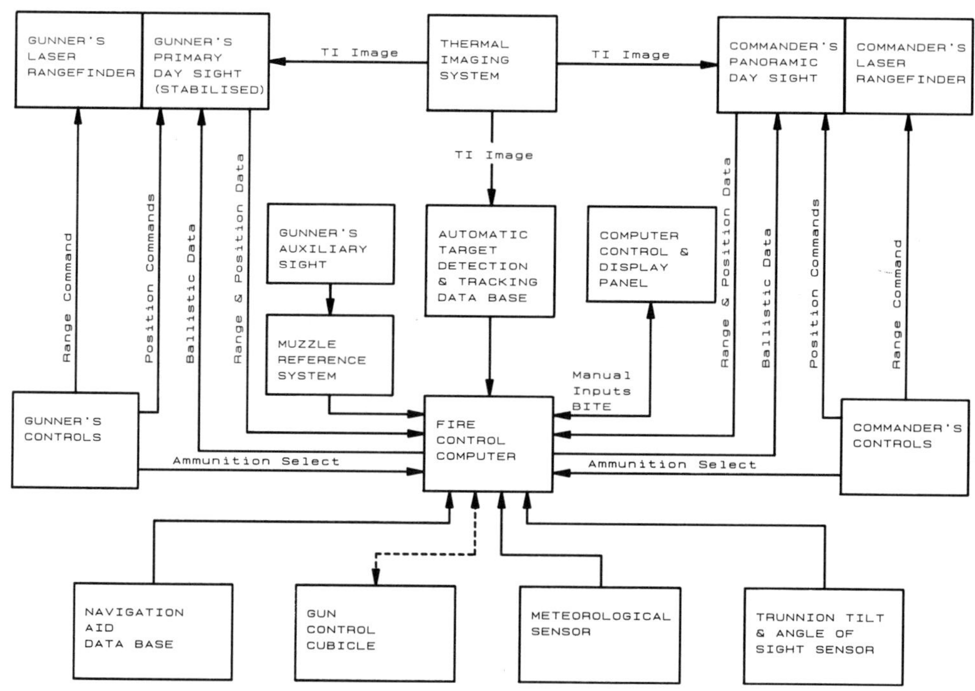

FIG. 3.29 A computer based Fire Control System.

Typically, the following data is input:

Target range—input automatically from the laser rangefinder, with manual back-up in case of failure,
Ammunition type—manual input,

Target rate and direction (in both the horizontal and vertical axes)—automatic sensor input from sensors on the gun and turret, or from gyros,
Charge temperature—manual input,
Barrel wear—initial state manually input, with subsequent automatic update based on rounds fired,
Air temperature and pressure—automatic input from an externally mounted sensor, but with manual mode as a back-up,
Wind speed and direction—normally an automatic input from a roof mounted sensor; manual back-up can be provided, but accurate information is not easy to obtain,
Trunnion tilt and angle of gun—automatic input from a gun mounted sensor,
Vehicle movement—automatically sensed from the vehicle transmission, or a manual input.

The principle outputs from the system are:

Gun elevation and traverse angles required to achieve a first round hit,
Target tracking rate and direction,
Visual displays for the operator.

When the computer calculation is initiated, the system assumes that the gun and/or the sight are initially pointing directly at the target. The computer then determines the gun elevation and aim-off (left or right) required to bring the round onto the point of aim. In simple systems, the offsets normally appear as a computer-generated mark in the field of view of the sight and the gunner lays this over the target and fires. When the computer is linked into the gun control equipment, the gun is driven automatically to the correct position, where it can be fired by the gunner or by the computer. The use of the computer to fire the gun speeds up the engagement but it does deny the operator the chance to make any fine adjustments, should the system appear not to have functioned correctly. Hence, a fully automatic system will only be accepted if the operators have total confidence in its accuracy.

Against moving targets, it is essential that tracking continues up to the instant of gun firing, so that any last minute changes in target motion can be detected and taken account of in the lead angle calculation. With independent stabilised sights this can be done easily and accurately.

The Computer

The computer is the heart of any fire control system and both analogue and digital machines have been used for this purpose.

The analogue computer takes continuous physical inputs from various vehicle systems and manipulates them through electrical circuits, to produce a real time 'solution' to the ballistic equation. Because the analogue computer relies on built-in circuitry for its functions, it is not a simple task to 'reprogram' it for, say, a new ammunition. Unlike its general purpose digital counterpart, the analogue computer does not have a memory or use software and this means that it is normally designed to carry out a limited number of specific tasks. This lack of a broad programming flexibility is a disadvantage, but the analogue computer does have some positive features:

Great precision and accuracy can be built into the machine for its specific task,
The cost can be kept down by restricting the computer to only those components and functions needed for the given application,
There are no costly software programs to be written or maintained.

Nevertheless, despite these factors, the digital computer is now much preferred because of its greater inherent flexibility and its long term potential outside the weapon control area. In the digital computer, all the input parameters are fed in as, or converted to, binary numbers (composed of zeroes and ones), which can easily be represented by electrical impulses. The binary numbers can then be processed through a series of arithmetic and logical operations, using the program held in the computer memory.

Figure 3.30 illustrated a ruggedised digital fire control computer. The lower section contains the power module, which runs off the vehicle 28 volt DC supply. Above and to the right are the memory module and the microprocessor, while to the left are the input and output signal boards, which connect the microprocessor to the rest of the system. On the side of the casing can be seen the input/output sockets and the attachment points for the shock mounts, which help to cushion the computer from the effects of vehicle vibration.

Program Storage

There are various means of holding the program, but the most common system in current AFVs is based on integrated circuits called Programmable Read Only Memories (PROMs). The program is permanently 'blown' into the PROMs, which are often referred to as 'firmware'. As the name implies, the program on a PROM can be read by the fire control system but it cannot be directly altered in the normal course of use. To change a program, the PROMs must be replaced or 're-blown'—often necessitating their physical removal from the computer. Despite this drawback, PROMs are well suited to AFV use, being reliable, readily available to a ruggedised standard and comparatively free from program corruption.

AFVs have also employed Random Access Memories (RAMs) such as the core store fitted in the computer shown in Figure 3.30. Using a program-loading device, the RAM in the fire control computer can be readily re-programmed, without having to open sealed boxes or change components. This simple and rapid reprogramming capability can be very useful if the computer store is too small to carry all the available programs simultaneously or when a software upgrade is being developed and needs to be tested in the field. It also reduces the cost, time and disruption associated with a fleet-wide programme change. However, RAM can be more expensive and it is more vulnerable to corruption by transient signals.

As the use of computers in AFVs increases, there will be a constant demand for more memory capacity. To meet this requirement, alternative technologies such as optical discs and bubble memories will be considered, provided they can survive the harsh environment of the tank.

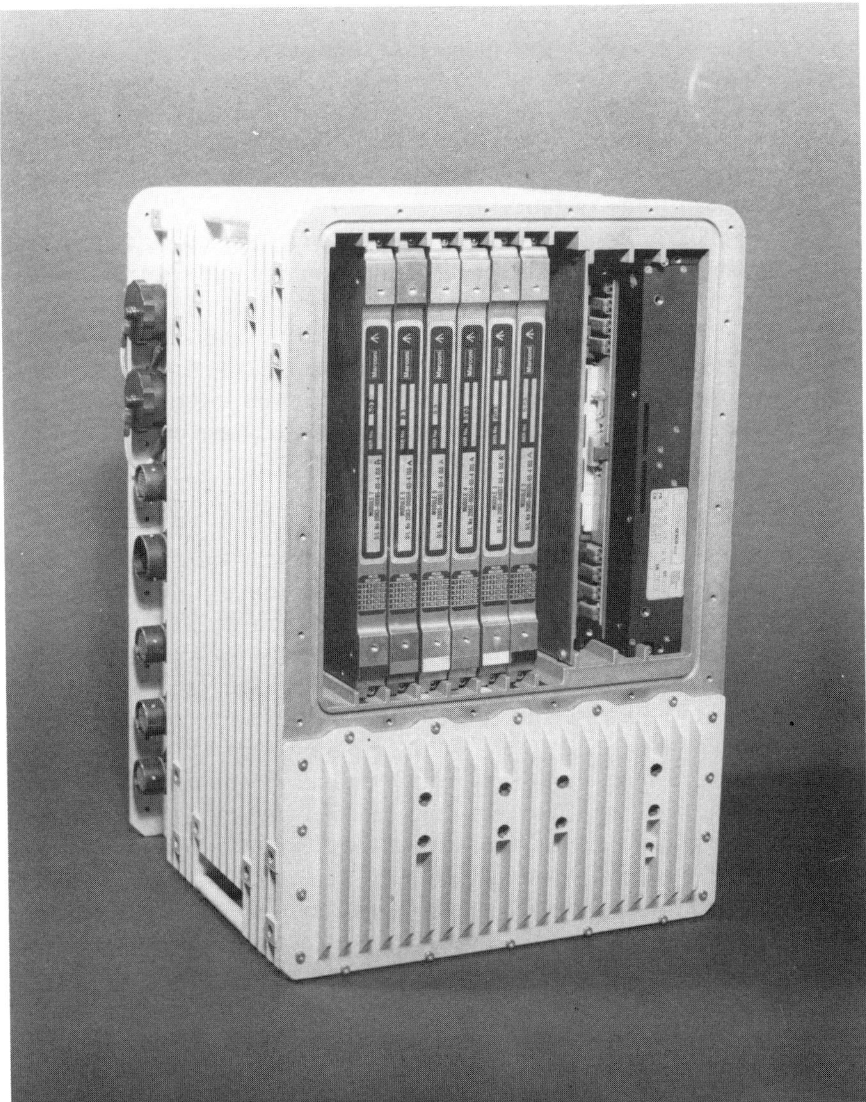

FIG. 3.30 A Digital Fire Control Computer.

Fire Control Programming Languages

Nowadays most fire control programs for digital computers are writen in a High Order Language (HOL), such as CORAL or Ada. HOLs are relatively simple to learn and to write, as they are based on comprehensible terminology rather than the complicated alphabetical/numerical sequence of Low Order Languages such as assembler codes. A compiler program is used to translate the HOL into machine code (the zeroes and ones), which the computer is able to process. In carrying out this translation, a compiler operates to a set of rules which may not always result in the fastest or most efficient set of machine code instructions. Hence, it may be necessary to insert into the program segments of assembler or machine code, specially written to achieve rapid program execution.

Ada was originally developed as an international standard computer language, which would be cost effective, readily transferable from one system to another, reliable and easy to maintain. Both the United States Department of Defense and the United Kingdom Ministry of Defence now specify Ada as the preferred language for key military systems.

Fire control programs can normally be divided into modules, covering for example the ballistic equations, the sensor inputs or the gun control signals. Each module is written as a self-contained package, with clearly defined input and output parameters which can only be changed within carefully controlled limits. This modular approach makes it easier to modify the internal features of individual sections, while maintaining overall program integrity—an important feature in weapon systems, where safety and reliability are critical.

Ballistic Model

A number of methods are available to calculate the ballistics of the round, including trajectory integration, polynomial equations and range tables.

Knowing the mass of the round and the laws which govern its motion in the atmosphere, the flight path of the round can be derived for a given launch angle, using trajectory integration. If the first calculation produces a theoretical 'miss', the launch angle is adjusted and the computer carries out a new integration, continuing with this process until a 'hit' is achieved. This iterative method produces very accurate results for all set of conditions and for flat trajectory KE rounds only one or two iterations are required. However, for high trajectory CE rounds, especially those fired at long ranges, numerous iterations are needed to achieve an accurate result—a time consuming process.

An alternative method is to use a series of polynomial equations, each of which replicates the flight of the round under a given set of conditions. Compared to trajectory integration, polynomial equations produce a solution more quickly, but they can be less accurate for the more extreme sets of condition and they do require more computer memory to store all the equations.

Ballistic data can also be stored in the computer as a series of range tables, similar to the system employed in the past for artillery. This method is quick and accurate, but a large amount of data must be stored to cover all possible sets of conditions. To overcome this latter problem, and yet retain the advantages of speed and accuracy, the computer can use the trajectory integration technique to calculate its own 'daily' range table, based on the conditions which apply at the time. As conditions change, the table can be updated and thus only a limited amount of data needs to be stored in the computer memory.

Additional Facilities

Most computer-based systems in current service offer facilities over and above basic weapon control, the main ones being training, self-checking and diagnostic testing.

The computer can be used to generate targets in the operator's field of view, enabling him to undertake 'dry run' training wherever the tank can be operated, such as in a barracks or on a non-firing range. Add-on training packages which use an eye-safe laser to simulate the firing of the gun can be integrated with the weapon system computer. The latter passes operational data (such as the 'lase' signal) to the simulator and receives information on the gunners performance, for analysis and display.

The majority of computers are programmed to carry out self-checks, either automatically or when the crew interrogates the system. The computer and its supporting sensors are exercised and their responses compared to predetermined criteria, with any deviations being identified by a code displayed to the operator.

Once a system defect is identified, the suspect LRU needs to be diagnosed to verify that it is faulty and to establish the likely cause, preferably without removing the LRU from the vehicle. The on-board computer is ideally suited to its task, but only if Built-in-Test (BIT) is engineered into the vehicle *ab initio*. Diagnosis usually requires access to internal LRU signals not needed for operational purposes. Thus, extra wiring sometimes must be built into LRUs and harnesses, to feed these signals back to the computer. For this reason, when fire control systems are retrofitted into older tanks and interfaced with existing hardware, only limited BIT can be provided. When designed into a new vehicle ab-initio BIT can be a powerful diagnostic tool, but even then only some 80% of possible faults are likely to be diagnosed. Attempts to diagnose the remaining 20% are not cost effective, since the additional wiring increases the cost of the LRUs, makes them more complex and, ironically, can reduce their inherent reliability.

Gun Control Equipment

Introduction

The modern MBT has a heavy, well armoured turret and a large calibre gun, yet it must be able to acquire, track and engage targets quickly and accurately, while itself being on the move. These requirements demand a correspondingly high degree of performance from the gun control equipment, which must have the following features:

A quick response time, to ensure that targets can be engaged the instant they appear,
High acceleration and rapid rates of traverse and elevation, to enable the gun to be brought to bear quickly and to cater for fast moving targets,
Precise control in traverse and elevation, to ensure accurate tracking of slow moving targets and to enable the gunner to lay precisely on target,
Accurate stabilisation to give a high hit probability when firing on the move.

The main elements which make up the system are:

The turret and gun drives,
The gyro stabilisation system,
The controllers.

Electro-hydraulic Turret and Gun Drives

Electro-hydraulic turret drives have been used in MBTs for many years and are still in widespread service. A pump produces high pressure hydraulic fluid which elevates and depresses the gun (by means of a hydraulic ram) and traverses the turret (via a hydraulic motor). The pump can be driven directly off the vehicle main engine, but in some vehicles it is electrically driven. With this latter arrangement, the pump can be located in the turret, which eliminates the need to pass high pressure hydraulic fluid through the hull to turret rotating interface, and power control can still be obtained using batteries, providing a useful silent watch capability. In the static firing mode, the hydraulic ram can be locked, to hold the gun firmly at the fire position.

Electro-hydraulic systems meet all the requirements noted in the introduction to this section, as they are very powerful and yet capable of providing fine control for accurate, slow speed tracking. In the past, electro-hydraulic systems tended to be smaller than electrical systems, but this advantage is now being eroded. The main drawbacks of the system are:

High pressure hydraulic fluid poses a fire hazard in the turret. To protect the crew, halon-gas fire suppression systems are sometimes fitted and these are very effective, but obviously they occupy valuable space and increase the cost of the tank,

The hydraulic fluid must be carefully filtered to ensure a smooth tracking performance,

The pipework occupies room in the turret, tends to leak and is not simple to repair in the field without introducing air and/or contaminants into the fluid,

The pump can be noisy and, like any mechanical device, prone to failure.

Electrical Gun and Turret Drives

Nowadays, most light AFV turrets are electrically driven, but for many years only British MBTs have been fitted with all-electrical turret drives, principally to eliminate the fire risk from hydraulic systems. Since the Second World War, therefore, the turret and gun drive on British tanks has been produced using metadynes, which are electro-mechanical amplifiers consisting of a coupled motor and generator. Electrical power from the on-board vehicle generator is amplified through the elevation and traverse metadynes and fed to the DC drive motors at the appropriate gun and turret drive gearboxes.

To produce a rapid response, the metadynes must be kept running at operating speed, even when the vehicle is on standby with the gun and turret stationary. Thus, on silent watch the metadynes can rapidly drain the vehicle batteries and, as with the hydraulic pump, they are noisy and prone to mechanical failure.

Modern developments mean that the metadyne can now be replaced by a Solid State Power Amplifier (SSPA) using High Power Transistor Stacks. The SSPA is a high efficiency device, almost silent in operation, and its standby current requirements is only 15% that of a metadyne. Thus, the SSPA enhances the silent watch capability and results in lower heat dissipation, reducing the vehicle's thermal signature. From standby, the solid state equipment provides full power within a few seconds of receiving a demand and its output is greater than that of the metadyne, resulting in reduced target switch times and an improved stability performance. It is also smaller and more reliable than metadyne-based systems. It can be seen that SSPA-based electrical turret and gun drives also meet all the system requirements noted above, but their added advantages mean that such systems are likely to become much more widely used in heavy MBTs.

Gyro Stabilisation

Basic stabilisation in elevation and traverse is normally obtained by fitting two rate gyros to the gun, one each to sense gun elevation rate and gun/turret traverse rate. If, for example, the vehicle turns right, the traverse gyro will precess and produce an output proportional to the rate of hull and turret movement. This output is amplified and fed to the turret drive motor through the servo loop. The motor will drive the turret leftwards back to its original position, so that the gyro output will be cancelled. This action continues as long as the vehicle is turning and trying to move the turret from its original position in space, thus stabilising the turret in traverse.

In order to improve stabilisation performance further, the modern tank can have 'feed forward' gyros fitted to its hull. When the vehicle moves, these hull-mounted gyros sense the disturbance first and their outputs can be used to drive the turret traverse and elevation gearboxes, keeping them 'out of the way' of the hull and thus minimising the effect of the hull disturbance on the turret and gun.

Control Handles

In most vehicles, control handles are provided for both the gunner and commander, enabling either of them to traverse the turret and elevate and depress the gun. When independent stabilised sights are fitted, the same handles are normally used to control the position of these sight lines, which keeps the number of control at the crew stations to a minimum and ensures that only one technique has to be learned for engaging targets.

Various designs of controller have been used in MBTs over the years, but the two-handed type appears to be favoured at present. It provides the operator with a means of bracing himself in a moving vehicle and, by applying counter pressure from one hand against the other, he can achieve an accurate slow speed tracking performance. However, one handed controllers and thumb controlled joysticks are also used and it cannot be said that there is a 'correct' answer to the controller question.

Weapon system switches, such as 'Fire Laser' or 'Select Ammunition' are often mounted on the control handles, so that engagements can be carried out without interrupting the target tracking and gun laying activities.

Irrespective of the type, it is essential that the controller should be able to meet the conflicting requirements of fast traverse and slow speed tracking. This is achieved by 'shaping' the controller output, either electrically or in the software, to produce a curve as shown in Figure 3.32. Near the null point, large movements

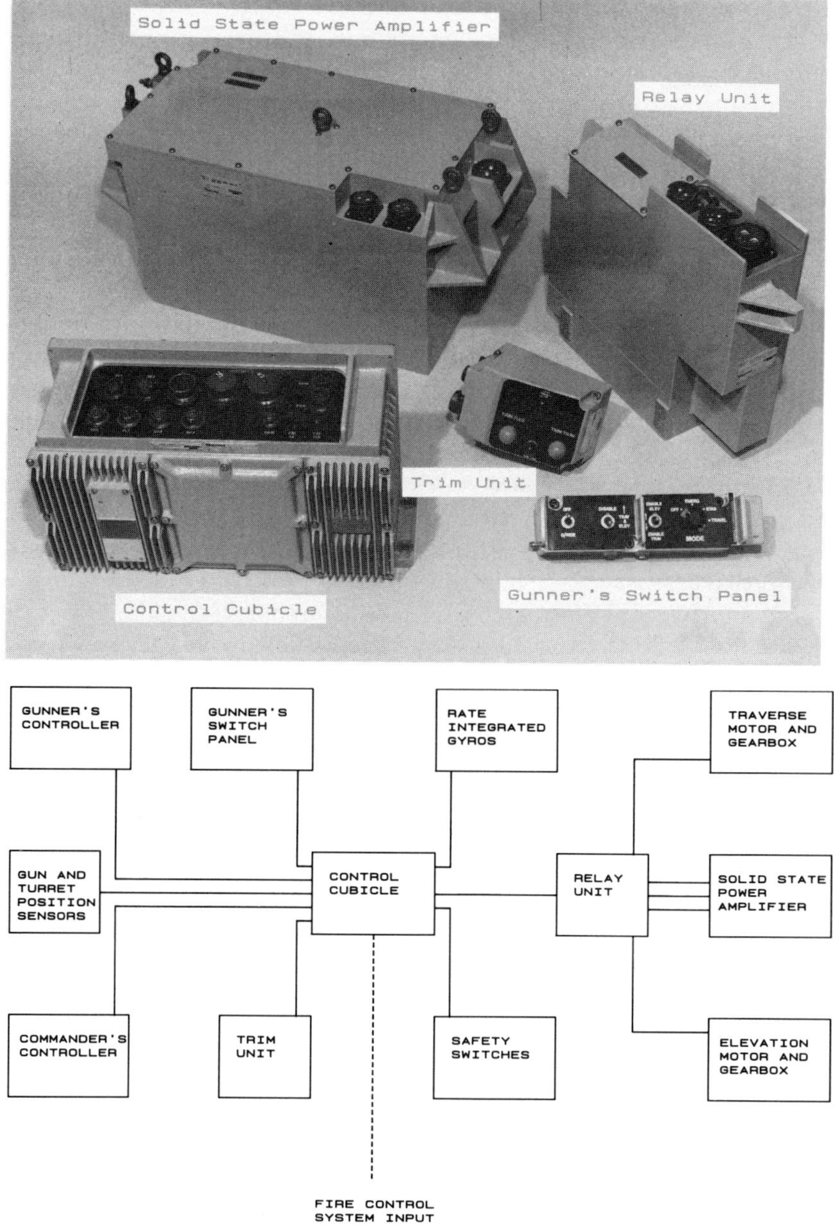

FIG. 3.31 Solid State Gun Control Equipment.

produce only small outputs, permitting accurate slow speed tracking. Further movement gradually accelerates the rate of output to produce fast turret and gun speeds. In some traverse systems a microswitch is fitted towards the limit of controller movement and when this is activated the turret automatically goes to maximum slew rate.

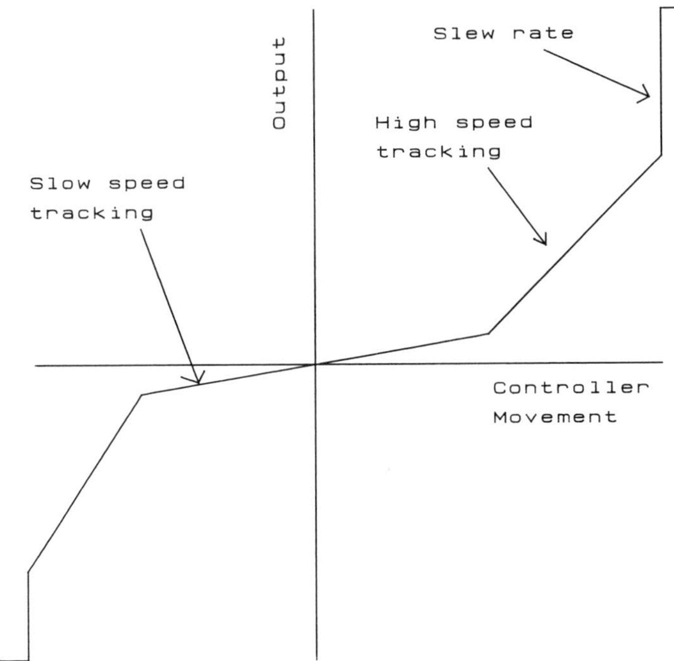

FIG. 3.32 Controller Output Shaping.

The Future of Tank Weapon Systems

Overall System Approach

Without doubt, the future of tank weapon systems is inextricably bound up with the development of the tank itself. As anti-tank weapons become more powerful and more varied in their mode of attack, it is clear that the tank needs to be better protected and more mobile. One way of meeting these requirements would be to reduce the overall size of the tank, but this would also reduce the space available for both systems and crew. Apart from the saving in volume, reducing the size of the crew is very attractive for other reasons, such as cost and the availability of suitably skilled manpower. However, the number of crew tasks is likely to increase rather than diminish and the inevitable result will be increased automation of the weapon system.

At the beginning of this chapter, the point was made that the weapon system must be considered as an entity if it is to function successfully. However, it must be said that even the most modern tanks are still made up of a number of discrete systems, each designed to its own standard, and these are actually integrated by the crew to produce a single fighting machine. There is little flexibility in the operation of the vehicle, in that control handles and switches are normally dedicated to one function only and, except in a few instances, each system can only be controlled from one crew station.

In future vehicles, the aim should be to have one common standard for all systems, with each crew member being able to carry out a very wide range of tasks, leading ultimately perhaps to the universal crew station. Some of the features of an integrated and automated system are discussed below.

Digital Data Bus

Until recently, cabling in all AFVs has been based almost exclusively on copper wire, with individual lines for each data signal and power source. Cables with over 100 individual lines have been used in AFVs and this has led to a proliferation of thick and unwieldly harnesses, which with their accompanying junction boxes occupy valuable space, especially in the fighting compartment. The result is often an ergonomic and maintenance disaster, particularly where new systems have been retrofitted in existing vehicles.

There will always be a requirement for substantial cables to carry power, but data signals can now be transmitted much more efficiently using a digital data bus. In this system, the parallel outputs from individual wires are fed onto the bus serially, so only one thin cable is required. To access the data bus, the inputs to and outputs from an LRU must conform to a standard set of protocols, but once these have been established a system with great scope and flexibility is created. Provided they obey the protocols, new facilities can be added and existing facilities changed or removed, without the need for extensive modifications or retesting. A second data bus can be fitted to provide system redundancy, for negligible cost.

Data busses can be based on either copper wire or fibre optics. The former are cheaper and since they carry electrical signals, more readily integrated with the vehicle's electronic LRUs. However, the fibre optic cables do have a number of advantages. In particular, they can transmit data at 10 MHz, (10 times faster than the copper bus), and they are not susceptible to electromagnetic interference. The main problem with fibre optics used to be the need to convert the light to electricity and vice versa. This has now been overcome by the use of ultra-sensitive light detectors in the data bus to LRU couplers, so that optical fibre data busses can now support 20 to 30 LRUs.

Automatic Target Detection and Tracking

The use of computers to enhance digital images has already been discussed, but this process can be extended to provide automatic target detection and tracking. The computer can be programmed to alert the crew to potential targets, by comparing the images seen by the sight with a library of likely target shapes. Having detected a likely target, the computer positions it in the centre of the field of view and then stores the digital pattern of the target zone. If the target moves, the computer will note the change and then scan the field of view for a pattern which most closely resembles the stored image. Having located the pattern, the computer brings it back into the centre of the field of view by moving the sight, thus tracking the target automatically.

Battlefield Management System

With a data bus fitted in the vehicle, the creation of a comprehensive Battlefield Management System (BMS) becomes a viable proposition. The primary purpose of the BMS will be to gather, organise and transmit the mass of data which already exists on the battlefield, and to present this information clearly to tank commanders and their superior headquarters. An important element of any BMS will be a navigation aid, linked into the data bus, such as the one shown in Figure 3.33.

FIG. 3.33 Inertial Measuring Unit and Control Unit for a Navigation Aid.

Starting with the individual tank, information such as own vehicle position, engine health, and ammunition and fuel state can be drawn together via the data bus and presented to the vehicle commander on a display screen. The screen will display written information as well as maps, to which can be added tactical information such as enemy dispositions, blown bridges or minefields. However, with the data bus linked into the radio, all this information can then be transmitted automatically to accompanying tanks or back through the chain of command. Thus, for example, without having to speak directly to either his squadron, troop or tank commanders, a tank regiment commander could quickly and accurately establish which tanks were running short of fuel and ammunition.

From the headquarters point of view, the BMS will allow information and orders to be transmitted directly to individual vehicles. Attack orders, for example could be presented as a map overlay, showing the start line, march route and enemy dispositions. All attacking tanks would receive the same information and would see as a glance how they were expected to operate as a group.

Conclusion

Since the early 1970s there has been a tremendous growth in MBT electronics and there is no sign of this ceasing. Apart from the technologies mentioned above, potential developments can be foreseen in areas such as;

Transmission of video data from front line tanks to unit headquarters,
Crewman's helmets with head-up displays, fed from externally mounted electronic sights, with weapon control being achieved by sensing head movement,
The use of millimetric wave radar to detect incoming anti-tank missiles.

In the final analysis, the scope of the electronics in future tanks is likely to be limited as much by cost as technical feasibility.

4

Critical Dimensions

Design Balance

A successful tank design should reflect a harmonious combination of the various characteristics of an armoured fighting vehicle—a design balance. There are many restrictions placed on a designer by the laws of physics; by the operational requirement; by the current state of technical development; by costs and other superimposed constraints. Tanks are heavy and complex machines and when the life cycle costs are calculated, the costs per kilometre are very high indeed. It is therefore essential that as high a proportion as possible of non-tactical movement should be undertaken either on tank transporters on roads or by rail on rail flats. In peacetime this helps to keep down costs, reduces maintenance and minimises damage to roads. Tanks can be moved long distances relatively easily and in wartime there is the operational advantage of having a tank arrive at its initial battle position mechanically sound and with relatively fresh crews. The overall dimensions of a tank will, therefore, be governed to a large extent by the operational need to move it by rail or road. It has been estimated that, on average, 12–15% of tanks will suffer some form of breakdown on the initial move to their deployment locations. This figure does not include between 5–10% of tanks which cannot be brought up to a serviceable state in time before deployment, assuming a 90–95% overall availability. In the worst case therefore, up to 20% of front line tanks may not even reach their initial battle positions.

Most countries, particularly in Western Europe, impose statutory limits on the dimensions of vehicles allowed on public roads. In the United Kingdom and on the Continent the most significant design limitation is the restriction on width to a maximum of 2.5 metres although special arrangements can be made for wider loads. Transportation by rail, however, poses more severe problems. Width and height of the tunnels are the most obvious restrictions but the need to keep vehicle side overhang to a minimum (the tank must be within the width of the rail flat on which it is transported) is also a requirement. If the tank is wider than the rail flat (as was the case with the British Conqueror tank) then the tank train may only be allowed to move on a 'down' line as long as there is no train on the corresponding 'up' line, as the railway authority may not permit trains to pass each other even when on different lines. While this may be acceptable in war, since the train timetables will be determined by the general staff, it poses unacceptable delays to movement and increased costs in peacetime.

There is a multitude of various rail gauges applying to routes and loads throughout the Continent but the loading gauge generally accepted as the limiting factor is the TZ gauge (see Figure 4.1) where the maximum width permitted is 3.54 m. Loads within this limit allow access to most rail routes in Western Europe, albeit with some restrictions. If the need to transport tanks by rail is accepted as part of the operational requirement, the height, width and the shape of the upper part of the vehicle will have to conform to the rail gauge requirements. The weight of a modern battle tank, about 40–65 tonnes, and the length do not pose any serious transportation or design problems. The rail gauge height limit applies only to equipment that is permanently fixed to the tank and not to items like the commander's machine gun which can be removed for transportation. There are many other factors which prevail on the tank designer to keep the height down of which the foremost is for the tank to offer the lowest possible silhouette to the enemy to avoid detection and to present the smallest target to anti-tank weapons if engaged. A glance at the Vehicle Data Table (Table II) (inside the back cover of this book) reveals the markedly different national trends with the Russian tanks being consistently the lowest and the American tanks consistently the highest.

Width and upper turret profile, however, become the dominant characteristics and if the TZ rail gauge limit is adhered to, imposes very considerable constraints upon the tank designer.

Choice of Weapon System

The previous chapter dealt with tank firepower and this chapter examines how the choice of the weapon is the dominant influence which decides the final dimensions of the tank. The logical starting point is the target. First, the target must be defined. If the tank is used to engage 'soft' targets, such as light wheeled vehicles and men in the open, then the gun would need a good HE performance and a high velocity round would probably not be needed. This would allow the selection of a light gun with relatively low recoil energy. As a further bonus it is likely that the ammunition will also be relatively small as the propellant charge weight will be low.

On the other hand, if the tank's primary role is to destroy other tanks or similar 'hard' targets then a high velocity gun will be required bringing with it all the attendant problems of heavy weight, large calibre and length. The high recoil forces will require large buffers and recuperators to absorb the energy and sufficient room in the turret to allow the gun to recoil at all angles of elevation and depression. The most restricting angle of elevation is when the gun is directly opposite the turret ring since above and below the ring the breech will have additional room to recoil into the space in the bustle or the hull respectively. It will also be necessary to provide stowage space for the much larger and heavier ammunition, particularly the longer fin stabilised long rod penetrators.

Once the calibre of the gun has been selected and the length of the barrel and other dimensions have been decided upon, the problem of fitting the gun into the turret can be addressed. A prime consideration is the position of the gun trunnions or mounting points and hence the inboard length of the gun. The trunnions are normally near the point of balance as this keeps the load and wear on the elevating mechanism to a minimum. The need to mount the gun near its centre of gravity is essential for tanks with electrically operated gun control systems. If the gun is

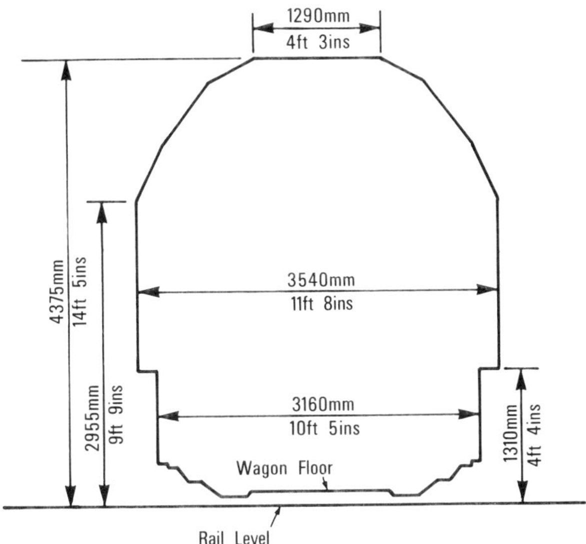

FIG. 4.1 The Continental 'TZ' rail guage.

designed to be inherently out of balance, for example in self-propelled field artillery, then a hydraulically operated elevation system will almost certainly be required because of its high power density and the lock-out facility provided by such systems. In either case, the tank gun will need to return to an index position if an autoloader is fitted.

The internal dimensions of the turret must allow the gun to be loaded preferably at all angles of elevation and depression. The amount of depression given to a tank is a prime factor in establishing turret height and hence overall vehicle height but its significance has major operational implications when the tank is in a fire position on the battlefield. A glance at Fig. 4.2.1 and Figure 4.2.2 show two tanks in

FIG. 4.2.1 Side view of two tanks in a fire position showing the operational implications of having limited gun depression.

fire positions, both aiming at the same target. The tank on the right in each case has only 89 mils (5 degrees) depression set on the gun whereas the tank on the left in both photographs has 178 mils (10 degrees). Since both tanks are aiming at the same target it is apparent that the tank with only 89 mils available for depression is

FIG. 4.2.2 Front view of the same two tanks in a fire position aiming at the same target.

forced to expose far more of its less well protected hull to enemy fire. Western nations consider that about 178 mils (10 degrees) to be the minimum acceptable depression limit for a gun but this view is not shared by Warsaw Pact countries who generally have about 89 mils in the interests of giving the tank a low overall height and silhouette.

If the need for about 180 mils depression is accepted, it must be provided over at least the 1080 mils (60 degrees) frontal arc to ensure that the gun clears all obstructions such as track guards and the driver's periscope. This 1080 mils arc usually matches the arc of maximum protection provided by the armour of a tank's turret. Obviously it would be a relatively simple matter to ensure adequate clearance for gun depression by mounting the turret well forward on the hull but other factors such as the space/volume requirements, the seating position for the driver and the need to provide a reasonable slope of armour for the front glacis plate will mitigate against this. The 180 mils depression could also be achieved by mounting the trunnions fairly high in the turret but recourse to this as a solution will inevitably lead to a high turret roof and so the final position of the trunnions becomes a matter of compromise. Details of the depression angles for Western and Soviet AFVs are given in Figure 4.4. Since it must be possible to load the gun at all angles of elevation and depression, its inboard length (in the fully recoiled position) plus the length of the largest indivisible piece of ammunition is another critical factor. In order to ease the problem for the loader in manually loaded tanks and in tanks such as T72 and Leclerc fitted with an autoloader, the gun control system automatically returns the breech to an index position for loading. It should be noted that the loading length is not necessarily measured from the rear of the breech but from the rear of the chamber in the case of a non-tied breech block which is the type used in most tank guns. One of the advantages of split or separated ammunition, as used in Chieftain and Challenger, is that the longest single piece is considerably shorter than fixed or single piece ammunition.

Turret and Mantlet

Before considering the effect on turret ring diameter, it is appropriate to look at some of the factors affecting the choice of mantlets. As the gun elevates and

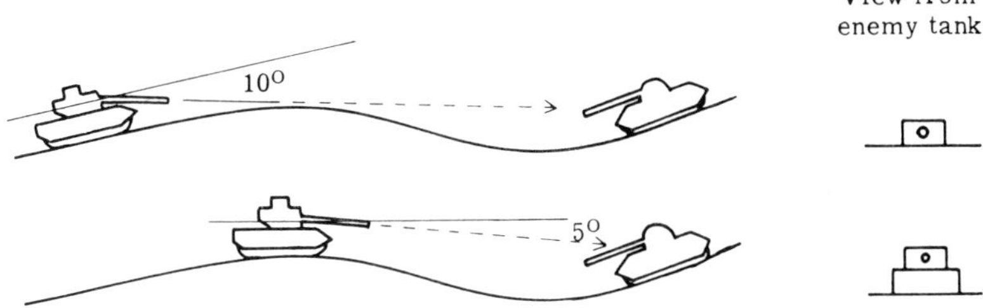

FIG. 4.3 A schematic representation of the effect of having only limited gun depression.

Western AFVs
Scorpion—178 mils (10 deg)
Leopard 1—160 mils (9 deg)
M60A1—178 mils
Centurion—178 mils
AMX 30—178 mils
Sheridan—132 mils (7.4 deg)
Chieftain—178 mils
Challenger—178 mils
M1A1—178 mils
Leopard 2—178 mils
Leclerc—150 mils

Soviet AFVs
T55/T62/T72—71 mils (4 deg)
PT 76—71 mils
JS3/T10—53 mils (3 deg)
T80—71 mils (estimated)

FIG. 4.4 Gun depression figures for Western and Soviet AFVs.

depresses it is essential to maintain the same level of protection for the crew. The role of the mantlet is to keep out all types of ammunition, from small arms to the main anti-tank KE natures, and therefore the hole in the front of the turret must be kept as small as possible. Various designs of mantlets have been tried over the years with the idea of providing the best protection at minimum weight and with the least mechanical complication. Mantlets can be classified either as interior or exterior and the diagrams of each type are given in Figure 4.5. The position of the trunnions and the size and weight of the mantlet will also affect turret balance. It is desirable that the turret should balance in the vertical axis about its point of rotation as this will reduce the loads on the turret traverse gear. In the extreme case where the out of balance forces are high or the tank is on a side slope, the traversing loads could make it difficult for the gunner to traverse the turret by hand or it might put very high energy demands on the power traverse system.

It will also be necessary to balance the turret about a horizontal axis if undue loading on the turret race ring is to be avoided. One method of achieving this and balancing the weight of the barrel at the same time is to provide the turret with a bustle at the rear. In the British Chieftain and Challenger this valuable extra space is used for the stowage of ammunition projectiles (not propellant charges), radios and the NBC system. In the more modern tanks such as Leopard 2, M1A1 and the Leclerc, the bustle is used to stow the majority of the single piece ammunition rounds. The Leclerc, due to enter service in the French Army in the mid-1990s, is the first Western tank to have a 3 man crew in which the loader is

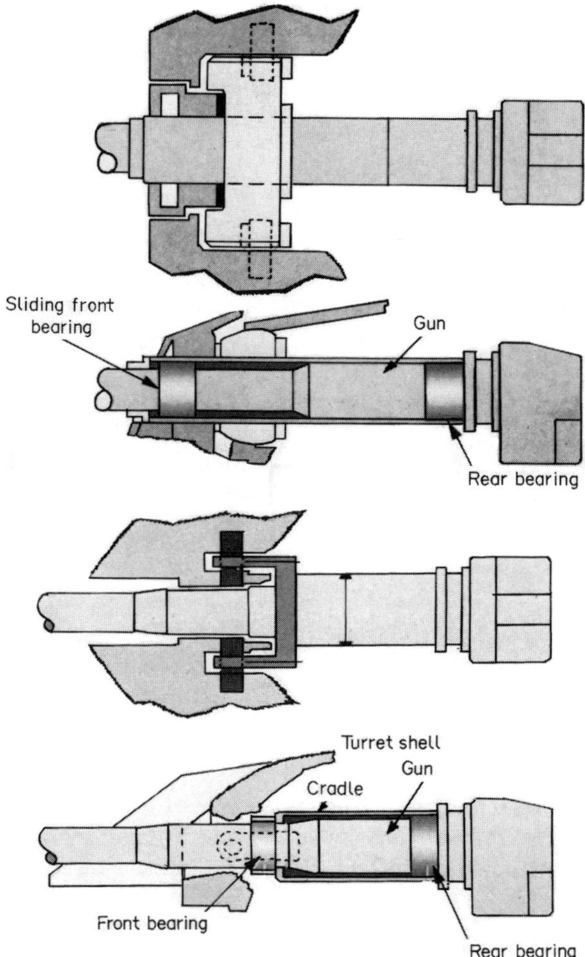

FIG. 4.5 Mantlet types. The exterior type with the gun cradle mounted on the rotor in the upper diagrams and the interior type (Chieftain and Challenger) in the lower.

replaced by an electrically operated autoloader mounted in the bustle. Though British design philosophy has traditionally been to mount all propellant below the turret ring, the United States and West Germany in their latest tanks, have resorted to blow-off panels so that, in the event of a hit on the bustle, the propellant gases are vented to the outside air.

As a general rule, the turret when complete with gun, represents about 20% of the total weight of a tank, so that mounting the turret and ensuring it can perform all its battle functions at any position and condition of movement is a complex engineering problem. The race ring must not only support the weight of the turret but it must also prevent the turret lifting off during cross-country movement when it is subjected to severe vertical acceleration. In addition, now that firing on the move at a moving target is possible with modern digital fire control systems, any backlash in the mechanical interface between the hull and turret will render the system inaccurate and will reduce the effectiveness of any precision, high cost fire control system. To ensure that the turret is securely mounted on the hull, designers have strengthened this area and have also sought ways to reduce or eliminate backlash by giving the turret gearbox a resilient mounting.

The race ring must be able to transmit the firing stresses of the gun to the suspension and ultimately the ground. These stresses could amount to 3–6 g, depending on the propellant charges used and the angle of elevation at the time of firing. All this must be achieved at minimum friction to keep the turret rotational loads as low as possible. There may be an additional requirement to provide a non-rotational air and water seal at the hull/turret interface for NBC protection and deep wading. The production of a suitable turret race ring calls for precision engineering of the highest order and it is not uncommon for the roller or ball bearing to break up or to develop flat spots or become lumpy—a phenomenon sometimes called 'Brinelling'. Perhaps future developments in the field of high efficiency magnets may lead to the turret being both supported and powered by linear motors.

Some means must be provided to allow electrical power, tank intercom, hydraulic fluid and filtered air, piped direct to the crew stations from the NBC filtration system, to pass between hull and turret. This is achieved by means of a rotary base junction containing all the necessary slip-ring contacts with perhaps the addition of a fibre optic or other digital data transmission facility in future.

Diameter of the Turret Ring

We have already seen how the choice of the gun affects the position of the trunnions and by reference to Fig. 4.6 it can be seen that if loading and firing at all angles of elevation are to be possible than the diameter of the turret ring is critical. If the turret ring is to be kept within the width of the track (Figure 4.7, upper diagram), then this immediately fixes the width of the tank to the maximum permitted by the appropriate rail gauge. Thus, the overall width of the tank is the diameter of the turret plus the width of the two tracks, suspension mountings etc. Once maximum width has been set, the tank designer must then take into account another design parameter. It is essential that the steering ratio be kept as near as possible to 1.5 and certainly below 1.8. The steering ratio, or L/C ratio, is defined as the ratio of the length of the track on the ground to the distance between track centres (Figure 4.8) and is, in effect, a measure of the tank's resistance to turning. If the L/C ratio (Figure 4.8) is low (below 1.5) the tank will tend to be unstable in the turns and unless a wide track is used, the Nominal Ground Pressure (NGP) (Figure 4.9) will be high leading to poor performance over soft ground. However, if track length is increased without a corresponding increase in width, the L/C ratio rises very sharply, as does the resistance to turning, requiring a disproportionate amount of power, especially in muddy conditions. The determination of the optimum range of the L/C ratio as lying between 1.5–1.8 has been largely empirical and history is replete with examples where designers exceeded that value only to find that the tank would not steer except on smooth tarmac or concrete where the resistance to turning is low. So the width of the tank must not exceed the rail gauge

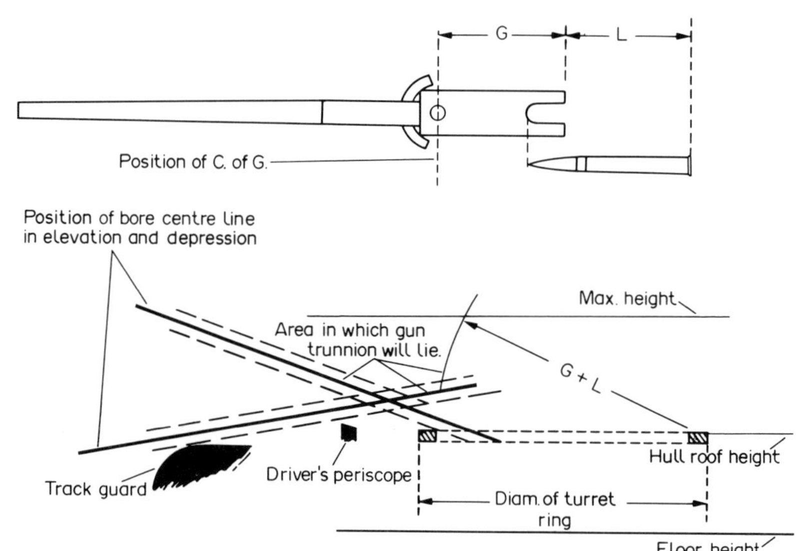

FIG. 4.6 Fitting the main armament.

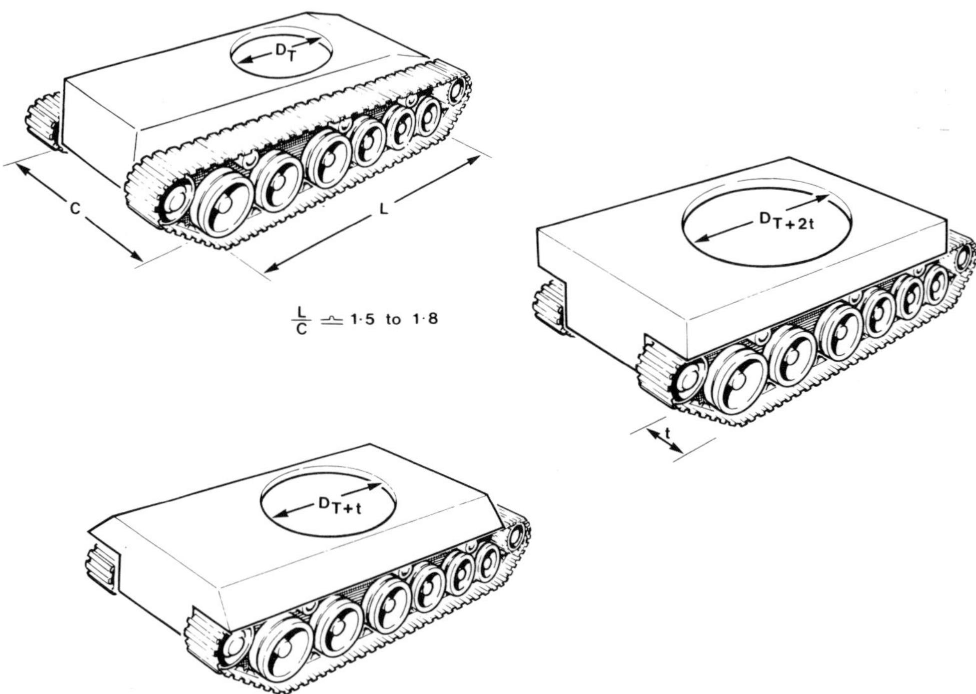

FIG. 4.7 Fitting the turret ring into the hull.

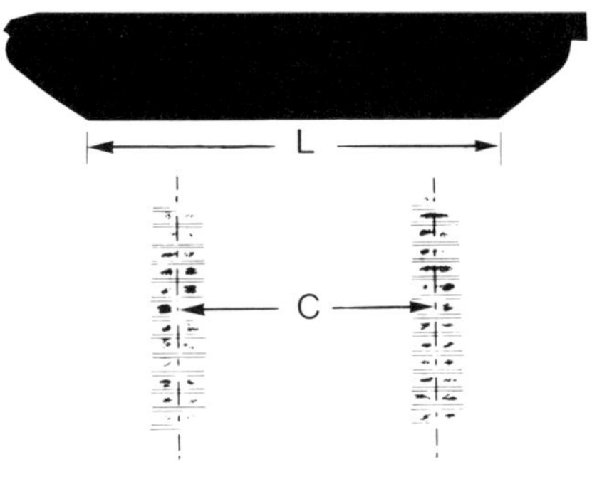

FIG. 4.8 Steering—L/C ratio.

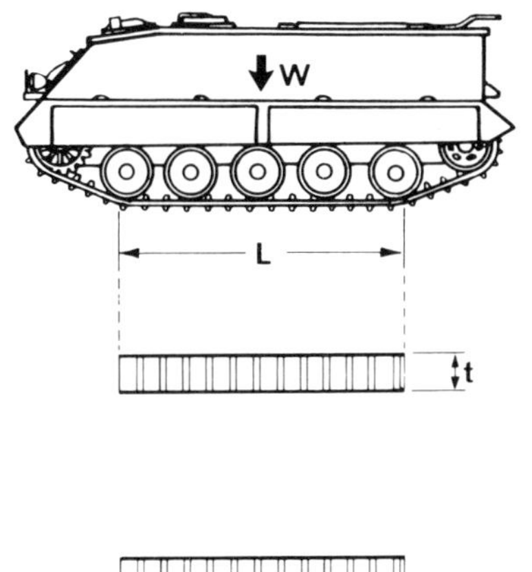

FIG. 4.9 Nominal ground pressure of tracked vehicles.

and is directly related to its length through the L/C ratio. If the restriction imposed by the rail gauge is to be adhered to and the turret ring diameter is to be kept within the inner limits of the track, then the maximum diameter permitted in Europe would be about 2.4 m (the diameter D(T) in Figure 4.7). The ring diameter can be increased by building sponsons over the track and in extreme cases this could mean that the turret ring could have a diameter almost as great as the overall width of the vehicle (the diameter D(T) + 2(t) in Figure 4.7 middle diagram). This solution means that the height of the tank is increased and that the hull sides in that area have vertical armour, a highly undesirable characteristic for achieving maximum protection. A compromise solution is normally adopted whereby the turret ring is raised above the upper track level by sponsons, but as the turret ring does not extend to the full width of the hull, it then allows sloping armour to be used, giving maximum protection within the weight limit.

Reference to the chart in Figure 4.10 will show how the features affecting the design of the turret are built up. In the past the thickness of the turret side armour had little or no influence on its size or interior volume. With modern composite or spaced armour the density is such that it may well be that the interior volume of the turret is dictated by a combination of the rail gauge and the thickness/volume of the armour required to defeat the threat. In modern tanks it is becoming increasingly difficult to mount all the sophisticated equipment necessary to fight the 24 hour battle (thermal imagers, navigation aids, panoramic sights, warning sensors for lasers and radars, chemical detectors etc) and give the gunner and commander room to operate his controls while ensuring that the tank still remains within the rail gauge. Careful thought must therefore be given to ergonomics in the turret at the design stage, the use of full scale mock-ups of the layout of each crew station and close user participation in the development process before any design is frozen and manufacturing starts. If the layout of the crew stations does not permit the crew to work to the best of their ability when under stress then the full potential of modern fire control systems in reducing engagement times and increasing chance of a hit will not be realised in battle.

Tank Height

There is a need to understand the difference between tank tactical height and actual height. The tactical height is that part of the tank that has to be exposed in order to engage the enemy whereas the actual height is normally taken to be the height of the tank from the ground to the highest point. This is normally taken to be the top of the commander's cupola but care must be exercised when comparing the relative heights of tanks to ensure that the same datum points are used. The position of the gun trunnions and the major influence it has in deciding tactical and overall height has already been stressed. It is now normal practice to provide a turret floor that rotates with the turret. This will have to be at some, albeit small, distance above the hull floor itself to allow room for the suspension torsion bars and bearings on which the floor can rotate. Provision must then be made for a standing loader wearing a helmet (about 1.8 m) unless an autoloader is fitted. Even in modern tanks, like Leopard 2 and M1A1 where it is possible to load sitting down using the ammunition stowed in the bustle, not all loaders chose to do so and therefore the turret height cannot be reduced. The only other alternative as practiced by the Russians is to select crews smaller in stature and to design the tank accordingly. As far as it is known, no Western nation selects tank crews on the basis of their height and they are therefore obliged to design tanks for the 95 percentile man. Therefore, loader height and the amount of gun depression will fix the height of the turret roof and thereafter it is a matter of national preference what other fixtures are added. A commander's cupola will be needed and the height of this can vary from the low, relatively crude systems seen on the earlier Russian vehicles; to the mini-turret, including a commander's 12.7 mm (0.5 in) machine gun, seen on some marks of American M60 tanks; to the separate, contra-rotating commander's turret fitted to the British Conqueror tank. A glance at the vehicle data table (Table II) shows the very marked differences in height between the Russian and American tanks at the low and the high end of the scale respectively. Although Table II does not show the relationship between the tactical height and

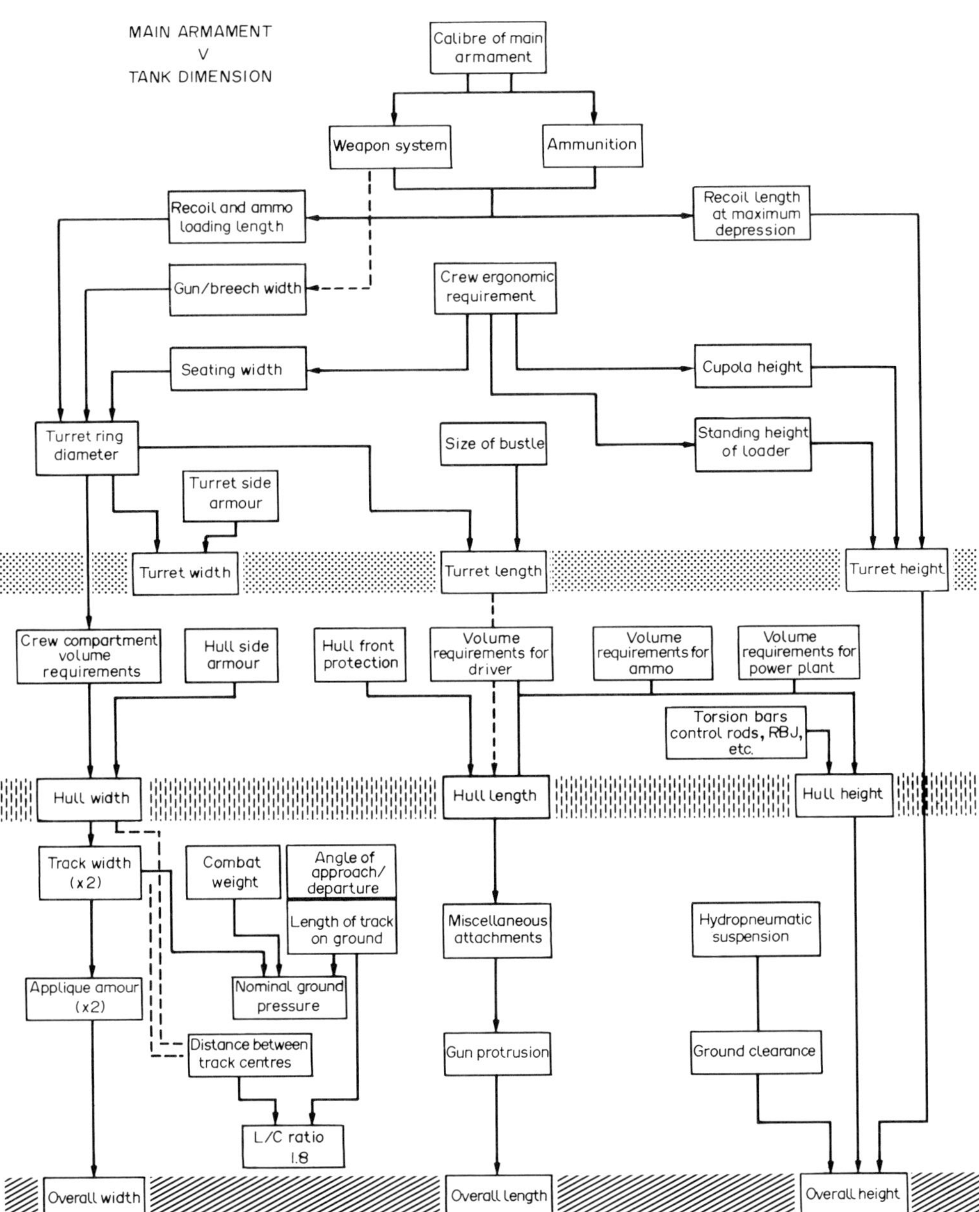

FIG. 4.10 Main armament and tank dimensions.

the actual height, there is a direct relationship and the higher the tank the greater the target it will present to the enemy on the battlefield. In essence, the height of the tank above the gun trunnions should be kept as low as is consistent with all the other requirements for maximum depression and so forth, described above. The practical effect of this is that designers should keep the height of the commander's cupola to a minimum as this will always be exposed when the tank is in a position to fire the main armament.

Hull Dimensions

Reference to Figure 4.7 shows that the hull width is related to the turret ring diameter while still staying within the rail gauge. With some tanks now fitting composite armour side plates (M1A2 and Leopard 2) the width can be significantly greater than the distance to the outer edge of the tracks might suggest. If composite armour is utilised, then it will probably be necessary to make special arrangements for rail movement. On Leopard 2, for example, provision is made for the front three side plates on each side to lift over on hinges and lie flat on the front track guards to ensure the tank fits within the Standard Rail Gauge.

The height of the hull is determined by a combination of several factors. At one time the critical factor was the need to accommodate a seated driver in an upright position but the introduction of the semi-reclining driver pioneered by Chieftain, has allowed the hull height to be reduced by up to 300 mm. However, with the demand for increased power/weight ratios and the restriction on the space available for the power pack (see Chapter 8), it could be that the minimum height of the engine will be a critical factor. It is a common feature of the modern tank to have engine deck height above the level of the turret ring. This does not pose a tactical constraint providing that the turret can rotate through 6400 mils (360 degrees without elevating the gun unnecessarily although it is obvious that there is little possibility of giving the gun any depression when facing to the rear.

If the tank utilises torsion bar suspension then allowance must be made for the bars and their protective covering to be laid transversely across the hull floor. This can add approximately 150 mm to the height of the hull and one advantage of suspension systems contained within the track envelope such as Horstman and the hydro-pneumatic systems fitted to Challenger and Leclerc is that they help to keep hull height to a minimum. Hydro-pneumatic systems also save weight and a current estimate is that both Leopard 2 and M1A1 would save about 600 kgs (1300 lbs) by replacing torsion bars with hydro-pneumatic struts.

A limiting factor would be a requirement to stow ammunition vertically below the turret ring but it is most unlikely that this would be allowed to influence hull height to any great degree as it is a relatively easy matter to stow ammunition horizontally. Other stowage areas, such as the turret bustle, could be found. At present even 120 mm single piece long rod ammunition does not pose a handling problem in current turrets. Should there be a need to move to a larger calibre in future or to use longer fin stabilised penetrators to achieve greater performance at current calibres then handling of single piece ammunition might be difficult. The solution might be to use two-piece ammunition. The determination of hull length will depend on a number of factors. Starting at the front, there is the armour thickness of the glacis and toe plate to be considered which may be appreciable with composite armour. There is also the need to accommodate the driver in a reclining position so that his periscope is still forward of the turret ring. The swept volume required by the turret basket and turret services have to be calculated with precision so that the basket does not come into contact with fittings mounted on the turret wall. This swept volume, known as the 'sacred circle' must be kept free so that nothing can come loose and jam the rotation of the turret. In order to devote a greater proportion of the tank's overall weight to armour, designers have been considering reducing the space taken up by the power pack. The solution adopted by Leclerc is to use a highly rated but small capacity diesel engine of about 16 litres (Leopard 2 has a 48 litre diesel engine). An alternative idea being considered by a number of nations is to amount the engine transversely i.e. across the hull. In each case the engine is mated to the gearbox (mounted transversely as before) via a specially designed transfer box. About 1 cubic metre (40 cubic feet) of space can be saved in this way, allowing room for more ammunition.

Although most tanks provide limited access between the turret and the driver's compartment at certain gun positions, the engine compartment is almost invariably closed off by a bulkhead. Sometimes arrangements are made whereby the engine can aspirate through the turret and this is particularly important if deep wading or schnorkelling is contemplated. It does, however, make it very cold for the crew. If the bulkhead is fixed at the rear of the crew compartment then the space available for the power pack is clearly defined.

The next chapter explains the need for the power plant to occupy the minimum volume but since the width of the vehicle is in direct relationship to the distance between the track centres (L/C ratio) then the length of track on the ground is related to the turret ring diameter.

Theoretically, provided the length of track in contact with the ground is kept within the limits of the L/C ratio (1.5–1.8), then the length of the tank hull could be extended to give it a larger overhang without penalty. Unfortunately, this is not so as there are severe limitations on the amount the hull can be extended forwards or rearwards over the track contact length, as we shall see.

The first limitation is the angle of approach and departure. If the hull protrudes beyond the track envelope in front, then the tank will have difficulty climbing banks or crossing ditches. Similarly, the rear of the tank should not extend beyond the rear sprocket or idler, although in practice this is not so important as the angle of approach. The relationship between the contact length and the overall length is called the pitch ratio and designers aim for a ratio of about 1.5 to 1.8. Anything above 1.8 is likely to be the major contributory factor to excessive vehicle pitching, causing motion sickness or crew fatigue and could become a limiting factor to the speed at which the vehicle is able to move cross country. A further effect of excessive overhang could be that the nominal ground pressure would increase as the overall weight of the tank would become greater without providing for a larger area of track in contact with the ground.

Design Balance

One of the areas where a balance has to be struck by the designer between the various user requirements is in the relationship of the Nominal Ground Pressure (NGP) to the L/C ratio (Figure 4.9). Nominal ground pressure is defined as:

$$\text{NGP} = \frac{\text{Vehicle Weight}}{\text{Area of tracks in contact with the ground}}$$

The units usually used are lbs/sq in (Imperial) or KPa (SI).

It should be noted that this is a nominal ground pressure as vehicles have flexible tracks and the few road wheels bearing on the track wheel path create peak pressures that are 5 or 6 times greater than the NGP. In extreme cases and under certain conditions these peak pressures can cause a collapse of the soil. Furthermore, this collapse tends to be cumulative and as each road wheel passes, it sinks further into the ground, the vehicle adopts a progressively higher nose-up attitude and the rear of the tank may 'belly' and touch the ground. At the other end of the scale, on hard going or on roads, only the grousers or rubber pads are in contact with the ground and this may represent only 50% of the nominal contact area.

In order to achieve a more accurate measure of the ability of a vehicle to move cross country, a method has been developed by the Royal Armament Research and Development Establishment (RARDE) in the United Kingdom to arrive at a Mean Maximum Pressure (MMP). This calculation takes into account the weight of the vehicle together with the area of the track in contact with the ground and the number, size of the road wheels and the pitch of the track. MMP aims to average out the peak pressures which occur directly under the road wheels and the minimum pressures between them. MMP gives a much more accurate measurement than NGP of a tracked vehicle's performance cross country but has yet to find international acceptance.

For good cross country performance, it is important that a vehicle's NGP (or MMP) is kept as low as possible. As there is a limit to the length of the track in contact with the ground due to the L/C ratio requirements, then the only way to increase the contact area and thus reduce ground pressure is to make the tracks wider. However, this can only be done to a limited extent as excessive track width will seriously inhibit the hull width if the rail gauge limitation is not exceeded. It would also make the tracks heavier, increasing rolling resistance and vehicle all-up weight, making it necessary for more robust, and consequently heavier, road wheels and suspension components. It also makes track adjustment and maintenance by the crew a more tiring task though hydraulic track tensioners, operated by the driver from under armour, are now available.

When it is paramount to have a very low nominal ground pressure, such as for an over-snow vehicle, a very wide, light track is used but the vehicle hull tends to be narrow and the payload has to be carried above track level. This is acceptable for logistic vehicles and highly specialised over-snow vehicles but would not be suitable for armoured fighting vehicles. A specialised vehicle is shown in Figure 4.11. The Haaglund BV 202 is made in Sweden and is the only military over-snow vehicle made by a Western country. It is in service with the armies of the United Kingdom, Canada, Norway and others. Despite having a long track in contact with the ground, the vehicle achieves its very low nominal ground pressure while still having an acceptable L/C ratio by an articulated joint in the middle. The engine is in the front section but all four tracks are powered via a power take-off through the articulated linkage.

The Design Spiral

The inter-dependence and inter-relationship of some of the physical aspects of the tank that affect the overall design are shown diagrammatically in Figure 4.12. Starting at the lower end and following the spiral upwards gives an indication how

FIG. 4.11 The Haaglund BV 206 over snow vehicle.

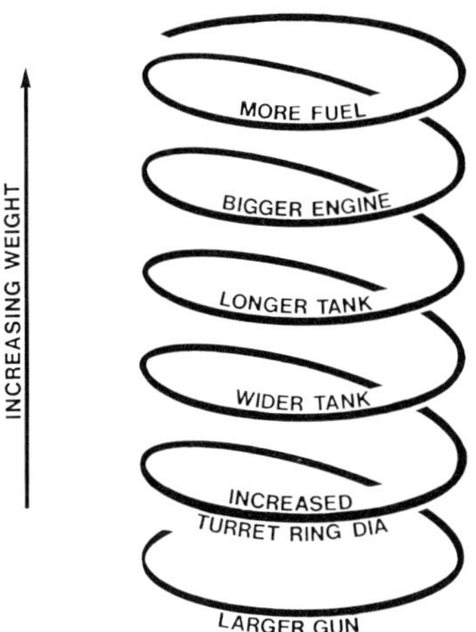

FIG. 4.12 The design spiral.

the tank has grown over the years—the larger gun demanding an increased diameter turret ring, leading to a wider, heavier tank which demands a larger, more powerful engine and so on. Here again, the law of diminishing returns comes into play. In their efforts to make the next generation of tanks significantly superior to the last, tank designers may have forgotten that a superior tank cannot use its superiority all the time and indeed may not even be able to exploit one of them fully; the less technically superior tank, particularly if it is reliable and available in greater numbers, may prove more effective in the end. The threat to the tank on the modern battlefield from 'smart' munitions, especially top attack, demands that the next generation should be designed with the reduction of all its various signatures as top priority. This will involve the use of 'stealth' technology to reduce radar reflectively, the reduction of thermal and, if possible, the magnetic and seismic signatures as well. But above all, the silhouette of the tank must be reduced to make it more difficult to detect; and if detected, to be hit. All tank signatures can be reduced but the only way vehicle size (but not necessarily vehicle weight) is likely to be reduced, while still keeping high levels of protection, is by the elimination of one or even two crewmen. Once this decision has been made, tank designers can begin to descend the design spiral—a smaller tank requires a smaller engine and less fuel and it can be made lower.

The next generation of tanks will need to be fitted with some form of active defensive countermeasures. We have already seen the first evidence of this in the fitting of reactive or explosive armour as an add-on to in-service vehicles and the next step will be to integrate both passive and active measures. In this way the 'mobile protected gun platform' will have a worthwhile role on the battlefield in the next century. Further details on protection are given in Chapter 5.

Additional Factors

There are two additional factors which have to be taken into account at the design stage of any armoured vehicle. They are Fightability and Availability. Both are critical in achieving a successful overall design and both are dependant on far more than just the application of formulae or the need to keep within agreed international standards or criteria.

Fightability

Mobility, capacity, survivability and firepower are characteristics which together enable the vehicle to perform as an effective fighting machine when manned by trained soldiers who must be capable of performing to a high standards under the stress of battle. The term 'fightability' or more properly, ergonomics, has been coined to cover the man–machine interface. No area of vehicle specification and design is more difficult to describe or to determine than fightability. Though fightability is based on general principles of the ability of the human body to perform certain functions using all the senses and hand and eye coordination, it remains, ultimately, a subjective exercise; what are good ergonomics to the right-handed gunner whose left eye is the master eye are very poor ergonomics the left-handed gunner who prefers to use his right eye. Nevertheless, a great deal of time and money is spent on the development of sophisticated fire control systems and at last it has been realised that unless the man can perform up to the limit of his capability when in battle, the full capability of the system will not be realised and money will have been wasted.

Availability

Availability usually expressed as a percentage, is the characteristic which determines the time a vehicle can be operated by the crew, ideally to the full extent of its operational capabilities. However, availability is not solely dependent on the vehicle and is subject to a number of outside influences such as the logistic support policy in force at the time; the quantity of spares provided; the manpower available for repair in the logistic support services and the ability of the crew to carry out routine servicing as easily as possible. Nevertheless, the higher the basic availability built into the vehicle from its inception, the greater will be the proportion of time it can be used by the crew.

Conclusions

The design characteristics of a vehicle are the framework on which its detailed specification design is based. They are determined by a careful analysis of the joint impact of; the threat faced by the vehicle and the crew who will use it; the tactics; the organisations in which the vehicle will be used and the training to which its users will be subjected in preparing for battle.

5

Protection

Man has always attempted to protect himself against the weapons of his adversaries but this has been balanced by his need to remain mobile. Over the years, as body armour increased steadily in weight, so mobility decreased, until the longbow using the first long rod penetrator, the arrow, made the armour protection available at the time a worthless and cumbersome disadvantage. The key to greater survivability lay in the reduction in weight and hence an increase in mobility.

A similar development cycle can be traced to armoured protection for fighting vehicles. Early First World War tanks were built of relatively soft boiler plate, riveted to an inner frame of angle iron. Demands for ever higher levels of protection in the 1939–45 war led inevitably to the production of tanks such as the British Churchill and the German Tiger where the weight of armour compromised the overall design balance. The result was that these vehicles were unreliable, slow and, paradoxically, became more vulnerable to anti-tank fire despite their increased protection.

The tank has no friends on the battlefield and must therefore attempt to provide a measure of protection against every weapon arraigned against it. The threat can be from FGA, helicopters and 'smart' sub-munitions delivered by artillery guns or rockets primarily directed towards top attack; from vehicle-borne guided missiles and hand held anti-tank weapons; other tanks, belly attack and track cutting mines with increasingly sophisticated fuzes and, in the future, from laser damage weapons. In addition, the tank must provide the crew with a high degree of protection against the effects of Nuclear, Biological and Chemical (NBC) warfare.

Levels of Protection

Protection can be divided into three levels. The first is personal body armour. This is used increasingly for internal security operations but has no application to vehicle technology. Secondly, there is armour for light vehicles but, at this relatively low weight, it is impossible to consider protection against all likely forms of attack. In general, protection will be designed to resist penetration by cannon fire or similar APC mounted weapons. Finally, heavy protection, requiring the maximum protection that can be provided within the constraints of weight and other limitations over as wide an arc as possible.

There are four basic principles to ensure vehicle survivability on the battlefield:

DO NOT BE DETECTED. The tank must reduce all characteristic signatures.

The most important are thermal, magnetic, radar, seismic, acoustic and, of course, visual. Much can be learned from the air and sea systems experience, especially in the design stage, by careful attention to detail. For example, avoiding the use of right angles will reduce the radar reflectivity. The work carried out to diffuse the jet efflux of helicopter engines and thus reduce the thermal signature has direct application to tank engine exhaust design.

IF DETECTED, DO NOT BE HIT. The second principle requires the tank designer to consider every possible way to make the tank difficult to hit. This will include making it as small a target a possible, perhaps reducing the number of the crew from four to three or less. The tank must limit its exposure time to the minimum when moving from one fire position to another. A high power-to-weight ratio will be required to provide good acceleration and maximum agility. A good suspension system will be able to translate the high power-to-weight ratio into high cross country speed while maintaining a stable gun platform.

IF HIT, DO NOT BE PENETRATED. The third principle requires the tank designer to consider every possible method, both active and passive, to protect the tank from being penetrated when hit. The first priority is to prevent penetration of the crew compartment.

IF PENETRATED, SURVIVE. Finally, every advantage must be taken of modern developments to minimise the behind-armour effects. This will include anti-spall liners to reduce the effect of the HEAT jet and protected charge magazines to reduce the chance of hot fragments igniting the propellant charges. If the propellant itself is stored in the turret bustle, as in M1A1 and Leopard 2, blow-off panels to vent the gas to atmosphere will reduce the chance of an ammunition explosion. Halon fire suppression systems are used in some tanks but it should be noted that all propellants contain oxygen as part of their chemical composition. Halon, an inert gas, suppresses a fire by excluding oxygen and will work successfully against fuel fires in the engine compartment and will counter any secondary fires in the crew compartment; but it will not have any effect against propellant fires. Finally, consideration should be given to providing tank crewmen with some form of flak jacket and fire-proof overalls to reduce the chance of injury from flame, spall and armour fragments.

Early Developments

Early tanks had an equal level of protection all round the vehicle. This was necessary and sensible as they were subject to attack by a variety of weapons from all angles. At that time the attack was non-specialised because no weapons had been developed specifically to attack armoured vehicles. As weapons developed, so did the materials to resist attack but it quickly became apparent that the sheer weight of the armour would make it impossible to provide all-round protection at the higher levels. Common sense dictated that the majority of the attacks would be directed towards the front of the vehicle, normally facing the enemy, so the preponderance of armour tended to be distributed over the frontal arc.

Whittaker's Directional Probability Variation (DPV)

The first serious attempt to analyse the probability of attack from any given direction was undertaken by Lieutenant-Colonel Whittaker in 1943. He examined the theoretical attack by anti-tank guns against a single advancing tank and his report gave rise to Whittaker's Directional Probability Variation (DPV). The theoretical findings were confirmed by data obtained in the Second World War and the DPV generally still holds good, although modern analytical methods are more complex and precise.

Figure 5.1 is a diagrammatic representation of Whittaker's DPV in which it can be seen that 33% of all attacks lie within the frontal 800 mil (45 degree) arc and 45% of all attacks will be within the 1,066 mil (60 degree) arc. The chance of attack decreases significantly outside this arc. Thus provision of a similar level of all-round protection would incur a significant weight penalty. The diagram shows Whittaker's DPV and an elliptical DPV derived from it. The latter is more regular in shape and so is amenable to more detailed mathematical analysis. British tanks have followed the policy of providing protection against the major anti-tank weapon threat over the frontal 1,066 mil arc but with certain qualifications. It is accepted that the turret does not conform to the same DPV as, although the hull may normally be pointed in the direction of the threat, the turret may spend a significant amount of time traversed to one side engaging flanking targets. The other implication to be derived from the DPV is that it is better to reduce the limits of the frontal arc providing maximum protection rather than reduce the level of protection overall.

The Effect of Modern Weapons on the Directional Probability Variation

The threat to the tank on the modern battlefield is now omni-directional, notably from top attack with the next generation of 'smart' munitions using infra-red, millimetric or other forms of guidance (Figure 5.2). While still having the preponderance of armoured protection over the frontal arc, the designer must now take into account dive and top attack weapons and bomblets and expand the DPV upwards, more into the shape of a hemisphere to take into account the three dimensional aspect of the threat. A diagram of a possible refinement of the original directional probability variation to include the three separate protection requirements, kinetic energy, anti-tank guided weapons and top attack is shown in Figure 5.3. In the past, the top of the tank has been required to give protection only against artillery shell splinters, usually 155 mm, exploding at about 10 metres distance. In general terms this has required about 18 mm of Rolled Homogeneous Armour (RHA) to give adequate protection. This is no longer sufficient and modern turret top armour must be able to achieve about 250–300 mm RHA equivalent protection. Clearly armour plate thickness alone will not be able to provide this without an unacceptable weight penalty and some other form of light-weight protection such as Explosive Reactive Armour (ERA) described below will be required. The turret shown in Figure 5.3 has had the sides raked by 265 mil (15 degrees) as an aid to providing increased flank protection. The effect of raking

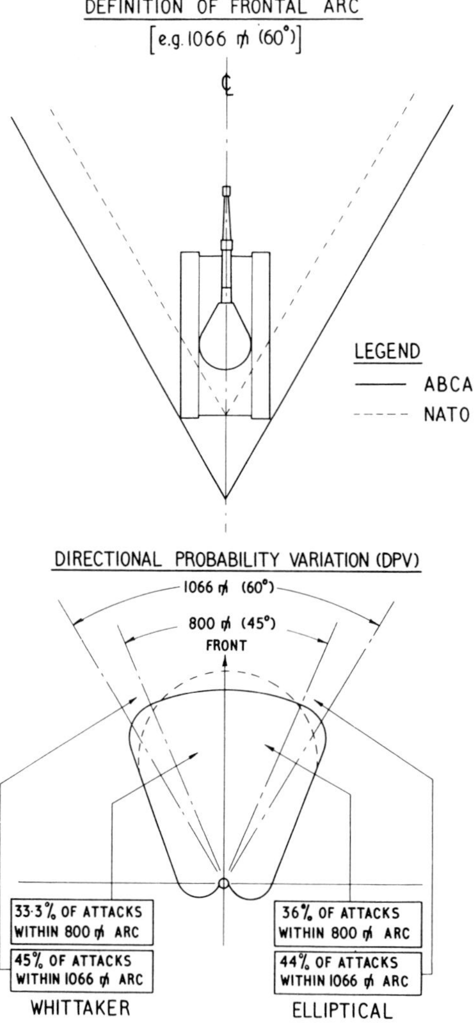

FIG. 5.1 Whittaker's Directional Probability Variation (DPV).

back and sides in this fashion is to add to 18 mil (10 degrees) to the effective frontal arc i.e., to increase it from 1,066 mil to 1,243 mil (60 to 70 degrees) with minimal effect on internal turret volume.

Structural Requirements

Any fighting vehicle must be inherently strong to carry its payload (crew and fighting equipment) as the ground conditions, particularly cross country, impose considerable strains on the structure. The stress placed on the hull when a 50 tonne tank hits a bump at 50 kph is very considerable so there is a requirement for a strong basic structure or 'chassis' quite apart from the strength needed for armoured protection. The stresses imposed by firing the main armament are also

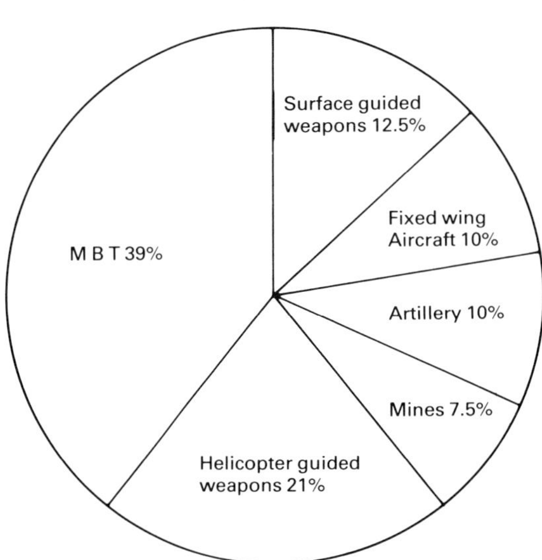

FIG. 5.2 The future threat spectrum.

very large and these have to be absorbed initially by the recoil mechanism, transmitted through the turret ring, the hull, suspension and ultimately to the ground.

Conventional steel armour normally provides sufficient inherent structural strength but even if an effective unconventional and extremely lightweight armour could be produced there would be a limit to the amount of weight that could be saved because of the need for reinforcing or structural support.

Armour Materials

Rolled Homogeneous Steel

The classic material for vehicle armour is a range of special nickel/chrome alloy steels. Steel is a very versatile material and can be produced in a variety of forms but more recent practice favours the use of homogeneous plate which has the same hardness and structure throughout. The production of plate involves a rolling process to bring it to the correct thickness and to induce some desirable metallurgical properties. The armour produced by this method is known as Rolled Homogeneous Armour (RHA) and is used as the current standard of comparison for protection levels offered by other materials. However, different nations have different ways of calculating depth of RHA penetration and care must be taken to compare like with like.

Thin Plates

For thin plates, up to approximately 25 mm, a fairly hard steel of approximately 350–400 Brinell is used. As this is not intended to provide protection against the larger anti-tank weapons, there is some advantage in providing a face-hardened

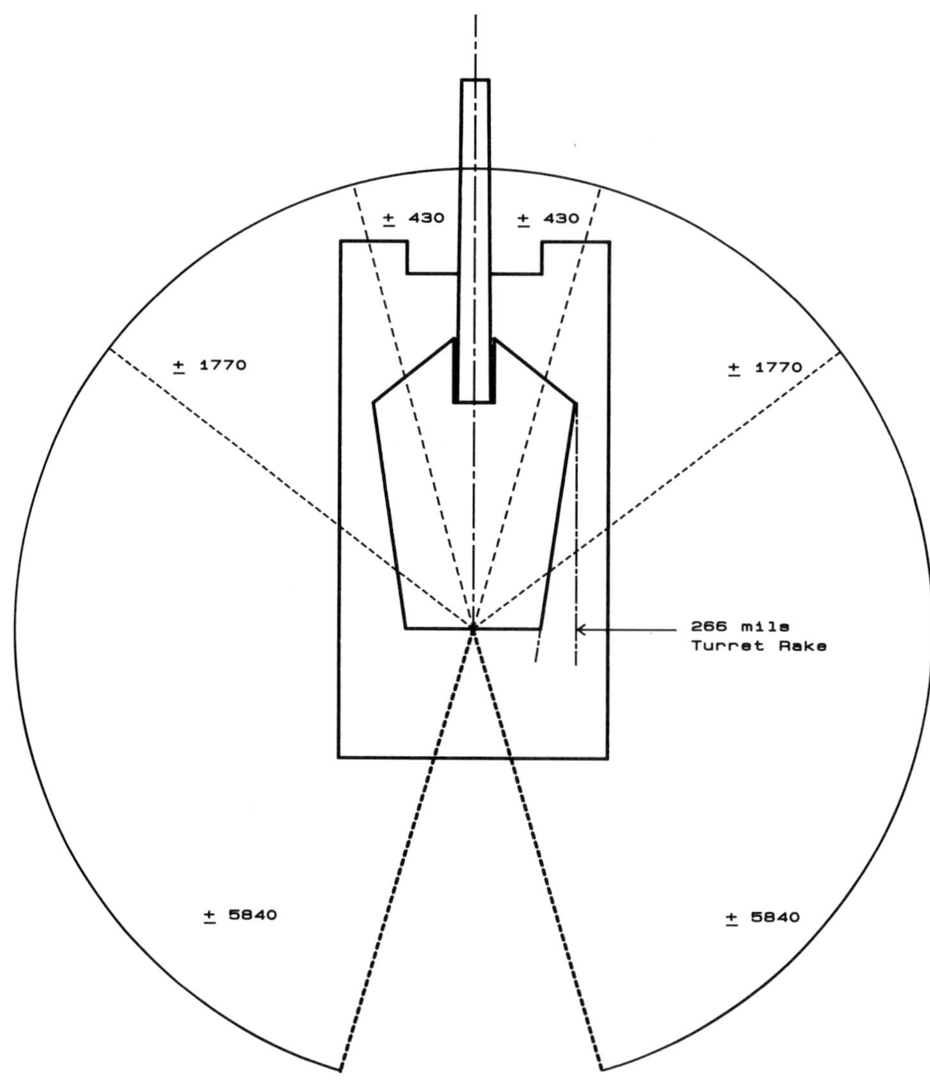

FIG. 5.3 A modern interpretation of the directional probability variation to take into account top and dive attack weapon characteristics.

outer surface. This tends to shatter small projectiles and can provide added protection without an increase in weight. However, this material is notoriously difficult to fabricate and weld; consequently it can only be used in the simplest of structures. Another grave disadvantage is that if face-hardened plate is overmatched it tends to fail catastrophically. If RHA plate is defeated by KE attack the projectile will penetrate, bringing debris with it. The resultant damage will depend largely upon the energy remaining after penetration but is normally sufficient to put the vehicle out of action, particularly if larger calibres are used.

Thick Plates

For rolled thick plates, usually defined as plates over 25 mm thick, the steel is normally in the 275–325 Brinell hardness range. Because of the nature of alloy steel, special welding techniques have to be employed and electric arc welding is mandatory. A major problem is the distortion that occurs when large amounts of heat are put into the parent plate by the welding process. A very carefully controlled welding operation is essential during manufacture and every weld sequence must be identified and agreed beforehand; welders must be trained in new techniques and must be tested periodically during the manufacturing process; those that fail must be retrained and tested again. All this is a complex, time-consuming and hence expensive business. The importance of the weld in retaining the ballistic integrity of the structure when under attack is paramount and it is therefore essential that the welds between the major armour plate of the vehicle are fabricated in as near ideal conditions as possible and are replicated for every vehicle in the production run. Modern tank factories employ plasma arc cutting equipment with the armour plate submerged under water to eliminate plate distortion in the area of the cut. Roll-over jigs are required to ensure that all welds are 'down hand' (metal flow is with, and not against, gravity) and modern automatic welding machines ensure that the long, multiple weld runs in the hull side and belly plates are laid evenly and with minimum heat transfer.

Cast Armour

If a complex shape is required which cannot easily be fabricated from RHA, then cast armour must be used. Until recently, cast armour was almost universally used in the construction of turrets, especially the nose piece. Although complex shapes can be cast with a wide variety of thicknesses and curvature it is more difficult to control exact thickness and some degree of over-provision must be made to ensure that no casting is ever below the minimum thickness in any area. For a given level of protection, castings need to be about 5% thicker than RHA plate as the compostition of the metal, by the nature of the casting process, is less dense.

Aluminium Alloy Armours

Aluminium is now well established as an armour material, particularly for the range of lighter armoured vehicle used for reconnaissance and the various types of infantry combat vehicles. Although work on aluminium armour started in the early 1940s, it was not until a need for airportable vehicles was established in the 1950s that this work was pushed to a successful conclusion.

Aluminium in its pure state offers very few advantages and it needs to be alloyed with other metals to give it the necessary properties desirable in an armour material. It was found that by adding a certain quantity of magnesium in work-hardened plate, the ballistic protection offered by plates of comparable areal density (weight per unit area) to steel plate was at least as good as that for steel against low-level KE attack but considerably better than steel against HE fragments. However, during the manufacture of the ubiquitous American M113 armoured personnel carrier, the other advantages that this material had to offer were confirmed. Because of its lower density, the aluminium alloy plates are thicker and give the vehicle inherent stiffness which reduces the number of internal bracing members needed. The alloy is also much easier to machine but requires special welding procedures and a high standard of skill if the ballistic integrity is to be maintained. Lighter components make fabrication easier and all these factors combine to make production simpler and help keep costs down.

In the mid-1960s, the United Kingdom introduced a range of tracked, light reconnaissance vehicles suitable for deployment by air. A new aluminium/zinc/magnesium alloy which combined good welding properties, good ballistic protection and showed weight saving advantages of between 6–20% when compared to steel was used.

In the last few years, some other less desirable aspects of aluminium have come to light. The alloy is used extensively in the construction of the superstructure of most modern ships in order to keep the overall weight down and the centre of gravity as low as possible. Uninformed press reports during the Falklands War stated that the alloy superstructure of Royal Navy ships had ‘burned’ when hit. The metal alloy itself does not burn but the intense heat generated by the other combustible material caused the alloy to melt and, to the uninformed, gave the appearance of having burnt away when the wreckage was examined.

Other Armour Materials

Titanium

At one time it was thought that titanium alloys would be increasingly used to provide armoured protection as the ballistic protection provided by this material against small calibre attack showed approximately a 30% saving in weight compared to steel. However, titanium is still a relatively rare metal; it is difficult to weld and fabricate and is about ten times the cost of steel. It does not show sufficient improvement in protection to justify its greatly increased cost.

Ceramics

Ceramics are another group of materials that have been used extensively for body armour and are particularly interesting for the vehicle designer as they show most promise for the protection for light vehicles. They had been used extensively in the space programme where their light weight, high strength and resistance to extremely high temperature make them ideal to protect space craft during re-entry.

To date all ceramic armours, of which the most common are boron carbide, silicon carbide and alumina, are extremely hard but are also brittle. However, recent developments in Japan and elsewhere have shown that it is possible to make a ‘flexible’ ceramic—that is, to eliminate much of its brittleness. The process to increase the flexibility is still subject to certain commercial security restrictions. It is too early to say whether this new ‘flexible’ ceramic will provide any more protection for armoured vehicles then its more brittle counterpart.

Ceramics provide protection against KE attack because their extreme hardness causes the projectile to shatter as the ceramic tile itself shatters. Because of their ability to withstand very high temperatures, they can also be used to protect against HEAT. Inevitably, ceramic armours offer one-shot protection. If continuous protection is required, then the tiles must be capable of being easily replaced. This in itself is a drawback to their use in most armoured vehicle applications. The size of the tile is critical. If the tile is made too large, then when it shatters it will leave a large area unprotected. If the tile is made small, then although the area affected by each shot is reduced, the total area of the joins between each tile is increased, reducing the degree of protection offered. Larger individual tiles reduce the problem of securing them in place but smaller tiles increase the chance of being able to cover the more complex, contoured armour shapes such as the front of the turret.

In sum, although ceramic armours offer good levels of protection for very low areal densities, at present they are expensive to manufacture and are currently ineffective against large calibre KE attack. Ceramics are therefore ideal for protection of specific areas in aircraft and helicopters where the need to save weight it paramount. Their use in future as one element in a composite armour matrix on tanks cannot be discounted and they could readily be adapted for use as appliqué kits for the protection of unarmoured light vehicles.

Composite Armour

If the form and type of attack is known, then it is possible to optimise tank armoured protection to give the highest protection levels against the specific attack. If, as is more usual, the tank has to protect itself against several varieties of attack then the choice of a suitable armour becomes a more difficult problem. If each separate threat were to be given the highest protection levels in the design without regard to other design factors, then the combination would undoubtedly give the best all-round performance but the penalty would be an excessively bulky and heavy armour leading to an impractical vehicle design.

Recent advances in material technology and a better understanding of their capabilities against both kinetic and chemical energy attack has led to the development of spaced armours. Details of the design and construction of 'Chobham' armour are still highly classified but published information indicates that this type of spaced armour offers greatly enhanced protection against a wide spectrum of the threat including kinetic energy fin stabilised long rod penetrators. The announcement by the United States that their M1A1 tanks in West Germany would be fitted with depleted uranium armour plates from 1989 onwards gave some indication of the type of materials that can be used to achieve the best possible protection within the limits of size and weight.

Inevitably, there is a penalty to pay. The manufacturing process for modern spaced armour is more complex and has to be carried out under secure conditions so that details of its composition and construction are known only to a few men in the factory who actually assemble the armour itself. Also, because it is not homogeneous the armour is bulky and therefore its characteristics must be considered as part of the original vehicle design.

Explosive Reactive Armour

Perhaps the single most important aspect of Explosive Reactive Armour (ERA) is that it can be used to enhance the protection of existing vehicles though it is likely to be more effective if its characteristics are taken into account at the vehicle design stage. ERA armour consists of a series of individual panels as shown in Figure 5.4 bolted onto the sloping surfaces of the tank hull and turret. Each

FIG. 5.4 Photograph of the separate panels that comprise explosive reactive armour.

panel is made up of a layer of explosive material sandwiched between two metal plates. These panels, which are attached at an oblique angle to the vulnerable areas of a tank's superstructure will on attack from a shaped charge warheard, explode, dispersing the HEAT plasma jet generated on impact (see Figure 5.5). A number of countries market ERA armour under various proprietary names. Claims for their effectiveness vary but a useful rule of thumb is that they can provide protection equivalent to ten times the weight of homogeneous rolled steel armour and that penetration of the charge jet can be reduced by more than 75%. Though designed primarily to protect against chemical energy warheads they provide some small additional protection against kinetic energy attack.

ERA can be easily and quickly applied to a wide range of vehicles. Even though each panel has only a 'one-shot' capability, their modular design and light weight enable them to be exchanged in the field. A simple fixing system also enables ERA to be retro-fitted to existing vehicles, giving an extremely cost-effective improvement in armoured protection. The need for high standards of safety has been taken

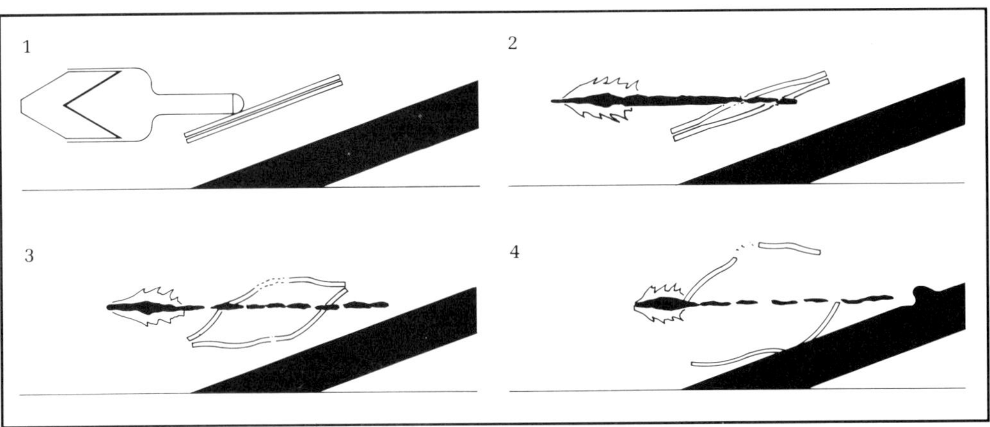

FIG. 5.5 Schematic diagram of the principle of operation of explosive reactive armour.

FIG. 5.6 Soldiers fitting ERA packs to a tank turret in the field.

into account in the design of the explosive material used between the plates. ERA represents a major departure for many armies in that explosive will be carried on the external surfaces of a tank and there are may be environmental objections in some countries to mounting ERA on tanks in peace. Special insensitive explosive has been developed to ensure that the panels can be handled, cut, drilled and welded without risk and that small arms fire and rough usage will not detonate them. When attacked by a hollow charge warhead the panels are so designed that there is no risk of sympathetic detonation of the other panels in close proximity.

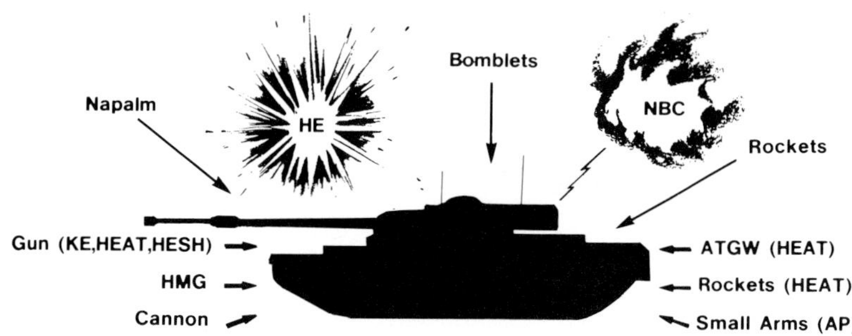

FIG. 5.7 The threat to the tank.

The Sloping of Armour Plate

If the aim of the designer is to produce a vehicle which encloses the largest interior volume for the least weight, this could be linked directly to the surface area of the vehicle. Theoretically a sphere offers the largest interior volume for the smallest exterior surface area. Although this is impractical for a vehicle, it is easy to see why a hemi-spherical turret is so attractive.

In Figure 5.8, the armour facing the most likely direction of attack is placed vertically so that the projectile would strike it at normal. The thickness it would have to penetrate can be represented by T_N. If the plate is then sloped at an angle β and reduced in thickness so that the horizontal thickness remains the same, then the weight remains the same but the surface area of the plate is greater because 1 is now greater than h.

Equivalent Thickness

The saving in weight does not stem from the simple sloping of the plate but from other consequences that arise. If the plate in Fig. 5.8 represents the plate in front of the driver's compartment, the sloping armour saves weight because there is a reduction in top and side armour. To give a measure of comparison, the thickness of armour is normally expressed as EQUIVALENT THICKNESS which is the path length a projectile would have to travel to penetrate if it struck the target horizontally and at 0 mil azimuth angle of attack. Referring to Fig. 5.8, the actual thickness of the armour material can be established by the formulae:

$$T_\beta = T_N \cos \beta$$

As cos 60 degrees of 0.5, it is easy to realise that armour plate sloped at 60 degrees (1,062 mil) has an equivalent thickness of twice its actual thickness.

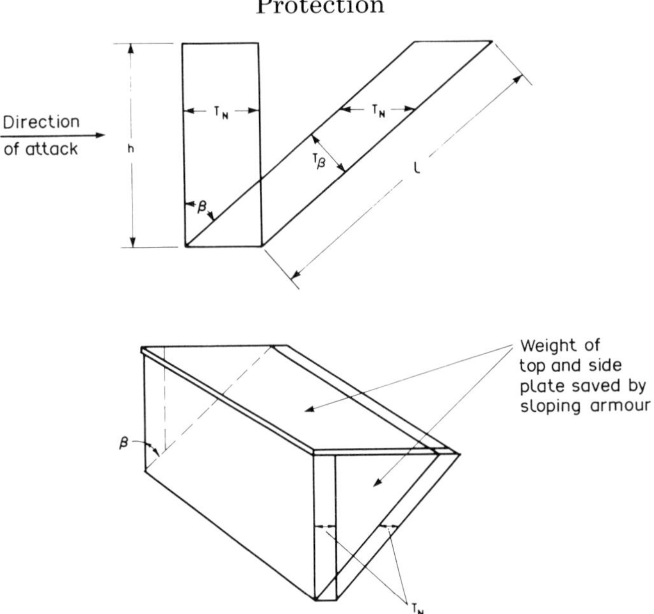

FIG. 5.8 Equivalent thickness.

Effect of Vehicle Attitude

It is extremely unlikely that a projectile will hit a target exactly head on, and although KE shot may be regarded for all intents and purposes to be travelling horizontally, it is quite likely that the target will be inclined at an angle at the moment of impact. Therefore the angle of attack will be a compound angle of the actual slope of armour relative to the vertical at the moment of strike.

If the armour is sloped at an angle β from the vertical and the projectile strikes at an azimuth angle α, then the compound angle can be found from the expression:

$$\cos C = \cos \alpha \quad \cos \beta$$

Differing National Notations

It should be noted that the angle of slope is the angle from the vertical because armour was originally placed at the vertical. It is important to establish the basis for measuring the slope as some nations measure it as the inclination from the horizontal. This can be misleading for the cosine law for equivalent thickness cannot be applied directly and another formula must be found to equate measurements made under one set of conditions to another.

Additional Effects of Sloping

Some of the weight savings achieved by sloping the armour have already been mentioned but there are other equally important effects. The mechanism whereby a solid KE projectile, be it APDS or a long rod penetrator, defeats sloped armour is a very complex matter but in neither case is the path taken by the projectile a

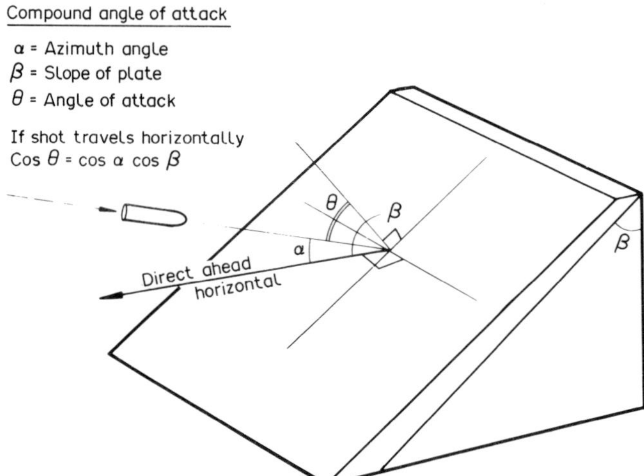

FIG. 5.9 Compound angles of attack.

continuation of its original line of flight and the path length is discernibly longer. Thus, the projectile is forced to give up more energy to the armour material than would be the case if it continued in a straight line. The protection offered by sloped plate is always slightly greater than that calculated by the cosine law.

More importantly, once armour is sloped in excess of 1,062 mil (60 degrees) there is a good chance of inducing a ricochet. The exact angle at which ricochet occurs depends on a wide variety of factors but the design and nature of the projectile is the most important.

The Ideal Material

Requirements

There are several factors to be considered in the search for an ideal armour; but the major consideration is that the armour should be effective. It must do the job it is designed to do and it should be light but, above all, the armour must be cost effective. There is little advantage in developing some exotic material which is so expensive that it would make the vehicle prohibitively costly. Other considerations are that the armour should be amenable to modern construction techniques, easily weldable and capable of being cast into a variety of shapes if required.

The Steel Solution

For many years various alloy steels have measured up to this requirement very well. It is a tough material, the technology of dealing with it is well understood and it can be made with various properties by changing the proportion and type of the alloying elements. It is readily available and inexpensive and the technique of fabrication is well understood. Although it is a heavy material with a high areal density and offers high levels of protection against kinetic energy weapons, its performance against chemical energy weapons, as an homogeneous structure, is limited.

Most alloy steels contain some or all of the elements of manganese, nickel, chrome, molybdenum and vanadium to give the correct blend of high strength and resistance to fracture or rough treatment.

The specific composition of the steel and the heat treatment afforded to it will depend whether it is to be rolled or cast. Most armour steels are manufactured to specifications in the IT series. IT 80 is the specification for rolled steel and IT 90 for cast.

The Future

The Need for a Defensive Aids Suite (DAS)

With the exception of explosive reactive armour, the tank's protection is provided entirely by passive systems which rely on various types of steel and composites to defeat a chemical or kinetic energy threat. However, even reactive armour, as its name suggests, reacts to the threat and is not a truly active protection system. If a tank is to survive on a future battlefield, it will have to turn to active systems in order to give it the protection it needs. That is to say, it will be necessary to detect and destroy an incoming missile before it can hit the target vehicle (in the same way that SEAWOLF protects a warship at sea).

It should be borne in mind that any active system will give protection only against HEAT warheads mounted on guided and unguided weapons as it is difficult to postulate a system that can detect, react and deploy an effective kinetic energy counter-measure in view of the very short time of flight. Three basic principles of a three-phase defensive process are:

WARN. A passive system will be required to detect the launch of a missile at ranges up to 4 kms. This warning device will alert the tank commander that a missile is on the way. Flying at 300 m per sec, this will give a minimum of about 12 seconds warning. Of necessity, the warning device must have a wide field of view including at least 80 mil (45 degrees) elevation.

CONFIRM. The confirmatory phase will be required to locate the missile accurately at a minimum distance of 1 km.

REACT. The third and final phase will use active systems, employing any method to destroy the missile.

6

Configurations

Crew Duties

Problems of Defining the Requirement

In the past, many armoured vehicles have failed to live up to expectation because the crews have not been able to operate them to their theoretical maximum efficiency. There are many reasons for this, partly because the study of the man/machine interface was not understood and partly because there was a communication failure between the designer and user. Most countries now operate a sophisticated 'User Statement of the Requirement' system which translates the military requirement into a document which can be understood by the designer. With the best will in the world, matters may still go awry as the tactical picture may have changed since the requirement was originally stated. In this age of expanding technology, as new capabilities arise so quickly, it is often difficult for the soldier to visualise the application of a particular technology to the tactics likely to be used on a future battlefield. In many cases it is not possible to define the way the equipment will be used until hardware is produced and it is put into the hands of the user for testing.

The Command Function

There are several aspects to be considered but the most important is that layout of the vehicle, particularly the fighting compartment, must be governed by its intended tactical role and that the vehicle commander must be able effectively to exercise his command function. This is important for the commander of any fighting vehicle but it becomes a vital factor if a tank commander is also the troop, platoon or squadron commander.

The Scope of Crew Tasks

Additionally, there will be a number of minor tasks which have to be completed to maintain the vehicle at maximum efficiency. These tasks are normally shared amongst the crew and will not significantly diminish in magnitude or number if the crew size is reduced. A reduction in crew numbers will usually mean an increased burden on the remainder, notably in the 24-hour battle.

Apart from the prime task of manoeuvring the vehicle on the battlefield and firing the main armament, the other tasks to be undertaken in action are loading and maintaining the machine guns or other armament, operating the radio sets, cleaning and maintaining vision devices, making running adjustments and servicing ancillary equipment such as the NBC filters.

With the improvement in night viewing devices, the ability of armoured vehicles to fight a 24-hour battle has increased with a consequent increase in crew fatigue. This could mean a reduction in the time available for the crew to undertake the tasks usually performed during a lull in the battle or when the vehicle was withdrawn during the hours of darkness. These tasks include replenishment of ammunition, fuel, food and water; maintenance of the main armament; servicing of the turret and automotive system. Finally, at every halt of more than a few minute's duration, camouflage must be erected and stowed again before the next move.

In addition to these chores, the crew will need to rest and eat. It is normal for vehicle crews to be self-contained for their eating arrangements as it gives greater flexibility but it does impose an extra burden on the crew. As any wife will tell you, the last thing she wants to do at the end of an exhausting day is to cook a meal! A reduction in routine maintenance tasks is therefore a high priority so that the crew themselves will be able to remain more efficient. Consultation between the user and the designer will be required at all stages of development to ensure the correct layout of the equipment and that it is ergonomically designed to be operated correctly and quickly under the stress of battle.

Further guidance on defining the requirement is given in Chapter 12.

Crew Numbers

After the First World War and for a greater part of the Second, it was thought that a five-man crew was essential for the efficient manning of a tank. This allowed for a commander, gunner, radio operator/loader and a driver, with a fifth crew member as a hull gunner/co-driver.

More often than not, the numbers of crewmen needed was dictated by the type of armament carried. The M3AL General Lee tank was an American medium tank under development in 1940 and very soon saw action in North Africa. It had an unusual configuration because the main armament was a 75 mm gun, with very limited traverse, carried in a sponson on the front right hand side. The upper turret, which had all-round traverse, contained a 37 mm gun. This arrangement required a crew of 6 men to man it efficiently.

Most nations at that time favoured a 5 man crew as they believed that the extra member was essential as a co-driver. The tanks of those days were not simple vehicles to drive. There were no power-assisted controls and steering tillers and the manual gearbox required great physical effort. If a long approach march had to be undertaken or if the driver had been in the seat for a long period, a relief driver was essential. In addition to his stand-by duties, the co-driver was expected to double up in most of the other crew positions. He was also invaluable in maintaining morale by providing quick snacks or a cup of tea as the diaries of tank crewmen written at the time will testify. Usually he was located alongside the driver and was given a machine gun to fire, with questionable effectiveness, through a rudimentary vision block. The Soviet Union quickly gave up the fifth man, the KW 85 being their last five-man tank. In this respect they have led the world. They were the first to reduce to a four-man crew and they have also been the first to reduce to a three-man crew in all their tanks since T64.

The Germans remained committed to a five-man crew throughout the Second World War and it was not until the introduction of Leopard 1 in 1965 that the crew size was reduced to four. Similarly the Americans, with some exceptions, persevered with the five-man crew right through until the M48 entered service in 1952.

The British were also firmly wedded to a five-man complement although in some tanks that had been upgunned, such as Crusader 3, fitted with a 57 mm gun, they had been forced to accept a three-man crew because the available space under armour had become limited. Even Comet, introduced in 1945 as a successor to the Cromwell, still retained a five-man crew. When it was decided to abandon the Cromwell-Comet line and develop an entirely new concept, based on the lessons learned during the Second World War, it was apparent that if the tank was to have a sloped glacis plate and be able to accommodate all the new equipment, there would be no room for the fifth crewman. By then the need for the fifth man was being questioned and the elimination of this crew position eased the designer's problems.

A tank should be capable of being operated in an emergency by one man less than the number for which it was designed. For example, a four man tank should be capable of being operated by three, and a three man tank by two. But there are very few tank commanders who will deny that an extra man in war is of great benefit especially as the 24 hour battle is now very much a reality.

Battle Tanks

A conventional four-man crew consists of commander, gunner loader/radio operator and driver. Most modern main battle tanks still have a crew of four although Russian tanks, the T64, T72 and T80, as explained, all utilise an autoloader to replace the loader, as does the Swedish S tank and the new French tank, the Leclerc. Some variations on the four-man, conventional crew layout are shown in Figure 6.1. Before considering various possible combinations of tasks, it is important to examine the role of the most important crew member, the tank commander. In peacetime it is often felt that he is not used to his full capability as realistic fire and movement exercises have to be limited in scope for environmental and safety reasons. This has lead to the loading of more and more tasks onto the tank commander in the mistaken belief that he is the only crew member capable of taking them on. Under battle conditions, however, a very different picture emerges.

In battle the commander must be able to continuously monitor the tactical picture whether the tank is in contact with the enemy or not. Total awareness of the immediate tactical picture is paramount if he is to react to orders correctly and swiftly and if he is to interpret events and pass back accurate information to his superior. His ability to do this relates directly to the tank's chance of survival. Once the tank is in contact with the enemy, he must use all the skill and knowledge gained in training, assisted by the equipment in the tank, to acquire a target,

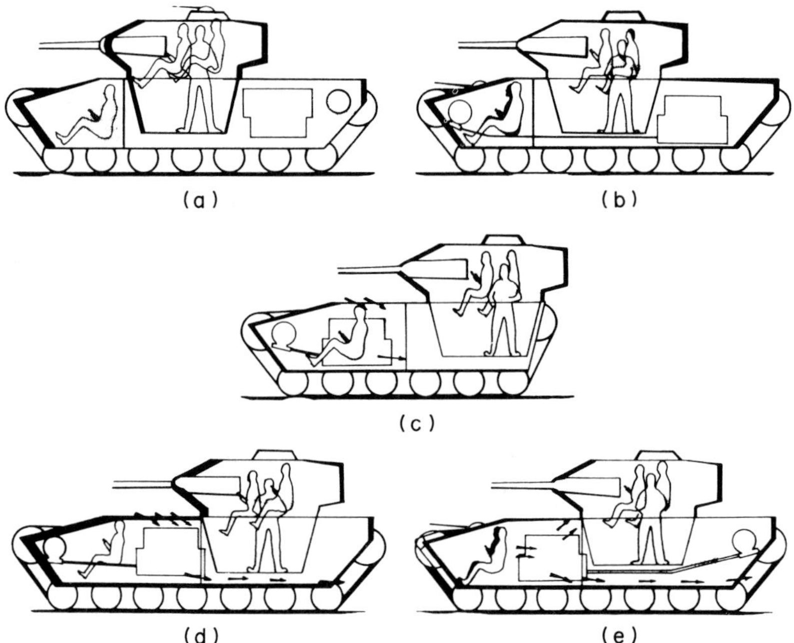

FIG. 6.1 Some typical four-man tank crew layouts.

initiate a fire order and destroy it as quickly as possible. While all this is going on, he must ensure that he is aware of the changing tactical situation around him (other tanks, dismounted infantry, supporting arms etc.); he must consider what his next move or moves should be, what the enemy is likely to do and whether he should modify his plans accordingly, what his current ammunition state is and so on. All this must be done while dealing with the normal two-way passage of information and directing the driver to a new fire position.

Possible Crew Combinations

Commander and Gunner

As shown in Chapter 6, it is important to keep the volume under armour as low as possible in order to reduce the size of the vehicle and so make detection on the battlefield more difficult. The simplest way to do this is to eliminate one crew member and either re-allocate his duties to the others or find mechanical, electronic or other means of carrying them out. There are six possible combinations for a three-man crew although some of them are not practical possibilities:

Commander, gunner and driver (with autoloader)
Commander, loader and gunner/driver
Commander/driver, gunner and loader
Commander/gunner, loader and driver
Commander/loader, gunner and driver
Commander, gunner and driver/loader

The most practical combination is the commander/gunner concept. In many modern tanks most of the gunner's controls are duplicated at the commander's station, giving him the same ability to fire the main armament. When there is a gunner, the commander acquires the target and then there is a small but finite time lapse as he hands it over to the gunner to finish the engagement. Time can be saved if the commander himself fires the main armament. However, if this combination is adopted, it means that the commander cannot acquire other targets while the gunner is engaging the first. Furthermore, many of the commander's tasks cannot be undertaken simultaneously with his responsibilities as a gunner, so the overall result is a net loss in efficiency and hence a probable reduction in overall survivability.

Commander and Loader

The commander/loader combination is perfectly acceptable for vehicles where the weight of the main armament ammunition is such that the commander can load it easily, preferably with one hand. It is immediately apparent that this is out of the question for 105 mm and 120 mm main battle tank ammunition and although just possible to do so for calibres up to 90 mm, it is still likely to increase engagement times and reduce the rate of fire. It is a solution most often found in light vehicles, like the UK's CVR(T) 76 mm Scorpion reconnaissance vehicle, where firepower does not have the overriding priority it has in the main battle tank.

Commander and Driver

The commander/driver option in a conventional turreted tank is not a combination that needs to be examined in any detail as the commander would be unable to fulfil any of his functions from the driver's station in the hull. If the driver's station is moved to the turret, the combination is worth consideration but the argument that the commander cannot command while he is driving is still valid. It would be extremely difficult to fire the gun while the vehicle was on the move, particularly if the target required that the gun and turret be traversed away from the general direction in which the vehicle was travelling. If, however, the gun is not free to traverse in relation to the hull, as in the Swedish 'S' tank, some of the objections are overcome. Indeed, within the tactical limitations imposed by a fixed gun configuration, the 'S' tank solution whereby the commander and gunner have identical driving controls seem to be acceptable.

The conventional Turreted Tank

Since the Second World War, it has been generally accepted that a central turret position was best suited for a main battle tank design but within this constraint there are several possibilities. The most common arrangement is for the driver to be seated in the front, as shown in Figure 6.1(a)); behind him is a central fighting compartment with a turret; finally the engine and transmission compartment are to the rear. This presupposes that the tank has rear sprocket drive but in some configurations, notably the American Sherman series, the drive was through a front sprocket necessitating a complex drive shaft from the rear engine compartment under the floor to the front final drives. This particular configuration as shown in Figure 6.1(b) was evolved as a result of the decision to utilise the well-tried and proved Wright Whirlwind, a 9 cylinder 340 hp radial engine, although the diagram shows a conventional engine. As might be expected of an aeroplane engine, it had a high power-to-weight ratio but posed considerable installation problems and produced a tank that was very high, a major disadvantage on the battlefield.

The central turret position gives the best balance of features, allowing the driver a good view, 6400 mil traverse and the possibility of giving the gun a full 180 mil (10 degrees) depression without unduly raising the height of the turret roof. Its major drawback is that with the modern requirement for high energy tank guns and the consequent large size of the ammunition, the volume needed under armour in the fighting compartment is increasing. This not only increases the overall size and weight of the tank but also increases the target area. Most designs have been directed towards reducing the target size while still retaining the power and efficiency of a conventional tank design.

The Cleft Turret

The true cleft turret should not be confused with the narrow, high turret of the M60 A1E2, a tank using the 152 mm gun from the unsuccessful Sheridan reconnaissance vehicle programme. The true cleft turret has a shape rather as if one had taken half an orange, placed it on a flat plate and then pressed a pencil down into it so that the upper part of the pencil was level with the orange. The diagram in Figure 6.2 give some idea of how this looks.

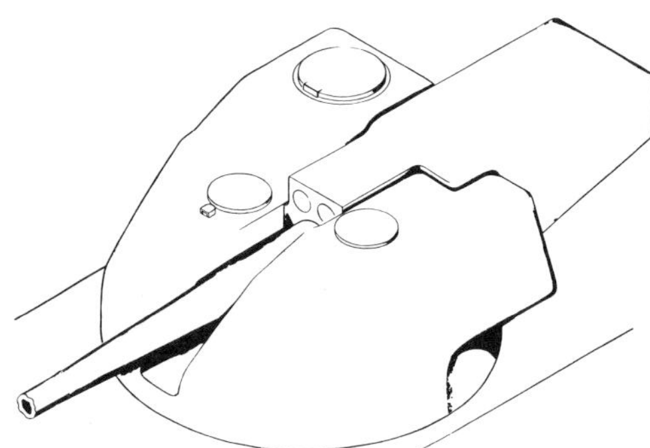

FIG. 6.2 The cleft turret.

Advantages

The particular advantage that this system bestows is that the gun can depress fully without the constraint of the turret roof. If the height of the turret roof, or strictly speaking the height of the turret either side of the cleft can be reduced then the weight of armour required to provide the desired level of protection can also be reduced. As the breech of the gun is lying in the valley between the two sides of the turret it is afforded a measure of protection.

Disadvantages

Despite the fact that the cleft affords some protection, it also causes some design problems. Elevation, and not depression, of the gun now becomes a major limiting factor, the turret ring below the turret (engine decks) being the limiting factor. As the gun is now disassociated from the crew, loading and servicing is difficult. Also, trials have proved that the isolation of the turret crewmen on their separate sides of the turret creates psychological problems which have to be taken into account, especially when operating the tank for long periods closed down. An external autoloader becomes essential and care must be taken to ensure that the elevation of the gun is not obstructed by spent cases and debris. Because servicing the gun is virtually impossible without getting out of the turret, reliability is of paramount importance.

As the gun is lying in the cleft of the turret and gun recoil is not constrained by turret ring diameter, it may be possible to reduce the size of the tank, as shown in Chapter 3. However, by its very nature, the gun divides the turret in two halves which can lead to crew control problems. However, as two identical crew stations are required, crew duties, particularly for surveillance, can be relatively easily exchanged.

In the larger calibres, the weight savings are negligible and the 16-tonne American T92 was one of the few tanks to get beyond the drawing board and into the prototype stage. In the end, the need for an airborne tank, mounting only a relatively small calibre gun, disappeared with the increased reliability of anti-tank guided weapons and the vehicle never went into production. It is not impossible to imagine a cleft turret AFV in the future, but the disadvantages are formidable.

Oscillating Turret

The Germans are credited with being the first nation to produce a tank with an oscillating turret. This design was chosen for their 30 mm twin gun anti-tank aircraft 'Kugelblitz' tank but it was not followed by any other designers until it appeared in the French AMX 30 tank and the Panhard armoured car. In essence, the oscillating turret is a two-piece turret where the bottom half allows a 6400 mil rotation on a conventional turret ring but the upper part is mounted on trunnions at either side of the turret. The gun is fixed within the upper part of the turret and gun elevation or depression is obtained by tilting the whole of the upper part of the turret. A diagram of the general arrangements is shown at Figure 6.4. After the Second World War, when the French still had considerable overseas interests, they decided to develop an air transportable light tank. At that time there were no suitable air freighters in service but some were projected that would be capable of lifting aproxiately 15 tonnes. In the event the AMX 13 was never used as an airportable tank but its 75 mm high velocity gun made it a very effective tank

FIG. 6.3 The American T92 tank with a two-man cleft turret.

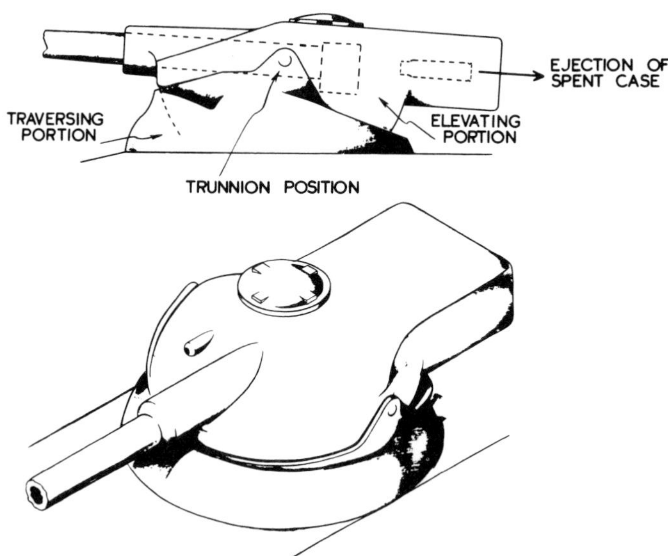

FIG. 6.4 Oscillating turret.

destroyer. Although the protection offered would not be acceptable by modern standards, in 1949, when the first prototype appeared, the level of protection was comparable with some of the main battle tanks then in service. As a light and highly mobile vehicle, it offered a relatively inexpensive but effective solution that found favour in some nineteen countries. Later variants for the French Army mounted a 90 mm gun and a 105 mm gun was made available for export.

Advantages

The main advantage from this system accrues from the gun being fixed in relation to the upper turret. The sighting and fire control system are greatly simplified as there was no need for complex mechanical linkage between gun and sight (in a modern application the linkage would be electronic) since both are mounted in the upper part of the turret and move together. As the gun is fixed to the upper turret the swept volume requirement inside the turret due to the elevation and depression is also greatly reduced.

The gun can be mounted close to the turret roof and so reduces the frontal area presented to the enemy when engaging a target with the main armament. Because the gun is fixed in relation to the upper turret, a human loader would have a very difficult task and therefore an autoloader is essential. The loader can be eliminated, reducing the silhouette of the tank and enhancing protection.

The attraction of a simple autoloader is lost if the magazine is positioned anywhere except in the bustle, where the ammunition maintains a constant position relative to the gun and breech. Problems then arise in light tanks where there is a limit to the number of ready rounds of ammunition available. Ammunition magazines mounted on oscillating turrets usually have to be replenished from the outside and if the magazine has a small capacity the need to expose the crew to reload could be a serious operational disadvantage for a tank in battle though it would not be of such critical importance for a tank destroyer.

Disadvantages

Apart from the limitations on the quantity of ready rounds that can be stowed in the turret bustle, the weight problems are multipled very considerably when the vehicle is scaled up to MBT levels. The sheer weight of the upper turret, which includes armour, gun, ammunition and autoloader, necessitates very considerable gun trunnions and large amounts of hydraulic or electrical power for stabilisation. These trunnions have, in turn, to be supported by a substantial thickness of metal in an area where the protection levels (the sides) would not necessarily require such thickness.

NBC protection is particularly difficult to provide in an oscillating turret. Practically all AFVs rely on crew compartment over-pressure as a means of countering the inevitable leakage mainly from the hull/turret interface. However, the gross leakage caused by the inability to seal effectively the upper and lower halves of the turret and the turret ring itself renders it impossible to utilise a collective NBC protection system.

To provide the protection at maximum elevation, the curved skirt must necessarily have a large swept volume making it difficult to make full use of the fighting compartment. A minor complication is the transfer of the various services from the hull to the upper turret and vice versa. There is a need for the rotary base junction beween lower turret and hull but there is also a need for a second set of slip rings between upper and lower turret.

The apparent advantages of low tactical height and simplified sighting systems are soon outweighed by the increasing weight penalties if MBT protection levels are imposed: the United States T69 experimental medium tank utilising an oscillating turret was abandoned in the late 1950s. It would seem that this concept is only suitable for light vehicles where there is no requirement to have MBT levels of protection.

Driver in the Turret

Advantages

If the driver can be removed from the hull, then certain restrictions no longer apply. The turret can be brought forward as the space the driver previously occupied in the hull and in front of the turret ring is no longer required. If the turret is mounted forward on the hull it becomes much easier to achieve a 180 mil (10 degree) depression without the need for unnecessarily high gun trunnions. This in turn leads to a reduction in hull height (and overall vehicle height) because the driver is no longer the limiting factor on hull height.

Mounted in the turret, the driver has an excellent view whether opened up or closed down. This can be a considerable help to the tank commander as he does not need to give as much guidance to the driver as before, particularly at night or in difficult terrain. If the driver is placed forward in the turret and the commander to the rear in a superior position, all is well if the tank is travelling forward with the gun forward but once the turret traverses to left or right or towards the rear, severe disorientation problems for the driver occur.

Disadvantages

First and foremost, it is obviously necessary to provide a contra-rotating system for the driver so that he is always facing forward in direct line with the hull. All the controls and instruments the driver requires to perform his task relate to operations within the hull compartment and thus signals have to be transferred through the hull/turret interface (the rotary base junction) and a second interface between the turret and the driver's independent contra-rotating console. This inevitably leads to a complex and expensive solution.

As the turret rotates, further problems arise in having to keep the driver facing forward. Unless his position is exactly central, which is not feasible because of the gun, he moves in relation to the hull which makes it very difficult to drive the tank properly. A more serious problem arises over the allocation of the arcs of vision. It is readily apparent that it is not possible to give both the commander and the driver all-round vision and one or the other must accept that his vision will be blocked over certain arcs.

Having all members of the crew in the turret fighting compartment does help with sharing of crew duties and prevents any member of the crew being isolated, as in the cleft turret configuration, but this is small compensation for the extreme complexity of the system. The United States and Germany embarked on a joint venture to produce the MBT 70 tank which had such a configuration; it involved the use of 88 electrical and 11 hydraulic slip rings in the rotary base junction! Such complexity inevitably leads to high cost and coupled with doubts about the main armament, the 152 mm Shillelagh gun/missile system, led to its cancellation as a joint venture. The United States endeavoured to continue the development of this concept with XM 803, but escalating costs and continuing technical problems forced them to abandon the project.

FIG. 6.5 US/FRG MBT 70.

External Gun

Reduction of Silhouette

Of all the unconventional concepts considered so far, the external gun shows the most promise. If the crew can be contained entirely below the turret ring then their chance of survival is greatly enhanced. The gun is mounted on a plinth which is itself mounted on a rotating platform. Thus, the target presented when engaging the enemy is remarkably small. As the gun is entirely supported by the external trunnions, the height of the turret roof does not come into the calculations and the tactical height of the tank can be reduced considerably.

Weight Advantages

A typical tank weight analysis is shown in Figure 6.6 where it can be seen that the total weight of armour represents about 46% and the weight of the turret can be 75% of that figure. Any savings that can be made in this area will have a direct and significant effect on the overall weight of the tank. As a large percentage of the turret weight is due to the need to provide protection for whatever volume is to be enclosed, an external gun mounted on a rotating platform offers considerable savings in the weight normally required for turret crew protection. It is generally accepted that the system would lead to a smaller and lighter vehicle compared with a tank mounting a gun of comparable calibre; this is well illustrated in Figure 6.7.

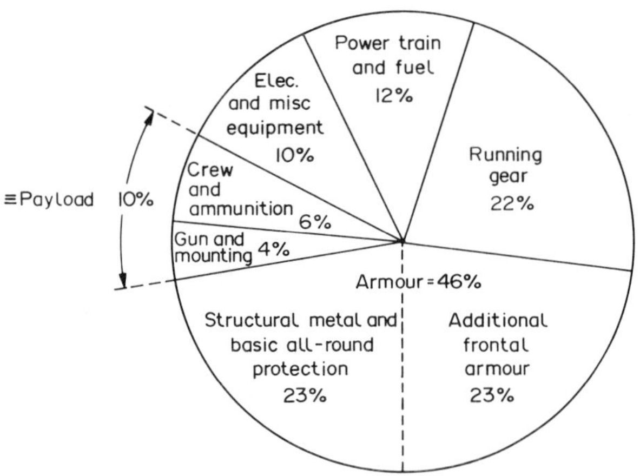

FIG. 6.6 Typical weight analysis main battle tank.

FIG. 6.7 Bofors external gun on a Marder chassis.

Importance of Reliability

The reliability of the system becomes paramount because servicing on the battlefield is impossible except during a lull in fighting. The obvious position of the machine gun is for it to be co-located in a weapon pod alongside the main armament. This raises even greater problems of access as, to date, machine guns are not noted for their reliability.

Sighting and Vision Devices

Perhaps the greatest problem to overcome is the design of suitable sighting and vision systems. With the crew in the hull, below the turret ring, and the gun trunnions a metre above them, the situation is something akin to the position of a submarine commander and his crew. It is difficult but not impossible, to devise a gun-sighting system with a sight head alongside the gun barrel. However, it becomes more difficult to give the commander all-round vision. It is essential that he is provided with a means to view the battlefield not only to acquire targets but also so that he can gather information on what is happening around him and be in a position to make command decisions affecting the deployment of his tank in battle. Implicit in the decision to field an external gun tank is the acceptance that the commander will never be able to view the battlefield directly through his eyes and will always have to be dependent on some form of vision device, be it television, a thermal viewer or a fibre optic. In all the trials done to date, using remote devices to pass information to the commander while denying him direct observation of the battlefield, the consensus view has been that remote vision devices are not sufficient on their own.

Although not so vital for the effectiveness of the tank, but just as important for its survival, is the need for some vision arrangement to assist the driver to reverse. Normally this is achieved by the commander using the panoramic vision device located on the top of the external gun mounting but there is no reason why he cannot be provided with his own separate rearward facing viewing device such as a solid state TV camera.

Forward Engine and Transmission

In the early design of tanks the engine was placed centrally. Consequently the centre of gravity was near the middle of the vehicle. It also allowed easy access for maintenance. As designs progressed, it became advantageous to place the driver in the most forward position and to locate the fighting compartment in the centre. A rear engine normally led to rear sprocket drive but sometimes other factors, such as the power, shape, size and availability of engines. As we have already seen, the Curtiss Wright radial in the Sherman led to a design incorporating a rear engine but forward transmission and front sprocket drive.

Roles for which a Forward Engine is Desirable

If each access is a high priority, such as in an APC, then it becomes essential to mount the engine and transmission in the forward position. In light vehicles, where the power pack is comparatively small, it is relatively easy to locate it forward of the fighting compartment with the driver either alongside, as in the British CVR(T) series shown in Figure 6.8, or behind the engine compartment. If it is intended to produce a series of vehicles based on the same chassis, then the forward engine and transmission configuration is the only practical option which permits unrestricted rear access.

The forward engine configuration is even more advantageous if the chassis is used as the basis of self-propelled (SP) gun. 155 mm ammunition is both bulky and heavy and easy access to the gun is a prime consideration. An SP gun with rear access allows loading onto the floor of the fighting compartment at most of the likely gun firing positions. Ground stacked ammunition can be passed easily into the vehicle, either directly into the gun when firing at intensive rates or to replenish the internal ammunition stock.

It is in the range of light and medium AFVs that the forward engine location finds most favour as it is in these weight classes that vehicles are designed from inception as part of a series or family of vehicles. The advantage of unrestricted rear access for personnel carriers, ambulances and command vehicles is immediately apparent. Rear access for a command vehicle allows an extension canopy to be fixed onto the rear. This increases the space available for map displays and briefings, all part of the normal functions of a command vehicle when stationary. It is normal practise for this extension to consist of a light tubular frame covered with waterproof fabric. Any form of ballistic protection is impractical so this system has limitations, notably when there is an air or NBC threat. However, being light and not permanently fixed to the vehicle, it can be left behind if the command post has to move quickly in an emergency.

Forward Engines for Main Battle Tanks

Placing the engine and transmission forward of the fighting compartment will enhance the protection provided for the crew as the path length which any armour piercing projectile has to travel will be increased. The only example of this configuration in an MBT is the Israeli Merkava (Chariot) tank as seen in Figure 6.9. The prime consideration in the design of this vehicle was to achieve the highest possible survivability for the crew. A comprehensive fire suppression system is fitted as the Israelis found that the highest proportion of tank crewmen casualties was caused by burns and not by direct injury from fragments.

The Merkava design allows access to the crew compartment through two vertically mounted clam-shell doors at the rear of the hull which make ammunition replenishment a simple task. It also allows protected access to the back of the tank without the need for the crew to climb over the top of the turret. When a tank is in a defensive position for any length of time and there is a need for the crew to leave the vehicle, they can do so without the need to expose themselves to the enemy and without the tank withdrawing from its fire position. The large compartment in the rear of the vehicle is also a bonus. Although it would be possible for a small infantry section to be carried for a short time in considerable discomfort, the greatest advantage of the design is that it permits the carriage of a considerable quantity of ammunition.

Fig. 6.8 Alvis CVR(T) Scorpion.

Fig. 6.9 Israeli Merkava tank.

Until some of the limitations of this system are examined, it is difficult to see why this design has not been copied. The main problem is to arrange for the gun to have a 180 mil (10 degree) depression without placing the gun trunnions inordinately high in the turret and raising the overall height of the tank. As shown in Chapter 3, the further the turret is moved towards the rear, the more difficult it becomes to obtain sufficient depression with the gun. With the fighting compartment to the rear of the engine and transmission, the optical path of the gun sights will be through the hot air rising from the radiators, causing heat shimmer. The problems are not insurmountable but add considerably to the designer's difficulties as he strives to ensure that the tank can achieve a high chance of a hit in all circumstances.

Perhaps the major problem with the Merkava configuration lies with the balance of protection. Because the engine and transmission are in the front, the surface area to be protected is larger when compared to the conventional, central turret layout. Inevitably this adds to the overall weight of the tank. In addition, the engine and transmission, while providing extra protection, do so at the expense of their own vulnerability—almost any projectile that penetrates the frontal armour is likely to achieve a Mobility kill. However, as the Israelis have recognised, trained crewmen are their most valuable asset whereas tanks can usually be repaired in a matter of days or even hours.

Fixed Gun Tank

The concept of fixing the gun to the chassis is very attractive. It offers a simple method of automatic loading and would permit a longer barrel to be used than would be possible in a turreted tank of similar size and weight.

The vehicle is essentially simpler as the complexity of a fully rotating turret is eliminated, a three man crew is possible and the reduced volume permits high levels of armoured protection to be achieved for a given weight. The only tank in service using this configuration is the Swedish Bofors 'S' tank and the diagrams in Figure 6.10 and Figure 6.11 show the general arrangement and the crew stations.

The commander and gunner have controls with which they can steer the tank when driving and traverse and elevate when firing. These controls are identical; thus, if necessary, either the commander or gunner alone can drive and fight the vehicle without changing crew positions, making it operable by one man in an emergency. The third crewman, the radio operator, faces rearward and is responsible for driving the tank backwards.

Because the gun is fixed in relation to the hull, the gun is aimed in azimuth by traversing the whole vehicle. The steering system allows the traversing velocity to be continuously variable, giving fine control of gun traverse rates. Elevation is achieved by raising or lowering the front and rear road wheels. The fixed gun tank offers the advantage of a lower silhouette because the gun can be placed close to the turret roof. The design will normally allow for the glacis to be given a large angle of slope. As in the external gun tank, the compartment can be given a very high level of protection and because the crew are all co-located, this configuration offers the best possible protection for a given weight of vehicle. However, the design suffers from one very considerable disadvantage in that it is impossible to fire on the move. At a time when fire control systems make this, and the more difficult task of firing at a moving target when on the move a possibility, to surrender these capabilities does not make operational sense. The concept has some attractions as a tank destroyer but even then it seems to fall between two stools. The complexity of the sophisticated suspension system will make this a very expensive vehicle and will certainly rule it out as tank destroyer on those grounds alone.

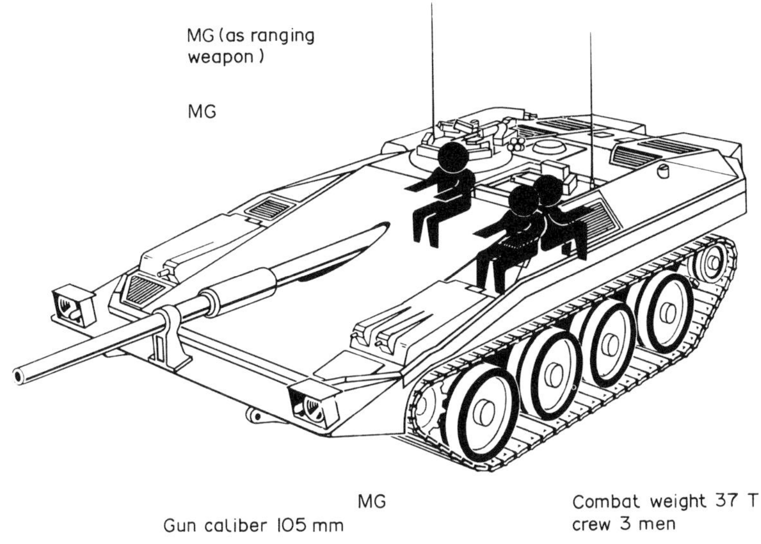

FIG. 6.10 'S' tank—general arrangements.

Future Developments

The future of some form of mobile, protected gun platform in the latter part of the twentieth century and the early decades of the next is assured; or at least as assured as it ever has been since the tank first appeared. As in the past, the emerging threat and the operational concept will dictate its future shape and form.

Two things are clear. The increased sophistication of the threat, especially from top atack by 'smart' munitions launched at long range will dictate that the tank must take active measures to protect itself on the battlefield. However, the first rule of self-protection is DO NOT BE DETECTED, so the tank designers will have to make some fundamental changes in order to reduce tank signatures. A reduction in overall size is perhaps the most important, as so many other advantages come in its wake—a smaller tank is more difficult to see, requires a smaller engine, uses less fuel, will have a reduced thermal signature, will have reduced radar reflectivity and so on. The adoption of a three-man crew will achieve all these highly desirable attributes but only two nations, Russia and France, have decided to adopt this configuration at the moment. Fortunately, the technology

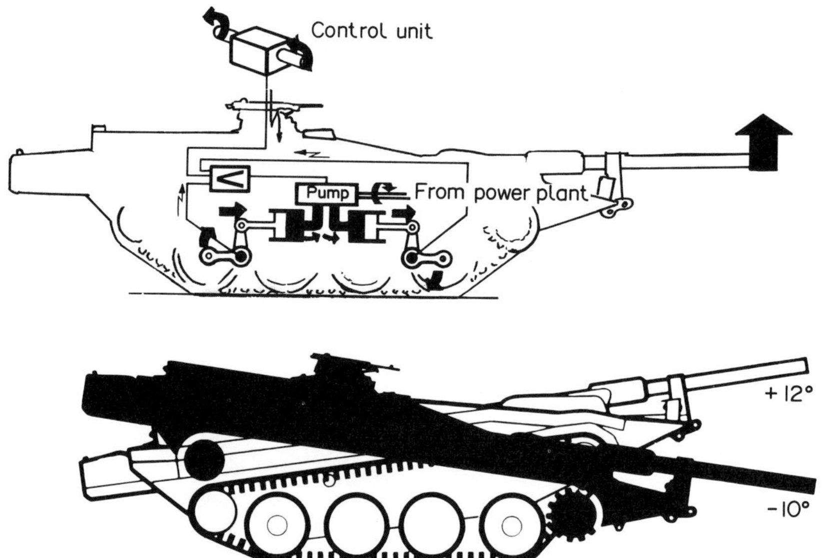

FIG. 6.11 'S' tank—method of gun elevation.

FIG. 6.12 The latest version of the 'S' tank, the Strv S (103G).

that will enable a three-man crew to function effectively in a 24 hour battle is available today—all that needs to be done is for a far-sighted decision to be made. But the inability to take an objective view of the future has bedevilled the tank right from its birth in the early part of this century and will no doubt persist to the next.

Writing in 1938 in a book entitled *The Tank in the Next War* before the tank battles of the Second World War had taken place, Major E W Sheppard said:

> 'It is a military truism to say that to every weapon of war there is a counter; but to deduce from that axiom that the weapon thus countered has lost all its value and must incontinently be relegated to the scrap heap is neither valid in logic nor true in practice.'

7

Light and Ultra-Light Armoured Vehicles

Introduction

The focus of previous chapters has been on main battle tanks rather than on light armoured vehicles for two reasons:

Their role is to fight; it is their *raison d'être*.

Their design is more complex as their success on the battlefield demands that they operate at the highest levels of performance that can be provided within the limits imposed by technical and budget considerations.

However, there exists another type of armoured fighting vehicle, more numerous than the main battle tank, but one that is also highly significant if only because, in aggregate, more money is spent on it. This type can be classified conveniently as the Light Armoured Vehicle (LAV). The term LAV comprises armoured personnel carriers and their derivatives and specially designed vehicles such as light reconnaissance vehicles. The vast majority of light armoured vehicles do not have a primary fighting role but they provide other essential capabilities, such as mobility, survivability, carriage capacity and firepower to the troops using them. They must be designed to accommodate those differing requirements from the start.

Light Armoured Vehicle Types

Four factors have led to the proliferation of light armoured vehicles on the battlefield: the increasing hostility of the battlefield; the development of new armours which make it possible to produce lighter vehicles still offering reasonable levels of survivability; the development of low-recoil guns, which make it possible to mount larger calibre weapons on relatively light chassis and the narrowing of the gap in performance between wheeled and tracked vehicles.

The intensity of the modern battle requires every soldier to have some form of protection, either a trench or building with overhead cover or a mobile armoured vehicle. Commanders, staff officers, liaison officers, signals despatch riders, telephone line crews, and military policemen have, over the last few decades, used a variety of wheeled open-topped 'jeep' type vehicles which provide little or no protection to their occupants. The requirement for vehicles on the battlefield has increased considerably and unprotected wheeled vehicles issued to the infantry so that they could achieve some mobility are no longer considered adequate.

Light armoured vehicles used instead of jeep-like utility vehicles can be called Light Armoured Utility Vehicles (LAUV). Vehicles providing mobility with some limited protection can conveniently be designated Ultra-Light Armoured Vehicles (ULAV). The recent development of lighter armours has made it possible to design small vehicles, typically carrying no more than four men, which can offer levels of protection similar to those provided by armoured personnel carriers. Designs for such vehicles are proliferating as more and more armies recognize the requirement for some level of protection. The French have led the Western armies when they accepted the Panhard M11, shown in Figure 7.1. It is worth noting that they see the M11 as both a combat and a utility vehicle. Tracked ULAVs are also available. The

FIG. 7.1 The Panhard M11 Vehicule Blindé Leger, a wheeled ultra-light armoured vehicle.

Engessa Ogum is an example, see Figure 7.2. However, the normal constraints faced by designers of ULAVs are much more stringent than those faced by designers of infantry section carriers, not least in that their stretch potential is more limited. The third factor promoting the proliferation of types of light armoured vehicles is the improvement in the design of guns which permit them to be mounted on lighter vehicles. The 105 mm light-recoil tank gun can now be fitted to both wheeled and tracked infantry section carriers and combat vehicles (see Chapter 2). The result of this development is that more manufacurers are including tank-destroyers in their stable of vehicles based on a common design or 'family'

FIG. 7.2 The Engessa Ogum, a tracked Ultra-Light Armoured Vehicle.

concept. Even though the 105 mm gun is no longer considered to be adequate for a main battle tank, there is no doubt that when mounted on a wheeled vehicle and firing kinetic energy ammunition, it is still a formidable weapon, especially as its relatively low cost allows it to be fielded in large numbers. Figure 7.3 shows the Steyr-Daimler-Puch tank-destroyer mounting a 105 mm gun. The final factor generating the increase in the numbers of light armoured vehicles is the improvement in the cross-country capabilities of wheeled vehicles when compared to tracked. Multi-wheeled vehicles using modern variable pressure tyres, differential locks and improved suspension have all led to the narrowing of the difference in performance between wheels and tracks. As before, tracks and wheels will continue to have their advocates and both types will be required for the tasks each do best; there will never be a 60 tonne wheeled tank and similarly, a tracked vehicle would find it difficult to move 500 kms in a day over roads and tracks.

Nomenclature of the Light Armoured Vehicle Type

The proliferation of vehicle types has led to confusion over their nomenclature. In general, they can be categorised by reference to their weight or function, the former being more usual; but how light is light, since there is no industrial or NATO standard? Therefore, for the purposes of this Chapter, ULAVs are defined as vehicles under 5 tonnes. Since it is not the custom to label tracked vehicles other than a tank as 'heavy', the qualifying term 'medium' for armoured personnel carriers has recently been introduced in the United States for vehicles between 15 and 30 tones.

Designating vehicles on the basis of function avoids these problems but introduces other difficulties. What exactly is an armoured personnel carrier? Is it an infantry section carrier or is it any vehicle whose function requires it to carry

FIG. 7.3 The Steyr-Daimler-Puch tank destroyer.

personnel, such as command post or repair and recovery vehicles? How does one decide if a vehicle which carries an infantry section actually is a combat vehicle? Does the addition of firing ports transform a vehicle from a personnel carrier to a combat vehicle? Is an APC with either a cannon or a guided weapon a true infantry combat vehicle? Are all vehicles so armed combat vehicles?

A third aspect of confusion is caused by the tank-destroyer. In the past these vehicles were specifically designed to engage tanks from static fire positions and did not take part in mobile combat. They normally mounted a high-velocity gun and relied more on being sited in enfilade positions (firing into the flank of an attacker) for their success. But should not this designation be extended to include systems designed to engage tanks with guided missiles instead of guns? There is no apparent reason why not, but there appears to be a marked reluctance to do so.

There is no easy answer to any of these questions and different armies have different terms for the same type of vehicle: mechanised combat vehicle, infantry combat vehicle, mechanised infantry combat vehicle and armoured infantry combat vehicle are some examples.

Types of Forces Using LAVs and ULAVs

Introduction

As suggested above all military forces operating on land take advantage of the capabilities provided by light armoured vehicles. These forces can be divided into two categories: army units, and other forces including police forces.

Army Units

The full range of units and sub-units making up a conventional land army routinely use light armoured vehicles. There are several types of infantry, all of which could use LAVs and/or ULAVs. These are:

Armoured Infantry. Some armies, notably the Soviet, American and West German, differentiate between armoured and mechanised infantry. Armoured infantry is organised, equipped and trained to operate integrally with, and in support of, tanks. Their tasks include clearing defiles, carrying out small-scale attacks on localised pockets of resistance during an advance, holding ground and local protection of tanks in defence. As shown later in this Chapter, their requirements for light armoured vehicles are different from those of their nearest cousins, mechanised infantry.

Mechanised Infantry. Mechanised infantry are the main heavy infantry in those armies which do not have special armoured infantry units. They are organised, equipped and trained to operate both with tanks and on their own, if this proves necessary. They support tanks during the advance and are the main ground-holding element of the army in the defence. Their requirements for light armoured vehicles are similar in scope to those of armoured infantry, differing only in the emphasis put on specific aspects of the vehicles' basic characteristics. These differences will be covered in more detail in the section on Basic Characteristics.

Light Infantry. Most armies recognise the requirement for less heavily protected and armed infantry, if only because of budgetary considerations. Light infantry units can reinforce mechanised infantry and operate on their own (with additional support from other arms) in mountainous, jungle and swampy terrain, and for special tasks such as rear area security. They too, have requirements for light armoured vehicles, but these differ markedly from those of armoured and mechanised infantry.

Airborne Infantry. A special type of light infantry. Many nations designate certain light infantry units as airborne because of the strategic and political advantages gained by having units which can be deployed by air when speed is essential. These units, which require airborne supporting elements, also have requirements for light armoured vehicles, which may or may not be met because of the very large extra cost of providing the transport aircraft. The recent development of light armoured utility vehicles and all-terrain mobile platforms are likely to have a greater impact on the combat effectiveness of airborne infantry than on any other element of the field army.

Other Forces

Those elements of the maritime forces which normally operate on the land, such as marines, commandos, naval landing parties and shore police, also require light armoured vehicles. The ground elements of the air force require them for airfield protection as do the various types of police for riot control and anti-terrorist operations. The requirements are becoming more numerous and more varied.

Conclusions

Several conclusions can be drawn. Firstly, light armoured vehicles vastly outnumber tanks in any conventional army and represent a vastly greater expenditure of defence resources. They may not have the glamour of the main battle tanks but they merit the same detailed consideration when drawing up the operational requirement and when formulating a concept of operations for battle.

Secondly, it should be clear that while the infantry may be the prime user of light armoured vehicles, the number of these vehicles used by other elements of the army is likely to be significantly larger. Every element in the army, as well as special groups in both the air force and navy, have a vested interest in these vehicles and may wish to have a say in the determination of the requirement.

Thirdly, a distinction needs to be drawn between a variant and a Specially Equipped Version (SEV). A variant is a vehicle whose characteristics are so different from those of the basic vehicle on which its design is based that the chassis is itself different. Figure 7.4 shows a variant of the M113, the M577 command post vehicle. An SEV is a standard vehicle, such as the infantry section carrier, which is fitted with a kit to allow it to perform a special function. Figure 7.5 shows an M113 which can be fitted out internally as an ambulance. Figure 7.6 shows a list of possible variants and SEVs based on the conventional infantry section carrier. Figure 7.7 shows a list of possible variants and SEVs based on a hypothetical ULAV chassis.

FIG. 7.4 The FMC M577 command post vehicle, a variant of the M113.

FIG. 7.5 The FMC M113 infantry section carrier.

Variants

Reconnaissance	Command post
Anti-tank guided missile	Engineer/pioneer
Mortar	Tank-destroyer
Light tank	Recovery
Repair	Artillery/mortar observation
Counter-mortar radar	Electronic warfare
Armoured ammunition	Armoured fuel replenishment
Armoured communications	Armoured flame-thrower

Specially Equipped Versions (SEV)

Ambulance	Company command post
Armoured general stores	Anti-aircraft point-defence detachment
Tactical command post	

FIG. 7.6 Some possible variants and specially equipped versions based on an infantry carrier chassis.

Variants

Basic command and liaison	Reconnaissance
Anti-tank guided weapon	Anti-light armour cannon
Signals line repair	

Specially Equipped Versions (SEV)

Despatch
Special tasks (VIP and nuclear convoy escort)

FIG. 7.7 Some possible variants and specially equipped versions of a light armoured utility vehicle.

Basic Characteristics of Light Armoured Vehicles

Introduction

Light armoured vehicles require certain characteristics which reflect the capabilities demanded by the type of troops by whom they are used. The four most obvious are mobility, survivability, carriage capacity and firepower. However, two additional characteristics must be added to this list: fightability and availability. The former defines the ease with which the vehicle and its major systems can be operated effectively under the stress of battle. Availability is the extent a vehicle remains operable, allowing the soldiers to use its capabiity to the full. Some explanatory notes on each are below.

Mobility

Mobility consists of three distinct components: strategic, tactical and battlefield. The relative priority accorded to each in the staff requirement has a very significant impact on the vehicle's design.

Strategic mobility

is the ability to move forces to a theatre of operations. Thus, it is strategic mobility which allows vehicles normally stationed in one country in peace to move to the theatre of operations either by road, rail or ship in a period of tension. Note that a vehicle may itself not have strategic mobility but it must not inhibit it; an amphibious vehicle stationed in North America would not be expected to swim to North Norway for operations or exercises, but it must not preclude deployment by whatever means is required. For deployment by air, the vehicle must be capable of being airlifted in a certain type of aircraft and for a minimum distance. Similar considerations apply to vehicles moved by sea but weight and size restriction seldom apply. The differing requirements for the air, road and rail components of strategic mobility place very differing demands on a vehicle's design and must be carefully thought out by the operational requirements staff.

Tactical mobility

is the ability to move about within a theatre of operations. This is a prime requirement for combat vehicles since forces in peacetime are rarely deployed in, or even near, their battle positions. Tactical mobility has several components closely matched to those of strategic mobility. These include movement by road and track; by ferry, bridge, swimming or wading; by tactical fixed-wing transport aircraft; and by helicopter as an under-slung or internal load. Clearly all these requirements have a direct bearing on the design of the vehicle.

Battlefield mobility

is the ability to manoeuvre in order to win the encounter battle. This is the prime requirement for combat vehicles. Battlefield mobility demands many of the same design requirements as tactical mobility. In order to win the manoeuvre battle, a vehicle will make use of roads and tracks; it will have to cross ditches and streams but the main requirement is for it to be as mobile as possible within the constraints of overall vehicle design. Battlefield mobility is the capacity to negotiate, at reasonable speed, most types of terrain while ensuring that the soldiers remain fit to carry out their task, both inside the vehicle and when they have dismounted.

Carriage Capacity

Carriage capacity for men or equipment represents the fundamental characteristic of any vehicle; if it is not defined, the vehicle will have no role. It thus represents the payload of the vehicle in the original meaning of the word—the cost of the revenue-producing element. Carriage capacity also needs to be specified; for equipment and stores such as anti-tank weapons, mines, wire, and digging tools and for combat supplies (rations, water and ammunition).

Specifying carriage capacity is not easy. Great care needs to be taken in order to keep both the range and quantity of the equipment that the user might like to carry within reasonable bounds. Also, a decision will have to be taken early on which equipment should be stowed under armour (inside the vehicle) or outside. The greater the requirement for the former, the greater will be the armoured volume of the vehicle and hence its weight and cost.

Survivability

The basic requirements for AFV protection are set out in Chapter 5. Survivability of a light armoured vehicle needs to be defined with care. All armoured vehicles must be capable of surviving on the modern battlefield and the tank is the best equipped to achieve this. However, not all vehicles can be protected against the anti-tank threat to the same extent as the tank and it is in this area that misunderstanding occurs. No medium, let alone light, APC will be able to protect the 9 or 10 infantrymen inside to the same level as a tank crew; to do so would require a vehicle weighing perhaps 80 tonnes or more, so clearly this is impractical. However, the vehicle designer must be tasked to provide the best protection available within the weight limit set by other requirements (air, road or rail maxima) while making the vehicle as small as possible to minimise being hit and achieving good battlefield mobility.

Firepower and Targets

In general, the targets for the weapons mounted on these vehicles can be classified as:

Personnel
Other light armoured vehicles
Tanks
Helicopters and other 'slow' aircraft
Fixed-wing and other 'fast' aircraft

Personnel Targets

All armoured vehicles carry some form of anti-personnel weapons just as all fighting soldiers carry a personal weapon. Targets may be in the open (in direct line of sight), in the open but in dead ground (out of the line of sight) or behind some form of protection such as defensive works or the walls of buildings. Their location determines the type of weapon to be used.

Troops in the open and in line of sight are best engaged by direct automatic fire or air burst artillery, which invariably makes them dive for cover. When in the open and out of the direct line of sight, area weapons are more effective. Either vehicle-mounted mortars or automatic grenade-launchers are the preferred weapon, both fairly recent additions to the land arsenal. A related aspect of the anti-personnel role is the counter-ambush weapon, which raises the chance of the vehicle's survivability when it is caught in an ambush. These weapons are uually based on anti-personnel grenade launchers, mounted on the periphery and activated by the commander, which surround the vehicle with either smoke or small fragment-ejecting grenades or a combination of both.

Troops located behind armour are a more difficult target. Nevertheless, armour-piercing shot and explosive shell are effective, though shaped-charge warheads require a relatively large calibre if they are to be effective. Further details are contained in Chapter 2.

In war, when political sensibilities are dulled, the favoured weapon for use against well dug-in infantry is the vehicle-mounted flame-thrower. However, few Western armies maintain this type of weapon in peace, though a manportable system is available in the Warsaw Pact forces.

There is now a plethora of weapons available to the infantry section but since there is a limit to the number which can be mounted on a single vehicle, distributing weapons between vehicles is usually the only answer. Thus in a mechanised platoon the headquarters vehicle might mount a grenade-launcher while the others might mount the heavy machine guns. All vehicles would probably carry counter-ambush weapons.

Light Armoured Vehicles as Targets

Light armoured vehicles customarily mount weapons to engage other light armoured vehicles and two different types of engagement can be envisaged: self-defence in a chance encounter and providing defensive anti-light-armour support.

These two functions differ essentially in their tactical objective and range of engagement. Because chance encounters occur at short range where survival is the prime requirement, a range of perhaps 500 m or 600 is adequate. This range is also consistent with that of other company and platoon weapons. In the dedicated defensive role, the engagement and defeat of opposing light armoured vehicles from a prepared defensive position is the objective. A range of probably 2000 m is desired and is consistent with that expected of infantry anti-tank guided missiles. Examples of vehicles with weapons serving these two purposes are, respectively, the American M113, usually mounting a .50 in machine gun and the GKN Sankey Warrior, which mounts a 30 mm Rarden cannon, see Figure 7.5 above and Figure 7.8 below.

FIG. 7.8 The GKN Warrior, an infantry combat vehicle mounting a 30 mm Rarden cannon.

In the past, engaging light armoured vehicles called for heavy machine guns but as the armour on these vehicles became thicker, the calibre necessary for achieving a kill became greater. Some light armoured vehicles now mount 60 mm or even 90 mm guns. A gun can engage a wider variety of targets as its calibre increases and thus the drive towards larger calibres derives as much from the need to engage a multitude of targets as it does from the need to defeat the best protected.

While in most armies a great deal of effort and money is devoted to the defeat of tanks, far less appears to be spent on the defeat of light armoured vehicles—a far more numerous target. Few armies dedicate units or sub-units to this role, relying on weapons such as heavy machine guns, artillery or even tanks to take on this task. Only recently have larger calibre weapons been mounted on light personnel carriers and even then the latest American version mounts only a 25 mm cannon. We will explore the arguments on the need to dedicate weapons to the anti-light-armour role in a later section.

To engage a target successfully requires both a high probability of a hit and a high probability of achieving a kill, given a hit. Details of the method of calculating chance of a hit are given in Chapter 2. However, the principles are the same for defeating the thinner armour of light armoured vehicles; indeed scaling down the technology of penetrators designed for tank guns to smaller calibres is perfectly feasible (e.g. the 30 mm armour piercing discarding sabot Rarden round) and gives the light armoured vehicle a significant additional capability.

Achieving behind-armour destructive power is, of course, the objective in the defeat of armour. The obvious way to achieve this is to penetrate the armour with an explosive shell but the additional requirement in the defeat of light armoured vehicles is to kill as many as possible of the troops inside. A kinetic energy or shaped charge round may well penetrate the armour and kill one or two men in its path but is unlikely to kill the entire crew except possibly by secondary effects such as the initiation of an ammunition fire. However, it is possible, by using a high explosive special effect shell to achieve maximum behind armour effects.

Tanks as Targets

Light armoured vehicles have often been employed in the anti-tank role either as tank-destroyers, as dedicated anti-tank guided missile vehicles, or as a hybrid such as the Bradley, which mounts machine guns, a 25 mm cannon and a TOW anti-tank guided missile, see Figure 7.9. The defeat of tanks poses a severe technical challenge. The engagement of tanks by LAVs, which are far more vulnerable to tank gun fire than are tanks to the majority of their weapons, means that the risk of defeat is far higher. Nonetheless, if tank-defeating weapons can be mounted on much cheaper chassis and the vehicles can be fielded in sufficient numbers, then the odds become more favourable. The armoured corps of most armies do not favour the concept of the tank-destroyer because their separate roles are often confused by those who do not understand the difference between the use of the tank in mobile operations and the tank-destroyer in static defence. The tank-destroyer and tank may look very similar and may well mount an identical gun but if there is to be only one type of vehicle, tank soldiers would want it to be a tank rather than a tank destroyer.

Aircraft as Targets

Light armoured vehicles can be called upon to engage helicopters. Hovering or slowly moving helicopters can be engaged with a cannon so long as it has sufficient range and lethality. A target acquisition system suitable for engaging ground vehicles would suffice. When the helicopter moves appreciably faster, engaging it without a more sophisticated target acquisition and fire-control system is unlikely to achieve a hit. The problem therefore, is not one restricted to light armoured vehicles but is a matter of developing the right fire control system and mounting it on a chassis capable of accommodating the very considerable weight. Such a vehicle is almost invariably very expensive.

Conclusions

The relative priority between the various basic characteristics of a vehicle determines its design and its performance. This priority can only be determined

FIG. 7.9 The FMC Bradley Fighting Vehicle mounting a machine gun, a 25 mm cannon and TOW anti-tank guided missile.

after a number of operational issues have been resolved. The next section deals with these issues and recommends ways in which their resolution can be achieved.

The most convenient way to outline these characteristics is to express them in a value tree, a figure which displays not only the vehicle's individual basic characteristics, but also their components and the relationship between them. Chapter 12, on stating the requirements for armoured fighting vehicles, provides guidance on how to construct a value tree and how to use it in the procurement process.

Operational Isues

Introduction

A number of operational issues arise during the determination of the requirement for light armoured vehicles. These are: wheels versus tracks, swimming versus fording; carrier versus anti-armour functions in the infantry section carrier; the need for firing ports, devices for clearing scatterable mines and self-entrenching devices. Each of these require examination and, eventually, justification.

Wheels versus Tracks

Whether a light armoured vehicle should be wheeled or tracked is an issue on which a great deal of rhetoric has been expended. Regrettably much of this has been ill-informed or, worse, prejudiced.

The advantages of wheeled vehicles, as normally asserted by their protagonists, are:

They provide much greater tactical mobility since, provided they can operate on roads or tracks, they can travel at higher speeds for longer distances with lower likelihood of breakdown.

They provide a better ride since the tyres provide a cushion between the vehicle and the ground.

Since most light armoured vehicles have six or eight wheels, and since their weight is usually distributed fairly evenly between them, the vehicle is not likely to be immobilised by a mine which destroys a single wheel station.

Since the internal frictional forces to be overcome in the drive-train are lower, fuel consumption is lower and power available at the wheel is proportionally higher.

Lower maintenance and operating costs combine to give significantly lower operating costs.

Since most adults are familiar with driving wheel vehicles, their training requirements tend to be more easily met.

They can be used in internal security operations, where the presence of a tracked vehicle of any sort could provoke a hostile reaction from the crowd or from politicians.

They are usually quieter then tracked vehicles. This is of value in the reconnaissance role.

The advantages of tracked vehicles are:

Tracked vehicles provide higher levels of cross-country mobility, their single most important advantage.

They accept higher loads since their ground pressure is lower as the weight is distributed over the whole area of the track and not just under the wheels.

Since power is transmitted through a single sprocket on each side, rather than a multiplicity of shafts, one to each wheel station, the drive trains of tracked vehicles tend to be simpler and less costly. Note, however, that this is offset by the additional cost of the track, which over the life of the vehicle can be significant.

Because of the simpler drive train, the provision of a large, internal volume in the hull is usually easier.

Generally speaking, for very light vehicles of about 5 tonnes or less, wheeled vehicles provide a greater advantage in tactical mobility than they surrender in battlefield mobility. This is reflected in the use to which vehicles of this modest weight are put in field armies. Though there are exceptions, wheeled vehicles demonstrate a balance of advantage in the weight range from 5 to 15 tonnes. Above that limit, tracked vehicles usually have the advantage when cross-country mobility is required.

However, advances in both fields have blurred the distinction between tracks and wheels. There are at least two wheeled 155 mm self-propelled guns weighing in excess of 30 tonnes in service. Tracked vehicle designers too, have had their success. The reliability of tracked vehicles has improved and cost has been reduced. Further details can be found in Chapters 4, 10 and 11.

Swimming versus Fording

The requirement for crossing water obstacles exists in three quite different settings: the continental, in which the requirement applies mainly to the army; and the marine, where the requirement applies to amphibious assault units who must move many troops ashore from ships as quickly as possible; and the island state, where the requirement applies to the army and the police, both of whom must be able to deploy rapidly from one island to the next. The obvious answer to those requirements is to have vehicles that swim.

Meeting this requirement is not technically difficult; virtually all manufacturers of light armoured vehicles provide them in amphibious configurations. To do so, however, places an upper limit on the 'density' of the vehicle since it must float if it is to be amphibious. An equally critical requirements is that its centre of gravity and centre of buoyancy must be in equilibrium with each other; the vehicle must float right side up and with adequate freeboard, a fact that impinges directly on both the design and the loading of the vehicle.

The fact that a swimming capability places this limit on the density, and thus the protection and firepower that can be accommodated on the vehicle, immediately raises the issue as to whether the tactical benefit is worth the cost. For marine use and in island states, the answer seems to be that it is. While helicopters can assist in deployment from ship to shore and between islands, their expense makes total reliance on them unacceptable. There is simply no alternative to having vehicles that swim. For continental armies the answer is not so straightforward.

Amphibious assaults offer one conspicuous advantage to the swimming vehicle: the beaches over which vehicles must move tend to slope gradually into the water and assaults are planned on that basis. However, this is not the case when crossing rivers. Water obstacles, rivers and canals are much easier for an amphibious vehicle to enter and cross than to exit as steep, muddy slopes do not provide the traction necessary for the vehicle to pull itself up out of the water. Detailed reconnaissance of the far bank is almost invariably required, followed up in most cases by extensive bank preparation. While specially designed engineer vehicles, such as the Royal Ordnance (UK) Combat Engineer Tractor, shown at Figure 7.10, have a limited capability to handle this task under fire, their acquisition represents another expense and they are usually in short supply. If far bank preparation is required, any semblance of achieving surprise in the assault is usually lost.

FIG. 7.10 The Royal Ordnance Combat Engineer Tractor (CET), an amphibious engineer reconnaissance vehicle.

Many vehicles in the field army do not swim, notably main battle tanks, standard wheeled load-carriers and utility vehicles, such as jeeps and command and communications vehicles. Bridging or ferrying will be necessary if these vehicles are to cross a water obstacle. Once the policy decision has been made to fund such a water crossing capability for heavy AFVs, light armoured vehicles, which will be able to use the same facilities, will not need to have an integral amphibious capability. For this reason, the requirement for an amphibious capability is likely to diminish in significance over the next few years and many armies have already decided not to incorporate it in the next generation of vehicles.

The Carrier versus The Anti-Armour Functions for Infantry Section Carriers

The Issue

It is technically feasible to mount both an anti-light-armour weapon and an anti-tank guided missile on every infantry section vehicle; both the Soviet BMP and the

American Bradley Fighting Vehicle are so equipped. It is also possible to mount only the anti-light-armour weapon, as is the case with the UK's Warrior. But in many armies, infantry section carriers mount neither type of weapon.

The Factors

Ultimately, the two factors bearing most fundamentally on this issue are weight and volume. Volume must be provided for the crew, for the weapons and for the ammunition; and armour must be provided to achieve protection. However, several tactical factors are significant.

The first is the role of the vehicle. The requirements of the section carrier are normally best met when the vehicle is tucked down behind hard cover, out of sight and direct fire. To assign either fire support or anti-tank roles permanently to the vehicle means that it must expose itelf to direct fire from the enemy. This represents an additional risk, not only to the vehicle itself but to its continued availability to perform the carrying function. Also, it endangers the lives of the men inside unless they have dismounted. In that case they have been stranded on the battlefield, with neither the transport, the protection nor the firepower provided by the vehicle itself. In effect, the imposition of a multiplicity of roles for one vehicle, while being attractive in reducing costs, requires the vehicle to occupy positions or perform tasks which are, at best, dangerous and, at worst, compromise its primary role.

Although the armoured personnel carrier has been given the ability to give fire support with its cannon, the problem of how this new capability should be commanded has not beeen solved. Who should remain with the vehicle and who should dismount? Should the section commander also be the vehicle commander? Is it more important for the dismounted troops be commanded by the most experienced individual or is the firepower of the vehicle more important? Inevitably, the solution is a compromise. The vehicle has a role to perform even when the troops have dismounted and the firepower may well be used to give fire support.

Splitting the command in a way that allows one soldier to command the vehicle and another the troops when dismounted adds little to the efficiency of the section in war. Continually changing command appointments at vehicle level is not the way to prepare for battle. When the normal turnover in personnel in an infantry battalion is taken into account, the training task becomes onerous and costly.

The Alternative

An alternative being pursued by some armies is to split the anti-armour and infantry section responsibilities. It is normal to establish an anti-tank platoon in a battalion, equipped with light armoured vehicles mounting anti-tank guided missiles. It should be just as logical to recognize the anti-light-armour function as of equal importance and to establish a similar, complementary anti-light-armour platoon. The sections of these two platoons, which each might comprise four sections of three or four vehicles, would be deployed together to reinforce the mechanised companies covering the most likely light-armour tracked approaches.

Additionally, the platoon headquarters of the anti-light-armour platoon becomes an ideal comand headquarters for a highly mobile reserve when reinforced with anti-tank guided-missiles and one or two infantry platoons.

The dedicated anti-light-armour vehicle is likely to have operational characteristics that are almost identical to those of an infantry reconnaissance vehicle. Thus, the former does not introduce a new vehicle requirement into the inventory with all the logistics and training implications.

A range of 1,000 m for the weapon can be provided at low cost since at that range costly target acquisition systems are not necessary. Furthermore, sophisticated weapon stations demand considerable space within the vehicle, to the detriment of its primary role of carrying a mechanised section into battle. The weapon will be able to contribute significantly to the defensive fire of the company and will also be able to bring suppressive fire to bear during the advance and the attack. It will unquestionably be a more effective weapon than the heavy machine gun normally mounted on section carriers in the past. However, choosing a solution may well entail accepting those disadvantages which are the least objectionable.

Firing Ports

Many armies fit their section carriers and mechanised infantry combat vehicles with firing ports which either allow personal weapons to be fired through them or specially-fitted small arms to be fired from within the vehicle. As the installation of these ports takes up valuable interior space and radically alters the seating positions, their advantages and disadvantages bear further examination.

Firing through ports is unlikely to be very accurate particularly when the vehicle is moving cross country. Even assuming that careful aim can be taken, holding a sight picture will be impossible and realistically only the general direction of fire can be controlled. The fire from firing ports is only likely to be effective when the vehicle is caught in an ambush in which case neutralising fire may distract the attackers and affect their aim.

However, firing ports do offer one advantage. The psychological effect on the infantry soldier riding about cooped up in the back of a section carrier with little or no view of the outside world is poor preparation for the shock of battle once he dismounts. The provision of firing ports permits the infantryman to build up his aggression before he dismounts by allowing him to take part, even if the effect of his fire is limited, in the battle. This will prepare him once he dismounts or at least will reduce the debilitating psychological withdrawal that enclosure within a noisy, jolting armoured vehicle can promote.

The inclusion of firing ports in armoured troop carrying vehicles adds considerably to their cost, reduces the armoured integrity and lowers the overall level of protection of the vehicle. Some other disadvantages are:

The troops must face outward to fire their weapons. This means that the space immediately around the firing ports cannot be used for the stowage of kit and equipment.

There is no central 'gangway' as the backrests form a V in the middle of the vehicle. Thus, it is more difficult to enter and dismounting will take longer, increasing the time the soldiers are exposed if under fire.

Access to the rear of the vehicle is also more congested when outward-facing benches are provided. Special installation kits to transform the vehicle for other uses such as ambulance or command post will be more complicated and costly. Finally, sealing the vehicle to permit an over-pressure NBC system (to prohibit the entry of toxic gases and radio-active particles) is more complicated, will require a higher capacity fan and is less likely to be reliable, since the firing ports require some form of sealing arrangement.

If some form of self-protection is required, remotely fired grenade-launchers or small automatic weapons can be used. They are more simple to operate and cost less.

Devices for the Clearance of Scatterable Mines

One of the most significant recent developments in both tube and rocket artillery is their ability to lay down quantities of small mines which can destroy personnel and/or lightly armoured vehicles. They represent a serious and increasing threat to the mobility of mechanised units. The scatterable mine's greatest advantage is that it can be laid with great speed across the line of advance, usually achieving total surprise.

One effective counter-measure is to fit some or all vehicles with a device which will clear a safe lane through a minefield. These devices usually take the form of a small plough attached to the front of the vehicle and operated from inside, much along the lines of the dozer on the pioneer and engineer version of the M113, a photograph of which is shown at Figure 7.11. These mine ploughs add substantially to the cost of the light armoured vehicle fleet and this reason alone may well mitigate against their widespread adoption. Furthermore, the ploughs, by adding weight to the vehicle and by moving its centre of gravity forward, reduce significantly the chance that the vehicle will be able to swim. The mobility will also be reduced, the weight will increase. Overall, the mineploughs might be considered a mixed blessing. Nevertheless, their value in clearing a lane through a scatterable minefield at short notice may well outweigh the disadvantages. A balance must be struck, with only a proportion of vehicles being fitted with them.

Self-entrenching Devices

The tactical advantages of being able to achieve protection from artillery fire and concealment by using a self-entrenching device are clear. Once again, the policy whether all or just a proportion should be fitted with these devices must be decided by the operational staff; certainly, both a scatterable mine clearance and self-entrenching device cannot be mounted on the same vehicle.

The Impact of the Relative Priorities of Basic Characteristics and Related Decisions on Vehicle Design

The priorities of the various characteristics or armoured vehicles must be decided at the operational requirement stage as they will have a direct bearing on the design of the vehicle. But to emphasise the point, photographs of vehicles highlighting certain of the characteristics are shown in the following Figures.

FIG. 7.11 The FMC M113 Dozer pioneer and engineer section vehicle, developed by General Motors of Canada.

FIG. 7.12 The General Motors of Canada Light Armoured Vehicle LAV 25, a wheeled amphibious reconnaissance vehicle.

FIG. 7.13 The Alvis Stormer, a small vehicle which can be utilised in a variety of roles.

FIG. 7.14 The Vickers Valkyr, an infantry section carrier with good tactical mobility and easy access for internal security operations.

FIG. 7.15 The Haaglunds CV90, a mechanised combat vehicle with 7 roadwheels.

8

Power Trains

Requirements

Power trains cover the complete installation for the propulsion of any land vehicle, from the fuel tanks to the road wheels or sprockets. Major components include the engine itself, the change-speed transmission, and in the case of track-layers the steering mechanism.

Historically, the earliest practical tanks were conceived in time of war; provision of suitable engines posed a challenging problem. Aircraft engines were in critically short supply and the commercial vehicle industry not sufficiently mature to provide a source; consequently, special-to-purpose engines were developed. Throughout the subsequent three decades, however, piston aircraft engines, together with the truck, bus and car industries, provided the source. By the end of the Second World War and throughout the '50s and '60s, MBTs had power/mass of the order 9–12 kW/tonne, giving maximum road speeds of the order 40–50 km/h (25–30 mile/h). At this level, the complete power train occupies about 38% of the internal space (see Figure 8.1), and its surrounding armour is a major

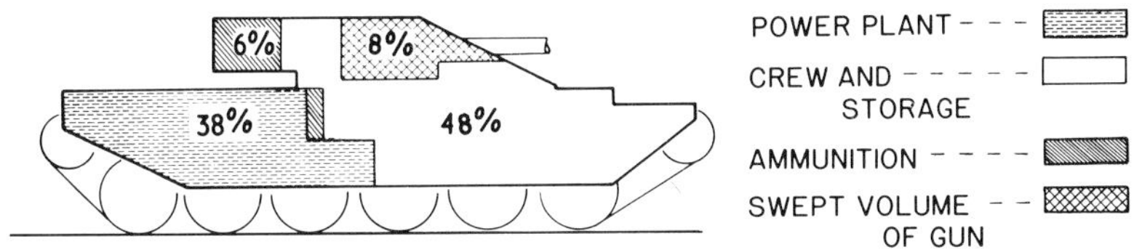

FIG. 8.1 Volumetric division of a typical battle tank.

contributor to the vehicle weight, more so than the power train itself. So it is important to achieve minimum bulk in the overall train, and in each of its components. Compactness is the greatest single virtue that a tank engine can have. From 1980 onwards, tanks entered service with power/mass about twice as high as their predecessors, and since there was no way that the current 38% could be allowed to escalate towards 76%, marvels of compactness had to be achieved. Lighter AFVs exhibit the same logic, but much less cogently. In a reconnaissance vehicle, the bulk of the crew is unlikely to be less than 75% of that in a MBT, but the total bulk may be 25% only. If crew bulk has become more significant, then power train bulk must be less so. In personnel carriers, the crew bulk is even more dominant. In all engine duties, compactness is desirable, but in none except the MBT is it crucial. Helicopters demand primarily high power/weight and mission reliabilty. Trucks are conceived around whole life costing, which leads to initial simplicity, long mean life between overhauls and extreme fuel economy; compactness has low priority. This one argument forces tank engine design ever further away from commercial practice. It is true that the situation in any one country at a particular time may appear to contravene this generalisation, but such would be a temporary and local trend only. Tank engines are 'military specials'. The power levels in wheeled AFVs are such that engines and change-speed gearboxes off the commercial shelf may be suitable; some manufacturers have found it possible to use commercial drive axles too. But really fast, big track-layers must integrate their change-speed and steering functions into one gearbox, and this too then becomes a military special.

Military vehicles cover the whole spectrum, from staff cars and low mobility trucks to MBTs. At one end, the equipment represents an almost unmodified commercial purchase; at the other, the vehicle and all its automotive components represent military specials, well removed from commercial practice.

Matching the Engine to the Duty

Resistances to Motion

When a land vehicle moves, it may encounter three types of resistive force:

rolling resistance,
air resistance and
gradient resistance.

The sum of these is called the road load. To overcome them, the power train must provide a driving force, the tractive effort, equal to their sum.

Rolling Resistance

Rolling resistance is encountered when a vehicle is pushed slowly over a level surface. It comes from friction in a variety of bearings and seals, rub between gear teeth, brake rub, distortion of tyres or tracks and distortion of the ground. On metalled surfaces, the last of these is negligible, and of the others, tyre/track distortion is the dominant factor for a vehicle in good condition. Under these conditions, rolling resistance in wheeled vehicles shows little speed sensitivity up to the maxima common in military vehicles, and is typically about 2–2½% of the weight. Rolling resistance so expressed, as a percentage or fraction of the weight, is called specific rolling resistance. For tracked vehicles it is typically 4–5% of the weight at low speeds, and rises towards about 8% at 90 km/h. On soft surfaces, ground distortion soon becomes dominant. Thus, even on firm turf whereon tracks just leave a neat print, about 2% is added to the values above. For ground still softer, it becomes very difficult to quantify the going type. On a ploughed field, rolling resistance can certainly be about 10% of the weight, but may range from about 8 to 18% with topsoil type, wetness and time since ploughing.

Air Resistance

Air resistance of a vehicle is governed by its frontal area, how 'streamlined' its shape is, and the square of its speed through the air. For on-road vehicles, air resistance is important; at 80 km/h (50 mile/h) on the level, it represents about half of the total road load for a typical private car. Large trucks have greater resistances, but their air resistance represents a smaller proportion of the total, typically about 15%. By comparison, armoured vehicles are densely packed and slow; this makes their weight and rolling resistance dominant compared with their frontal area and air resistance. So air resistance is insignificant for AFVs.

Gradient Resistance

Gradient resistance is given by $W \sin \theta$ (see Figure 8.2). Slopes are commonly designated in the form 1 in 5, or 20%, but this is ambiguous. It can mean either 1 up for 5 horizontal, or 1 up for 5 along the slope, giving $\theta = 11.3°$ or $11.5°$ respectively.

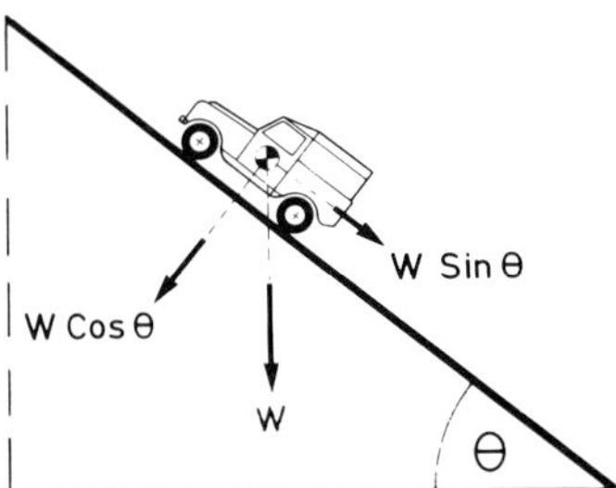

Fig. 8.2 Effect of gradient.

Since metalled roads rarely exceed 1 in 3 gradient, the difference is not serious. But for steeper slopes met in off-road operation, it is safer to designate slopes by the angle θ. On this basis maximum road slopes will be about 19°. Off-road, slopes of 30° to 40° may be encountered. Steeper slopes make resistance to motion $W \sin \theta$ greater, while grip on the ground, governed by $W \cos \theta$, lessens. On dry road, a slope of 45° is about the ultimate climbable, and this only at the expense of wheel or track slip and burned rubber. Off-road surfaces usually give less grip than road, so realistic limits for steady climb are about 28° only for all-wheel drive, and 38° for track-layers. With a flying start, steeper short slopes may be climbed. Starting from rest on a slope is another matter, introducing more complex considerations of clutch or coupling capacity.

For any given vehicle type, e.g. a fast track-layer, the power/weight ratio governs the maximum achievable road speed on level metalled surfaces. In this context, it is important to appreciate that the achievable maximum power at the road wheels or the sprockets, road power, is usually much less than the manufacturer's quoted power for the bare engine. Variations in the engine test-bed procedure affect power at the flywheel; installation into a vehicle can affect power losses via filters, silencers, etc., and losses in the transmission render the power reaching the road even lower still.

Constant Power Characteristic

Consider a MBT, having mass 55 tonne (weighing 540 kN), and a maximum power at the sprockets of 1080 kW, i.e. power/weight ratio of 2 kW/kN; this is rather better ratio than the best currently in service. It will probably be so geared as to be as fast as possible in high gear on a slight road upgrade; this avoids endless fussy gear changing in typical easy road running. Then it will be capable of about 80 km/h (50 mile/h) at maximum power, and probably a little more on the level or a slight downgrade as its engine runs onto its governor (Annex A, p. 207 refers).

If the going should become more difficult, due to upgrade or soft ground, the vehicle must slow down. But for optimum performance under these more arduous conditions it should still be possible to deliver 1,080 kW into the sprockets. The power train should ideally be capable of exerting its maximum power, on demand, irrespective of how fast the vehicle is moving, or of how fast its sprockets are turning. This ideal is called a constant power engine. Thus, if this MBT should now encounter a gradient of 38°, (limit for track-slip), with going such as to give rise to specific rolling resistance of 10%, it should achieve 10 km/h thereon (Annex A refers). These two running conditions are shown in Figure 8.3, plotted as specific

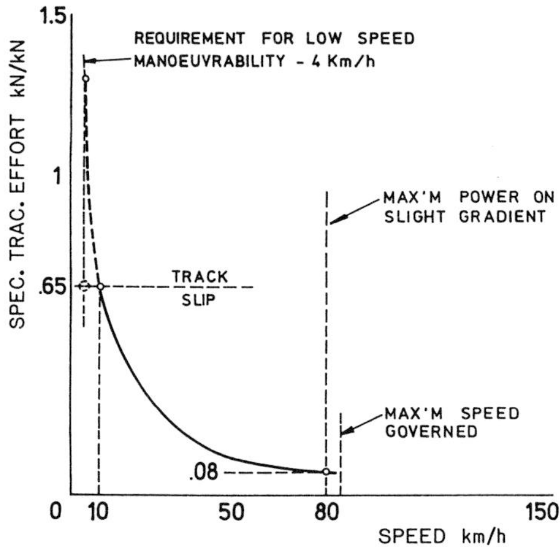

FIG. 8.3 Performance of a constant power engine.

tractive effort (tractive effort divided by weight) against road speed. All points on the curve between them represent 1080 kW. As the going worsens and the road load increases, the road speed must fall, and the resulting tractive effort increases to match the road load. At first sight it might seem irrelevant to provide specific tractive effort greater than 0.65, since track-slip would result. However, at this condition the vehicle would still be moving at 10 km/h, and operational circumstances will arise when this is too fast, e.g. moving with walking infantry. Military vehicles need to be able to move at speeds down to 4 km/h, under the worst conditions of going, for long sustained periods, without slipping a friction clutch. To maintain such a low road speed, either a very low gear may be provided or, alternatively, a hydrokinetic coupling/converter, which, by being able to slip continuously if provided with suitable cooling arrangements, can allow slow movement. For further detail on this see Chapter 9.

Real Engine Characteristics

Real engines can achieve nothing like this constant power curve: in almost all of them power will begin to drop when increased loading begins to force their speed down, even though they be driven flat-out all the time. Even when the circumstances demand something less than maximum power, piston engines cannot achieve anything like the range of speed (80 to 4 km/h) required by our hypothetical vehicle.

Figure 8.4 shows what might be expected from engines designed for MBTs.

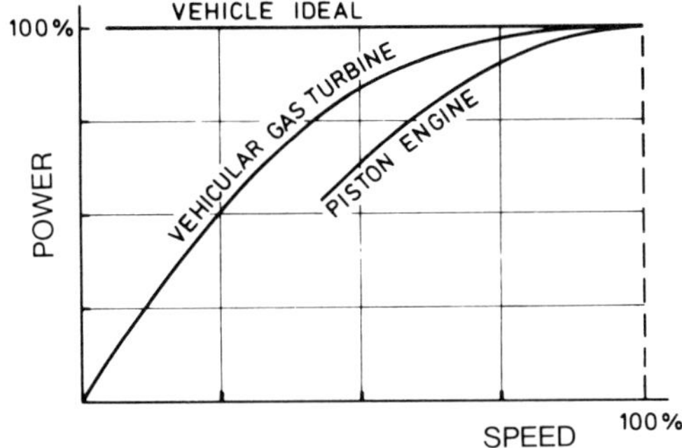

FIG. 8.4 Power/speed characteristics.

To retain something approaching maximum power availability over the whole range of road speeds, a limit must be imposed upon the range of engine speeds to be used in flat-out driving, though in easy driving the engine can and will be taken outside this range. This is achieved by changing the gearing between the engine and the road wheels or sprockets, so that the engine may be operated fairly close to 100% speed at any vehicle road speed. How many gears will need to be provided will depend upon the engine characteristic, how much power drop from 100% is acceptable, how and where the vehicle is to be operated, and how much driver skill may be anticipated.

Considering the first of these, the gas turbine can have a characteristic nearer to the ideal than the piston engine, and so may need less gears. In heavy road vehicles, the acceptable power drop would be less than 20%, and with a piston engine this leads to between eight and sixteen gears. For optimum performance on paper, the MBT would need a comparable number, but this is not practicable. Already gearbox bulk is comparable with that of the engine itself and, furthermore, cross-country going changes so rapidly that the driver, or the auto-change mechanism, would continually be confronted with decisions about changing through several gears at once. So an inadequate number of gear ratios must be accepted and, as partial compensation, a very rapid, hot-shift gear-change be provided.

Fuel Consumption

So far we have talked primarily about hard driving for performance, but in practice, land vehicles spend much of their time at light loads (even negative when the vehicle overruns in engine braking). Thus, to achieve long range with minimal fuel bulk under armour, and to minimise logistic problems, low fuel consumption at all powers is desirable. Most engines certainly burn less fuel when driven softly rather than hard; but to quantify this we must consider whether the fuel consumption drops *pro rata* with the reduction of power.

Engines burn some fuel when idling, just to keep running. Fuel is then burned for zero power output; this represents zero efficiency of conversion of the fuel's energy into useful work. Thus, engines have zero efficiency at idle. Generally, their efficiency is best at or near to full power, and then gets progressively worse as their output is restricted; the relationship is not linear.

In the world of vehicle engines, it is common to talk not about efficiency, but rather about the rate of fuel consumption divided by the power. This is called specific fuel consumption, sfc, and has units of the form kg/kW h. At idle, engines burn some fuel for zero useful power; sfc is then infinite. So low efficiency implies high sfc and vice-versa.

The duty of driving a land vehicle is hard on engines. They are expected to run over a wide range of speeds, and to produce near maximum power at all of them. They must run at light loads too, and accept continual see sawing wildly over the whole range of speeds and loads. They must be economical of fuel, not only on full power but at all lighter loads too. On top of all this, they must accept mechanical shocks, as in gear changing, and thrive on maintenance standards far lower than those of the aircraft world. Tank engines, in particular, are built in penny numbers, and never see enough in-service running to become properly developed before they are retired as obsolete. Finally, they are expected to be relatively cheap; we do expect a lot for our money.

Engine Types

Currently available engine types for AFV propulsion include spark ignition (SI, petrol, gasoline) engines, compression ignition (CI, diesel, oil) engines and gas turbines. Steam has been considered, but the bulk of the necessary cooling system eliminates it from free-roving vehicles in general and AFVs in particular. The same appears true of the Stirling, (hot-air) engine. So we will discount both these types. SI and CI engines are usually reciprocators, but could use Wankel rotary mechanisms. As SI engines, rotaries offer commendable compactness in larger powers, though suffering real, not necessarily insuperable, problems of gas leakage; these can lead to questionable life and inferior fuel economy. But SI engines are unattractive for future AFVs as explained below. Because of the compactness of rotary SI engines, determined efforts have been made to develop compact rotary CI engine, but the problems escalate, and these have not been successful. So we will discount rotary engines too.

SI reciprocators have been much used to power AFVs, but they have lost ground. At the powers required in small AFVs, they do have a compactness advantage over

CI, but less at MBT powers where bulk is critical. Commercial expertise in high-powered engines has evaporated with the demise of big piston aircraft engines; fuel consumption is heavy compared with CI, and the volatility of the fuel gives rise to greater fire risk by accident than with diesoline, kerosene or paraffin. Since most readers will be familiar with SI engines in cars, they do provide a useful entree to studying CI performance, but the future for AFV engines does not lie with SI.

Reciprocating Piston Engines

Four-stroke cycle

Most readers will be familiar with the mechanism inside a typical car engine and its nomenclature (see Figure 8.5); also with the four-stroke cycle (see Figure 8.6).

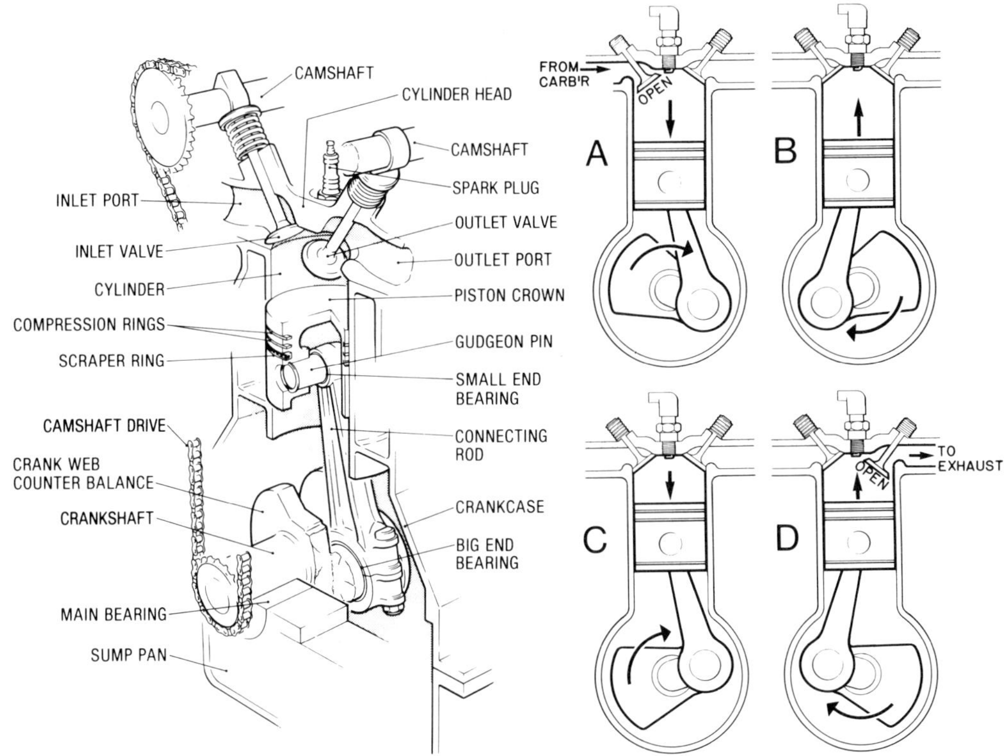

FIG. 8.5 Engine components.

FIG. 8.6 Four-stroke cycle.

At A, the falling piston INDUCES fresh charge from the carburettor via the open inlet valve, opened by the camshaft, now shown in Fig. 8.6. At B the rising piston COMPRESSES the charge, and near the top of this stroke, called inner dead centre or idc, the charge is sparked. The resultant combustion increases the gas pressure inside the closed cylinder, causing EXPANSION which drives the piston down at

C. At D the rising piston EXHAUSTS the spent gases through the open exhaust valve.

SI/CI Difference

In a SI engine, the fuel and air are pre-mixed in a carburettor, and enter the cylinder as a fairly homogeneous mix. Power is controlled by a throttle, acting on both fuel and air (see Figure 8.7). Petrol injection may be used instead of a carburettor. Usually this implies injection into the inlet manifold, upstream of the inlet valve (see Figure 8.8). The fuel is metered by the injection system and the air by a throttle, the two controls being suitably linked. Again, the charge within the cylinder is fairly homogeneous: such a charge will burn satisfactorily over a narrow band only of air fuel ratios. 12–17/1 by mass. In a CI engine, fuel injection is directly into the combustion space, via the cylinder head (see Figure 8.9). There is no control upon the air flow into the engine, the charge is not homogeneous, and the air/fuel ratio varies with the load, from about 20/1 upwards. Injection begins shortly before the piston reaches idc on the compression stroke, and ignition results from contact of the fuel with the hot air, heated by compression. From this difference in their modes of fuel admission stem all the main performance differences between SI and CI engines.

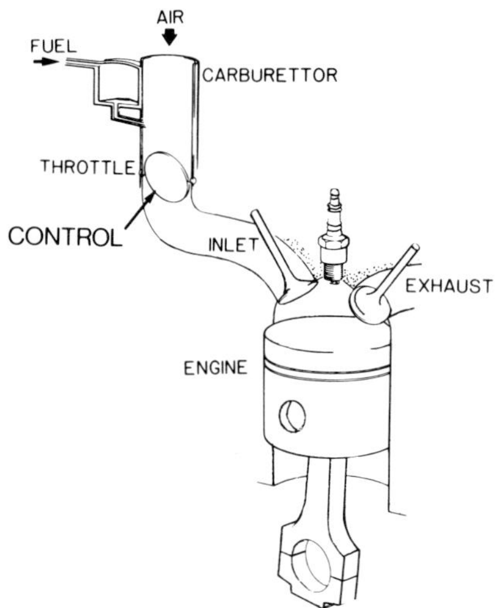

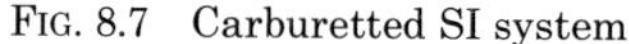

FIG. 8.7 Carburetted SI system.

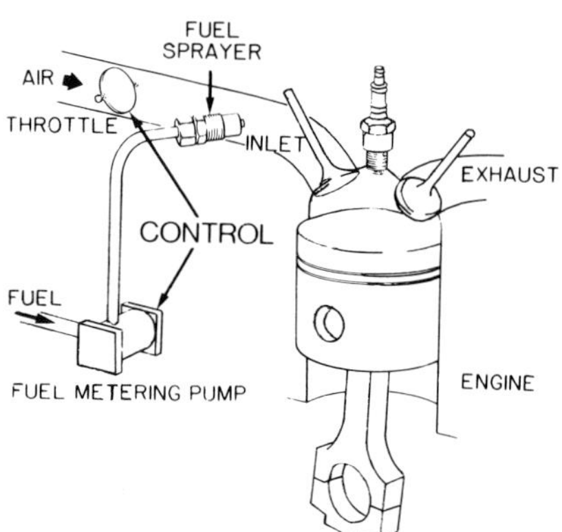

FIG. 8.8 Injected SI system.

To ensure a high enough air temperature for compression ignition of the fuel, CI engines need a high compression ratio (CR), typical CR being 14–25/1. Small cylinders suffer proportionally more heat loss from the air to the hardware and so need higher CR. In SI engines, fuel is present throughout compression, so high CR would risk premature ignition in part of the charge; typical CR is 8–10/1. High CR in the CI engine leads to high pressure, heavy mechanical loading and demands heavy build. Thus for given cylinder size, CI engines tend to be heavier than SI.

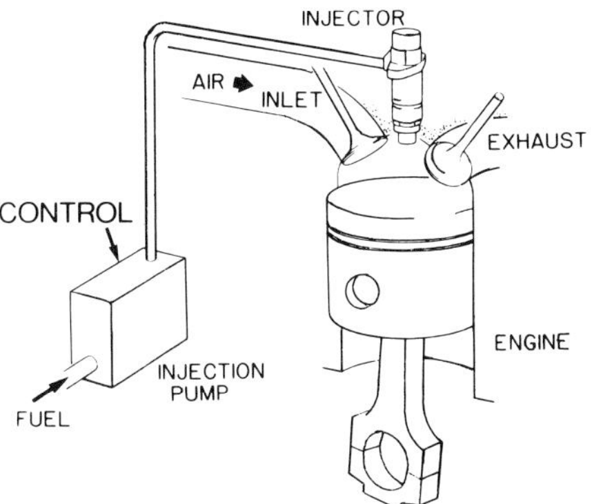

FIG. 8.9 CI system.

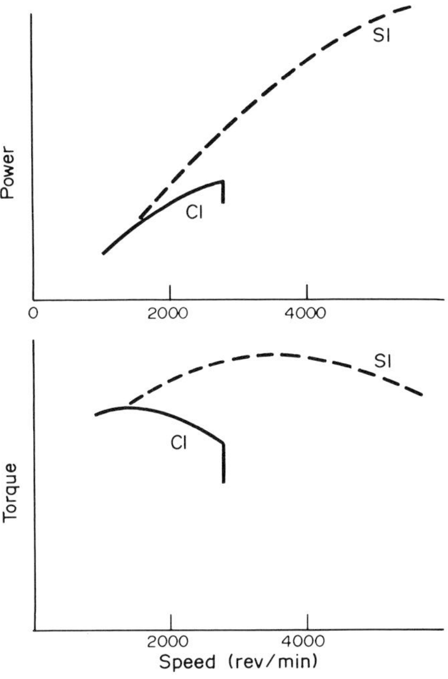

FIG. 8.10 CI and SI performance.

In SI engines, the fuel and air have adequate time for mixing. In CI engines, time is limited and mixing never complete. This leads to two problems:

Not all the induced air can be burned. This leads to a restricted work output per cycle from a given cylinder size.
Rotational speed must be kept down to maximise the mixing time.

Consequent upon less work per cycle and less cycles per second, the CI engine is less powerful and pulls less hard than a SI engine of the same cylinder size, i.e. has less Torque (see Figure 8.10).

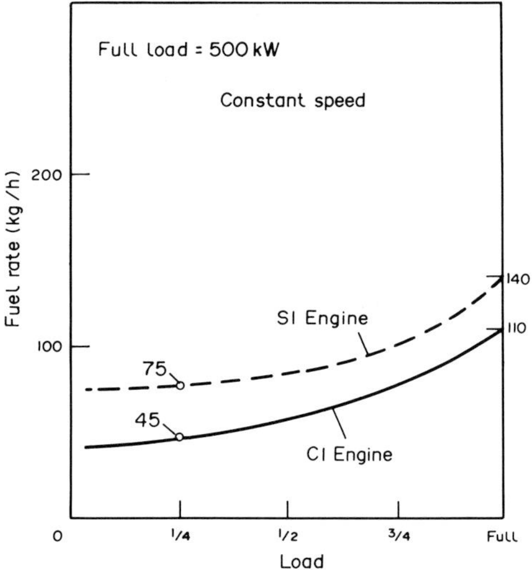

FIG. 8.11 CI and SI consumptions.

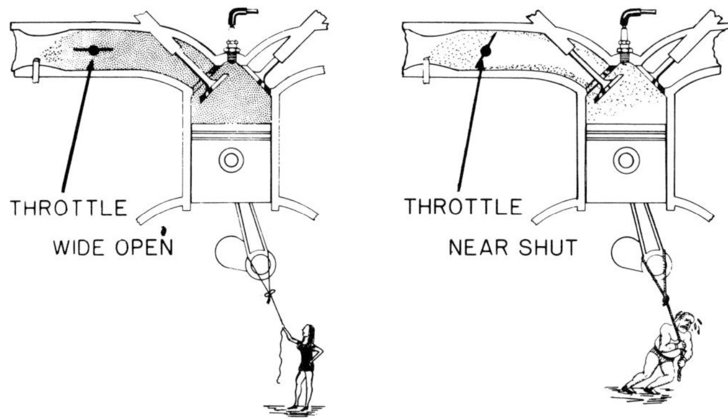

FIG. 8.12 Effect of throttling.

Figure 8.11 shows the CI engine to be more economical of fuel than an equally powerful SI over the whole load range, with its proportional advantage being most marked at light loads. This economy advantage arises from two causes:

> The leanness of the mixtures used in CI engines. Leanness spells economy in SI engines too, but with their homogeneous mixtures, attempts to reduce the fuel below about 80% of the correct amount lead to misfiring.
>
> The absence of a controlling throttle in the CI air intake. Throttling an SI engine introduces a waste of work during the induction stroke (see Figure 8.12).

The economy of CI engines has led to their general adoption in high mileage applications. These demand longevity too, and so the CI engine, with all its auxiliary equipment, is built to last and has acquired a deserved reputation for robustness in its commercial forms. But intrinsically it has the poorest power/bulk ratio of all the currently credible vehicle engines, in its simpler forms at least. It does not offer the compactness that is so essential a characteristic in engines for large AFVs and ways must be sought to circumvent this problem.

The reduction of fuel tankage for a mission in part offsets this, but nevertheless military engines must develop more kW from each m^3 of bulk than is commercially usual. Engines have irregular shapes, and so their bulk is difficult to quantify, but as a guide a modern truck engine achieves about 180 kW/m^3, and military CI engines are in the range 600–1000 kW/m^3, which underlines their 'special' status.

Minimising Engine Bulk

Since there is no foreseeable avenue for markedly improving the specific fuel consumption of CI engines, the development of more power has to mean the burning of more fuel, and hence of air. Again, there appears little likelihood of burning the induced air more completely, so the problem reduces to increasing the air-swallowing capacity of engines without commensurate bulk increase, possibly by:

Increasing cylinder size (swept volume) within the existing bulk.
Inducing more times per second (running the engine at higher speeds).
Filling the cylinder more completely on each cycle.
Increasing the density of the ingoing air charge.

Considering the first of these, the ratio of bulk volume/swept volume is about 100/1 in a four-stroke truck engine, and less than 50/1 in some military specials. The detail design changes leading to such compactness may militate against *in situ* maintainability, but this is not important if all maintenance is to be by removal of the complete power pack.

To achieve the second, the engine might be run faster, or operate a two-stroke cycle. The former is limited in CI engines by smokey combustion and offers little gain. At a given rotational speed, a two-stroke does cycle twice as frequently as a four-stoke, and this may offer some advantage in power/swept volume. But the need for a scavenge blower makes their ratio of bulk volume/swept volume high, and in the limit they are less well able to accept pressure charging than four-strokes (see below). So at the very highest ratings, two-stroke bulks compare unfavourably with four-strokes in the power range for military vehicles.

Considering the third, the use of many individually small cylinders, with tuned inlet/exhaust systems, along with valve timings accented towards high-speed performance can give a high-power/swept volume; racing-car engines exemplify this approach. But the resulting tendency towards a narrow operating speed range is ill-suited to a vehicle requiring a wide range of road speeds and having a limited number of gears.

Pressure Charging and Turbocharging

This leaves us with the fourth option. A compressor may be used to drive more charge into the engine, pressure charging; engines not so equipped are naturally

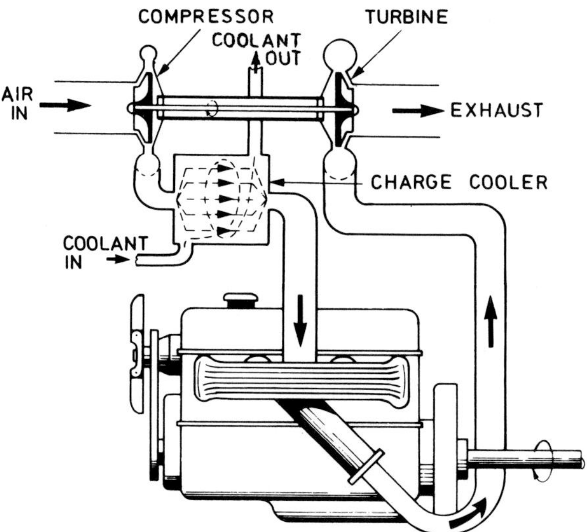

FIG. 8.13 Turbocharged system.

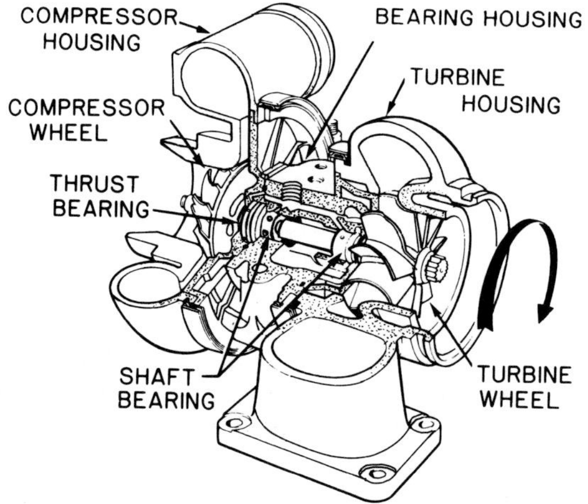

FIG. 8.14 Turbocharger.

aspirated. However, the compressor must be driven; the power for this may come from the engine crankshaft, mechanical supercharge, or from a turbine in the engine exhaust stream, turbocharge (see Figures 8.13 and 8.14).

In either case, the temperature as well as the pressure of the charge will be increased, and this is undesirable. It reduces the density increase achieved, and aggravates the stress level inside the engine. So a charge cooler may be fitted, cooling the heated charge either via the engine's cooling system or via atmospheric air. The former is more compact, but can cool the charge down to perhaps 100°C only. Air-to-air charge coolers can be bulky, as much as half as big as the engine radiators. But they can get the charge cooler, down to near atmospheric temperature.

Torque/Speed and Response Lag

Pressure charging aims for increase of power, not of efficiency. Turbocharging has small effect only upon efficiency, and this can go either way. Supercharging is intrinsically less efficient than turbocharging, because the compressor absorbs some of the useful engine power increase. This is particularly true at high-speed, light load conditions, when a mechanically driven compressor may absorb nearly as much power as at full load. Figure 8.15 illustrates the difference in fuel consumptions.

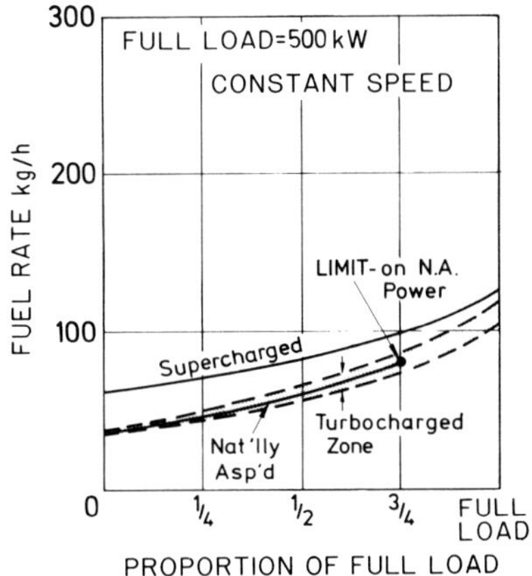

FIG. 8.15 Comparison of fuel rates.

But a disadvantage for turbocharging arises in the shape of engine power/speed characteristic to which it leads. It usually provides most power increase at high engine speed, resulting in an engine which does not pull well at low speed. Furthermore, at light engine load the turbocharger speed drops, and must rise again before the engine can accept full load; this leads to a lag in responding to sudden demands for increased power. If at the design stage smaller nozzles are fitted in the turbine housing, the gas flow is impeded and the pressure drop increased. So more power is taken from the gases, and the turbocharger is driven faster, giving more boost at all engine speeds. In the mid-speed range, power may now be satisfactory, but at high engine speed the engine may be over-boosted or the turbocharger over-speeded to destruction. To prevent this, a valve, wastegate, may be opened automatically as boost pressure rises too high, allowing some of the exhaust to bypass the turbine—see Figure 8.16. As a more complex alternative to small nozzles plus wastegate control, it is possible to make turbines of which the nozzle size is constantly variable while the engine is running. One possible mechanism for achieving this is shown at Figure 8.28 in the context of gas turbines.

The mechanism must operate reliably at bright red heats—which is not easy to

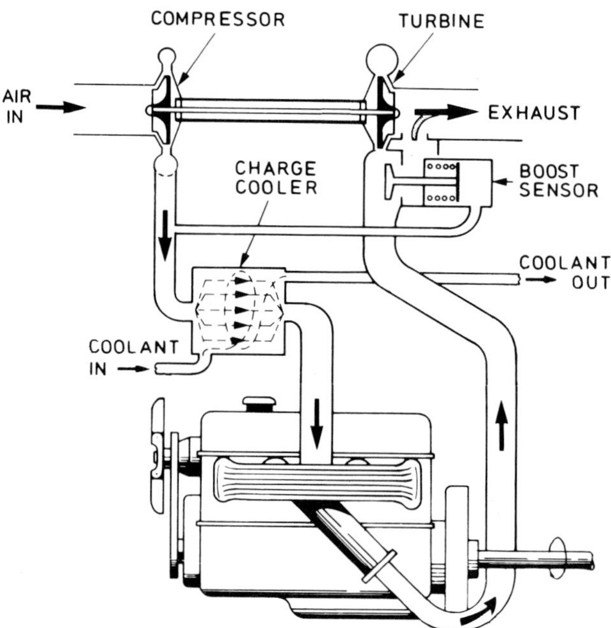

FIG. 8.16 Wastegate control.

achieve cheaply. Good control of the engine power/speed curve has been demonstrated, together with some reduction of turbocharger lag, on test-bed engines. The system is now beginning to become viable for production engines.

Stress Problems in Pressure Charged Engines

To achieve compactness, most MBT CI engines are fiercely boosted, well beyond the usual limits of commercial engine practice. This leads to both mechanical stressing within the engine, blowing it apart, and thermal stressing, burning/melting it. The designer must use all his skills to avoid trouble, including better detail design of cylinder head to cylinder joints, better layout of the internal cooling circuits, better materials in valves and piston crowns, oil cooling of the pistons, and charge cooling. But ultimately he has one card only left; he must lower the compression ratio (CR) within the engine.

In a hot, loaded engine, a compression ratio much lower than normal will ensure compression ignition; but low CR will introduce problems at cold start, and perhaps at sustained idle. To cater for these conditions, artificial charge warming may be necessary. There are at least four schemes for meeting this problem.

The first requires that the CR be continuously adjustable while the engine is running—high for start and low on heavy load. This can be accomplished by a special piston having two parts—a carrier attached to the con-rod in the usual way, and a shell bearing the piston crown and the rings (see Figure 8.17). The shell has a limited travel up and down relative to the carrier; so when it moves up, the crown moves further into the cylinder at idc, giving high CR and vice-versa. This

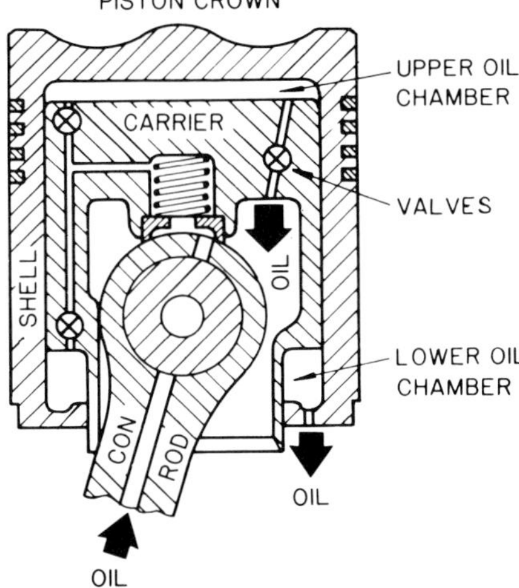

FIG. 8.17 Variable CR piston.

movement between the two piston parts is controlled by pumping oil in/out of two chambers between them. Typically it can control CR between about 8/1 and 16/1.

The other three schemes all build the engine with a fixed, low CR, and then provide for artifically warming the ingoing charge at start and idle as necessary.

The second scheme achieves this by spraying fuel into the ingoing air charge and igniting it electrically if engine temperatures are low enough to make compression ignition uncertain (see Figure 8.18). At high load conditions, this extra fuelling would be automatically turned off. Figure 8.19 shows the third scheme, Hyperbar.

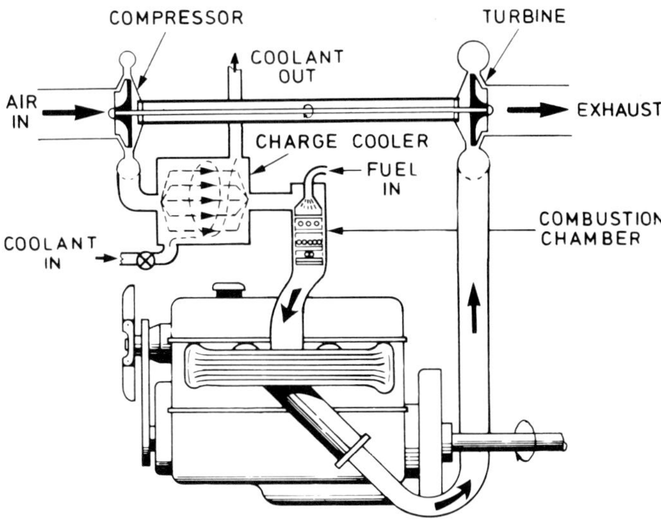

FIG. 8.18 Manifold heating.

Some of the air from the compressor is allowed to bypass the engine via an auxiliary combustion chamber. When this is fired, the turbine receives more energy and drives the compressor faster, so achieving more boost and a hotter charge. By tailoring the amount of bypass combustion, it may be possible to

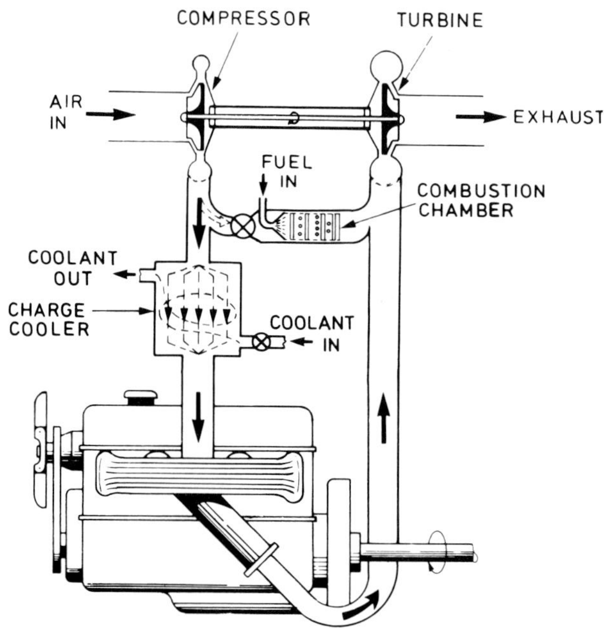

FIG. 8.19 Hyperbar system.

provide the preferred amount of boost at all engine speeds and loads, and so an attractive power/speed characteristic for vehicle drive. Also it maintains high compressor speed when the engine load is light, to achieve warm charge, and this helps to avoid the problem of response lag in accepting sudden power demands.

Figure 8.20 shows the fourth scheme which allows some of the hot exhaust gas to recirculate into the engine intake. Clearly this can maintain light load running indefinitely, but the achieving of cold start is less obvious. This is done by advancing the valve-timing of the engine during cranking. As a result, the not-yet-firing engine compresses its air charge on the compression stroke more than it expands it during expansion; so it pumps hot air back into its own inlet.

Three at least of these schemes are currently running in AFVs under development, but as yet the commercial world shows little more than polite interest in them. This highlights the gulf between commercial practice and military special engines.

Overall, the CI engine is a proven credible propulsion unit for AFVs, with known characteristics. Its greatest intrinsic weakness is its bulk, which does remain a problem despite remarkable advances. The future for it must rest with ever more intense pressure charging, leading perhaps to a 'combination' with the gas turbine.

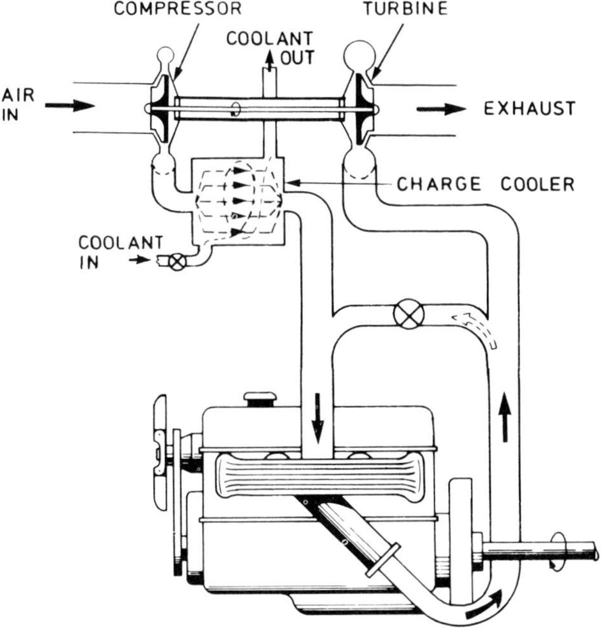

FIG. 8.20 Exhaust recirculation.

Gas Turbines

Components and Characteristics

In a piston engine, compression, combustion and expansion follow one another sequentially in the same space; in a gas turbine, all three proceed continuously and concurrently in different parts of the mechanism. This demands a separate compressor, combustion chamber and turbine (see Figure 8.21). The compressor and turbine may be radial flow machines, as in the turbocharger of Figure 8.14, or axial flow (see Figure 8.22). This shows an axial compressor; an axial turbine looks superficially similar, but it likely to have far fewer rows of blades.

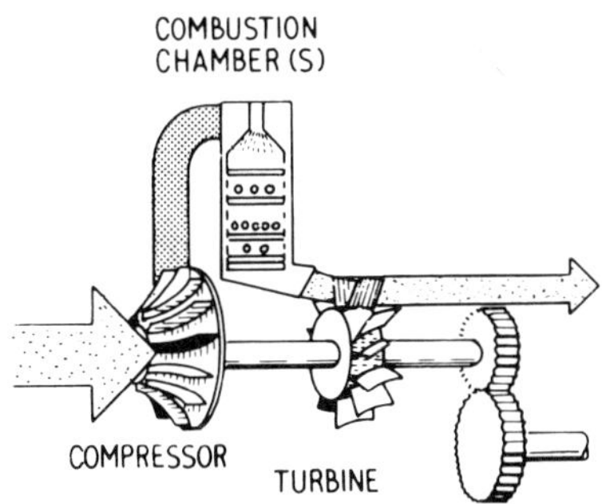

FIG. 8.21 Single-shaft gas turbine.

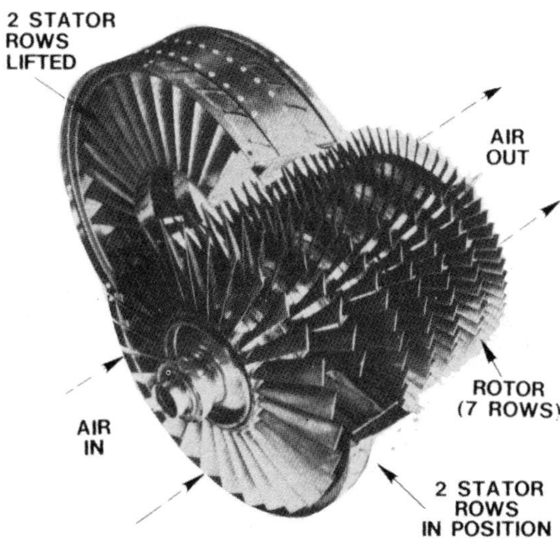

FIG. 8.22 Axial compressor.

Conceptually such a machine is simple; in reality it is much more difficult to ensure an excess of expansive, turbine power over compressive power than in a piston engine. So this engine type is very sensitive to design deficiencies and adverse environmental conditions. Because there are no valves, the flow is continuous and so the throughput is large in relation to engine bulk. Throughput relates to work output, and so the turbine is compact for its power. Again, no valves means no rise of pressure in combustion, unlike the piston engine. The maximum pressure in the engine is that achieved by compression only and so the construction is light by comparison with piston engines; thus it is a light engine for its power.

Because the gas flow and combustion are continuous, some of the hardware must experience temperatures comparable with the maximum gas temperature; in an intermittently firing piston engine, hardware temperatures are much less than gas maximum temperatures. Current blade materials restrict gas turbine temperature to around 1400 degrees K, about half of the piston engine value. The fuels burned are similar and so the air/fuel ratio must be much leaner in a gas turbine, typically about 55/1 compared with 20/1 in a CI engine. So the air throughput is large for a given power. This, taken with the sensitivity to adverse conditions, leads to bulky, low-pressure loss, air filters and inlet/exhaust ducting. But being internally aircooled, the gas turbine does not need the external cooling system that is associated with piston engines.

Twin-shaft Engines

If loading should cause the output speed of a piston engine to slow, the compression achieved is not affected; it is a function of the geometric build of the engine. But with the aerodynamic compressors used in turbochargers and gas turbines, the compression is very speed sensitive and so, if the compressor and output shafts are mechanically linked, a slowed output will lead to loss of compression. This makes the cycle ineffective, and so the output power of an engine of the type shown in Figure 8.21 decays steeply if speed is forced down, as shown in Figure 8.23.

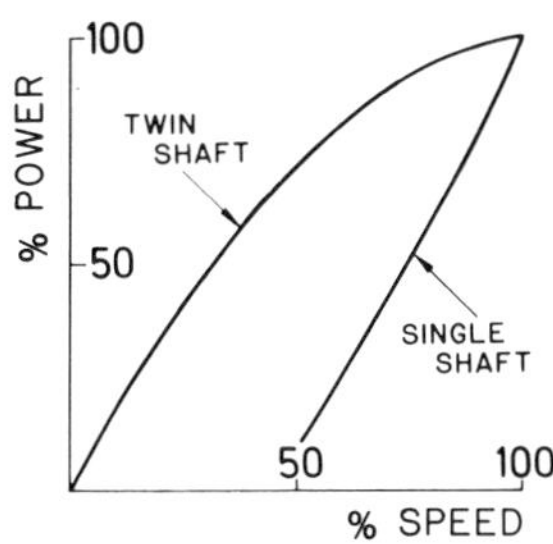

FIG. 8.23 Power/speed curves.

But if the single turbine be replaced by two mechanically independent ones, of which the first, high pressure, drives the compressor only, and the second, low pressure, the load (see Figure 8.24) the power/speed characteristic is changed.

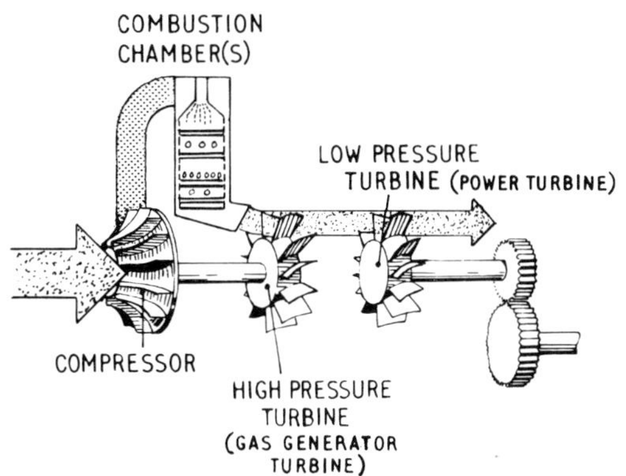

FIG. 8.24 Twin-shaft gas turbine.

Even if the output is loaded until it stalls, the compressor, or gas-generator, turbine can continue to run with speed only slightly reduced, providing an effective gas cycle; so the power is well maintained with falling speed (see Figure 8.23). Such a two-shaft engine has a power/speed characteristic automotively superior to that of a piston engine, and it is on this system that most automotive turbines are based.

Simple gas turbines can offer extreme compactness and lightness as bare engines. Their associated gas ducting and filters are bulkier than for piston engines, but this is more than offset by their freedom from an external engine cooling system and its associated cooling drive power. In two-shaft form they have an attractive power/speed characteristic, and having no pistons are relatively free from rubbing friction. So they are easy to crank at low temperatures and can have good cold-starting capability. Because their combustion is continuous, they are tolerant of a much wider range of fuels than either SI or CI engines.

But their greatest drawback rests in their fuel consumption. At all load levels they are thirstier than piston engines of the same power, but this is particularly so at low loads. In the quarter power region, where land vehicles spend much of their operating time, simple gas turbines are as much as three times as thirsty as CI engines of equal power. This is shown in Figure 8.25.

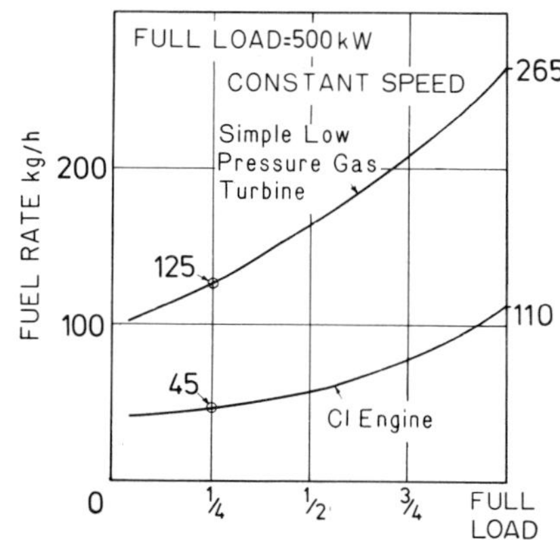

FIG. 8.25 Comparative fuel consumptions.

Heat Exchange

In the aircraft world, economy at near full load is the requirement, and this is met by engines combining a high pressure ratio with the highest gas temperatures that materials technology will allow; these are outside our interest. To achieve part-load economy as well, a different approach is necessary.

An inefficient engine must rid itself of its fuel energy somehow, either to its coolant or its exhaust. Gas turbines have no cooling system, so inefficiency reflects in a hot exhaust. If this energy be used to provide some part of the heating process after the compressor, the heating to be accomplished by the fuel is reduced, and hence the fuel consumption too. This is called heat exchange (see Figure 8.26).

The warm air from the compressor is heated by contact with the hot exhaust from the turbines. A heat exchanger can be either of two forms, a recuperator or a regenerator. The former has no moving parts; a car radiator provides an example of a hot-water-to-air recuperator, and it is easy to conceive a similar device working with hot exhaust gas and compressed air. Regenerators do have moving parts (see Figure 8.27). A disc(s), porous to air and gas flows is positioned with one edge in the warm air, the other in the hot gas, and rotated slowly. The disc material is continuously heated by the hot exhaust, and then moves into the air stream, where it gives up its heat to the warm air.

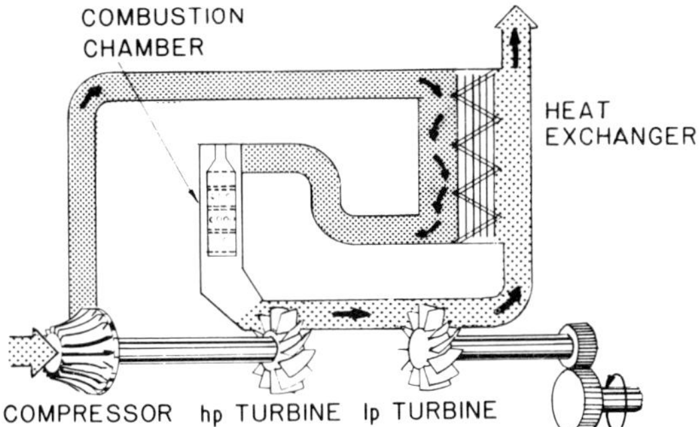

FIG. 8.26 Recuperative gas turbine.

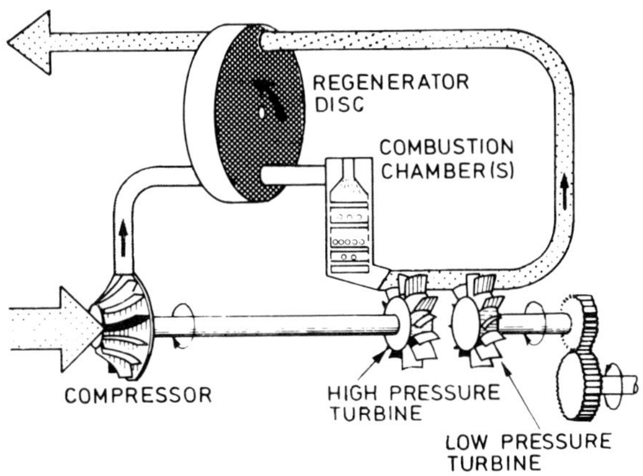

FIG. 8.27 Regenerative gas turbine.

Both of these systems have their pros and cons, and there is not yet enough practical experience of either in the gas turbine field to make firm choice between them. Recuperators tend to be bulky and difficult to keep clean in prolonged service. Regenerator materials must withstand continuous cycling, hot, then cold; ceramics are preferred. Rubbing seals must be provided over their surfaces to prevent the compressed air escaping directly into the exhaust ducts at atmospheric pressure. In practice, either sort of heat exchanger tends to rob the simple gas turbine of much of its compactness.

Variable Geometry

High gas turbine efficiency is dependent upon running with the highest possible gas temperature in the cycle. Much development effort has gone into developing the metal alloys currently available to withstand this, and continues to go into the development of viable ceramic components which will allow still higher temperatures. But inevitably, when an engine is driven lightly, the fuel input is reduced and consequently the top temperature tends to fall, with adverse effect on part-load economy. Recovery of waste heat via heat exchange certainly helps, but what is really wanted at part-load is a smaller engine, which may then continue to be driven flat-out, with high temperature and high efficiency.

Alternatively it might be possible to adjust the 'size' of the engine while it is running; the technology for doing this is called variable geometry (see Figure 8.28). Most automotive gas turbines include this system on their second, lp or free power turbine.

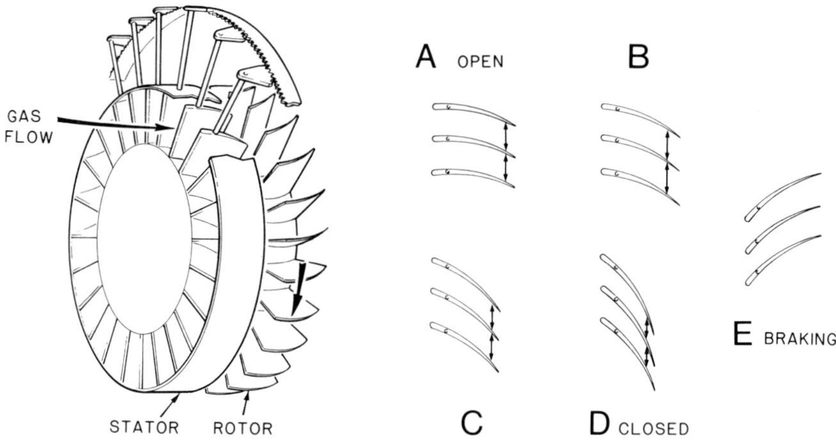

FIG. 8.28 Variable geometry.

In an axial turbine comprising one row each of stator and rotor blades, the stator blades are individually pivotted, their movements being geared together. As they pivot, the gas flow passage between them reduces from A through to D, effectively making the turbine 'smaller'. They are programmed to do this as the load is reduced and so, as the fuel flow is cut back, the air flow reduces too. So the gas temperature falls less than it would in an engine having fixed geometry; this helps to maintain good part-load economy. Furthermore, if the blades be pivotted round to position E, they tend to blow the rotor round backwards; this provides engine braking, otherwise lacking from gas turbines.

State of the Art

Most vehicular gas turbine prototypes incorporate heat exchange plus variable geometry on their power turbine at least. But currently they still cannot match the economy of a CI engine, as shown in Figure 8.29. So it is still not possible to buy such an engine commercially. But for propelling a MBT, economy is less important than compactness, and the Americans have decided upon a gas turbine in their M-1 or General Abrams vehicle. This engine incorporates both a recuperator and variable geometry, and is by any standards a sensationally compact unit. The bare engine has a bulk of about 1000 kW/m^3 compared with best CI military special values of about 800 kW/m^3; furthermore, it does not incur the bulk of an external

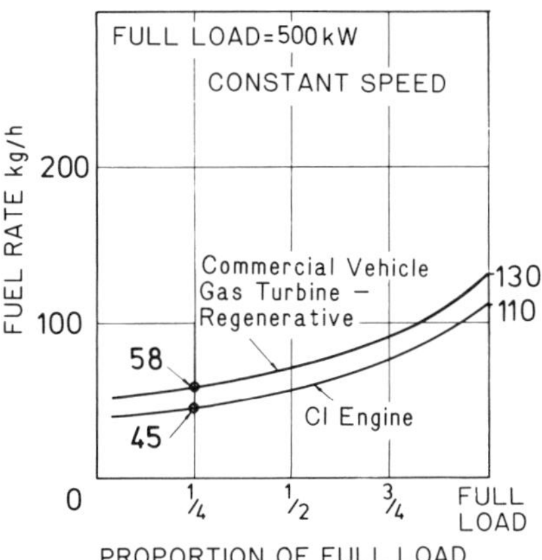

FIG. 8.29 Fuel consumption rates.

engine cooling system, nor the associated power loss to fan drives (8–10% of the bare engine power in a CI installation). But it remains thirstier than a CI engine, and when the bulk of a complete power train, including the fuel for a mission is assessed, the choice becomes unclear. At the present state of the art, the case for the gas turbine versus the CI engine in MBTs is arguable. Any fundamental difference is small enough to be subordinate to the development excellence of particular designs.

Overall, the technology of gas turbines is based in the aircraft world, whereas the development of piston engines tends to be centred in the ground vehicle industry. With present-day technology, it is true that gas turbines are intrinsically more expensive to manufacture, but no less important is the fact that the staff involved in their development have for the most part aircraft industry backgrounds, and as a result a quite different order of cost-consciousness. An engine of any technical type from such a background will be expensive.

Power-for-power, aircraft industry based gas turbines cost about five times as much as standard commercial vehicle CI engines; limited production military special CI engines cost about two to two-and-half times as much as their commercial counterparts. Commercial CI engines in their turn are about five times as expensive as car SI engines on a power-for-power basis. These cost differences reflect not only the differing degrees of complexity and differing standards of manufacture, but also the differing numbers of units produced in each type. Large military engines have to be 'specials', as we have stressed, but the cost of their procurement is high. Differences of detail design from commercial engines we must have, but we just cannot afford to embark upon the development of engines conceptually different from those developed for commercial roles.

Future Engines

Adiabatic and Compound Engines

There remains considerable development potential in both the gas turbine and the CI engine. For the former, the key to further progress lies almost certainly in the development of ceramic components for the combustion chamber and the turbine. These, by allowing operation at higher temperatures than metals, will lead to improved engine efficiencies and hence lower fuel consumptions. The use of similar materials in a CI engine might allow it to dispense with some or all of its cooling system: the resulting engine is called an adiabatic engine. By itself, this would not make the engine much more efficient; most of the heat saved from the coolant would come out not as extra work, but as a hotter exhaust. It would, however, save on cooling system bulk and fan drive power, and allow the engine to accept more boosting.

As CI engines are turbocharged more intensely, the available turbine power from the exhaust gases begins to exceed markedly the power needed to drive the compressor. Even at current boost levels, it may be found necessary to jettison exhaust energy at the higher engine speeds via a waste-gate to keep the engine out of trouble. As engines capable of withstanding higher boosts are developed, it may prove viable to extract all the energy available in the exhaust and, having taken that part necessary for driving the compressor, feed the rest into the output shaft—a compound engine, as shown in Figure 8.30.

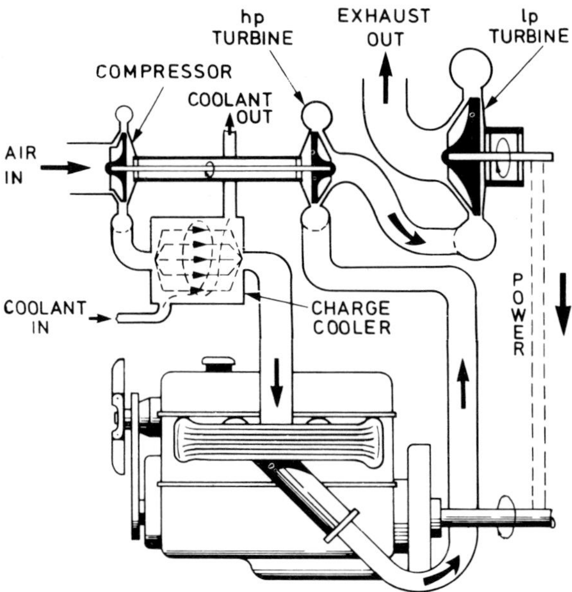

FIG. 8.30 Piston-turbo compound.

This concept is not new, but it does now seem to be nearing commercial viability. The idea lends itself to combination with the adiabatic engine; for then, the extra exhaust gas energy delivered by the latter could be recouped by the turbine(s). Fully developed, such an engine ought to have a specific fuel consumption about 18% lower than that of the best current CI engines. Indeed, it represents about the most economical engine concept at vehicular powers that is conceivable within the framework of our present technology. Furthermore, it should give engine bulks better than the best current CI values, and approaching those of gas turbines. But its appearance should not be anticipated much before the last few years of the present century.

The future for propelling military ground vehicle lies with IC engines, be they pressure-charged piston engines, gas turbines or compounds. Fossil oil will run out, but we have the technology to synthesise substitutes; it is only a matter of when it becomes economic to do so.

Annex A to Chapter 8

ANALYTICAL EXAMPLES

On earth, 1 tonne mass weighs 9.81 kN force (weight). Thus, a MBT having mass 55 tonnes weights 540 kN.

From experience, power/weight of 2 kW/kN (see page 00) implies a maximum road speed of about 80 km/h; at this speed, specific rolling resistance on road is about 8%.

Thus: Rolling resistance = W × Sp. RR = 540 kN × 0.08 = 43.2 kN.
For an AFV, air resistance is negligible (see page 00).
On a slight road upgrade, say 1 in 100 or 0.57°;
Gradient resistance = W sin θ = 540 kn × 0.01 = 5.4 kN
Thus: Road load = Rolling + Air + Gradient resistance = 48.6 kN
and: Tractive effort = Road load . . . to maintain steady motion.
Now: Road power = Tractive effort × Road speed
and: Given road power is 1080 kW (see page 00)
where: 1 kW = 1 kN m/s so Road power = 1080 kN m/s.
Then: 1080 kN m/s = 48.6 × Road speed
giving: Road speed at maximum power in high gear = 22.2 m/s
where: 1 m/s = 3.6 km/h so:
Road speed at maximum power in high gear = 80 km/h.
For the same vehicle on a 38° upgrade with Sp. rolling resistance of 10%:
Road load = 540 kN × (sin 38° + 0.1) = 386 kN.
Thus: Road speed at maximum power in low gear
= 1080 kN m/s ÷ 386 kN = 2.8 m/s
and since maximum engine power coincides with maximum engine speed:
Maximum road speed in low gear = 2.8 m/s = 10 km/h.

Referring to Figures 8.11 what is the sfc of the CI engine thereon, at full power of 500 kW, and at quarter power? A larger CI engine, of maximum power 1500 kW, has the same sfcs as the engine of Figure 8.11; what would be its rate of fuel consumption at full power?
Refer Fig. 8.11: Fuel rate at 500 kW = 110 kg/h.
Whence: sfc = 110 kg/h ÷ 500 kW = 0.22 kg/kW h.
Similarly at quarter power: sfc = 0.36 kg/kW h.
For 1500 kW engine with sfc 0.22 kg/kW h: Fuel consumption = 330 kg/h.

9

Transmissions

Requirements

Chapter 8 covered the engine as part of the power train. This chapter will deal with the drive-line, which distributes the engine's power to the road wheels or sprockets, modifying the torque/speed characteristic as necessary to match the engine output to vehicle demand. Major sub-systems in the drive-line include:

> Change-speed gearboxes; clutches, couplings and converters; universal and constant velocity joints; differentials; steering systems for tracked vehicles.

As the nature of the ground and the gradient vary, the speed of a land vehicle must vary, even if it be flat-out all the time. So we would wish that the complete power train should be able to develop its maximum power, on demand, at any output speed over a wide range of speeds, a constant power engine. All real engines fail to achieve this aim, as explained in Chapter 8 (see also Figure 9.1).

So the drive-line must provide the driver with the facility to keep the engine within a restricted range, not too far from the maximum engine power speed, over the whole wide range of vehicle operating road speeds. Changing gear achieves just this object. Figure 9.2 shows how, by using a five speed gearbox typical of modern private car practice, the engine's curve is repeated five times. The ideal 100% power level is now met five times instead of just once, and the power drop at the points in between is much reduced.

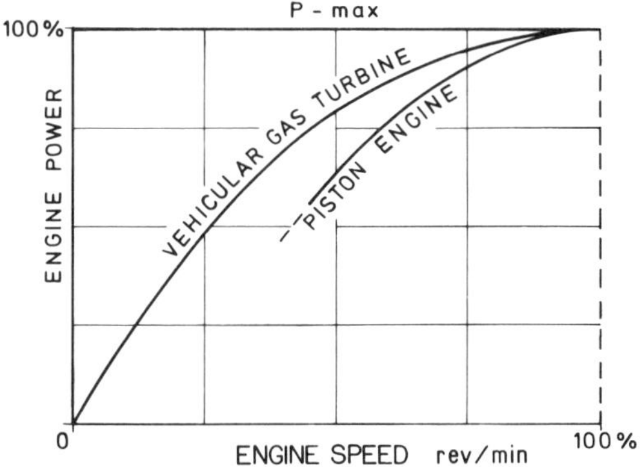

FIG. 9.1 Vehicle and engine performances.

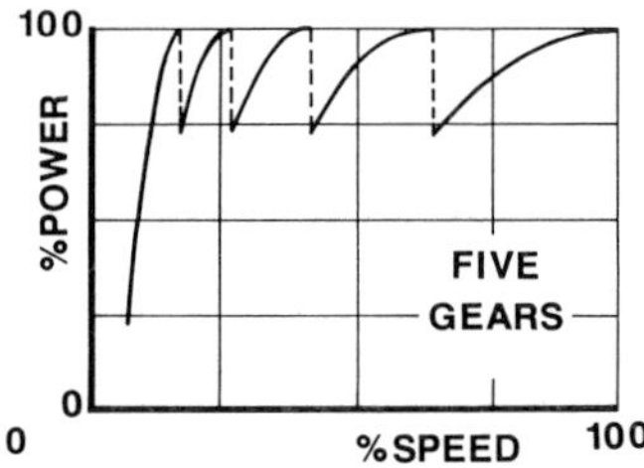

FIG. 9.2 Five gears.

It remains perfectly possible for the driver to operate the engine outside this restricted speed range if he so wishes; in fact he will often do so, when the circumstances demand a power a lot less than maximum. But if the demand for high power suddenly arises, he can have something not too far removed from maximum power available to him, by getting into the right gear for the road speed the vehicle has at the time.

Other vehicles might require a wider range of road speeds, or availability at all times of a greater percentage of maximum power, than does the private car. A fast tank may want its maximum power on tap over a range of ground speeds of as much as 20/1. A heavily laden truck, with a poorish Power/Weight ratio, cannot afford to be without more than about 15% of its best power at any speed. For either of these cases, the remedy is to provide more gears.

Figure 9.3 represents an imaginary vehicle with no less than forty gears! The power availability is very close to 100% of the maximum right down to about 3% of maximum road speed. But to drive it would tax the ingenuity of any driver, or any automatic change mechanism, and furthermore, it would spend much of its total running time in the process of gear changing, out of gear while so doing, and hence with no, or much reduced power at its wheels/sprockets. This would defeat the object of what we are trying to accomplish.

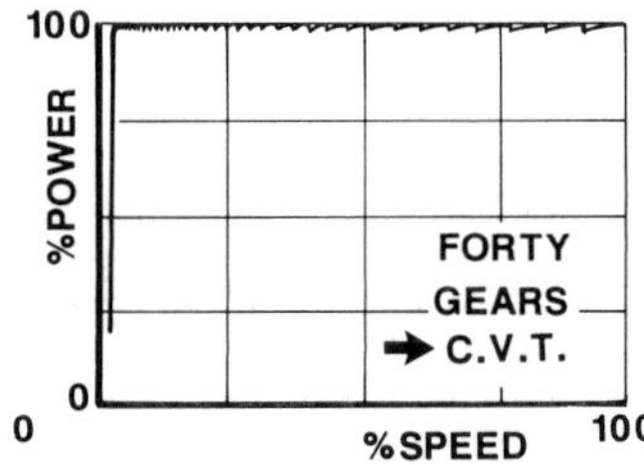

FIG. 9.3 Forty gears.

However, if the number of gears were increased *much* further, the steps between them would eventually become *infinitely* small, and the result would be a Continuously Variable Transmission (CVT), having no steps, no breaks in the power flow at all. The engine could then always be run at maximum power speed when performance was required, regardless of the road speed, or at maximum economy instead when the power demand was lighter. Such a system represents the ultimate drive-line, but it is not easy to make it work in practice. It is not uncommon in vehicles like mopeds, and is just entering the field of light private cars. But for MBTs, it is a long way off, not in this century anyhow. CVT must not be confused with the widely available automatic systems having *stepped* ratios, in vehicles like Challenger, Abrams and Leopard 2 and automatic private cars.

Change-Speed Gearboxes

The commonest form of gearbox employs spur gears, as shown in Figure 9.4. The gears may have straight-cut teeth, as on pair F-L, single helical teeth, as on the other pairs illustrated, or double helical teeth, not shown. Straight-cut gears are cheap but noisy. Single helicals are quiet, but develop big end-wise thrusts. Double helicals are quiet and thrust-free but expensive.

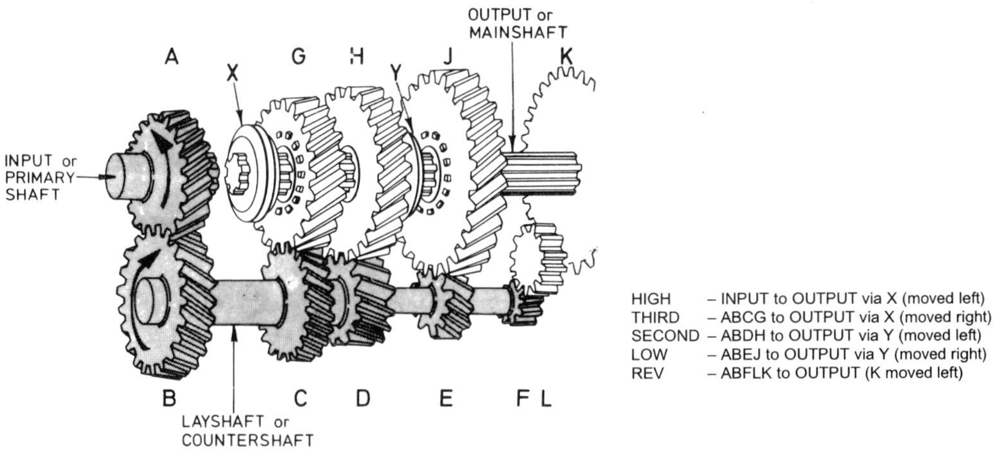

FIG. 9.4 Four-speed spur gearbox.

In the layout shown, power enters from the left, transfers down to the counter or lay shaft via gears A-B and leaves at the end remote from the input. Such a layout is ideally suited to a vehicle having front engine and rear-wheel drive. In other vehicles, transverse engined front-wheel drive, for example, it may be convenient to take the output from the centre of the second shaft. Such a gearbox does not really have an idle or lay shaft, but the term 'layshaft gearbox' is widely used to describe all spur gearboxs.

The gear pairs C-G, D-H and E-J run together continuously—constant mesh gears. Gear K is shown out-of-mesh with L; it has to be slid along the splines on the output shaft for engagement, sliding mesh gear. The constant mesh gears on the output shaft turn continuously, but transmit drive to the shaft only when the relevant dog-clutch X or Y is engaged. Figure 9.4 shows the engagement schedule. It is impossible to run with two different gears solidly engaged at once. So there has to be a short, but finite, interruption of the power flow while gears are being changed. As a new gear is engaged, the speeds of the components to be meshed will need to be matched. To make this easy, one end of the gearbox is disconnected, usually the input end, by means of a clutch. This is necessary for starting from rest too. The speeds can be adjusted, by driver skill or by small friction clutches, not shown, inside X and Y, synchromesh. These is also real current interest in adjusting the gear speeds by electronic control of the engine speed, with clutch engaged; this is not in general use yet.

In high gear, the gearbox of Figure 9.4 will rotate its output at the same speed as its input, direct drive. If gear C were given more teeth, and gear G less, they could drive the output faster than the input; this is overdrive. It allows fast, relaxed road running at low engine speed, which is conducive to good fuel economy.

Most automatic gearboxes are based upon epicyclic gear trains, as shown in Figure 9.5. If the sun be driven, and a load resists the carrier, the annulus will spin idly and no power is transmitted. But if now the annulus be locked, by some sort of friction brake or clutch, the carrier will be driven positively against the load, more slowly than the sun.

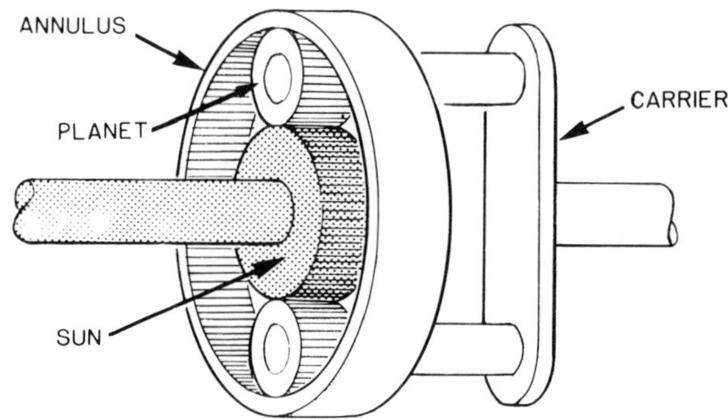

FIG. 9.5 Simple epicyclic.

Alternatively, the sun and carrier could be clutched together. Then the output would be driven positively at input speed. So this one gearset can offer two output speeds for one given input speed. If the output from its carrier were to be used as the input to the sun of a second epicyclic, a choice of four output speeds could result from just two gearsets.

Such a system promises compactness. Furthermore, gear changing does not demand accurate speed adjustments on intermeshing teeth; the change can be 'soft' and easy to manage, automatically if so required. Additionally, it is possible to begin the engagement of a new gear ratio before the one previously in use is completely released. This allows the transmission of some, not all, of the engine power throughout the duration of a change, referred to as hot shift. This point is very valuable in a vehicle experiencing high, off-road road loads. For in the very low gear then necessary, the range of road speeds attainable is very small, and if power is lost during a change, the vehicle may slow to such an extent that selection of the next gear becomes impossible. The drawback of epicyclic boxes lies in their power losses. Four speeds from two epicyclics would need four clutches. Two would be nominally disengaged, but incurring some rubbing losses. In complex epicyclic gearboxes, these losses, together with those from a large number of idling gears, can approach 20% of the input power.

Clutches, Couplings and Converters

Friction Clutches

When starting from rest, drive interruption is necessary between the engine and the gearbox. Most commonly, this is achieved by the use of a friction clutch, directly under driver control. Figure 9.6 shows the layout of a typical clutch for light vehicle duty.

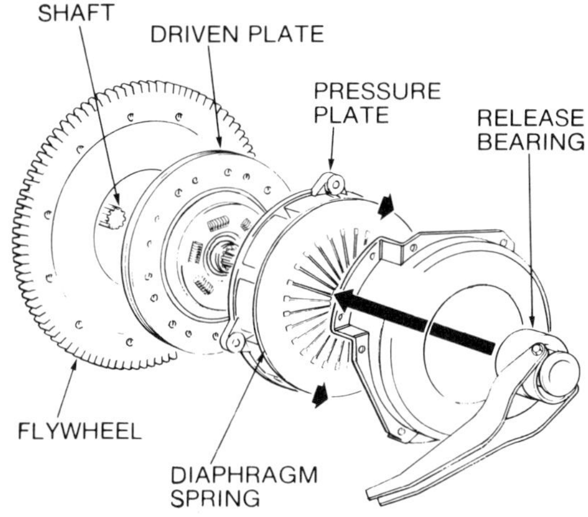

FIG. 9.6 Friction clutch.

The driven plate is splined to a shaft which drives into the gearbox. The drive comes from the engine flywheel and is passed by friction into the driven plate. To maintain this friction, the driven plate is sandwiched between the flywheel and the pressure plate, the latter being pressed to the left by the diaphragm spring. To release the clutch, the driver presses the release bearing to the left. Leftwards movement of the inner radius of the spring causes its outer radius to flex to the right, taking the pressure off the pressure plate and the driven plate. The connection between the driver's foot and the release bearing may be achieved mechanically or hydraulically.

Fully engaged, such a clutch transmits power with near 100% efficiency; the engine torque, or pulling effort, too is transmitted unchanged. When the clutch slips, the output speed and power are lessened. But the transmitted torque is unchanged. Clutches are not torque-converters.

Centrifugal Clutches

In some vehicles, a friction clutch is controlled automatically, rather than by the driver; British Chieftain and Scorpion are examples. The friction material is arranged as the outside of a cylinder, split axially into a series of sectors. These are driven by the engine, and restrained from flying outwards centrifugally by springs. But as engine speed rises, the springs are overcome, and the friction surfaces move out, into contact with the inside of a surrounding drum, which they then drive. So the clutch is free at engine idle speeds, but engages progressively as the speed rises. Because the driver cannot 'pre-rev' the engine, before the clutch begins to engage, ultimate starting ability on gradients is restricted by this system. But in any case the current trend is towards the use of a hydrokinetic coupling or coupling/converter between the engine and the gearbox.

Hydrokinetic Couplings and Converters

In a hydrokinetic coupling, or fluid flywheel, the engine drives a vaned wheel, the pump, which in turn gives whirling motion to oil; the moving oil then impinges on another vaned wheel, the turbine, and drives it. The layout and parts are shown in Figures 9.7 and 9.8. At idle engine speeds, this effect will be insufficient to drive the output and the vehicle, but as the driver accelerates the engine, the drive will be smoothly taken up.

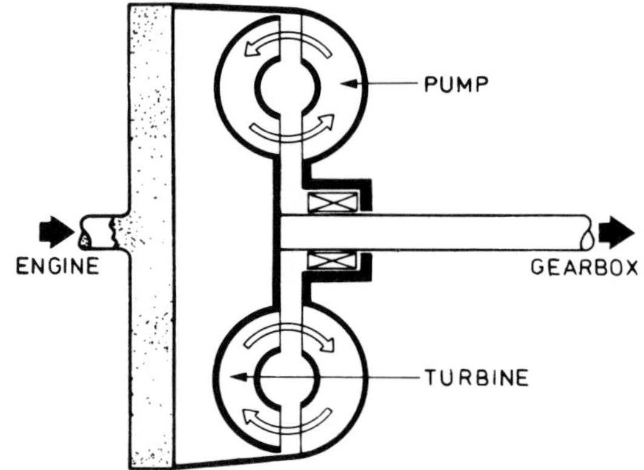

FIG. 9.7 Hydrokinetic coupling (schematic).

FIG. 9.8 Hydrokinetic coupling (photo).

The torque (turning effect) taken from the oil by the output is equal and opposite to that provided by the input. Were this not so, the oil would accelerate until it was. But the output speed will be less than the input speed; there is slip. As speed rises, the slip reduces, but output power is always less than input power and the difference appears as heat in the oil. But unlike the friction material in the plate of a clutch, the oil may be readily cooled externally; so prolonged heavy slipping can be made acceptable.

In a converter/coupling, often just called a torque-converter, there is a third member, the stator, as shown in Figures 9.9 and 9.10. When the oil is moving steadily, not accelerating, the sum of the torques on all three components has to balance out. So generally the torque on the output is not equal and opposite to that on the input alone; it can be more or less. In automotive designs it is made to be more. There is, of course, no way in which the output power could be made to exceed the input power, so when the torque is multiplied, the speed must be reduced; again there is slip.

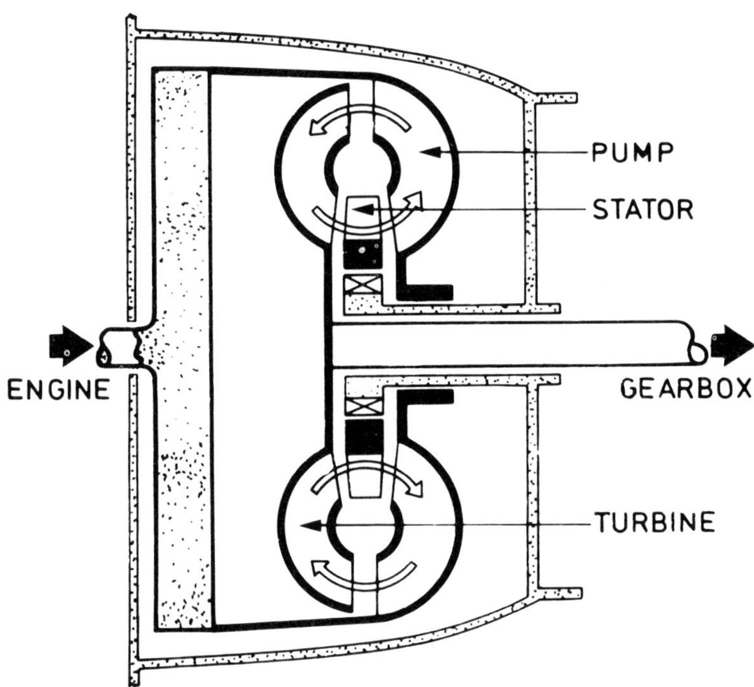

FIG. 9.9 Coupling/converter (schematic).

In practice an automotive torque converter can develop an output torque up to two or two-and-a-half times its input torque. This happens when the output is stalled, vehicle stationary, and the engine is driven hard. When the vehicle begins to move, and the output speed starts to rise towards input speed, the torque begins to equalise. The stator is now unnecessary. So it is usually mounted on a one-way clutch, or freewheel. At low output speeds it is locked to the casing, and contributes to the output torque; the whole assembly acts as a torque converter. At

FIG. 9.10 Coupling/converter (photo).

higher speeds the stator spins idly in the oil flow; it is now inactive, and the whole assembly acts as a fluid coupling.

Thus a torque-converter provides both an automatic clutch at starting from rest and a degree of 'lowering' of the gear in use, automatically without changing gear. In the latter capacity it is equivalent to perhaps one-and-a-half extra gears in the gearbox. If adequately cooled, it can also allow for continuous low-speed movement. It is usually combined with an automatic-change epicyclic gearbox, perhaps with manual over-ride, and the combination gives great ease of driving. On the debit side, however, when slipping it does introduce considerable power loss into the drive-line, additional to those mentioned earlier in epicyclic gearboxes. Not only does the loss degrade the power actually available at the sprockets for propelling the vehicle, but it adds to the heat load from radiators, charge coolers, etc. which has to be ejected from the hull. So the problem of achieving credibly armoured top-decks in AFVs is aggravated. For these reasons, torque-converters are often mechanically locked up solid when the vehicle is running in the higher gears. This leaves them free to exercise their greatest value in low gear, when starting from rest, particularly on steep upgrades, and when moving very slowly.

Hydrostatic Drives

In hydrokinetic drives, the power is transmitted by very large flows of oil, moving with fairly small pressure changes. Alternatively, small amounts of oil can be pumped through large pressure changes. The latter concept leads to hydrostatic drive. The principle is shown in Figures 9.11(a) and (b).

If the rotor in Figure 9.11(a) is driven round about its fixed central support shaft, the radial piston will move in and out, because the casing or stator is eccentric to the rotor. From 9 o'clock to 3 o'clock it will move out, and from 3 to 9 back in. As it moves out, the port at the top of the cylinder will be aligned with the inlet port on the top of the support shaft, and with the delivery port on the underside as it moves back in. So oil will be alterately sucked in and driven out. This is a form of oil pump.

Suppose now that high-pressure oil be supplied to the delivery port. It will try to

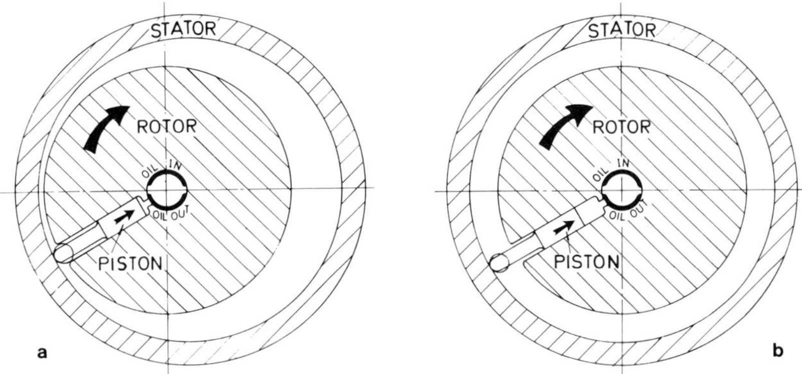

FIG. 9.11 Variable displacement pump principle.

drive the piston out, and this can be accomplished only by the rotor's turning anti-clockwise. So the same mechanism can double as a hydraulic motor. Two of them, interconnected by a pair of oil pipes, can transmit power over a distance. If the oil pipes are made flexible, relative movement between the pump and the motor becomes possible, leading to the concept of a separate hydrostatic motor at each wheel station, all energised by one common engine driven pump.

Now suppose the pump casing be moved to the left, as shown in Figure 9.11(b). When it becomes concentric with the rotor, the in-out motion of the piston ceases, and pumping stops. As it moves towards concentricity, the pumping is progressively reduced and, for a fixed pump rotational speed, the hydraulic motor will slow down. At constant input speed, this system can give continuously variable output speed. If the stator moves leftwards beyond concentricity, the motor output will reverse. This is exactly what we require for vehicular drive.

This looks like an ideal vehicle transmission system. Unfortunately, it cannot compete at present with mechanical systems in the matter of power loss. So its use is confined to a few special applications, including tracked vehicle steering, as we shall see. In practice, the system described would have not one but several radial pistons in the rotors of pump and motor. There are also very many other layouts of pump and motor for achieving the same effect.

The use of an engine-driven generator to energise electric motors at the wheel stations is another solution to the transmission problem, capable, like hydrostatics, of steplessly varying the transmission ratio. But it too fails to compete with mechanical and hydrokinetic/mechanical systems on grounds of power loss, cost and bulk. It has found limited application, diesel/electric rail traction for example, and at least one wheeled AFV. But it seems unlikely to become usual.

Universal and Constant Velocity Joints

Universal Joints

In general, the gearbox in a vehicle will be fairly rigidly mounted, while the wheel stations will be moving up and down on the suspension; additionally some or all of them may be required to steer. So the drive-line has to accommodate changes of both relative position and relative angle between its two ends. In a mechanical system, this demands universal joints of some sort.

The Hookes joint is widely used. Usually, the input and output shafts terminate in two-pronged forks, disposed at right-angles to one another. Their open ends are bridged by a cruciform member, pivoted in the fork ends. Each fork can pivot in one plane about the centre member, and taken together, these movements, at right-angles to one another provide complete articulation in any plant. This arrangement can transmit power with a large angular displacement between the two shafts. But if the input is rotated steadily, the motion of the output will undergo cyclic speed fluctuations, except when the two shafts are pefectly aligned.

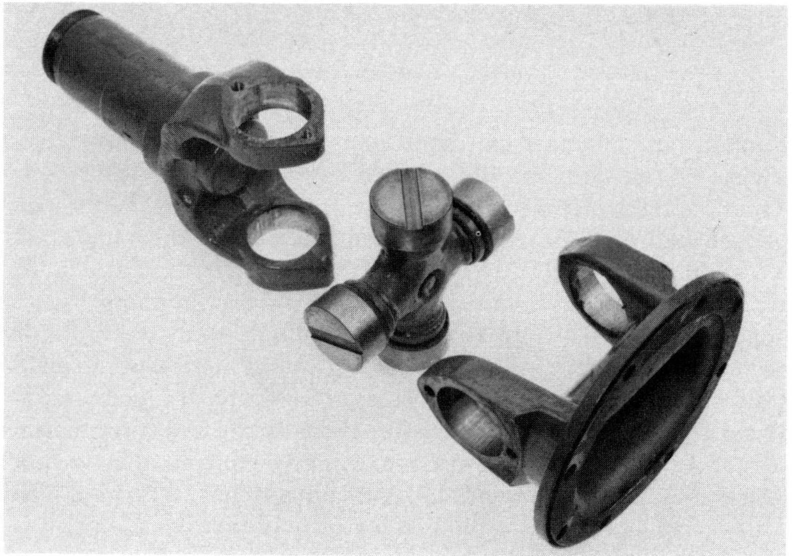

FIG. 9.12 Hookes joint.

To achieve steady rotation on the output, two Hookes joints may be used in series. So long as the angles made by the intermediate shaft with the input and output are equal, steady output will result. Such an arrangement can handle the problem of a driven rear axle, or a driven wheel station jumping up and down on the suspension. The deflection can be shared between the two joints. But if a driven wheel is required to steer too, the resultant angular changes will tend to be concentrated in the outboard joint. Then the angles are not equal, and the resultant speed variations in the driven, steered wheel may upset the handling of the vehicle.

Constant Velocity Joints

To overcome this problem, constant velocity joints may be used. Figures 9.14 illustrates a Tracta joint, which has been used in some wheeled AFVs. Although now obsolescent, and superseded by superior modern designs of joint, it is the easiest to understand.

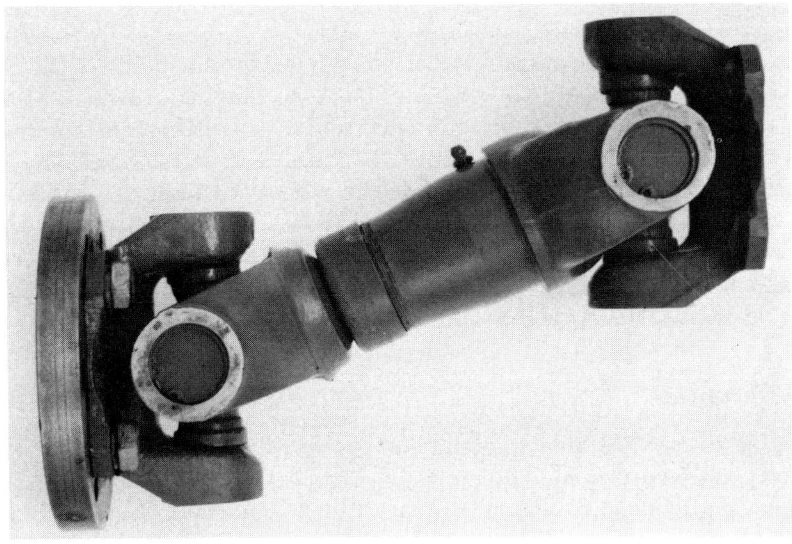

FIG. 9.13 Double Hookes joint.

FIG. 9.14 Tracta joint.

As in the double Hookes joint, the input and output shafts terminate in forks. In these, the two central members pivot; this gives articulation in one plane. But the two central members themselves can pivot about one another, in the other plane. Effectively, this is a double Hookes joint, with the central shaft greatly shortened. Thus the whole joint can fit into the hub of a steered, driven wheel allowing the steering angle changes to be shared between its two halves.

In a Tracta joint, the driving torques are transmitted via rubbing, sliding surfaces, and this incurs wear problems. More modern joints, Rzeppa for example, replace this sliding action by the rolling of balls in grooves. This makes them more mechanically viable, and it is this development that is largely responsible for the general acceptance of modern front-wheel drive cars.

Differentials

When a wheeled vehicle makes a turn, the wheels on the inside of the bend have less far to go than those on the outside, because they are turning at a smaller radius. Rather less obviously, with conventional front-wheel steer, the rear wheels will travel less far than the front ones, because, to some extent, they 'cut the corner'. If the drive-line does not allow the wheels to turn at different speeds, stresses will build up in the system, called 'wind-up'. Ultimately, these will be relieved by slipping of one or more of the wheels on the ground. These stresses can be very damaging to the tyres and the drive-line, and the ultimate slip can cause handling problems. Differentials can prevent them.

Bevel Differential

Figure 9.15 illustrates the most common of the differential mechanisms, though there are several other forms. The input drives a carrier, which carries bevel planet gears. These planets can rotate in the carrier, but in normal run they do not. They merely rotate with the carrier as though there were a solid part of it. So they force

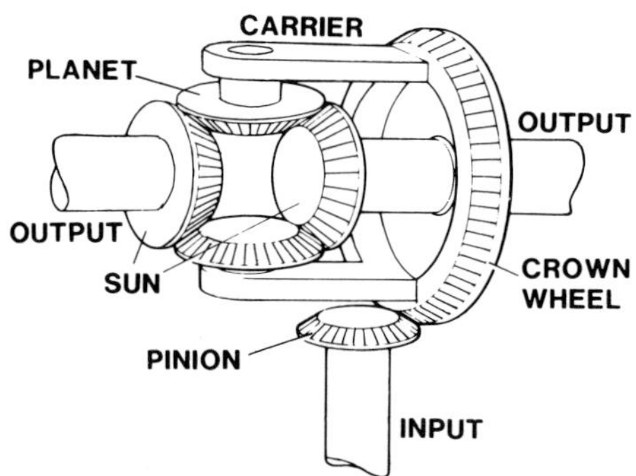

FIG. 9.15 Bevel differential (schematic).

the bevel suns to rotate, and these in turn drive the output shafts, at equal speeds. But should circumstances demand unequal output speeds, this can be accommodated. For then the planets can spin in the carrier; this causes one sun to speed up and the other to slow by equal amounts. This bevel differential is the mechanism found in the drive axles of the majority of road vehicles. Figure 9.16 shows an example.

Differential Lock

The provision of a differential between the drive wheels on the opposite sides of a wheeled road vehicle is very necessary, but it does introduce problems. Should tyre/ground adhesion be lost on one side of the vehicle, then there can be no torque transmitted in the output to that side. But a characteristic of simple differentials is that they transmit equal torques to both their outputs. So in this condition, no

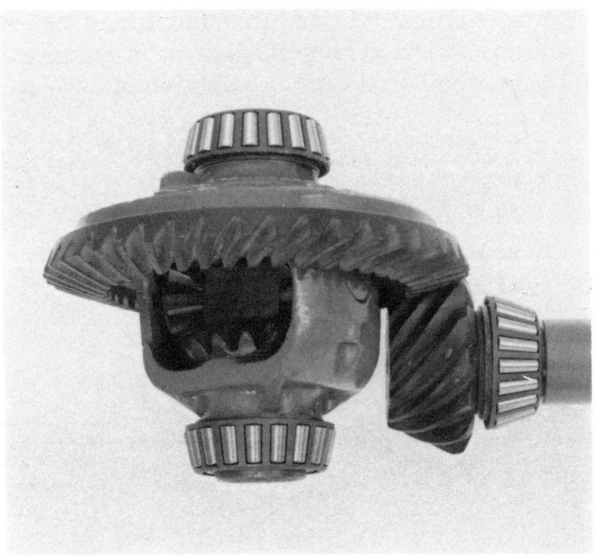

FIG. 9.16 Bevel differential (photo).

torque is transmitted to the other side either. Though the vehicle may still have good adhesion on one side, it can achieve no traction. In tracked vehicles, differentials often provide the basis of the steering system, as we shall see later, and if the going be such as to encourage the vehicle not to run straight, the differential will allow this. So tracked AFVs will often tend to 'drift' down the camber of roads, and require continual steering corrections to restrain them.

Sometimes differential locks may be built in. These may be directly under the control of the driver, or may operate automatically under high torque conditions, which are likely to provoke wheelspin. Lock is usually achieved by locking one of the outputs to the carrier. If that output is forced to turn at exactly carrier speed, then the other one will do so too. For driver control, it is usual to provide a dog-clutch on the outside of the main input gear to the carrier. When engaged, mechanically, electrically, pneumatically or hydraulically by the driver, it locks one output to the carrier. For automatic lock-up, friction clutches are provided inside the carrier, between the carrier itself and the back faces of the bevel sun gears. Under high torques, the interaction of the gearteeth between the planets and the suns tends to force the latter apart, and this action squeezes the clutch plates together, locking up the differential.

All-wheel Drive

In cross-country wheeled vehicles drive by more than one axle is usual. But if road use too is envisaged, differentials should certainly be incorporated on the axles side-to-side. To inhibit on-road wind-up, the various driven axles should also be allowed different speeds. This can be arranged by providing fore-and-aft differentials between them, or by using one drive only when road-running and declutching the other(s). Figures 9.17 and 9.18 illustrates two such schemes as applied to 4 × 4 vehicles. In the first, four-wheel drive is engaged only when LOW range is selected in the gearbox. In the other, selection of LOW range locks up the centre differential.

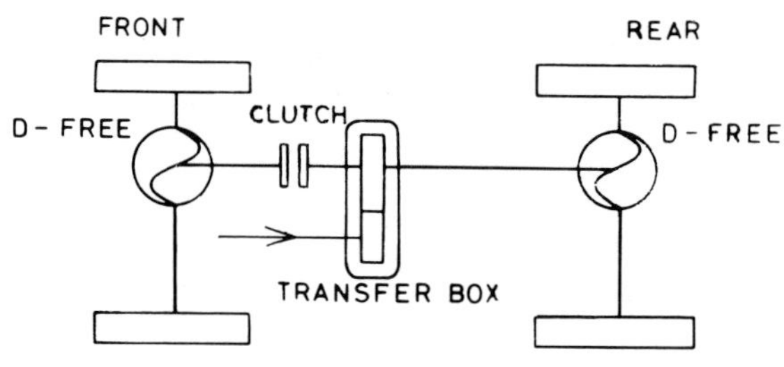

FIG. 9.17 4 × 4 layout.

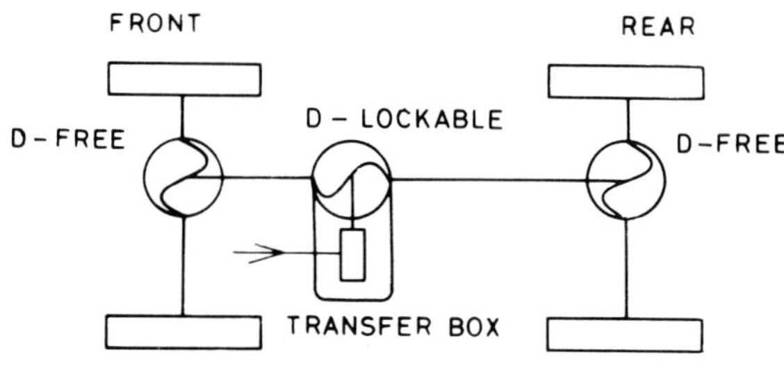

FIG. 9.18 4 × 4 layout.

To maximise off-road agility, all the differentials should ideally have lock-up available; this is true for tracked vehicles too. But considerations of cost and complexity preclude the adoption of this optimum solution in the majority of real vehicles.

Steering Mechanisms for Track-Layers

There are four systems available for steering track-layers:

Auxiliary steering wheels,
Track setting,
Articulation of the vehicle hull and
Skid steering.

In practice, many vehicles have incorporated more than one of these. For half-tracks, auxiliary steering wheels are the obvious choice. Track setting involves bending the tracks by steering some of the road wheels. It has been used on light vehicles, but needs back-up by some other system for making sharp turns. Articulation tends to be vulnerable and difficult to install in a fighting vehicle.

This leaves skid steer, which implies adjustment of the track speed on one side of the vehicle relative to the other, as the commonest system in tracked AFVs.

Clutch-Brake Steering

The simplest mechanism for skid steer is clutch-brake (see Figure 9.19). After the change ratio gearbox, the drive splits towards each sprocket, with a clutch and a brake included on each side. Disengagement of the left clutch would make the vehicle steer left. The sharpness of the turn would depend upon the severity of the

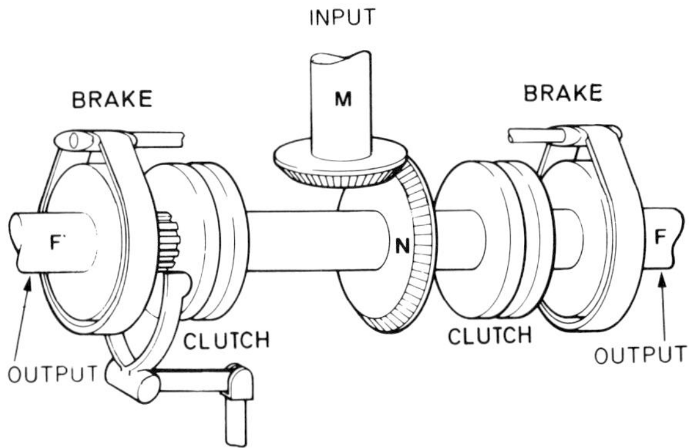

FIG. 9.19 Clutch-brake system.

going and the length/width (L/C) ratio of the vehicle; but usually it would be a gentle turn, and the left track would not stop moving forwards on the vehicle. This is a free turn. If the left brake is now applied hard, the left track stops and a relatively sharp skid or locked turn results. To make a turn of sharpness between these two, the brake might be applied partially, letting it slip. It would get hot, and this heat represents a waste of power. If systems can be devised wherein there are no slipping brakes or clutches during turns, such waste will be avoided, so the vehicle will maintain its road speed better while turning; furthermore, the problem of ridding the hull of waste heat will be reduced. Such superior systems are called regenerative; the clutch-brake system is non-regenerative.

With clutch-brake steering, a skid turn is the sharpest that can be made. But a system that could cause one track to reverse, giving equal and opposite track speeds, would make the vehicle slew about its own centre line, a pivot turn.

Clutch-brake provides a simple introduction to skid steering mechanisms and their nomenclature. Indeed it is still used in conjunction with other mechanisms; but it is crude. It provides little driver control over steer radii falling between those of free turn and skid turn. Attempts to achieve such intermediate radii are non-regenerative, and it can provide nothing sharper than a skid turn.

What is really wanted is a fully regenerative system, capable of a wide range of steer radii. In general, a vehicle should be able to turn very sharply at low speeds, to give good manoeuvrability. At the same time, there is not really much demand for an ability to make controlled large radius turns at low speed; a series of shortly held sharp turns will suffice. When running very fast, an attempted sharp turn would probably be disastrous; at best the vehicle would slide laterally, out of control, and it might well shed a track. A system providing sharp radius turns in low forward gear and soft turns in high comes close to what is wanted.

Twin Epicyclic Differential

Figures 9.20 illustrated a twin epicyclic differential. This mechanism achieves the same effects as the bevel differential in the drive-axle of a car. When the input is driven, both the annuli A must turn at the same speed. If the suns S are stationary, then the planet carriers, and the outputs F and F′ which are attached to them, will turn at the same speed as one another.

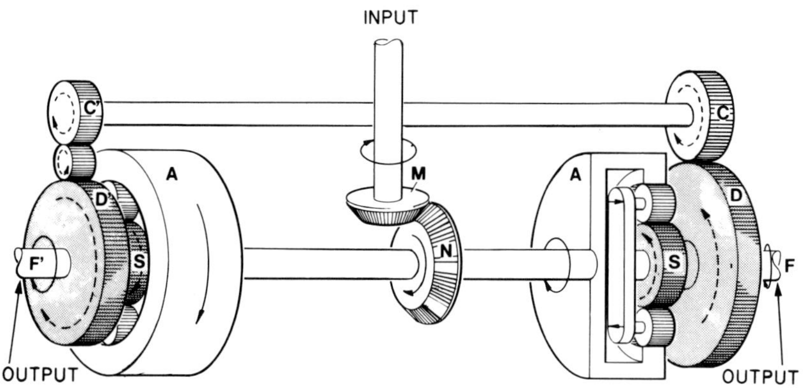

Fig. 9.20 Twin epicyclic differential.

Now suppose the suns were to turn as well. They are interlinked by the upper cross-shaft, and on the left side only there is an odd idler gear between C′ and D′; so the suns must turn in opposite directions—though the tooth numbers are such that their speeds will be arithmetically the same. Thus, the motion of one sun will add to its annulus, while the other will subtract. As a result, one carrier, and its associated output, is speeded up while the other is equally slowed. So like the differential in a wheeled vehicle, this mechanism can allow its two output shafts to rotate at different speeds; and when this happens, its cross-shaft rotates. If then the cross-shaft is forced to turn, the outputs will have to rotate unequally, and as a result the vehicle will go into skid steer. On this mechanism are based the Merritt double and triple differential steering systems, by which the majority of current large AFVs steer, e.g. Challenger, Abrams and Leopard 2.

Merritt Double Differential

Figure 9.21 shows again the twin epicyclic differential, but with additions. The cross-shaft linking C and C′ passes solidly right through a group of gears and clutches. Input M drives through N′, P and Q onto the annuli A as before, and if S and S′ are stationary, the vehicle will run straight. But if one of the two clutches is engaged, the cross-shaft will be locked to either N or N′, and these are turning, driven by M. Note that they turn in opposite directions to one another. So the cross-shaft can be driven at will in either direction. It then drives the suns and the vehicle is forced into steer, with choice of direction.

It remains to select how sharp the turn should be, without slipping any clutches or brakes, which would waste power. At any given engine speed on the input M, engagement of one of the steering clutches will give a fixed value of sun speed to S and S′. This creates a difference between the carrier or output speeds, and the ratio of this difference, one to the other, will depend upon how fast the annuli A are turning. If the annulus speed is high, the sun motion will have relatively little disturbing effect, and vice-versa.

Suppose P and Q to be just one of the pairs of change-speed gears in the gearbox. High gear will make Q, the vehicle and the annuli A run fast, so the suns will have little disturbing effect in steer, and the turn will be gentle; in low gear, the annulus speed will be low, and hence the turn sharp. As P and Q are changed from high forward gear to low, the ratio of the output speeds when turning increases, and this results in the turns becoming sharper.

This is the Merritt double differential steering system. The Merritt triple differential system achieves comparable results, and one or other of these two have served well in the majority of MBTs built since the early 40s. But now, new vehicles having significantly faster performances are beginning to appear, and these lead to a desire for still more steering finesse. It is now felt to be desirable to provide not only radius change with gear change, but superimposed on this, a limited range of continuously variable radius control in each forward gear.

Hydrostatic Steer

Generally this is achieved by a variant upon the double differential system, in which the cross-shaft is driven not mechanically by gears and clutches in a fixed relation to engine speed but by a combination of hydrostatic pump and motor, which can drive the cross-shaft in either direction over a limited range of speeds, continuously variable relative to engine speed. This is illustrated in Figure 9.22. Most of the power is transmitted mechanically through the change speed gears and the annuli, so the relative inefficiency of the hydrostatics is not too serious. The pump/motor can lock the cross-shaft, as well as drive it, and this makes the vehicle intrinsically straight-running when steer is not required. If a brake is added to the annulus shaft, pivot steer can be ensured when steer is initiated in neutral gear.

Systems of this type are in service in all the major tank-producing countries. They permit near-wheeled-vehicle steering finesse in fast track-layers, but they are wasteful of power, in straight-run as well as in steer.

For this last reason, there has recently emerged a resurgence of interest in purely mechanical steering systems, but having more steering finesse than that of Figure 9.21. The hydrostatic systems modulate the speed of their steer-shaft C-C′ steplessly; the latest generation of mechanical systems do it in steps, by the inclusion in its drive of a two or three speed auxiliary gearbox, and drive clutches that can withstand quite prolonged slipping. Their steering may lack the last degree of elegance of the hydrostatic systems, but does this really matter . . . in *war-time*? Their greater efficiency on the other hand will offer more automotive performance and/or less load on the cooling system, both very desirable.

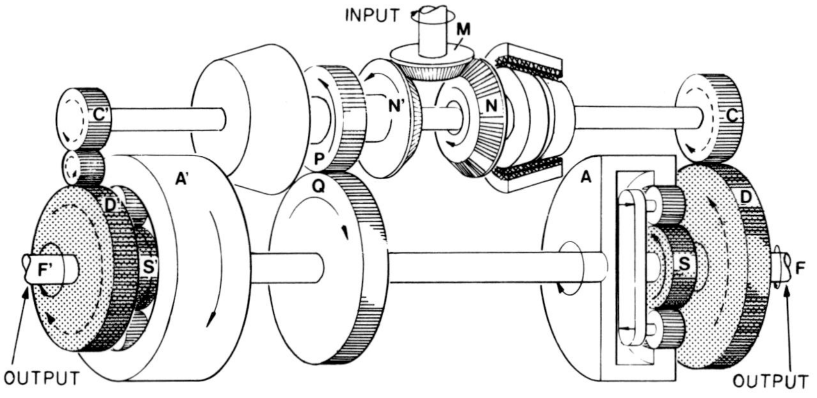

FIG. 9.21 Merritt double differential.

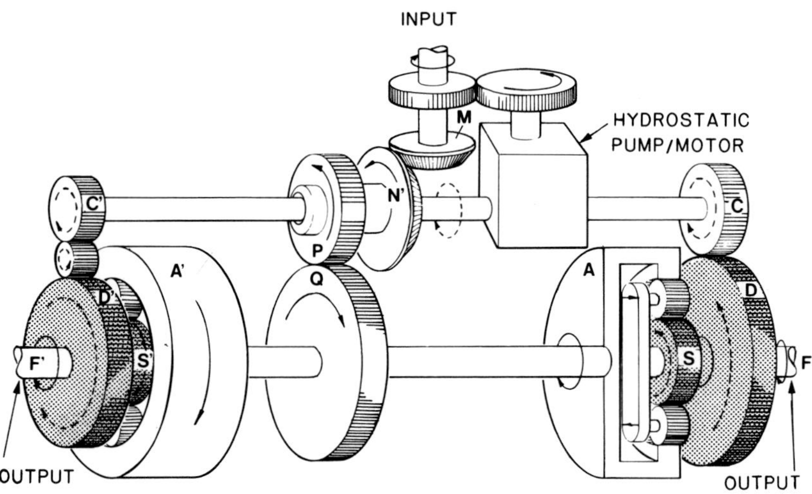

FIG. 9.22 Hydrostatic double differential.

There is *some* evidence that these *may* achieve pre-eminence in the heaviest vehicles, while the hydrostatic steer systems look likely to retain their position in medium and light weight tracklayers.

Conclusion

Many Second World War tanks combined an aero engine or one or two large truck engines with a road vehicle change-speed gearbox. Then, by the addition of a few clutches or brakes, or of a very simple steering gearbox bolted onto the back, they achieved a viable power train, for the sort of performance then deemed adequate. Those days have passed.

In its own peculiar way, tank engine development has now progressed well in advance of commercial vehicle requirements, and modern steering gearboxes are complex integrated mechanisms found nowhere else. The power train now represents a large percentage, perhaps 15–20%, of the total vehicle development effort, time and cost.

10

Running Gear—Tracks

Introduction

Whether it runs on pneumatic tyres or on tracks, the design of the running gear of an AFV must be dictated primarily by its requirement to operate away from smooth, paved surfaces. This is not to say that it has not still to be able to take its place amongst normal road bound traffic, providing safe handling and an acceptable ride to its occupants; it is however the peculiar need to maintain mobility over soft irregular ground, sand and rocks, steep gradients, banks and ditches, that is the predominant factor that governs the design of those automotive components that come between the hull and the ground—the running gear.

The role of the running gear can be considered in relation to the various hull motions that are affected by it. There are 6 of these 'degrees of freedom' in all, 3 of rotation and 3 of translation (Figure 10.1). For a vehicle to utilise fully the

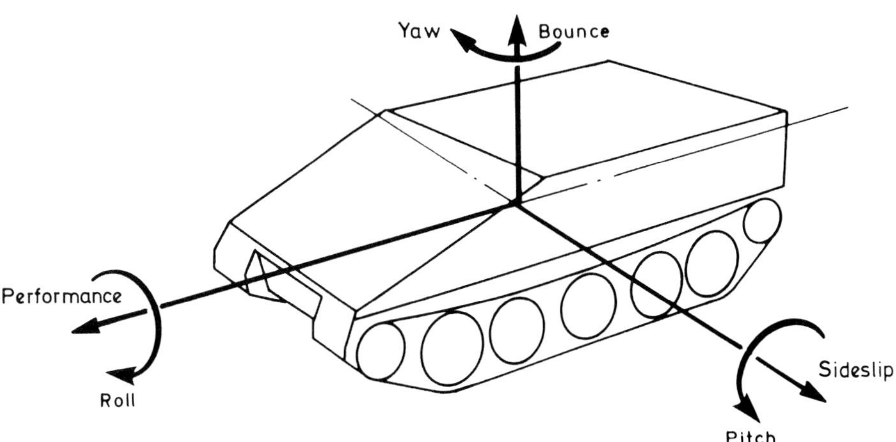

FIG. 10.1 Degrees of freedom of hull.

potential performance made available by the torque from the power train, acting on the sprockets or wheels, a well-matched design of running gear is essential. This will aim to provide optimum ride (pitch and bounce) and handling (yaw, sideslip and roll).

Performance

First, the aim must be to make the best use of the available grip offered by the ground, in order to take full advantage of the drive torque, and so maximise tractive effort and vehicle performance. This will call for correct design of the ground/vehicle interface components; that is the tracks of a tracked vehicle, or the tyres in the case of a wheeled one.

Perhaps less obviously, it will also be necessary to ensure that this tractive effort is spread over the contact area as evenly as possible to avoid localised over-stressing of the soil in shear. To ensure this the weight of the vehicle must be evenly distributed over the ground, and this will call for a large number of road wheels. However, since the ground will in general be uneven, it will be necessary, if all these wheels are to carry their share of load, to interpose some form of suspension between the wheels and the hull.

Attention to maximising tractive effort is only half the story. The effort put into achieving this will largely be negated if an unnecessarily high proportion has to be expended in overcoming rolling resistance. On a hard surface, in the case of a tracked vehicle, much of rolling resistance is due to the track itself and is affected by those components designed to guide its path, namely the idler, sprocket and top rollers (Figure 10.2). On soft going the greater part of the rolling resistance stems

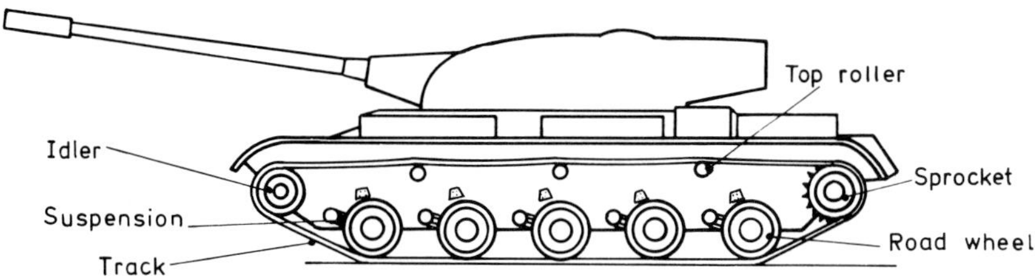

FIG. 10.2 Tracked vehicle running gear.

from the inevitable sinkage, up to the limiting point when the resistance matches the traction and the vehicle is immobilised. To minimise sinkage we must spread the weight over as large an area as possible: this is a matter of track/wheel design. We must also aim to make the ground pressure distribution uniform, which reinforces the need previously put forward for a form of wheel suspension.

Ride

Increasing emphasis on the importance of both tactical mobility and battlefield agility, in the overall design of the modern AFV, has resulted in a call for ever higher on-road and cross-country speeds: this requirement had been met in part by the rise in vehicle power/weight ratios now considered to be necessary. However, the achievement of these speeds is to no purpose unless the payload, be it crew or equipment, arrives at the end of journey in a fit condition to fight: this will be dictated by the quality of the ride imparted.

Furthermore, in the case of the MBT, the ability to fire on the move is nowadays considered essential. This is achieved by the servo-stabilisation provided by increasingly sophisticated gun control gear. The performance possible is, however, limited by considerations of power and weight and it is necessary that the control task should be eased by the provision of a reasonably stable gun platform.

To meet these requirements it is necessary to try to isolate the hull from the accelerations due to ground irregularity and vehicle motion, and this is a further task that falls to the suspension system. In the case of the wheeled vehicle, the tyres also will have a role to play.

Handling

The call here is for a design of steering system which will generate control forces at the tracks or tyres that result in predictable and controlled change of direction. This must be achieved at speed, under varying surface conditions, and should neither consume unnecessary power in the process, nor inhibit the mobility of the vehicle. As might be expected from their very different natures, it is in this area that the pneumatic tyre and the track differ most in their behaviour.

We can now summarise the functional requirements of the AFV running gear as follows. It must support the vehicle weight with a low ground pressure: such support should be uniform and independent of the irregularity of the ground. It must attenuate the shock and vibration transmitted to the hull by that irregularity when moving at speed. Interaction with the ground should produce optimum traction and control forces, and finally all this should be achieved with minimum power loss within the system. Subsequent sections of this chapter will look at each component part of the running gear of tracked vehicles in turn in order to see how these requirements can best be met. Chapter 11 will then examine the situation for the pneumatic tyred wheeled vehicle.

Tracks

Fundamentals

Until the advent of the self-propelled vehicle, the tractive limitations of the wheel on soft ground were of no concern. Its other shortcoming, namely sinkage, was apparently insufficient on its own to provide the impetus to devise a modification that would overcome this problem, perhaps because the ground pressure of the wheel was already no worse than that of the horse that pulled it. Thus it was not until the beginning of this century that the first practicable tracked vehicle was demonstrated, for agricultural use. The principle involved, of bridging the gaps between the wheels with a series of links joined to form a closed chain, was sufficiently developed by the First World War to make possible the birth of the tank, and continues unchanged in essence to the present day.

Compared with a wheeled vehicle of similar weight and size, the ground pressure of its tracked counterpart will be approximately one-third. The traction in cohesive soils, which is area dependent, will correspondingly improve by a factor of about three. Its ability to cross certain kinds of obstacle, particularly transverse ridges and steps, is markedly better. Furthermore, in contrast to the complication associated with all-wheel drive, the track only has to be driven by a single sprocket.

There are penalties to be paid in return for these undoubted advantages. Foremost amongst them is the problem of steering. As discussed in the previous chapter, the normal method adopted, skid steering, leads to a complicated special transmission. However, more important, from the point of view of mobility, is the requirement for high longitudinal forces to be generated between the tracks and the ground to overcome the slewing resistance; the implications of this will be examined later. Another problem, that has assumed major proportions with the high powers and road speeds of modern AFVs, is that of track generated noise and vibration. Levels of noise in a modern tracked AFV at speed on-road may surpass the threshold of pain and require special measures to protect occupants and equipment. Furthermore, the associated heat generated in the running gear adds significantly to the thermal signature of the vehicle.

Single-pin Tracks

Figure 10.3 shows examples of the track pin configurations commonly used today. In the case of the single-pin track, the lugs on the front of one link interlock with those on the back of the next and are connected by a single pin. It is a relatively light arrangement and, provided the number of lugs used is large, results in a strong track that is resistant to stretch and enemy attack. At its simplest, the pin turns in plain, unbushed holes in the lugs. It suffers the obvious drawback of high wear rate and associated large friction losses. Wear is minimised by incorporating a high manganese content into the steel of the links, giving a substantial degree of work-hardening. Nonetheless, the slack that it generates not only limits the life of the track and results in mismatch in pitch at the sprockets, but necessitates frequent tension adjustment by the crew. The hard manual labour involved can now be largely removed by the introduction of a variety of hydraulic track tensioning devices. However, when the limit of adjustment by moving the idler has been reached, the crew is still faced with the task of splitting the track to remove a link and then rejoining it. Bearing in mind that a single tank track link may weigh 35 kg, and that a worn pin will be deeply grooved, it is clear that here is considerable incentive to reduce wear if possible, quite apart from other considerations of cost and logistics.

The alternative to the dry-pin track is to make use of rubber bushes, similar to those universally used on modern car suspension links. Typically the rubber is bonded to an inner steel tube with a hexagonal hole through its centre and is then pressed into the body of the track link. The pin is now of hexagonal section, so that all relative movement between the links has to be accommodated by shear deformation of the rubber as can be seen in Figure 10.4.

With no rubbing components, the life of this part of the track is now limited by the life of the rubber. This is dependent upon the direct stress, caused by track tension, and the shear stress which results from the rotation between the links (Figure 10.5). The track tension which can be sustained, for a given permissible

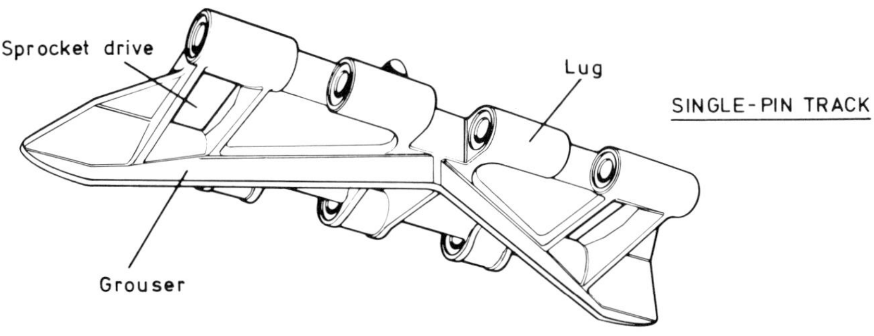

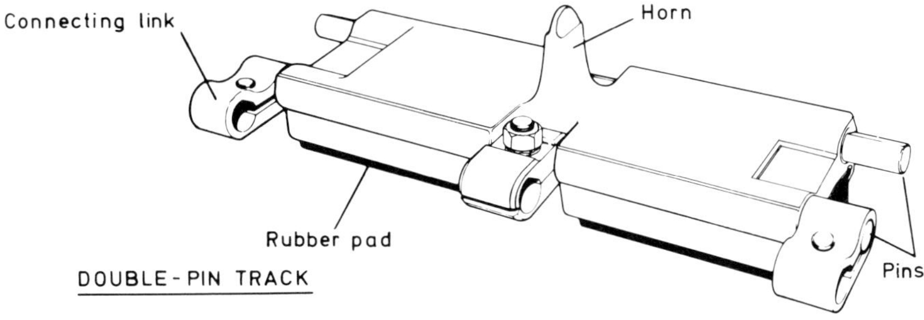

FIG. 10.3 Track link components.

FIG. 10.4 Rubber bushed single-pin link.

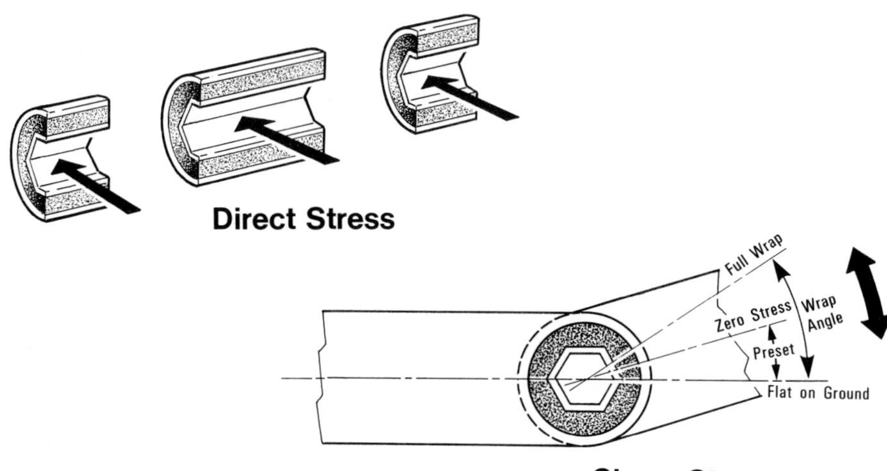

FIG. 10.5 Stress in rubber bushes.

direct stress, is limited by the length of the bushing which can be accommodated across a single-pin track. In practice it is not possible to increase the track width pro rata with the vehicle weight. This design is thus effectively precluded for heavy tanks, and it is usually met only on the lighter classes of vehicles. The shear stress is minimised by presetting adjacent links at an angle equal to half that required to wrap around the idler/sprocket; when a new track is laid out on the ground, this preset causes the ends to lift up, giving rise to the term 'live track'. Even so it is desirable to further reduce the shear if possible. Both these considerations lead to the idea of the two-pin link.

Double-pin Tracks

Referring again to Figure 10.3, it can be seen that now each link carries two pins: adjacent links are joined by separate connectors. The circular pins are bonded directly to the bushes, as they no longer need to be withdrawn to break the track: this is accomplished instead by removal of the connectors. Rotation of the pin within the connector is prevented by machined flats. The length of bushing is now almost doubled, whilst the rotation each bush makes will be approximately halved, compared with the single-pin track. With this configuration, therefore, rubber bushing becomes possible on the heaviest of tracked vehicles, although in these cases an extra connector becomes necessary in the centre of the link.

However, there are penalties. The extra rubber incorporated means that the track becomes unduly elastic, resulting in a tendency to jump the sprocket teeth. To get around this problem it may be necessary to run with a high tension, causing undue loading on other components. The weight will be greater: this is an important factor because tracks contribute 10% of the total weight of a tank. The manufacturing cost of double-pin tracks can be as much as twice that of single-pin tracks: but this is offset by much higher track mileage of around 8,000 km.

Guidance and Drive

The high lateral forces generated during a skid turn imply a strong tendency for tracked vehicles to shed their tracks. To prevent this, track links are provided with a vertical horn that runs between the pairs of road-wheels and engages on their inner surfaces. An alternative, utilising a pair of horns that run on either side of a single road-wheel, is sometimes met on lighter vehicles.

Drive is transmitted from the sprocket to the track by means of sprocket teeth that engage the links. Normally there will be a pair of sprocket rings for each track, and thus each link is driven at two points. Reference to Figure 10.3 shows that, in the case of a single-pin track, drive is taken on a pair of suitably shaped holes formed in the body of the link. The friction upon engagement and disengagement with the sprocket teeth is high, and the associated wear on the link can be the limiting factor in determining its life. On the other hand, the double-pin track engages the sprocket teeth between its end connectors. Again the wear rate is high, but in this case replacement is possible without scrapping the entire link.

Whilst the Americans and West Germans largely use rubber-bushed double-pin tracks and the British favour single dry-pin tracks, it is worth noting that the tank designers of the Soviet Union have succeeded, because of the relatively light weight of their vehicles, in producing a rubber-bushed single-pin track. A further point of interest with this track is that the drive is taken on the extremities of the links, where wear is less critical. This design also avoids holes which when packed with ice prevent engagement on the sprockets.

Ground Contact Surface

The requirement here is to maximise traction between the underside of the track link and the ground. To understand the basis for this, under the all-important unpaved surface conditions, it is first necessary to digress briefly in order to look at the nature of soils and the way that they transmit traction. The principles involved will be equally applicable to the design of tyre patterns.

Shear is transmitted between the surface of the ground and the bottom of the track by what is essentially dry (coulomb) friction; this is true whatever the nature of the soil. Within the soil, however, the transmission of shear is more complex, being in general made up of two components. One part is due to the friction between the soil particles and the other due to the 'cohesion', whereby certain types of soil contain fine elements that cling together when moist.

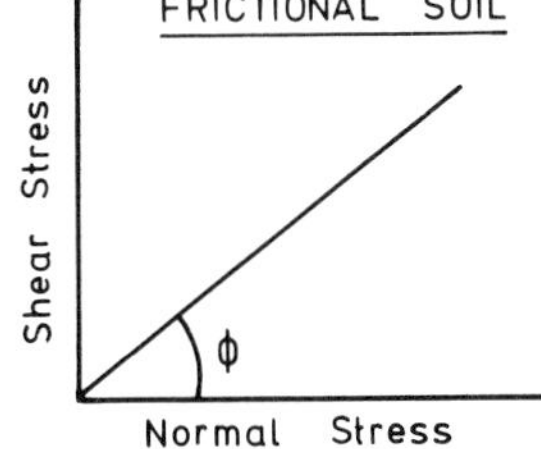

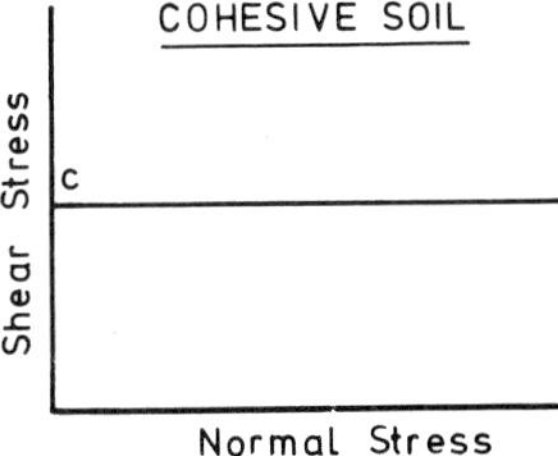

FIG. 10.6 Soil characteristics.

A frictional soil is characterised by having a shear strength proportional to normal stress (i.e. it follows the law of coulomb friction), and is devoid of any cohesion. It is typified by dry sand and can transmit a tractive force equal to about 60% of the load carried ($\Phi = 33°$). It is independent of the area of contact. Because the friction between track and sand is greater than that between the sand particles themselves, shear takes place within the sand itself and traction will thus be unaffected by the shape of the track surface. Indeed the effect of an aggressive track is detrimental, due to the disturbance it imposes upon the generally harder surface layers of sand. Thus the need here is for a comparatively smooth surface. Additionally, although it will not help traction, a large contact area will aid mobility by minimising sinkage and hence rolling resistance.

At the other end of the spectrum, we have the purely cohesive soil where the shear strength is independent of loading. This applies to all soil containing more than 20% clay, provided it is saturated, which is normally the case below the top few millimetres of the surface. The large majority of soils met in Europe fall into this category. The cohesion c is heavily dependent upon moisture content, ranging from near zero on very wet clay to 150 kN/m^2 or more on stiff clay. Because the shear force obtainable by friction between the track and the surface is usually less in this type of soil than that obtainable by cohesion within the soil itself, tracks are designed with a sharp aggressive edge, or grouser that will cut below the surface of the soil to utilise its shear strength. The tractive force will then be proportional to the area of soil being sheared, indicating the need for wide tracks and a large length of track on the ground. It will be noted that this is the same requirement as that for minimising ground pressure, and thus sinkage and consequent rolling resistance.

If it is assumed that operation will largely be over cohesive soils, what then is the problem in adopting these principles? First, widening the track, as a means of increasing contact area, will push up the rolling resistance for a given sinkage, as a greater volume of soil has to be deformed. Furthermore, if the overall width of the vehicle is not to be increased, the width between the track centres will be reduced. When this is combined with the expedient of lengthening the track on the ground, the designer will soon find himself up against steering limitations due to excessive L/C ratio as will be discussed later. Additionally, a wide track reduces usable hull width between the tracks and gives rise to high transverse bending stresses in the links.

However, perhaps the greatest limitation in practice arises from the damage that an aggressive track will inflict on a normal paved surface. The extent of this is such as to be unacceptable to civil authorities on peacetime, with the result that all modern track links are fitted with rubber pads on their underside. It is significant that on a frictional soil, as will be recalled from the earlier discussion, this absence of aggression will not affect the traction. As training grounds are usually located on these relatively infertile lands, the adverse effect of pads on mobility will tend to be masked. The designer is left with two options. He can rely on lateral projections beyond the pads to give some grip, when the sinkage is deep enough to engage them, which is usually when the need for traction is greatest. Alternatively, instead of moulding rubber into the body of the link, he can make the pads detachable so that, in a period of emergency, it becomes possible, at the expense of some time and effort, to regain the advantage of an aggressive grouser. Furthermore, since the life of the pads is only about one-third of that for the rest of a modern rubber-bushed track, detachable pads that can be renewed bring with them the additional advantage of allowing the higher potential track mileages of these designs to be realised.

Attachment of the pads is most usually by bolts, but Figure 10.7 shows an arrangement where retention is by a spring clip which is easily disengaged by driving a rod between the pad and body. To avoid the removal of all the 200 or so pairs of pads on a tank, it is recommended with this design that only one in six should be exchanged for the aggressive steel 'pad' shown. A further noteworthy point is the addition of extensions to the end connectors, designed in increase the contact area with the ground.

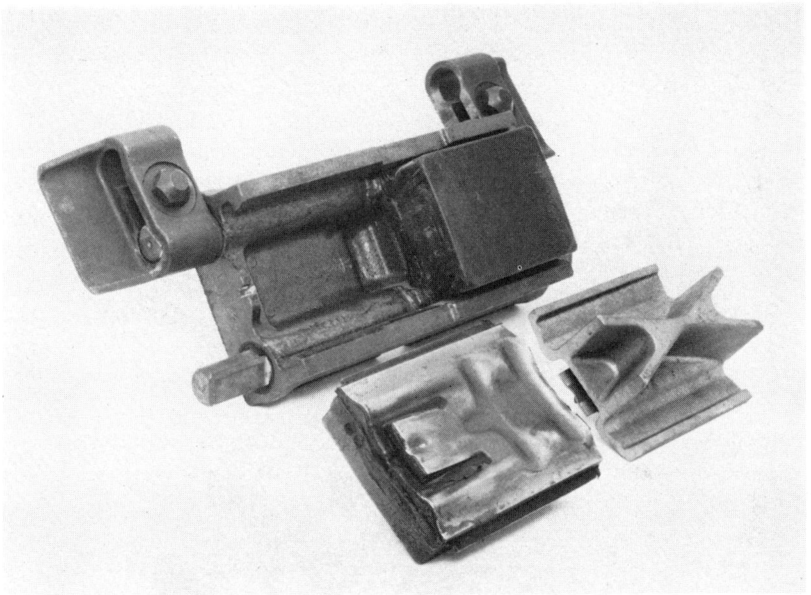

FIG. 10.7 Double-pin link with removable pads.

Track Developments

With tracks accounting for such a high proportion of the total weight of an AFV, there will be a good return on any weight savings that can be achieved in this area. One current line of development is examining alternative materials. Aluminium alloys have shown some promise, offering a 20% reduction in the weight of double-pin tracks. However, more recently advances in composite materials which combine the low density of aluminium with the strength of steel seem to have more to offer. Such composites as Boron/Aluminium or Silicon carbide/Aluminium have been found to combine high specific tensile strength and modulus with good damping and fatigue life.

Another line, that could be particularly advantageous in reducing vibration, is to replace a track made up of discrete links with a continuous band. Such tracks have long found application in very low ground pressure vehicles, such as those designed for over-snow use. However, improvements in the design, incorporating high tensile steel cables in a polymer matrix have extended the application to vehicles up to 20t with speeds in excess of 50 km/h.

Track Guidance System

Road Wheels

The fitting of tracks to a vehicle calls for a rather different design of road wheel, compared with its wheel-only counterpart. The need to engage a track horn has been mentioned, to provide positive lateral location. This results in modern AFVs all using a dual wheel design as shown in Figure 10.8. From this also will be noted

FIG. 10.8 Tracked vehicle with dual road wheels.

that the other main difference is the absence of a pneumatic tyre. In the case of the tank, the reason for this stems principally from the role of the vehicle, which exposes it to fire more often than the lightly armoured wheeled AFVs. However, additionally it is found that the size of pneumatic tyre needed to carry the loads involved would be too great to fit into the space available. As a result solid rubber tyres are used. Even these present a design problem: as tanks get ever heavier and their road speeds increase, the tyres become liable to overheat.

To minimise tyre rolling resistance, the need is for larger diameter wheels. However, in order to optimise soft ground performance, uniform weight distribution is needed, calling for a large number of wheels. The normal compromise is 6 or 7 road wheels per side on tanks, whilst smaller, lighter AFVs use 4 or 5.

Top Rollers

The top run of track could simply be left to hang in a catenary between the idler and sprocket; indeed this is the practice on a number of tracked vehicles. One objection to this is that the arrangement will limit the travel available before the wheels hit the top run, with consequent adverse effect on the ride. Another concerns the dynamics of the track itself, which results in lateral vibration resonances taking the form of a travelling wave moving from front to rear (Figure 10.9). These may reach violent proportions, and the resultant fluctuations in tension can cause an increase of as much as 20–30% in rolling resistance at certain critical speeds.

12 km/h No wave in top run

68 km/h Wavefront reached 2nd wheel

FIG. 10.9 Track dynamics of Scorpion.

By making the road wheels sufficiently large, the top run can be allowed to rest on the tops of the wheels. For reasons that are discussed later, the consequent increase in unsprung mass makes this an unsatisfactory solution for the higher speed vehicles, especially those with heavy tracks, and it will be found that modern tanks all use separate top rollers to support the track and to keep it clear of the wheels. a price has to be paid for these in the form of added weight, inertia and friction.

Sprockets and Idlers

If large road wheels are employed of a diameter comparable with that normally used for the sprocket and idler, then it is quite possible to replace either or both of these by the wheels of the end stations without producing an undesirable increase in flexure between links during wrap, and still maintaining an acceptable step-climbing ability.

However, the complication associated with transmitting drive to a suspended wheel has resulted in virtually all AFVs, either past or present, using a drive sprocket fixed to the hull. The case with the idler is not so clear cut, and a number of current tracked vehicles that utilise front sprocket drive make use of the rear wheel in place of an idler, as shown in Figure 10.10.

FIG. 10.10 Combat Engineer Tractor.

The decision as to whether to use front or rear sprocket drive will be based principally on the choice of engine location: there are no modern examples of drive being transmitted the length of the vehicle. However, tests have shown that the rolling resistance with a front sprocket can be as much as 50% higher than if a rear drive is used. This arises because the full track tension has to be transmitted around the rear idler, with consequential increase in friction losses at the pins and teeth. Against this, the tension in the top run will tend to inhibit track resonance, and the additional length prior to engagement of the sprocket will allow better clearance of mud and thus less chance of jumping the teeth.

Reference has been made to the use of the idler in the important task of adjusting track tension. This is achieved by mounting the idler on a swinging arm which is rotated manually by a screw, or hydraulically; in the latter case a neat solution is to use grease in the hydraulic cylinder, which can then be pressurised with a normal grease-gun. Such an arrangement will, however, only maintain the static tension. When moving over rough terrain, as the suspension allows the wheels to move up and down, the track tension will alter considerably. It may even become completely slack in front of the sprocket, with the accompanying danger of shedding. This is especially a problem with the increased wheel travel used in the modern AFV. To obviate this it is necessary to have dynamic tension adjustment and one solution, used by tanks in the United States, is to connect the swinging idler to the front wheel arm: such a solution is shown in Figure 10.11. As the wheel

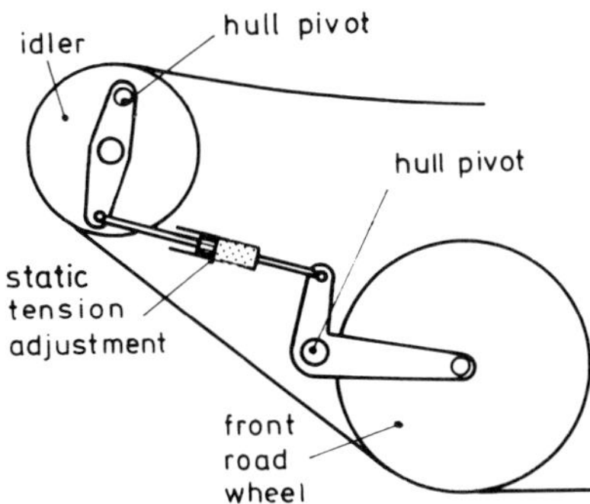

FIG. 10.11 Linkage for automatic dynamic track tensioning.

rises, the slack is gathered in by the idler moving forward. The track tension acting on the idler will be transmitted to push the front wheel down, and thus this arrangement gives increased resistance of the vehicle to pitching, especially during braking.

Steering of Track-Layers

The ideal steering system would allow the mobility advantages of the track to be combined with the efficiency, ease of handling, and life of the wheel. It should allow small radius, or preferably pivot, turns and should not intrude unduly on the hull width. These requirements are not all compatible and 3 solutions may be found in use today which all involve compromises on the ideal.

In each case the problem is to generate control forces F whose moment in the desired direction of turn is sufficient to overcome the very considerable resisting moments M that the ground is exerting on the track (Figure 10.12). If this control moment is insufficient then the vehicle will merely continue on a straight line path.

Half-tracks

Here the control moment is generated by the lateral force F acting on the steered wheels at the end of a moment arm l; for yawing we need $Fl \geqslant M$. This works well enough in conditions where the grip of the tyres is good, such as on roads. Under

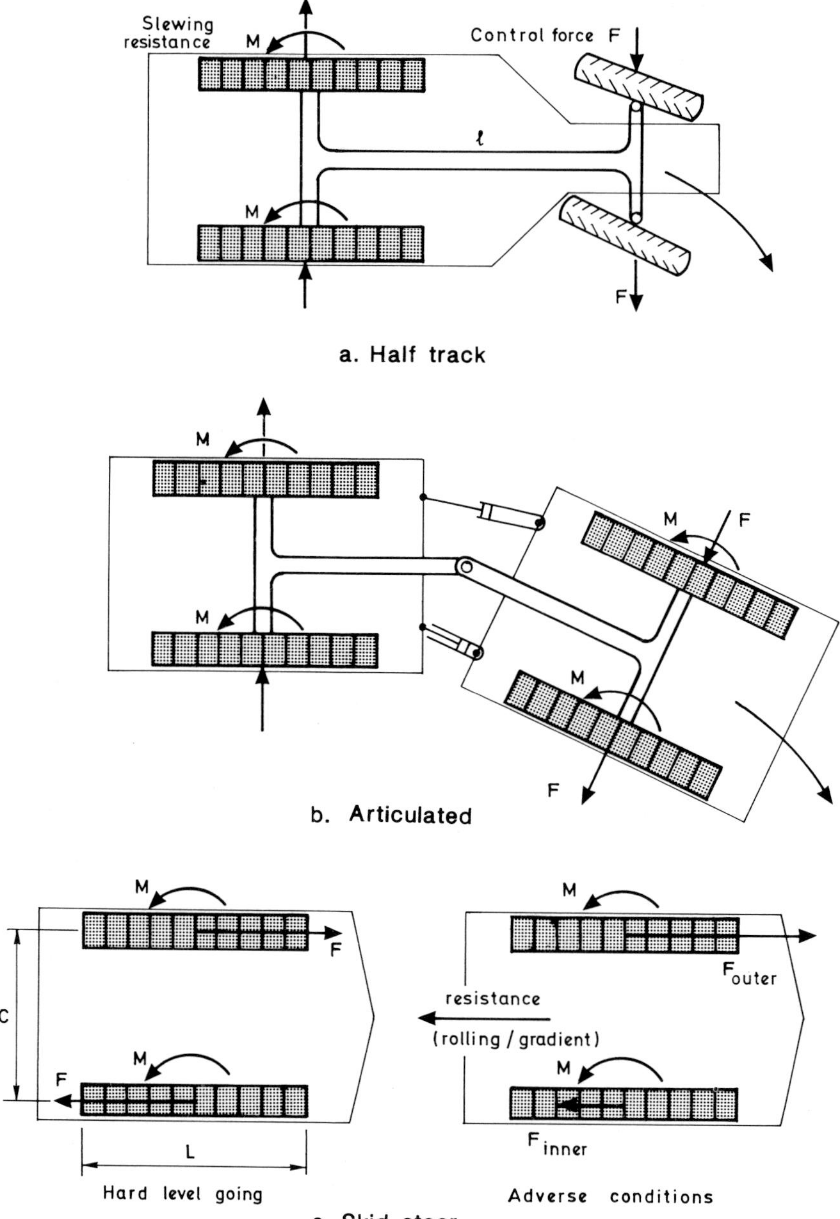

FIG. 10.12 Different approaches to steering tracked-layers.

soft going off-road, however, the tyres will tend to skid straight ahead and this is aggravated by the tendency for the front wheels to leave the ground due to terrain irregularity. As a result, it necomes necessary in practice to compromise the simplicity of the approach with the addition of some form of skid-steer mechanism, and this method of steering is no longer in widespread use.

Articulated steering

A logical development, to overcome the short-coming of the half-track, is to substitute tracks for the steered tyres, so increasing the control lateral force that can be generated. Thus each of the two pairs of tracks is mounted on a sub-bogey, either one or both of which may be turned about its centre in order to steer. A preferred alternative does not attempt to steer the tracks relative to the hull, but instead divides the hull into separate halves, each with its own pair of tracks; steering then is achieved by yawing one half relative to the other by means of hydraulic jacks between them. Allowing freedom for relative pitch additionally will ensure that both halves carry equal weight on irregular terrain.

It should particularly be noted that this principle does not demand any significant extra drive from the tracks, and these can be made as long and as wide as desired. It thus finds application where very low ground pressures are needed, such as with over-snow vehicles. A disadvantage is that the turning circle is large and pivot turns cannot be made.

Skid steer

In contrast to the previous approaches, where the control moment was generated by forces F lateral to the track, in this case the tracks are made to generate longitudinal forces. This is done by braking the inner track whilst continuing to drive the outer using one of the steer systems described in the previous chapter.

The control moment now depends upon the moment arm C, the distance between the track centres, and will equal FC. The slewing resistance is M per track, whose magnitude depends upon the length of the track on the ground; hence to turn we need $FC \geqslant 2M$. The magnitude of F will, for a given weight of vehicle, be reduced by placing the tracks farther apart (C), but be increased by lengthening the track on the ground (L). Thus for ease of turning a low L/C ratio is needed; however, it should be noted that this leads to wide tracks, more soil to be displaced, and associated high rolling resistance, whilst the short wheel-base results in pitching problems. For a typical MBT with a L/C ratio of about 1.7, as much as two-thirds of the ultimate grip of the track has to be used to slew the vehicle: this is, perhaps, 100 kN on average going. Considering now the situation where there is a drag force on the vehicle, either due to rolling resistance or an upgrade, there is very little spare traction available at the outer track. Thus, under what might be thought of as only moderately adverse conditions, the force on the outer track F (outer) soon reaches its limit of adhesion. Under these circumstances, pulling the steering lever merely induces track slip and sinkage, with the associated chance of bogging down, whilst the vehicle continues on a straight path.

Other disadvantages of skid-steering include the wear on tracks and road involved with lateral motion of the track links, together with the associated high transmission torques and power loss. Nonetheless, the essential simplicity and compactness of the method over-rides the other considerations for all but a few specialist tracked vehicles.

Finally it may be noted that this form of steering is equally applicable to wheeled vehicles, principally in order to benefit from the increased hull width that becomes available if individual wheels no longer need space to be steered.

Suspension and Ride

The Need

At the start of this chapter the purpose of interposing some form of suspension between the wheels and the hull was identified. It is to allow an even distribution of load on uneven ground and to minimise disturbance to the crew.

Let us look, for a moment, at a vehicle whose wheels are attached rigidly to the hull moving over rough terrain. By way of analogy, consider a stool that is set down on uneven ground; if it has two legs it will fall over, if it has three legs it will be stable with all legs carrying their share of the load, but if it has four legs then one will normally be off the ground. In the same way, the vehicle will, in general, even when stationary, only be carried on three wheels, the remainder contributing nothing to providing traction or lowering ground pressure. Although sinkage on soft ground, or the use of low-pressure tyres (which is in itself a form of suspension), may in practice allow further wheels sometimes to touch the ground. This will mitigate, but not solve, the problem. If the vehicle now moves at speed, the situation ceases to be static and contact may be reduced to two, one or even, at times, no points.

The effect on the hull of being supported at three points which follow every contour of the ground will be a complex motion made up of three components: vertical displacement (bounce), a rotation about the transverse axis (pitch), and rotation about the longitudinal axis (roll). In a military cross-country vehicle it is found that it is the first two that have the predominant effect on the crew and are used to describe the quality of 'ride' (recall Figure 10.1).

To gain some quantitative idea of the problem, consider a vehicle moving over undulating terrain which for simplicity will be taken as having sufficiently long wavelength λ in relation to the wheel base that bounce can be considered on its own—say $\lambda = 10$ m. At a speed $\upsilon = 10$ m/s (36 km/h) the frequency of the disturbance will be $f = \upsilon/\lambda = 1$ c/s and, assuming a quite moderate trough to crest height of $2H = 25$ cm, the corresponding maximum vertical acceleration can be calculated from the expression:

$$a = (2\pi f)^2 H = 4.9 \text{ m/s}^2 \text{ or } 0.5 \text{ g.}$$

The effect of this is that, even at those wheels which are in contact with the ground, the reaction will be halved as the vehicle passes the crests. At the same time, the crew are being subjected to a level of vibration which, as will be seen later, can only be endured for a very short time without loss of performance.

Although enough has been said to show that a suspensionless vehicle cannot provide a satisfactory answer at speed, it should be remembered that the first tanks only moved at walking pace and hence the ride accelerations were negligible. That left the problem of load distribution, and it was with a view to improving this aspect of the first generation of tanks that suspension designs were initially introduced. Since the principle involved will still be found on some tanks today, it is worth starting by taking a look at this class of suspension.

Bogey Suspension

If the weight of the vehicle is to be shared equally amongst the wheels, independent of the ground contour, then it becomes necessary to reduce the effective number of points of suspension of the hull to not more than three or, considering bounce and pitch only, two on each side. This can be done by placing pairs of wheels at either end of a pivoted beam, so that the load carried at the pivot must be shared equally between them, up to the limit of displacement. The principle is shown for a vehicle with four wheel stations in Figure 10.13 from which

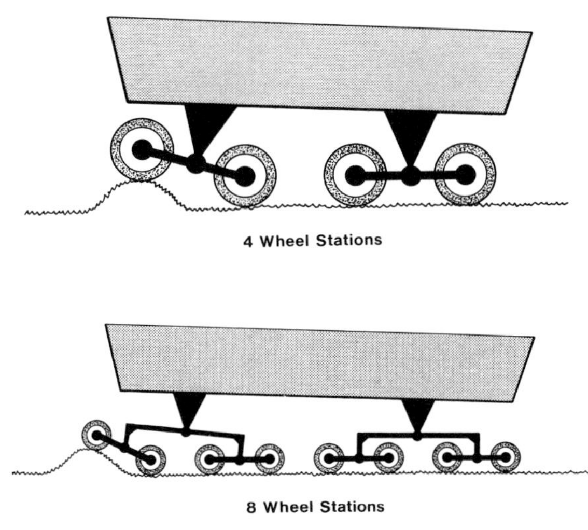

FIG. 10.13 Bogey suspension layouts.

it can also be seen how the idea can be extended to greater numbers of wheel stations. Although intended primarily to improve ground contact, the averaging effect of bogey layout will also reduce the motion transmitted to the hull by short bumps: in the two examples, the vertical lift of the centre of mass of the hull is reduced to a half and a quarter respectively of what it would be with no suspension.

Nonetheless, it was not long before tank speeds had increased to the point where considerations of ride necessitated the introduction of some form of resilience into the suspension. In a variety of layouts, this sprung bogey has been widely used in tracked vehicles up to the present day. In particular it has been favoured by British heavy tank designers in the form known as the Horstman suspension, which is shown in Figure 10.14. One advantage is that, being a self-contained externally mounted unit, it can be exchanged relatively easily if damaged. Also, although this tends to be a heavy design, it is cheap to produce. One of the principal drawbacks is that it is difficult to accommodate the sort of wheel travel necessary for present day speeds: for example, Chieftain has a bump-to-rebound travel of 215 mm, compared with 450 mm on Challenger. Another problem is that as speeds rise, the inertia of the linkage within the bogey means that the statical balance between the wheels is upset and the loads are no longer equalised as intended.

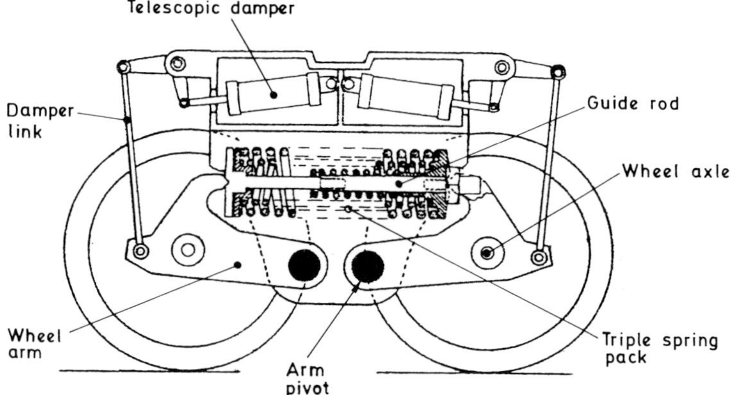

FIG. 10.14 Chieftain tank bogey.

Thus, although the bogey suspension has given good service on tanks with speeds up to 40 km/h, the increased emphasis on mobility has meant that all present designs are based upon independently suspended wheels. These will now be looked at with a view to deciding what sort of characteristics such a suspension should have.

The Perfect Suspension

An ideal suspension characteristic might be imagined as one which transmits no acceleration to the hull, but provides a constant force, just sufficient to carry its share of the weight, independent of wheel movement. The force/displacement characteristics of such a zero rate suspension would appear as shown in Figure 10.15. Closer examination shows up a number of snags if this proposal were to be adopted.

The first of these arises due to the practical limitation on wheel travel. Because of this, the vehicle will not be able to travel at a constant altitude, but will need to follow gradients and long wavelength undulations. It is also likely to encounter from time to time short bumps that are outside the range of the suspension. In these cases the hull will have to be accelerated vertically, implying the need for an extra force over and above that resisting the weight.

The next snag is the response to body forces. These are defined as inertial or gravitational forces on the hull and will arise due to braking, accelerating, cornering or change of static load. Because the zero rate suspension offers no pitch or roll stiffness, a body force will deflect the hull up to the limit of suspension travel. Again the implication is that an extra vertical force has to be provided under any of these circumstances.

Finally there is the problem caused by fluctuation of ground contact. After a wheel hits a bump at speed, a large downward acceleration is required as it comes to the top, in order to maintain contact with the ground. The force to produce this will depend upon the 'unsprung mass', which means that wheels should be kept as light as possible. However, that provided by the zero rate suspension remains constant even when the wheel leaves the ground and flies upwards towards the hull.

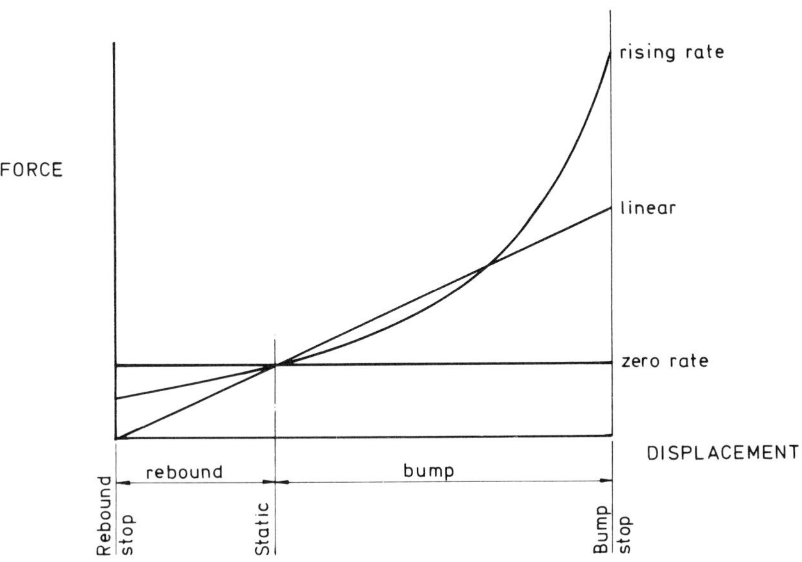

FIG. 10.15 Suspension characteristics.

This would result in the wheel frequently hitting the bump stop, with resultant shock, and would also have a bad effect upon traction and steering. Once more a suspension that offers an increasing force, in response to a rising wheel, is indicated.

Passive Suspension

The most straightforward solution to the problem outlined above is to use a suspension that provides a force that increases with deflection in a chosen and fixed manner. Such a response is provided by any of the various forms of spring whose characteristics cannot be altered, i.e. which are 'passive'. Most commonly, the force increases linearly as the wheel moves from rebound, through static, to full bump as can be seen in Figure 10.15.

The cost of departing from the zero rate spring is, however, that now any wheel movement alters the force in the suspension, even when this is not needed, and thus produces an acceleration on the hull. The lower the suspension rate, the less will be this effect, but the greater will be the problems arising from limited wheel travel, body forces and unsprung mass. Thus designs using passive elements will always be a compromise between these conflicting interests.

A measure that mitigates the problem is to adopt a spring that offers a rising rate (see Figure 10.15). To avoid hitting the bump stops too frequently, it has been found that a force at full bump equal to about five times that at the static position is desirable in a high-speed off-road vehicle. With a linear rate this cannot be achieved without adopting an undesirably stiff spring and reduced rebound travel. Adoption of a rising rate is seen to allow a soft spring (represented by a small slope) around static, with a gradual transition to hard at bump. With this arrangement it is possible to have a spring with high energy storage potential (represented by the area under the curve) but a low stiffness for much of the time.

Although, over the years, many different types of springing media have been used on military vehicles, these have been reduced to three types on current tracked AFVs: torsion bar, coil and hydrogas. The choice amongst these is influenced by wider design considerations than just their effect on ride, and it is of interest to examine the characteristics of each with this in mind.

Torsion Bar

Here the wheel load is made to apply a torque to a circular section steel bar whose twist in response provides the required compliance. Since tracked vehicles universally locate their wheels on leading or trailing arms, it is convenient to use these as levers with the torsion bar running across the hull, splined to rotate with the arm at one end, and to a fixed anchorage on the opposite side plate at the other. The resulting layout is simple, light and relatively inexpensive. As a consequence, the torsion bar has grown in popularity since its introduction on the German Panther in the Second World War, until the present time, when it is to be found on all but a handful of tracked vehicles.

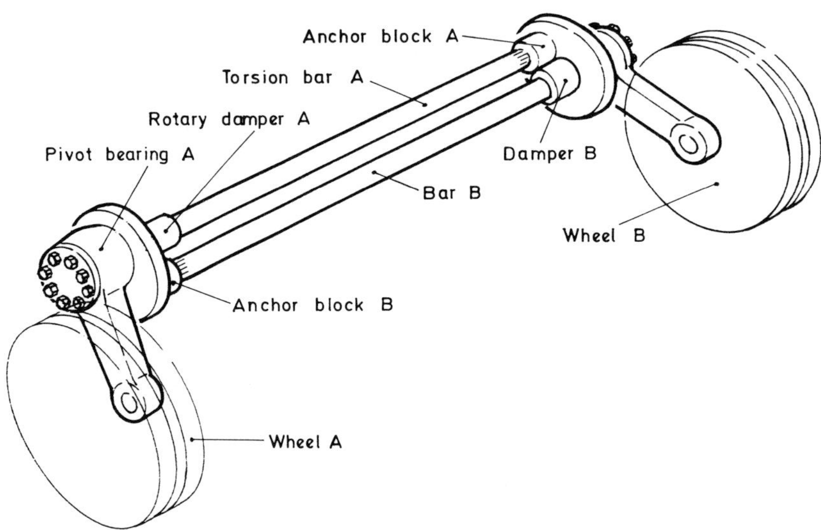

FIG. 10.16 Torsion bar layout.

There are, however, a number of associated drawbacks, foremost amongst which is the difficulty of obtaining sufficient travel. Properly designed, and for a given stress limit, travel is proportional to bar length and this in turn is limited by the hull width. With the steels available on early designs, bump movement was confined to about 130 mm. To improve on this, double-length, hair-pin bars were sometimes used. The principle has been pursued up to the present, but avoiding the undesirable introduction of bending stress by replacing the return bar by a torsion tube concentric with the first bar. Manufacture of the tube to the necessary high standards of accuracy and finish presents formidable problems, however, and the result is expensive (Figure 10.17). The other line to pursue, in the search for increased wheel travel, relies on the fact that this travel is proportional to $(\text{stress})^{4/3}$. From the start, special treatments have been specified in order to increase the stress limit. Shot-peening the bar, for example, will introduce compressive stress into the surface, nearly doubling the fatigue life for a given stress limit. Protection of the vulnerable surface, where stress is highest, by wrapping or running the bar in a light oil-filled tube is desirable. However, the principal factor that has allowed the torsion bar still to be used, despite the ever-increasing stress demands, has been the continuous improvement in steel. Using electroslag refined (ESR) steel the modern tank can now have a bump travel of as much as 385 mm using a single bar design.

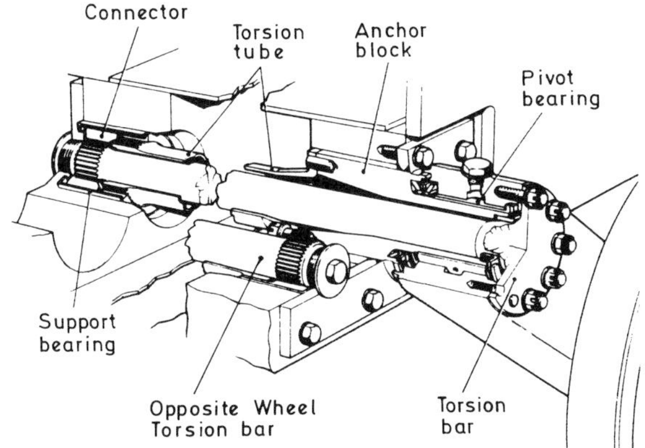

FIG. 10.17 Tube over bar suspension.

The essentially linear spring characteristic of the torsion bar means that, for the reasons previously discussed, it is difficult to obtain a sufficiently high force at full-bump. This may be resolved by use of a well-designed bump-stop having sufficient resilience to act as a helper spring. A more gradual transition can be achieved by introducing a second torsion bar acting in parallel with the main bar, but not brought into play until the wheel arm has rotated through a certain part of its bump movement. One application of this idea, tried in the United States, utilises a transverse torsion tube over half the hull width. A neat alternative, used by Vickers in the United Kingdom, is to run the second bar within the hollow wheel arm, a simple pair of levers being used to transfer rotation of the arm into twist of the bar.

Another problem concerns ease of replacement. Although it is true that, being under armour, the bar is protected from direct attack, nonetheless the design has proved to be vulnerable to the hull distortions likely to arise from mine blast. Under these circumstances, it is usually the front bars that need replacing. As these are rather inaccessible, removal of the broken bar from its anchorage, into which it is quite probably corroded, can present considerable problems. An answer seen in the latest designs is firstly to strengthen the hull over the front bars, and then so to design the anchorage that bar removal can be performed from outside the hull.

A further important result of internal springing is that it becomes necessary to raise the hull height by some 100 mm, with associated consequences to the vehicle silhouette.

Coil Spring

Used in compression, a coil spring may be thought of as being a torsion bar wound into a helix. Although this disposes of the problem of length, the space in the centre makes it bulky and, as a result, the coil spring has normally been found on externally mounted suspension units. A good example is that of the bogey shown in Figure 10.14. Here the central space is well-used by fitting three coil springs concentrically, the third being somewhat shorter than the other two so that its delayed action contributes to a desirably rising rate overall, despite the linear characteristics of the individual coils. The variation of stress between the inside and outside of the coils, together with the difficulty of treating all surfaces equally, means that the stress that can be employed in this configuration will be reduced by perhaps as much as 25% compared with the torsion bar. As a result, it will be considerably heavier for a given resilience and has largely gone out of favour at present on tracked vehicles, although it finds continuing application on wheeled AFVs.

Hydrogas

The principle of using the compressibility of gas as a springing medium has long been applied in the air springs to be found on many commercial vehicles. These operate at low pressures of approximtely 7 bar static and as a consequence are bulky, vulnerable and quite unsuited to AFV application. By operating at much higher pressure of about 100 bar static, the energy storage for a given unit mass becomes highly attractive, offering weight savings of perhaps 12 kN on an MBT as compared with a coil spring bogey design, whilst retaining the merit of being suited to installation outside the hull. The gas laws take care of the requirement for a rising rate, a bump-to-static force ratio of 5 being quite easily obtainable without compromising the desirable soft rate around the static position.

The pressure at bump, which would be 500 bar in this example, presents sealing problems if a piston in cylinder arrangement is used to compress the gas directly. An easier way would be to use a flexible diaphragm in place of the piston, but then it would be impossible to apply the wheel load uniformly to the diaphram. The answer is to use an actuator piston separated from the gas piston or diaphragm by a volume of oil, as shown in Figure 10.18. Sealing is effectively confined to the actuator piston and since it is now oil that is being sealed, the problem is considerably eased.

Adoption of this hydrogas spring, as opposed to a purely gas spring, carries with it a further number of significant bonuses. Foremost amongst these is that damping can easily be built into the design (this aspect will be discussed shortly). If the

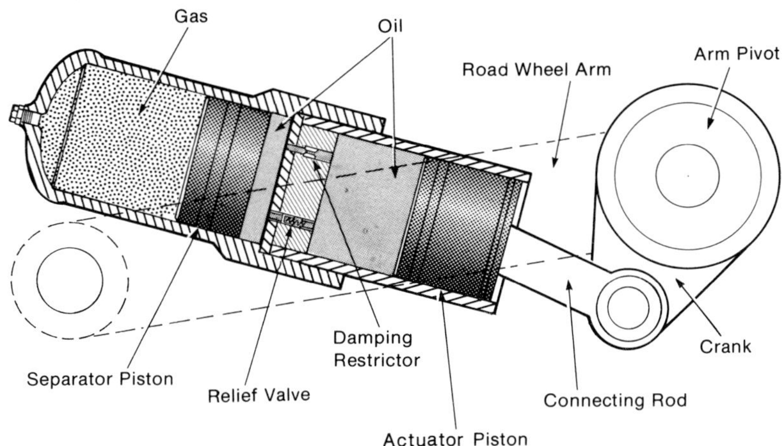

FIG. 10.18 Hydrogas suspension (Challenger).

damper orifice can be closed completely by external control, then this will allow the suspension to be locked up, which is advantageous for consistent firing in the case of a gun vehicle, or earth-moving in the case of an engineer vehicle. The addition of an external hydraulic supply piped to each suspension unit will allow the vehicle to be raised to provide additional ground clearance, or lowered to improve the silhouette. Perhaps of still greater advantage is to use the system to pitch the vehicle. This will give additional gun depression for firing from a reverse slope, the effect of which on the overall design has been discussed in an earlier chapter. In the extreme case of a fixed gun design, such as the Swedish 'S' tank, this pitching can be used as the sole means of elevating the gun.

Disadvantages of hydrogas include the increased cost, perhaps half as much again, compared with rival designs. The variation of gas volume with temperature will lead to fluctuation of track tension which can be significant not only due to diurnal changes but also to heating over rough ground when oil temperatures can reach 130° or more. Maintenance will be more complicated with hydrogas, because special charging arrangements for the oil and nitrogen will be needed. Finding room for the cylinder between the road wheel and hull side can present a problem if it is to be made large enough to keep operating pressures within bounds. In this connection, an interesting recent design proposal places the gas and oil cylinders one above the other within a monobloc which also acts as the wheel arm; rotation of the cylinder relative to a fixed crank then operates the piston via a connecting rod.

Resonance and Damping

Earlier the compromise inherent in adopting a finite rate suspension was discussed; it allowed the hull to be accelerated to follow the long wavelength (low excitation frequency) undulations whose amplitudes are outside the range of the wheel travel, at the expense of transmitting unnecessary force when travelling over relatively small, short wavelength (high excitation frequency) undulations.

FIG. 10.19 'S' tank with hydrogas suspension.

Unfortunately, when the dynamics of the situation are analysed, it is found that between these extremes there will exist a range of excitation frequencies over which the adoption of a spring will actually amplify the hull response to the ground input, in some cases to an alarming degree.

To see why this is so, let us look, for simplicity, at the bounce motion alone, so that the vehicle may be taken as a mass suspended on a single spring as shown in Figure 10.20. Now imagine this model being driven over terrain, the wavelength of which is progressively reduced, so that the excitation frequency rises. The success, or otherwise, of the suspension will be measured by the ratio of the amplitudes of hull displacement to ground displacement. At low frequencies then this ratio is united as the hull follows the terrain, whilst at high frequencies it drops towards zero as the hull remains inertial. Before this desirable state of affairs can be reached, however, there occurs a condition when the frequency of excitation coincides with the natural frequency in bounce of the vehicle, and resonance occurs between them. This natural frequency f_n is what would be observed were the vehicle to be pushed straight down and then released and allowed to oscillate. It is given by

$$f_n = \frac{1}{2\pi}\sqrt{\frac{k}{m}},$$

a stiffer spring thus increasing f_n, whilst a heavier vehicle will decrease it. Figure 10.20 shows the behaviour just described plotted graphically, and two important conclusions are clearly indicated.

First, the introduction of a spring will only be of benefit when the frequency ratio exceeds $\sqrt{2}$ (i.e. when $f > \sqrt{2}\,f_n$); up to this point it merely serves to amplify the input. To reach this condition as soon as possible means that f_n should be kept low

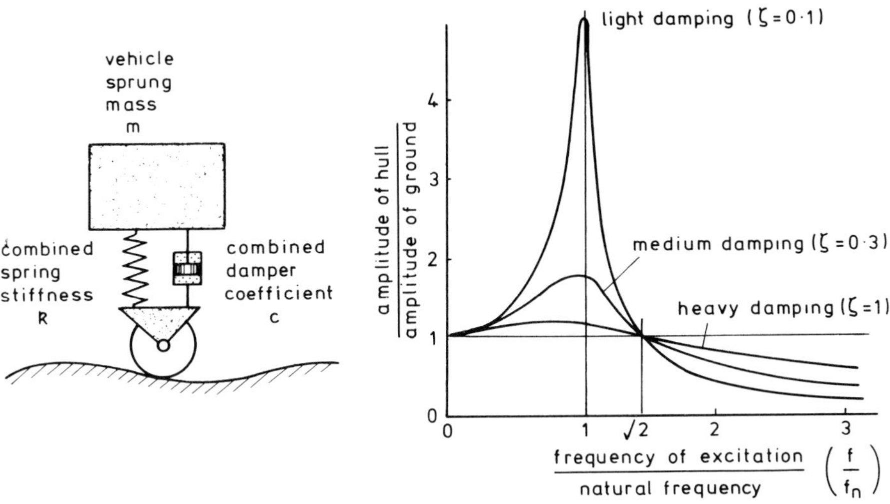

FIG. 10.20 Frequency response (displacement) of vehicle in bounce.

by the use of a soft spring and that the forward speed should be as high as practicable.

The second conclusion concerns the control of the resonant condition. The only way of limiting the resonant response is to introduce some form of energy dissipation into the system. A certain amount of this is inherent in any suspension, due to friction between rubbing parts. However, too much stiction is undesirable, as it locks up the suspension over small disturbances, and it becomes necessary to add a device whose sole purpose is to dissipate energy; this is called a damper. To avoid the problems of stiction it should provide a resisting force only whilst it is moving. If this force is directly proportional to velocity, the behaviour is termed viscous and is quantified by a damping coefficient c (lbf per ft/s or N per m/s). It can be approximated in practice by the pressure drop associated with the flow of a fluid through a restricting orifice. Unfortunately it can be seen that control of resonance by the introduction of damping is only achieved at the expense of increased amplitude ratios at higher frequencies, due to the additional force transmitted through the damper. Thus again, as with the spring, the choice of rating for a passive, that is a fixed characteristic, damper must be a compromise.

The level of damping in any particular spring/mass system if measured by the damping ratio $\zeta = c/2\sqrt{km}$. The amount by which different values of ζ will reduce successive amplitudes following a disturbance is shown in Figure 10.21. In practice a damper that gives a reduction of not less then 3:1 is found to be necessary for satisfactory ride, that is $\zeta \geqslant 0.35$.

The speed of early tanks was so slow that they operated well below resonance for most conditions, and the inherent friction was perfectly adequate without the need for any additional damping being apparent. As speeds increased and supensions were made softer, resonance became a problem and designers began gradually to include a purpose-built damper into their units, especially at the end stations, where they are most effective in controlling pitch. The problem of heat dissipation

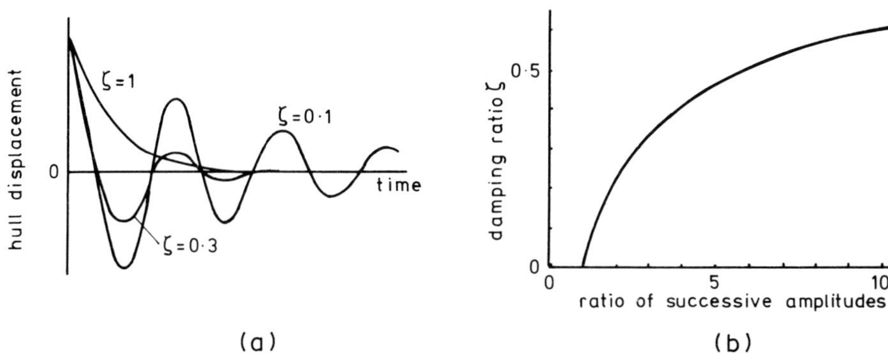

FIG. 10.21 (a) Vehicle response following a disturbance, for different levels of damping. (b) Relationship between damping ratio and rate of decay of oscillation.

when moving at speed over rough terrain has meant that AFVs have still usually tended to be underdamped, and it is only the latest generation of high-speed vehicles that have, of necessity, achieved satisfactory levels.

The telescopic type of damper commonly found on road vehicles has often been used on military track-layers. Its performance, however, has been strictly limited, especially in the case of heavy MBTs, by the lack of a good heat conduction path: cooling has principally been achieved by convection alone, as can be seen in Figure 10.14. In the case of those of the latest designs of AFVs which utilise torsion bars, the solution shown in Figure 10.16 has been found by building a rotary damper into the wheel arm bearing support unit. Because they are bolted directly on to the side plates, which provide the necessary heat sink, these units can be rated to levels not previously achieved. The mode of damping can be hydraulic, as in Figure 10.22, or may utilise suitably surfaced friction discs, as in the Leopard 2 MBT. If the spring is by hydrogas then, as has been seen, a damping restricter is easily included in the design, whilst again the complete unit may be bolted direct to the side plate and heavy damping is thus possible.

Being velocity proportional, the force generated by these highly rated dampers at present-day cross-country speeds can be very large and to avoid damage to them it is necessary to fit a pressure-limiting relief valve. Under these conditions the damper is acting as a buffer, usefully augmenting the spring and bump stop to prevent the suspension reaching full bump. This action leads to the alternative name for this component—a shock-absorber.

Human Response to Vibration

Referring back to Figure 10.20, when considering the frequency response of the vehicle, it was tacitly assumed that a sufficient criterion on which to judge ride quality was the hull displacement. In practice, this represents an over-simplification of the situation: it is the effect of motion on the ability of the crew to perform their tasks efficiently that is the final measure of the success of the suspension.

Figure 10.23a shows the results of tests in which the subjects were exposed to

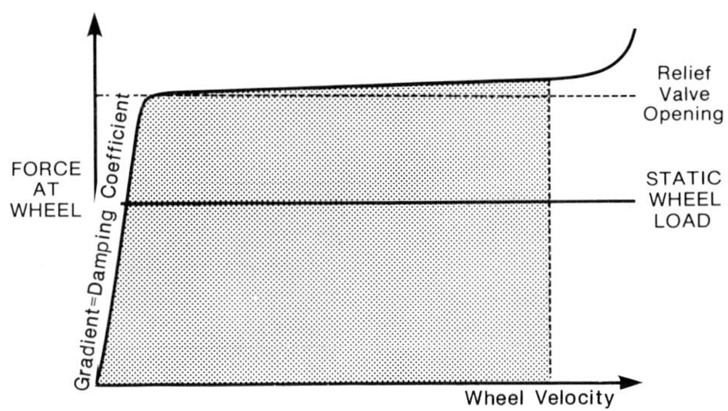

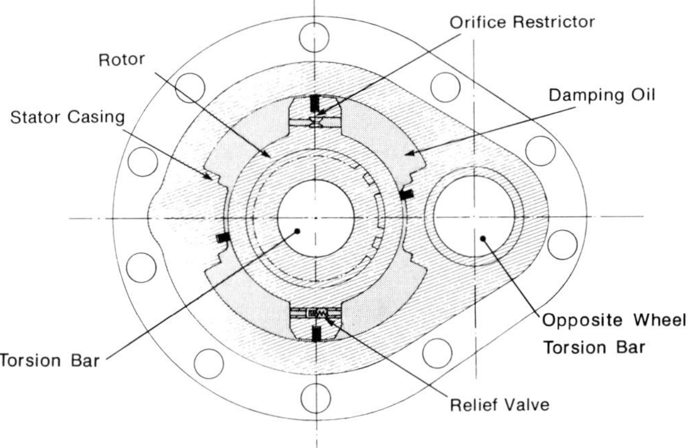

FIG. 10.22 Rotary damper (Warrior).

vibration of varying intensity and frequency, and their proficiency in the performance of a set task monitored. It is seen that the human response to vibration (HRV) is frequency as well as amplitude dependent. Man is most susceptible in the range 4–8 Hz, within which fall the natural frequencies of a number of principal parts of the body including the abdomen, thorax, pelvis, heart, upper torso and shoulder girdle. Consequently the acceleration of the hull should be minimised as far as possible over this range.

The hull displacement response in Figure 10.20 has therefore been replotted as an acceleration response in Figure 10.23b, and the general shape of the HRV curve superimposed. It can be seen that in order to minimise the overall effect of the disturbance on the crew, the HRV curve should be fitted in as low as possible whilst remaining above the curve of hull acceleration. Again, the importance of choosing the right amount of damping is apparent; too little results in high resonant acceleration, whilst too much transmits high-frequency forces. A damping ratio of around 0.3 is indicated; the best position for the HRV curve is then somewhere about as shown, with the 4 Hz point coinciding with a frequency ratio of 1.6, indicating a desirable maximum for f_n of about 2.5 Hz.

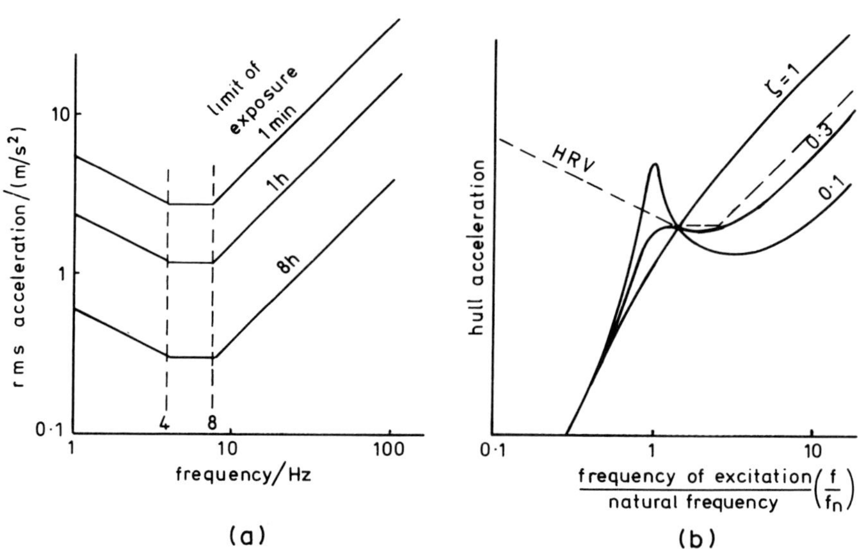

FIG. 10.23 (a) ISO recommandations for effects of vibration on Fatigue Decreased Proficiency (FDP) in man. (b)Frequency response (acceleration) of vehicle in bounce with FDP line.

Active Suspension—the Future

In this look at suspension design for military vehicles, the emphasis has been upon the passive suspension, because it is the only type in production up until the present. However, considerable work has taken place, and a number of research vehicles have been built to investigate the possibilities of incorporating a suspension whose characteristics, instead of remaining fixed under all circumstances, can be altered to optimise the ride under the prevailing conditions. Such an 'active' suspension may provide an escape from the compromises seen to have been necessary in choosing the spring and damper rates of a passive suspension. With conventional suspensions approaching the limits of performance, further advances in this aspect of mobility may be expected to rely increasingly on this approach.

In the block diagram in Figure 10.24 the elements of an active suspension are indicated, although not all the control inputs shown will always be present. The suspension itself will usually need a power supply which, for reasons of compactness, will normally be hydraulic. Variation of the suspension characteristic can then be performed by an electrical signal via an electrohydraulic servovalve which controls the flow of oil to and from the unit. The required control signal can be computed from any of a number of pieces of information concerning the motion of the wheels, the hull and even the terrain, derived from appropriate transducers.

In a purely active system, the suspension unit simply consists of a hydraulic jack or actuator which supports the hull mass. The problem with this approach is that every wheel movement due to ground irregularity is accompanied by hydraulic flow pumped to or from the actuator, with an associated power requirement. With a

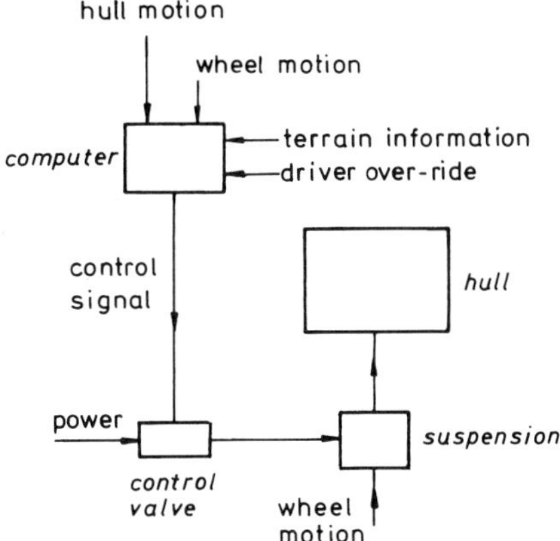

FIG. 10.24 Elements of an active suspension.

heavy vehicle, such as an AFV, moving fast over rough terrain, the pressures and flow rates needed would call for quite impracticably high power inputs.

The answer is to combine the active hydraulic supply and control elements with a passive spring, invariably a hydrogas unit, to form a semi-active suspension. Under conditions of straight running over rough ground, the unit behaves passively, with no hydraulic flow, and by making the gas spring very soft, a ride quality approaching that of the zero rate suspension can be attained.

Let us now review the problems identified earlier when discussing the zero rate suspension. Excessive deflection due to load changes can be dealt with by sensing the wheel-to-hull displacement, and using this to vary the hydraulic pressure and volume in the hydrogas strut. Similarly, excessive roll and pitch in cornering and braking can be eliminated, using signals from transducers, such as accelerometers and gyroscopes, that will sense these conditions before the unwanted movement has time to develop.

As a first stage in meeting the problem of limited wheel travel, provision can be made to utilise that available to the full, so that the approach of a large bump is anticipated by moving the front suspension to its bottom limit. This 'preview' can be provided by the driver operating a pitch control. Finally, as speeds rise further, it will become necessary for the driver's function to be taken over by an inbuilt system of terrain preview, perhaps using a laser or radar scanner. Such a system would come close to offering the ride of a zero rate suspension by only increasing the force on the hull if an obstacle were sensed that was outside the range of the wheel travel. The problem associated with unsprung mass would also then be overcome without recourse to large additional suspension forces, by lifting the wheel in anticipation of the bump. Since the force required is inversely proportional to the square of the time taken to raise through a given height, increasing this time by a factor of perhaps five reduces the force by some 96%. Such systems have received considerable attention, but this has largely been confined to theoretical studies and they would be extremely expensive to develop and make reliable.

Semi-active systems without preview are, however, another matter. Every automotive manufacturer around the world is currently working on these, and a number are already on the civilian car market. This investment in terms of cost and technical resources, may be expected to hasten the future application of active suspensions to military vehicles should improved off-road mobility receive the necessary priority.

11

Running Gear—Wheels

Introduction

At the start of the previous chapter the general requirements for running gear designed to meet the needs peculiar to the AFV were discussed. The application of these to the particular case of the tracked vehicle was then considered. In this chapter it is the turn of the AFV which runs on wheels fitted with pneumatic tyres—or wheeled AFV for short. A typical layout showing the principal components of the running gear for a wheeled AFV may be seen in Figure 11.1. Before going on to consider these in detail, however, the general attributes associated with the adoption of a wheeled solution can be summarised.

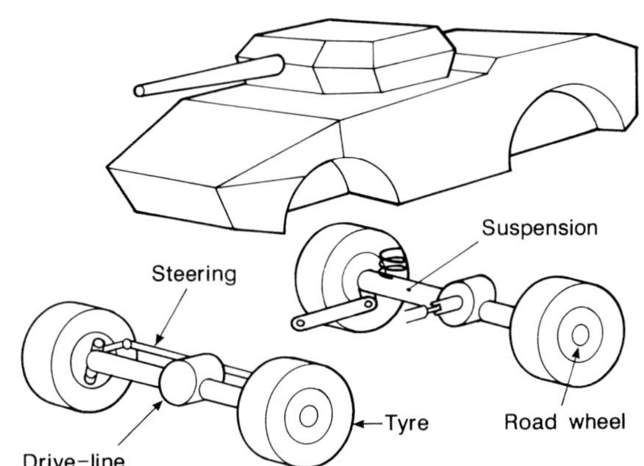

FIG. 11.1 Wheeled armoured fighting vehicle running gear.

Performance

This aspect shows up the principal disadvantages of discarding the track, namely the reduced area in contact with the ground and the correspondingly increased ground pressure. The resulting loss of mobility over soft ground can only partially be mitigated by fitting as many wheels as the space allows, normally six or eight on a high mobility AFV. Even then the ground pressure will be about three times that of the comparable tracked vehicle. Likewise, if the relatively poor obstacle crossing capability of the wheeled vehicle is to be kept to an acceptable level, then a minimum of six wheels is needed. Of course, all these wheels are needed only occasionally, and there are several examples of vehicles which are normally 4 × 4, but that can become 6 × 6 or 8 × 8 by the expedient of lowering a set of driven centre wheels, for example the French Panhard ERC (6 × 6) or the Soviet BRDM (8 × 8).

The reduced contact area of the tyre also means less traction in cohesive soils and to minimise this disadvantage, it is necessary to ensure that all wheels are driven, with associated complications to the drive-line. It is because, in this context, the distinction between the drive-line and the suspension can become rather blurred, that the drive-line (strictly part of the transmission covered in Chapter 9) is included amongst the components shown in Figure 11.1.

The advantage reverts to the wheel when on-road performance is considered. Here the internal rolling resistance inherent to the track may be three times that of the pneumatic tyre, with resulting penalties in terms of speed and fuel consumption.

Handling

It is a matter of common experience that the on-road handling behaviour of a vehicle fitted with pneumatic tyres, with correct design, can be made predictable, safe and effortless with minimal wear on tyres or road. This is because, first, the skid-steer approach of the tracked vehicle is discarded in favour of a steered wheel layout which does, however, carry with it a penalty in terms of associated linkages and space. Secondly, the pneumatic tyre responds to cornering force with a lateral compliance which can be used by the designer to adjust the handling of the vehicle to suit his requirements; this aspect will be examined in some detail later.

Off-road, the advantages of the tyre become less marked. The high external rolling resistance due to sinkage in soft ground can be exacerbated, when following a curved path, by the tendency for each wheel to cut a fresh rut; this can be mitigated by suitable design of steering at the expense of further complication. Discarding skid-steering means that pivot turns are no longer possible; indeed, even the tightest practically achievable turning circle may well prove to be an operational embarrassment.

Ride

The pneumatic tyre was first invented with the object of improving the ride of vehicles. Since then, roads have improved. However, with increased speeds, the tyre still has a vital role to play, not just in attenuating the transmission of road irregularities through to the hull, but also in keeping to a minimum the fluctuation of the contact with the ground, so maintaining the vital traction and cornering control forces. The problem of excessive levels of noise and vibration generated by a track on-road have been discussed; a military tyre designed for off-road use will certainly not be noiseless, but the level will now be such that it can be tolerated without discomfort over the long distances that may be dictated by strategic mobility requirements.

Suspension

The schematic nature of Figure 11.1 tends to mask the mechanical complication associated with most wheeled vehicle suspensions. This is especially the case if the wheel is independently suspended, driven, braked, and also steered. To illustrate this point, examine Figure 11.2 and then contrast that with Figure 10.8 which

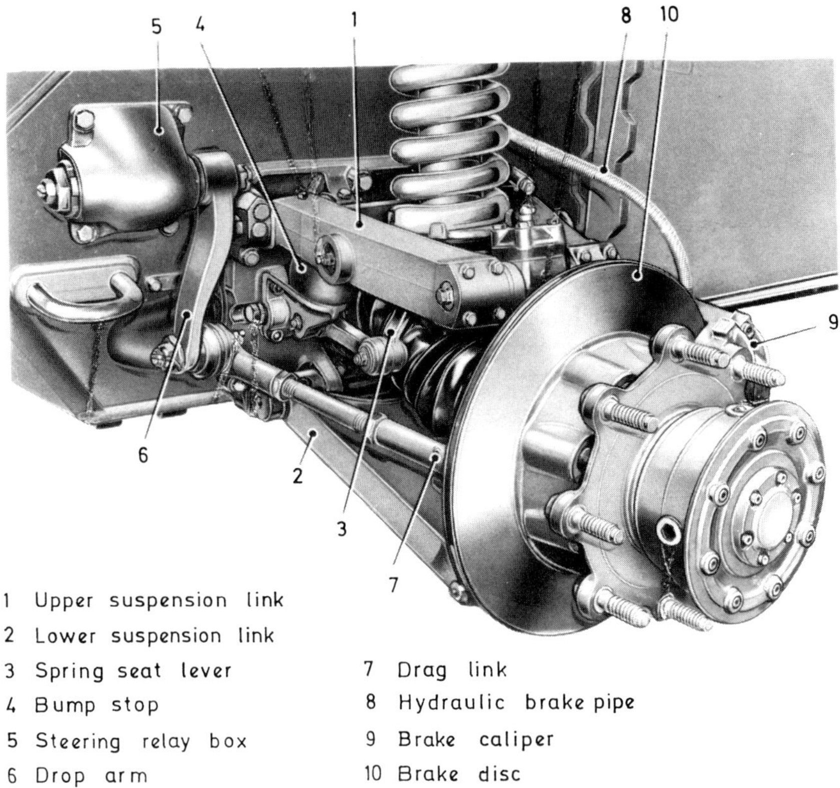

FIG. 11.2 Steered independent suspension unit for a wheeled armoured fighting vehicle.

shows the suspension of a typical tracked vehicle. In passing, note the drive (not annotated) via a bellows-protected shaft with constant velocity joints (see Chapter 9) at either end, terminating in the hub-mounted epicyclic reduction gearbox at the outmost extremity. The complication of the braking system can also be seen, and its vulnerability contrasted with the single inboard brake needed on each side of a tracked vehicle.

The suspension itself can be considered on two parts; the linkage that is needed to locate the wheel relative to the hull, and the components that transmit forces between them, that is the spring and the damper.

Suspension Linkages

Wheel locating systems fall into two categories. Independent systems, as illustrated in Figure 11.2, allow each wheel to move on its own without interconnecting with the remainder. Alternatively, a pair of wheels may be arranged so that the movement of one is relayed to the other. An example of the latter is the bogey suspension described in the previous chapter, and this principle (see Figure 10.13) may also be found on wheeled vehicles, usually longitudinally interconnecting a pair of adjacent unsteered wheels e.g. the rear 'walking-beam' bogey utilised on the Brazilian Engesa 6 × 6 range of vehicles. Most commonly met in this context, however, is the use of a transverse beam axle on the ends of which are mounted the wheels. If the wheels are to be driven, as must be the case for an AFV, then the axle contains within it a pair of drive-shafts and a differential (see Chapter 9); it is then known as a 'live axle'. Examples of two live axle configurations may be seen in Figure 11.3. The more familiar of these, because of its almost universal use on commercial vehicles, is that utilising leaf springs which also serve to provide location for the axle. The result is simple, inexpensive and robust and it may often be found on vehicles whose off-road mobility is of secondary importance, such as the British Saxon APC, intended primarily for internal-security duties. However, although these advantages are passed on in the application of this proven design to AFVs, the extension of its use to an off-road environment shows up a number of serious shortcomings.

First, on soft ground, the effect of sinkage on mobility is aggravated by the limited ground clearance, dictated by the bottom of the differential, and the subsequent high drag offered by the axle in deep mud. In the same way, over boulders the differential is highly vulnerable to damage. In contrast, an independent suspension will allow the bottom of the hull to be designed smooth and flat. This will have the added advantage of being less vulnerable to certain types of mine attack.

The next problem with adopting leaf spring location concerns the limitation that this imposes upon the wheel travel that can be obtained. A bump travel of perhaps only 70 mm may well be adequate for on-road use, but under cross-country ground conditions needs to be around three times that figure if the maximum speed possible, without undue contact of the bump stops, is not to be severely curtailed. In order to increase the available travel, it is necessary to discard the leaf springs in favour of an alternative form, usually coil springs. Since these cannot provide location, a linkage has to be used, typically of the form illustrated in Figure 11.3 as used in the West German Luchs reconnaissance vehicle. Here the axle is located by a pair of longitudinal links together with an 'A' bracket that takes lateral loads and, being above the two links, acts with them to resist rotation of the axle about its own axis under braking or drive. This arrangement will clearly carry a penalty in terms of added complication, cost and vulnerability. It will also aggravate the problem of the clearance space swept out by the suspension that has to be provided by hull cut-outs. These reduce the

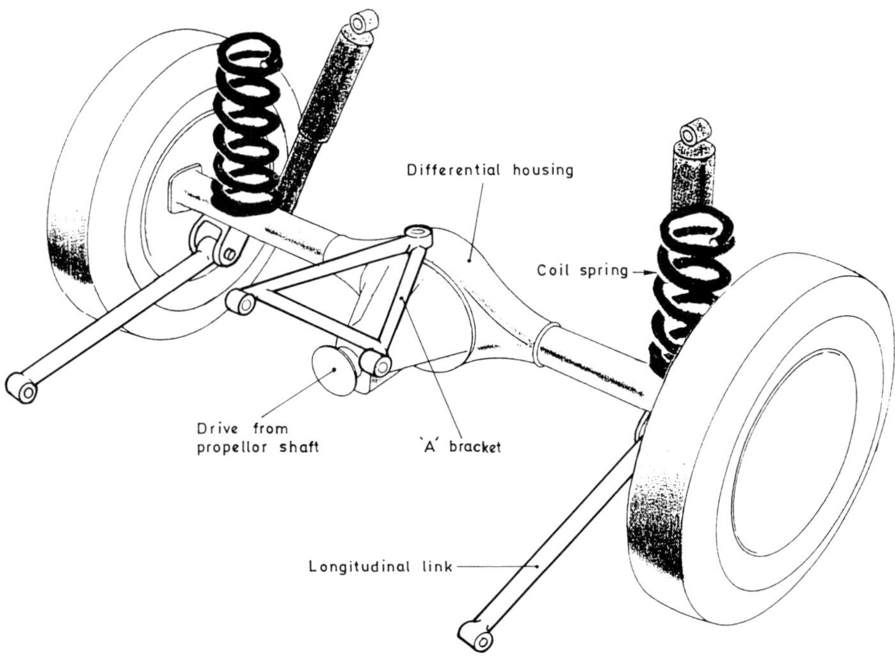

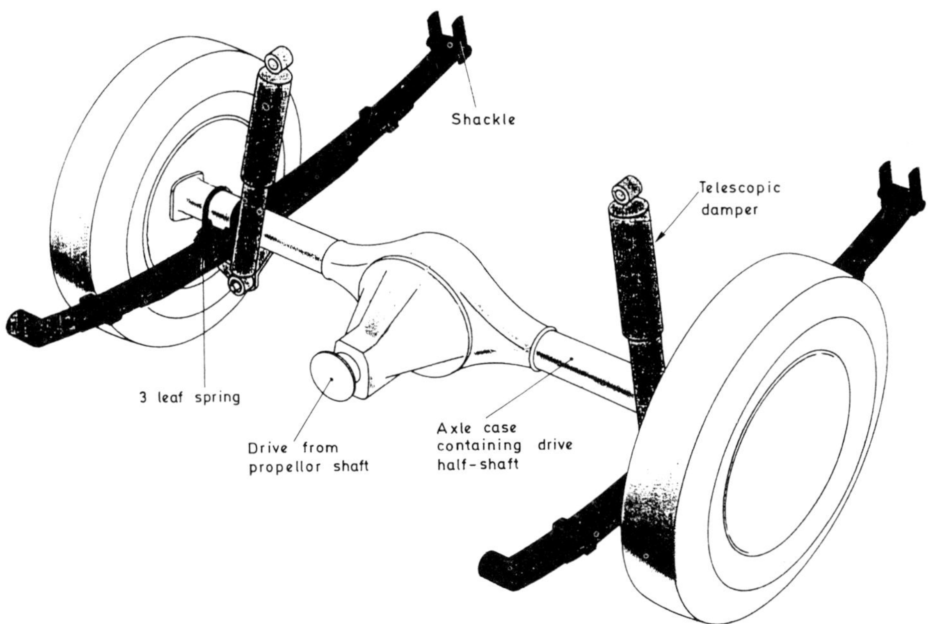

FIG. 11.3 Live axle configurations. (a) Coil springs with location by longitudinal links and an 'A' bracket. (b) Leaf springs also provide location.

useable internal volume and lead to a high silhouette, perhaps an increase of 400 mm in the case of a large AFV, compared with independent suspension. Further problems inherent to live axles concern their effect on handling. In the previous chapter the importance of a low unsprung mass in maintaining ground contact was discussed. As much as 20% of the total weight of a vehicle may be attributable to the wheels and axles of this form of suspension. This compares with about 8% using independent location. Additionally, if the axle is steered, when the wheel on one side hits a bump, both wheels will roll and the resulting gyroscopic couple will result in an unwanted steering input, further limiting off-road performance. Another point concerns roll of the hull during cornering. Excessive roll is undesirable, both because of its effect on the crew, and also its interaction with the steering and suspension geometry. Roll is resisted by the roll stiffness provided by the suspension; a beam axle with its narrow spring spacing, offers only about half the roll stiffness of the corresponding independent suspension and thus will roll through twice the angle.

Independent Suspensions

From the foregoing discussion it may be inferred that, to obtain the best possible mobility for an AFV, an independent suspension is desirable. Three linkages that give this are commonly to be found.

In the case of tracked vehicles, the trailing arm was seen to be universally used; it is compact, robust, and simple. For the same reasons, a number of wheeled AFVs use trailing arms for their unsteered rear wheel stations, where the potential interference of the arm with steering lock is no longer a consideration. An example of this is the 8 × 8 LAV-25 used by the United States Marine Corps, with trailing arms and torsion bars on its rear two stations. Two further types of independent suspension linkage are shown in Figure 11.4. These are the AFV configurations most commonly met and one or other will always be found where the wheel needs to be steered because, being transversely located, the links do not limit the turning circle at full lock. The double transverse link (sometimes known as the double wishbone) needs careful design of its geometry to ensure that the wheel remains as upright as possible, and the wheel track remains nearly constant, for both bounce and roll movements of the hull. This is achieved by making the lower link some 30% longer than the upper, and by inclining it upwards towards the hull.

The alternative is the strut suspension (also known as the McPherson strut), a variant that dispenses with the upper link by mounting the stub axle on the end of a near vertical telescopic strut whose upper end is directly pivoted on the hull. Although this does not allow the latitude in design geometry of the double wishbone linkage, it so happens that the arrangement gives near optimum layout in any case. Further advantages are the better packaging possible, with the damper incorporated in the strut, surrounded by the coil spring, and with the strut serving as the swivel axis for steering. It is also possible to widen slightly the usable hull width with this design. Its application is exemplified by the Italian Centauro 8 × 8 tank destroyer, which utilises struts at all stations.

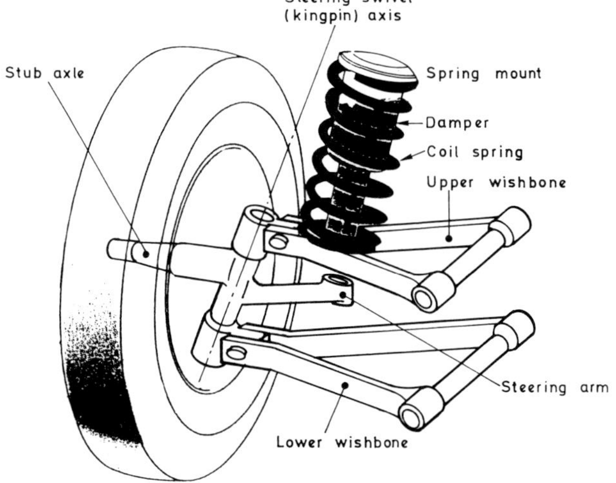

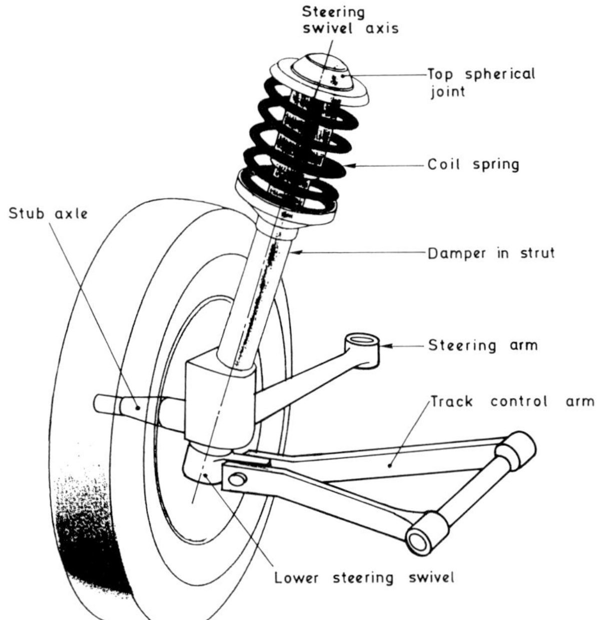

FIG. 11.4 Independent suspension with steered wheels. (a) Double wishbone. (b) Strut.

Suspension Geometry

Although independent suspension confers many advantages, its increased complication does call for accurate geometrical setting for its correct functioning. This will tend to be vulnerable to accidental or enemy-inflicted damage and needs careful maintenance. The principal settings for the suspension linkages, and also for the associated steering geometry, are shown in Figure 11.5.

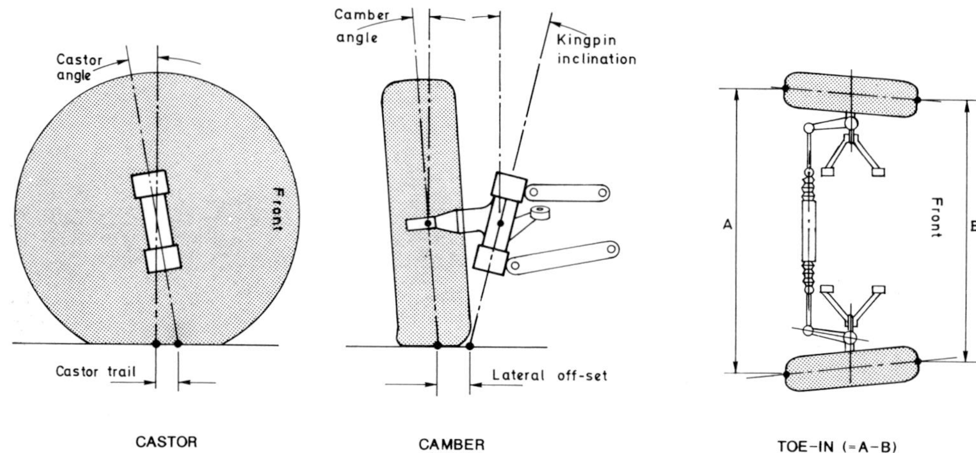

FIG. 11.5 Elements of steering geometry.

Castor

This refers to the fore-and-aft inclination of the axis about which the wheel swivels in order to steer—the kingpin axis—through an angle known as the castor angle. By arranging for this axis to intersect the tyre contact area ahead of its contact centre, the lateral force from the tyre on the ground during cornering will act behind the axis by an amount known as the castor trail. As a result there will be a moment applied to the wheel tending to align it with the direction of travel. In order to maintain the cornering force it is therefore necessary to apply a resisting moment via the steering system. This provides useful force feedback to the driver, enhancing the feel of the handling, and the self-centering on releasing the steering wheel is also a necessary safety measure. Too much castor will, however, make for excessively heavy steering, especially at low speed when large steer angles may be used.

Kingpin inclination

The kingpin axis is also inclined when viewed from the front. This is in order that it should intersect the contact area as near to its centre as possible in a lateral direction (centre-point steering), so ensuring that the tyre does not move fore-and-aft when turned. Again, excessive inclination is to be avoided, in the interests of keeping the wheel as upright as possible during steering. In practice, due to the difficulty of fitting the kingpin inside the wheel, positive lateral offset usually has to be accepted. This is undesirable since it means that braking or drive forces on the tyre will have a moment about the kingpin axis that will need to be resisted by the driver and will result in kick-back through the steering over rough ground.

Camber

The pneumatic tyre performs at its best when held perpendicular to the ground, zero camber angle, rather than leaning inwards or outwards. Thus ideally the suspension should be set up with zero static camber. However, sometimes a small angle may have to be incorporated in order that, when the outer wheel rises relative to the body as it rolls during cornering, it should become upright under these more demanding conditions. If the camber is outwards, then this will help to reduce the lateral offset (see Figure 11.5).

Toe-in

A pair of wheels, with positive lateral offsets, will tend to take up any compliance in the steering linkage such as to steer the wheels either towards each other (if they are driving wheels), or apart (if undriven). To anticipate this, wheels may be set up statically with either toe-in or toe-out respectively, thus ensuring that the wheels point straight ahead under running conditions. Because of the very small angle involved, this measurement is usually quantified by the difference between the track dimensions at the front and rear of the wheels or of the tyres.

Springs

Leaf

The use of the semi-elliptic leaf spring, in conjunction with a live axle, has been discussed earlier. Although it is simple and robust, the limitation that it imposes on wheel travel and packaging normally restricts its application in AFVs. Nonetheless, technological advances are being made. These include the use of taper rolled single leaf springs, and the introduction of fibre reinforced composites to replace steel in the interests of weight saving, and to prevent separation in the event of breakage, an important consideration with the leaf acting as a location for the axle. Use of two such leaves of differing curvature, so that the lower leaf is only engaged by the flattening of the top leaf under heavy loads, results in the rising rate shown to be desirable in the previous chapter (see Figure 10.15).

Torsion bar

This may be employed in a similar suspension layout to that in tracked vehicles, namely a transverse bar with trailing arm. However, with layouts based upon transverse links, that is the double wishbone and strut, a longitudinal disposition is the natural one, using these links as the lever arms. Again, the problem is to fit in sufficient length of bar to give the required wheel travel, especially with 3 or 4 wheels per side. One answer utilised by the British Alvis range of 6 × 6 vehicles, is to employ the tube-over-bar system (see Figure 10.17).

Coil spring

This is the most commonly met form of wheeled AFV springing; the application to independent suspensions may be seen in Figures 11.2 and 11.4, and to beam axles in Figure 11.3. For further details the reader should refer back to the previous chapter.

Hydrogas

The advantages of this form of springing again were identified in Chapter 10; rising rate, built-in damping, variable ground clearance, compactness and low weight. In addition, looking to the future, the introduction of any form of active suspension will need to be built around a hydrogas unit. In the case of wheeled vehicles, the hydrogas cylinder can quite simply act as the strut in that type of independent suspension, making for an attractively light, compact arrangement. In this form it is used on all wheel stations of the Spanish BMR-600 IFV.

Dampers

The telescopic damper, as found on most civilian vehicles, is also almost universally used on wheeled AFVs. The velocity/force characteristic will differ, however. With road vehicles it is normal to have nearly all the damping during the rebound part of the stroke, in the interests of minimising force transmission over small bumps. Conversely, off-road, where large bumps beyond the capacity of the wheel travel are encountered, it is vital to minimise contact with the bump-stops and so the damping will be biased towards the bump stroke.

Steering

Ackerman Linkage

When a vehicle is under steady state cornering, each wheel will move along a circular path. The centre of the circle will be the same for all wheels although, in general, their radii of turn will differ. In order to prevent lateral slip of the tyres, it is necessary to arrange for the plane of each of the wheels to lie tangential to its respective circle by suitable steering. In fact, the wheels at one chosen station may remain unsteered, since the remaining stations can then be steered relative to that one. Thus, in the case of a four wheel vehicle, it is normal to steer only two, usually at the front for reasons of controllability. Because the inner and outer wheels run at different radii, they need to be steered through different angles. To achieve the correct relationship for all angles of steering lock would require a complex linkage. In practice a good approximation is obtained using the Ackerman linkage illustrated in Figure 11.6, wherein a track-rod connects the steering arms of the two wheels, these arms being angled towards one another so as to intersect at the back axle. If the wheels are independently suspended, use of a one-piece track-rod means that vertical wheel movements would result in the wheels being steered relative to one another. To minimise this, the track-rod is divided into three parts, the outer two having about the same length as the transverse links of the suspension. In the case of the AFV, it is necessary to locate the central portion within the hull, which leads to the further complication of relay boxes and drop arms. (see Figure 11.2).

Steering Geometry Options (Figure 11.7)

Although pure rolling at all wheels can be obtained by steering all but one of the stations, there are often good reasons for adopting either more or less than this.

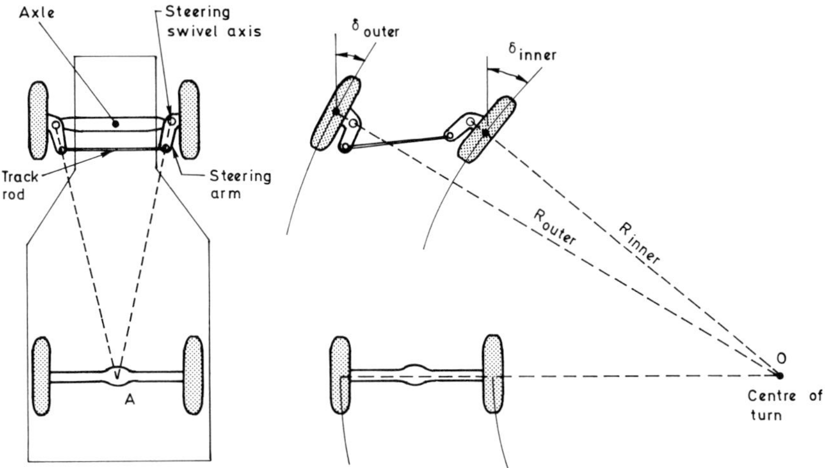

FIG. 11.6 Ackerman steering linkage allows inner and outer wheels to circle the same centre.

Consider again the 4-wheel vehicle. Suppose that, additionally, the rear wheels were to be made steerable. Such an arrangement is currently arousing considerable interest amongst car manufacturers, with the purpose of using this 'active steering' to adjust the handling of the vehicle automatically according to circumstances.

Of much greater importance, however, in the context of the AFV, is the use of 4-

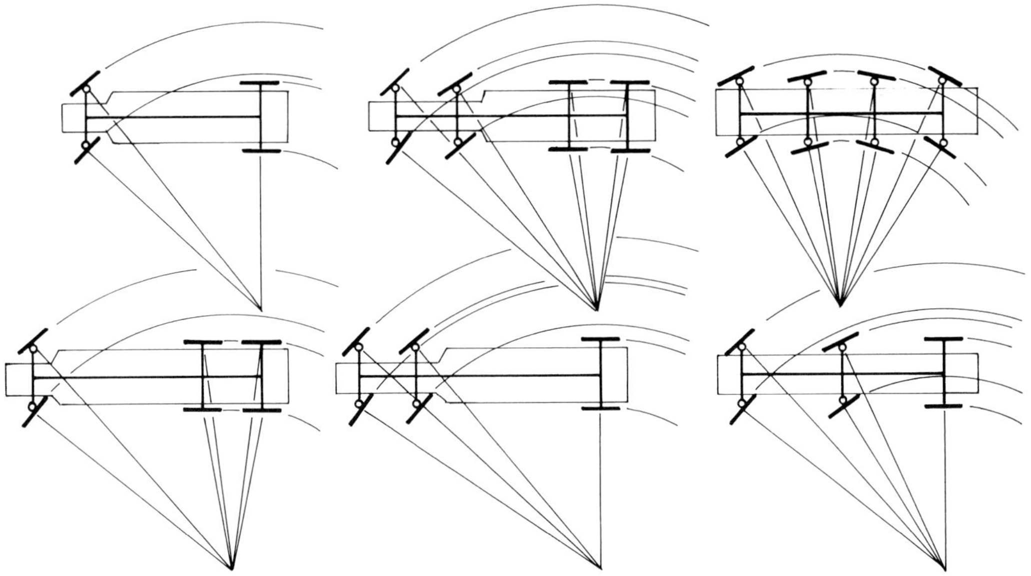

FIG. 11.7 Steering geometry options for 2 and multi-axle armoured fighting vehicles.

wheel steer to reduce the turning circle by almost half by means of a mechanical linkage that moves the rear wheels by an amount equal and opposite to those at the front. There is a further advantage to be gained by this when the vehicle is negotiating soft ground; the front and rear wheels on each side will run at the same radius and hence will cut only a single rut, thus reducing the rolling resistance. The principle may be extended to a greater number of stations than four. Thus the Spanish VEC 6 × 6 reconnaissance vehicle steers front and rear stations by equal and opposite amounts. The FRG Luchs 8 × 8 steers all stations (see Figure 11.7), the centre ones by a suitable fraction of those at the ends. This vehicle also has a facility for disengaging steer to the rear two stations when this is not needed, such as is normally the case on roads.

On the other hand, provision of steering can only be achieved at the cost of reduction in usable hull width and added complication. There is a good case for avoiding it if possible. Thus, although a 6 × 6 with equispaced stations will need two of these to be steered, if the two rear stations are closely spaced and well separated from that at the front, then it is acceptable not to steer either of them and accept the small amount of lateral scrub on the tyres that this implies. Such an arrangement is frequently adopted in AFVs, for example on the US Commando V-300 6 × 6 APC. Finally, mention should be made of the use of skid steer in wheeled AFVs. This works in the same way as on tracked vehicles and carries with it the same advantages (absence of linkages, robustness, tight or pivot turn capability, maximum usable hull width) and disadvantages (poor steering in adverse conditions, poor on-road handling, high tyre wear, increased power consumption). Although its use is generally to be found on lighter vehicles, skid steer is successfully employed on the French AMX-10RC 6 × 6 16t reconnaissance vehicle.

Tyres for Wheeled Vehicles

The pneumatic tyre provides the only contact that a vehicle has with the ground. Through it alone must be transmitted tractive forces for acceleration, braking and negotiating gradients, and lateral forces for cornering and on side slopes. Besides maximising these control forces, it will also be required to attenuate the vertical disturbing forces from ground irregularities. It must achieve all this on both paved surfaces, wet or dry, and off-road under a variety of soil conditions. It should not limit the vehicle speed, either by excessive rolling resistance or over-heating, nor should it incur excessive fuel consumption. Furthermore, since we are talking here about vehicles that will be exposed to enemy fire, the ability to withstand damage whilst maintaining some mobility is essential. Not surprisingly, the tyre is a complicated component and compromise between the many conflicting requirements is necessary.

Construction

Tyre build starts with a pair of hoops wound from steel wire. These ‘beads’ form an inextensible base which will remain tight on the wheel rims under inflation pressure and hence transmit cornering, traction and braking loads to the wheel. Between them are laid a number of sheets of reinforced rubber (plies) to form the carcass, every ply wrapping once around the circumference. Each ply consists of an array of unidirectional cords set in a rubber matrix. The cords may be of rayon, polyester, nylon or steel.

For many years construction consisted of plies, all of which ran the full width from one bead to the other. To give strength both in the circumferential and radial planes, the cords had to run at a compromise angle between these extremes, typically with a crown angle of 35° (see Figure 11.8). For symmetry, an equal

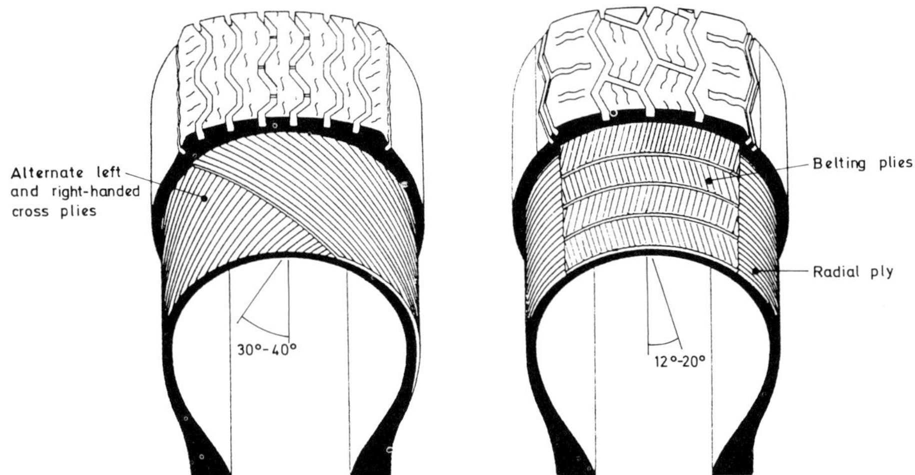

FIG. 11.8 Tyre carcass constructions.

number of left and right handed plies was used, as many as 12 on an AFV tyre. This construction is known as 'crossply' and it is still used on many military vehicles today, although it is fast being superseded by the radial ply tyre which has long been supreme in the civilian market.

The radial seeks to overcome the compromise, inherent to the design of the crossply, between the need for compliance in the sidewalls under vertical load (for a soft ride), and stiffness in the crown under lateral load (for positive handling). This is achieved by separating these two functions. No more than one or two full width plies are used, with their cords running in the radial plane (radial plies) together with a larger number of plies (perhaps four or six) confined to the tread area and with their cords running nearly circumferentially (belting plies).

This reinforcement of the crown area brings with it further advantages, over and above the better handling. Because the tread is well-supported, there will be less movement between rubber and road when the tyre flattens in the contact area, leading to less wear, especially in corners. Rolling resistance will also benefit, both because of this and the more flexible sidewalls. Ground pressure will be more evenly distributed, giving better grip both on-road and in soft going. Against this must be reckoned the increased vulnerability of the thin side-walls to accidental damage and penetration. Use of a flexible carcass allows inflation pressures to be varied widely according to the needs of the going. The Soviets especially have adopted this principle extensively: their vehicles are fitted with a central tyre inflation system (CTIS) feeding each tyre through hub-mounted pneumatic slip-rings. The pressure range used varies from 320 kPa on-road down to as little as 50 kPa in marshy terrain. The resultant doubling of ground contact area nearly doubles the tractive force obtainable. Tyre damage is avoided by lowering the operating speed with tyre pressure, although some reduction in life has to be accepted. Another way of decreasing the ground pressure is to use a low aspect ratio (defined as: section height/section width). This trend has been noticeable for some time amongst normal road vehicles for other reasons, but the use of low profile tyres in off-road vehicles (as low as 50% or less in special cases) has been primarily because of the large contact area made possible. The drawback with this approach is that, for a given sinkage, the ground deformation (and thus rolling resistance) is proportional to the tyre width. If an arched profile is used (see Figure 11.9), then the active width of the tyre will be regulated by the sinkage. Thus not

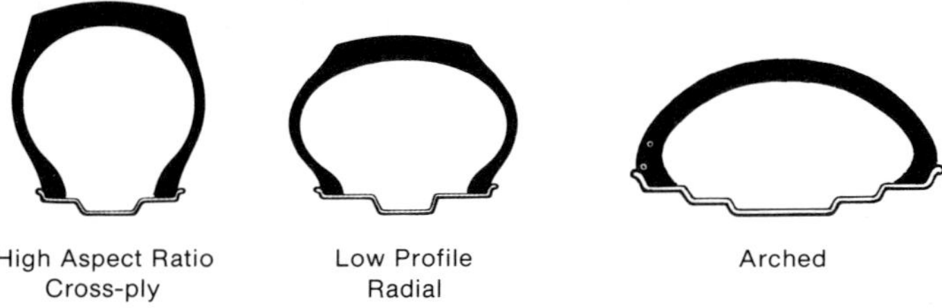

FIG. 11.9 Cross-country tyre profiles.

only will rolling resistance be minimised, but also the available traction automatically adjusted according to need. Such tyres have found application in a number of military vehicles, e.g. the West Germans' lightweight Kraka, but again it is in the Soviet Union, with its large unpaved distances, that they are most common. An inflation pressure range about half that quoted for conventional profile tyres is used. Mobility is consequently still further improved and there is an added bonus in the form of better tyre life.

Tread Pattern

For use on paved surfaces, the requirement is for as large a dry contact area as possible between the tyre and road. The sole purpose of the pattern is to remove water from under the tyre by a dual process of bulk displacement through large grooves, followed by elimination of the remaining film by knife-cuts in the tread, acting as a reservoir. Unfortunately, when it comes to off-road usage, the need is for something rather different. To understand the basis for cross-country tyre pattern designs it is necessary to recall the nature of soils and the way they transmit traction, as established in the previous chapter.

Thus over sandy (frictional) soils, traction is limited only by the coulomb friction available between the sand particles themselves. Nothing is to be gained be penetrating the surface layer and so a sand tyre will be smooth treaded, with perhaps a few circumferential grooves as a concession to possible occasional use on wet, paved surfaces. On the other hand, over damp clay (cohesive) soils, a smooth tyre will find little grip on the surface. It is thus necessary to design the tyre with a series of aggressive lugs, corresponding to the grouser of the track link, with the aim of digging into the clay and then using its considerable shear strength to provide traction.

The design of the lugs varies widely: some examples are shown in Figure 11.10. In general, they must be a compromise between the necessity for aggressive penetration of the soil on the one hand and mechanical strength on the other. By

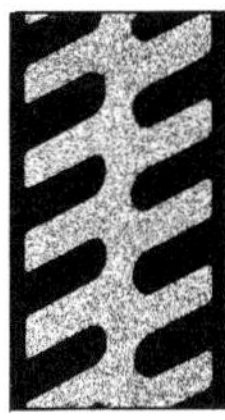

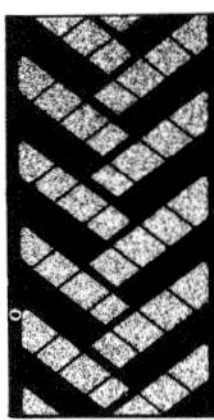
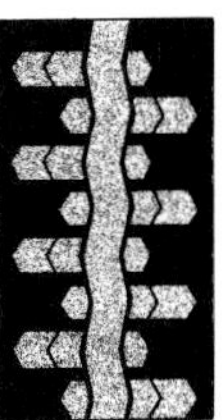

FIG. 11.10 Tyre tread patterns for cohesive soils.

adopting a chevron pattern, with the direction of rotation such that the soil between the lugs tends to be extruded outwards, a degree of self-cleaning is possible. The chevron will also give better stability on a side-slope and the continuous line of contact around the periphery, unlike a transverse bar pattern, makes for a smoother ride. In this context, mention should be made of the use of tyre chains, as a means of improving aggression and thus traction in cohesive soils, which can offer a performance comparable with that obtainable from tracks. It is also relevant to note that, if the vehicle is required to swim, aggressive lugs will bring a considerable improvement in propulsion.

In general, however, a penalty has to be paid when it comes to using these cross-country tyres on roads. They will have poor adhesion, especially in the wet, due to the small amount of rubber on the road, and the absence of provision for water film elimination. They will also tend to generate structural vibration and noise, and have poor lateral stability.

Low Vulnerability and Run-Flat (RF)

The conditions under which a wheeled AFV is expected to operate make it essential that some mobility should be maintained, despite the penetration of one or more of its tyres. The first problem, following loss of air pressure, is to keep the beads in place on the rims of the wheel. This can be achieved by fitting a simple spacer between the beads, such as the thick band made of rubber used on the British Army RF, which will, however, necessitate the use of a split wheel for fitting purposes. An alternative is the Swedish Trelleborg device that uses 6 metal segments within the tyre cavity that can be assembled from outside the tyre so as to clamp the beads to the rims once the tyre has been fitted using the conventional wheel well.

This tyre also sets out to solve the second problem, namely the provision of a limited RF capability. Each segment carries a plate formed to the arc of a circle so that, when in position, the six segments together form the smooth periphery of an inner wheel onto which the tyre can collapse following deflation. It requires for its implementation a tyre with flexible side-walls, that is of radial construction. Being rigid, this device will not provide a good ride. Also the difference of diameter between the inner and outer surfaces results in a cyclical slip between them in the contact area which may be 20% of the vehicle speed, resulting in heat generation and rapid wear.

The ride can be improved by making the inner wheel compliant. This is the approach adopted for the French Hutchinson VP.PV RF insert, a device that has achieved widespread acceptance amongst the manufacturers and users of wheeled AFVs. Here an inner core of rubber is moulded to contain a large number of independent cells which are inflated during manufacture to a specific pressure, depending upon the intended tyre load. Sufficient clearance is left between the tyre carcass and the core so that, during normal operation, the load is carried entirely by the tyre. The handling characteristics of the tyres will be unaffected, and the tyre inflation pressure may be varied to suit operational conditions, perhaps through a CTIS. The problem of heating and friction in the core is mitigated by incorporating a lubricant within each cell. Attrition of the core under RF running release this fluid and speeds of 55 km/h can be maintained for 55 km. However, the device is heavy and relatively costly, needing replacement after deflated running.

An alternative approach is to make the tyre sufficiently rigid for it to be able to carry its load without needing to rely on internal air pressure. This is the basis of the British Army RF, which is still widely used, although now being superseded. The tyre is of cross-ply construction with thick stiff sidewalls, so that it is heavy, and offers a poor ride. The top road speed is limited under normal operation due to overheating; whilst running deflated at 50 km/h the tyre consumes some 16 kW. A major drawback is that its insensitivity to inflation pressure limits the use of CTIS to improve mobility. Against all this, it is extremely robust for everyday use, and has an acceptable deflated and post-ballistic performance, broadly comparable with that of the cored type.

Rigidity can be obtained by completely filling the tyre cavity. The Hutchinson VP adopts this approach, as does the foam filled RF fitted to Brazilian wheeled AFVs. Again the fixed pressure means that vehicles so fitted are best suited to a predominantly on-road role, such as for IS tasks.

Summary—Tracks or Wheels for AFVs

In the process of examining the nature and attributes of AFV running gear in the last two chapters, comparisons have inevitably emerged between vehicles based upon tracks and those that rely instead upon the pneumatic tyre. It has been seen that there are significant technical differences in most of the components of the running gear. In turn, these differences will be reflected in the operating characteristics of the AFV. It may be found helpful to end by summarising the principal technical and operational arguments governing the choice of tracks or wheels.

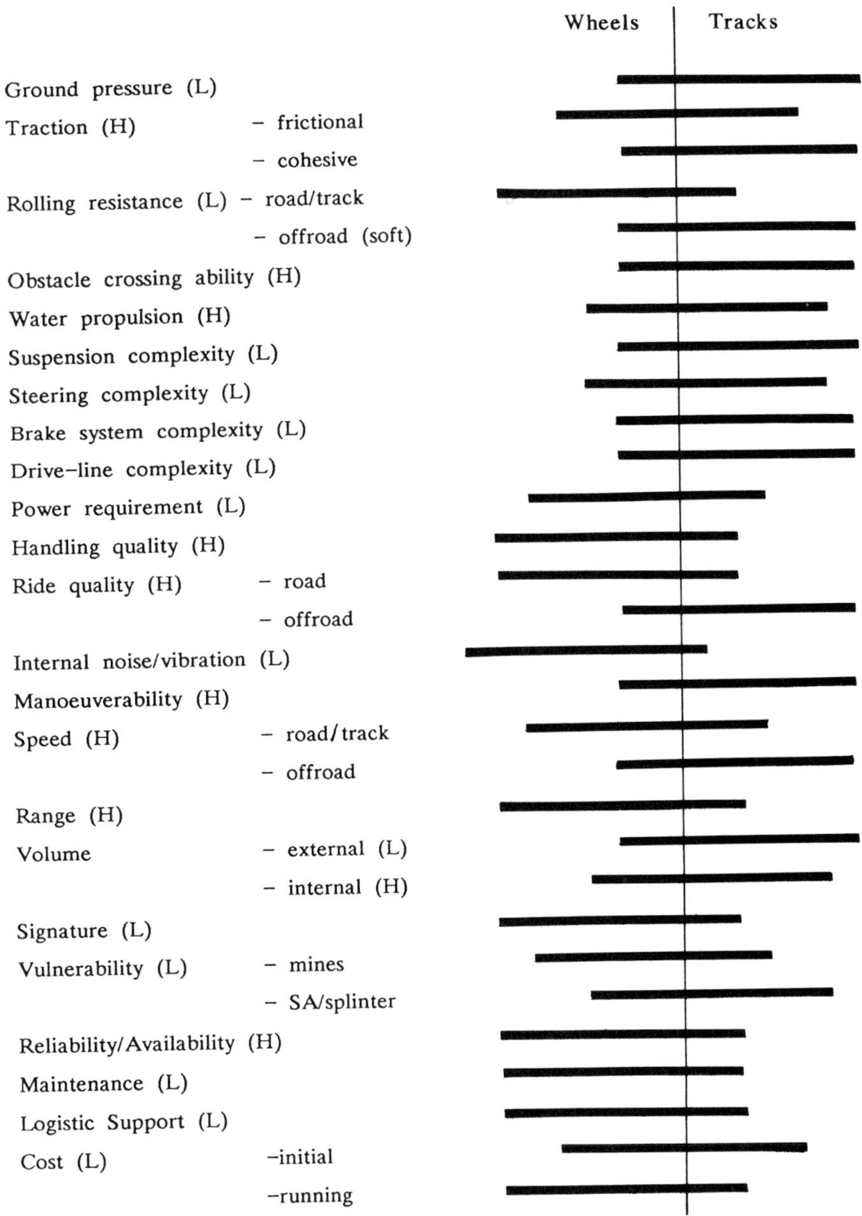

FIG. 11.11 Wheeled and tracked AFVs compared.
(H) High or (L) measures desired.

Were the issue clear-cut, it would not have been a matter of such heated debate over so many years. However, it is possible to establish some general guide-lines, and the important points that have to be considered where the choice still remains in doubt. The key factor must evidently be the operational role for which the vehicle is intended. Consider the MBT; its role dictates a level of armament and protection that means it must weigh some 45–60 tons, and if it is to have the required soft ground mobility, then the necessary ground contact area can only be obtained by use of tracks. If, however, the offensive nature of its role is relaxed, allowing a substantially lower level of protection, then a wheeled solution becomes a possibility. Such an AFV will weigh perhaps 30 tons or more and, despite running on eight large wheels, will still have a ground pressure that is substantially worse than the MBT of twice its weight. It will be large, and this will spread the already diminished armour still more thinly. But, provided some limitations are accepted, it could still carry a high pressure 105 mm turretted gun. For operations over long distances, running on unpaved, but firm, surfaces, the wheeled solution has attractions that have resulted in its adoption in several cases. It is relevant to reflect that most of the heaviest off-road construction vehicles run on wheels.

However, now suppose that we need a soft ground mobility that will match that of the MBT, evidently a further weight reduction is called for, in practice to about 20 tons. At this upper limit for high mobility wheeled vehicles, the power of the armament and the level of the protection will both need to be still further reduced, and will compare unfavourably with a tracked vehicle of the same weight.

Other things being equal, as vehicles get smaller, their weight decreases at a greater rate than the ground contact area. Thus ground pressure becomes less of a problem for wheeled AFVs below 20 tons, until at weights less than about 10 tons most AFVs are wheeled. The ground pressure advantage of tracks still remains, however, and where exceptional soft ground mobility is required, such as over bog or snow, then they become a necessity.

It is thus in the weight bracket 10–20 tons that the choice between wheels and tracks is most open. A list of the factors that might influence the decision is given in Table 11.1, together with an indication of the bias in favour of one type of running gear or the other. These ratings have, of necessity in the restricted format, to be of a somewhat generalised nature. Nonetheless, they provide a useful summary of the relative attributes of the contenders, and the reasons that lie behind them may be found in this chapter and the last. Specifically, it can be said that if the operational area includes a high proportion of soft ground, and if the role is such that unrestricted off-road mobility is paramount, then a tracked solution has to be adopted. On the other hand, if long distances on roads and tracks are likely, then wheels are indicated. This is especially so if prolonged independent operation, away from maintenance and logistic backup, is likely.

12

Stating Requirements for Armoured Fighting Vehicles

General

Previous chapters have described the operational and technical factors which impinge directly on the design of armoured fighting vehicles. This is appropriate because the acquisition of armoured vehicles is a complex and costly business, the aim of which is to provide the user with the capabilities needed to fight the battle. These capabilities, therefore, must be accurately described.

Documents for this purpose are usually formally structured as to title, format and content but certain basic principles apply regardless of the country of origin or the procedures laid down in a particular army. This chapter offers guidance on how that requirement should be stated.

In the United Kingdom the document performing this function is called the Staff Requirement (Land), (Sea) or (Air) depending on the originating Service branch. In other countries titles such as Statement of Requirement (SOR) or Required Operational Capability (ROC) are used. The title is not as important as the preparation of the document itself. However, it is important to ensure that the capabilities required by the user are accurately described before the expenditure required to design, develop, prove and procure the equipment is sought.

In the procurement process it is usual that a second, more detailed, technical document is produced and it is against this document that the performance of the vehicle is designed and assessed. This document is called the Technical Specification (TS) or Required Technical Characteristics (RTC) and translates the descriptive statement of the requirement into a specification that can be understood by the vehicle designer. Whereas the SOR states the requirement in general terms without recommending a particular solution, the Technical Specification defines the solution in precise engineering terms.

The sword is no longer used in battle as, over the years, technology has provided more effective weapons. On a more sophisticated level it has been stated that anti-tank systems such as the attack helicopter, remotely-delivered sub-munitions and scatterable mines have made the tank obsolete. Before authorising the costly replacement of in-service vehicles, the operational requirements staff must justify that the capability is still required and that it cannot be performed by other, cheaper means. The fact that the current equipment is obsolescent does not, in itself, justify its replacement; the high cost of new equipment demands that this sort of examination is carried out on behalf of the taxpayer.

Preparation of the Requirement

Confirming the Capability

Several options must be examined each time the acquisition of new equipment is proposed:

Does the requirement still exist or should the capability be eliminated?

Can the capability be given to another arm or equipment; for example, can the role of the tank be performed by the helicopter?

Can the current equipment remain in service and still carry out the task satisfactorily, possibly after a refurbishment or updating programme?

If a new equipment is required, will its technical superiority over its predecessor permit it to carry out tasks performed by other equipment; for example, can the new tank engage helicopters rather than having a specific anti-helicopter vehicle?

Quality versus Quantity

Having decided that a particular capability is still required on the battlefield, the operational requirements staff must then define the function and decide how they should be specified without prescribing the solution. They must also decide on quantities since it is not automatic that a new vehicle should replace the old on a one-for-one basis. The determination of equipment quantities is not an easy task and operational analysis and war gaming are used extensively, taking due account of the threat, quantity versus quality, the balance of investment, the operational plan and other factors. In deciding total quantities to be procured, one must remember that a technically superior vehicle is not able to use its superiority all the time. A simple, robust vehicle may win the day because it is available in greater numbers.

Defining the Characteristics

The selection of the essential characteristics of a new equipment is determined, in the first instance, by whether the vehicle is a main battle tank or a medium battle tank or a medium or light armoured vehicle. The reason should be clear in that the role of the tank requires it to have a certain level of firepower, mobility and survivability whereas a reconnaissance vehicle's prime characteristic might be surveillance and for a personnel carrier, capacity. The reader is referred to previous chapters for guidance on which parameters to include in each case.

The preparation of a statement of requirement for an armoured fighting vehicle requires far more than a blank piece of paper, enthusiasm and imagination, although these are essential prerequisites. Below is a list of some of factors that need to be taken into account in the formulation of a SOR:

The threat
Operational and training concepts
Force structure and organisation
Operational analysis
Reliability
The vehicle's value tree

A few comments on each will explain how each one contributes to the SOR and that they cannot be considered in isolation.

The Threat

The threat makes two important contributions to the SOR; the nature of the enemy against whom the vehicle will be used and the probable extent to which the enemy threat is likely to change during its in-service life.

The nature of the enemy includes his equipment and its performance, his organisations and his operational procedures in battle. A correct assessment of the threat is the first and most important building block in the formulation of the SOR. Every army has technical intelligence staff whose job it is to acquire and analyse the threat and to make forecasts for future developments. Intelligence staff must be invited to produce their assessment of the enemy's capability at the start of the process. However, nothing remains static and the enemy, like ourselves, constantly improves tactics, organisation and of course equipment performance. In consequence, the operational capability or performance required of the new vehicle must take into account growth or future stretch potential and provision to cater for it must be made in the SOR.

Operational and Training Concepts

Having decided on the present and probable future capabilities of the enemy's forces, the operational requirements staff must then determine, in the timescale of deployment of the new equipment whether the current tactical procedures and organisations will be able to exploit fully the capabilities of the new equipment. Furthermore, the training aspects, both the hardware and training procedures, need to be adapted to ensure that full advantage can be taken of the new equipment's performance. The SOR and the value tree (on which more below) must both include this.

Force Structure and Organisation

Concepts studies indicate what should be done on the battlefield in order to maximise the capability of new equipment. Studies on new organisations need to go hand in hand with the new concepts and focus on obtaining the best from the scarcest and most expensive of all resources—manpower. These force structure studies must indicate how to organise the army in the field so as to maximise combat power at minimum cost in both financial and manpower terms. In drafting the SOR, the operational staff must demonstrate the potential for manpower savings in two prime areas. First, it may be possible by using new technology, to achieve enhanced capability but with fewer men; an example is the next generation of tank with improved firepower and speed but having only a three man crew. Secondly, the logistic staff must show that the maintenance of the new equipment can be accomplished with fewer men by specifying higher levels of basic reliability and insisting that they are achieved by the manufacturer. Finally, by ensuring that spares availability matches the rate of build up of new equipment entering service.

Operational Analysis Studies

As the practical experience of using weapons in large-scale, high intensity war decreases in Western armies, the importance of the role played by operational analysis increases. Very rarely will a new, expensive weapon system go through the full panoply of the approval process without first being subjected to rigorous operational analysis scrutiny. It is still the only way to determine the balance of investment between various weapons. In the anti-tank field, for example, there is a plethora of weapon systems, all with their advocates and all competing for a share of the limited defence budget. How should the capability of an indirect fire weapon firing anti-tank sub-munitions be assessed against the capability of the anti-tank helicopter; or against a direct fire-and-forget missile; or the tank itself. How many of each weapon system should the operational requirements staff recommend as the minimum necessary to fulfil the battle plan.

Operational analysis techniques are now being refined to assess what the balance of investment should be when more than one capability is involved—the example given in the above paragraph is of a single capability area, namely anti-tank. More complicated and difficult decisions have to be faced when the assessment crosses capability boundaries. For example, how much should be spent on airborne surveillance to locate targets for weapons like MLRS for long range attrition of tanks as against the amount spent on shorter range direct fire weapons.

Operational analysis was first used in war games conducted on maps or sand tables with wooden models representing the tactical elements but these procedures were slow and required large staffs to move the models, assess the engagements and calculate the result. With the introduction of the computer, programmes were developed which permitted wargames to be played quickly, and more importantly, over and over again. Changes can be made to the characteristics of a particular weapon system (range, lethality, armoured protection etc.) or mix of systems (3 tanks in a troop or 3 tanks and one ATGW vehicle) and the sensitivity of the result to those changes can be determined. The more times the engagement is run, the greater the confidence that the outcome will replicate a real engagement. In the final analysis, confirmation that operational analysis was right can only be gained by using the weapon in battle and wars like Vietnam, the Falklands, Afghanistan and the Gulf War have been used as proving ground for both the theory and the practice of weapon system design.

Reliability and Availability

Availability of equipment, the ability of a weapon to perform its role when required, is a prime battle-winning factor. However, it is difficult to specify this in an SOR as availability, while based on reliability, is a product of many other factors such as spares provisioning, logistic support policy, manpower levels for maintenance and repair and the like—all of which are matters outside the remit of an equipment SOR to determine. Basic reliability levels, however must be specified in an SOR but scant attention has been paid to this in the past as the attainment of high reliability in service can only be achieved by proper attention to it during development. This usually means longer timescales and higher development costs which do not find favour with financial staff. Quite rightly, they require evidence that these higher development costs, with more financial provision made for reliability, will reduce maintenance and whole life running costs. The absence of any comprehensive system for assessing whole life costs has meant that development programmes, particularly for land systems equipment, have been underfunded, with insufficient prototypes and inadequate time in development to demonstrate reliability growth. Inevitably, development has had to continue after the vehicle has entered service at increased cost, loss of operational capability and with the user inevitably losing confidence in the equipment. Reliability must be designed into the equipment from the start and thoroughly tested during the development programme.

Research

Research has a very important role to play in the evolution of armoured fighting vehicles since it is the earliest stage in which some indication of future technical enhancements can be given to meet the intelligence staff's estimation of the future threat. Information on basic research assists the operational requirements staff to understand what is possible technically and what is not and to determine the trade-offs that may have to be made in formulating the SOR. The operational requirements staff must use every possible avenue to gain information on basic research—a process in which they can be greatly assisted by the procurement officials who ultimately have to turn the SOR into a technical specification. Assistance can come from government sponsored research agencies and establishments both at home and abroad, from collaborative programmes, from universities under contract or carrying out their own research or, as is becoming more common, from industry.

The Vehicle's Value Tree

The final input to the statement of requirement is the value tree of the vehicle. Conceptually this is a statement of the value that an army attaches to the various capabilities of a particular vehicle. Furthermore, it determines the relative importance the army attaches to those capabilities; which should predominate at the expense of the others and to what extent. The conventional way to express this relationship is to list the basic characteristics of the vehicle in an order of priority.

For example let us assume a tank's characteristics are, in order, firepower, survivability and mobility. The priorities are clear but we are told nothing of the relative priorities within each characteristic; is the last element of firepower to have precedence over the first element of survivability, a crucial distinction that must be communicated to the vehicle designer so that he is able to determine trade-offs while still meeting the operational requirement. Value trees, a relatively new concept in management techniques, can go a long way towards resolving this difficulty.

Value Trees

The Concept

The concept of a value tree is best explained in a familiar setting, the choice of a new family car. The choice requires that the members of the family establish a comprehensive set of guidelines that take into account the income, the size of the family, the sort of driving they expect to do, the preferred colours, style and performance and any other factors they consider important. In compiling the list, they would soon realise that most, if not all, these characteristics could be divided into sub-headings which would express their preferences more accurately. This process of sub-division could continue for several levels until the separate members of the family's individual desires for a new car are accurately and comprehensively described. The final document would assign a 'value' of the characteristics of a new car to the family as a whole, expressed in a 'tree' which related each aspect to every other in a logical fashion.

Having decided on the elements in the tree, the family would want to decide the relative priority that they would assign to each element in the tree. How to express these relative priorities is not altogether obvious, but one easy way would be to assign to each characteristic a percentage figure that represented the family's views with the total of these figures equalling 100% at any level on a limb. The resulting value tree might look like Figure 12.1 below. Some comments might be of assistance. First, the tree is divided into levels covering all aspects of the characteristic in the next higher level of that limb—transmission is sub-divided into automatic and manual, for example. It might appear at first glance that some of the characteristics are mutually exclusive though this become difficult to maintain as one goes further along any limb of the tree. For instance, if the family has 6 children, the size of car is likely to impinge directly on its cost whereas if there is only a single child, this might not be the case. Since the family may get larger over the expected life of the car, it must reflect its needs over a number of years and not just on the day the purchase was made. In military terms, the value tree must reflect the need for growth or stretch potential throughout the vehicle's expected in-service life.

Value Tree Characteristics

Value trees have the following characteristics:

The tree has levels which denote increasing levels of detail.

COLOUR—15%
- Exterior—75%
  - Base—50%
  - Trim—50%
- Interior—25%
  - Base—50%
  - Trim—50%

STYLE—23%
- Saloon—60%
- Hatch-back—10%
- Station wagon or shooting brake—30%

COST—28%
- Initial price 45%
- Cost of loan—25%
- Cost of maintenance—30%

PERFORMANCE—34%
- Reliability—26%
- Power—12%
- Transmission—20%
  - Automatic transmission—95%
  - Manual transmission—5%
- Ride—20%
- Handling—20%
  - Front wheel drive—90%
  - Rear wheel drive—10%

FIG. 12.1 A value tree for a family automobile.

The tree has limbs with elements or nodes, each of which describes a particular aspect of the value of the item.

At the first level, the nodes provide a description of the value of the item itself and at lower levels, successive nodes provide comprehensive coverage of the next senior node from which each is descended.

Relative values attached to the nodes at any level along a limb are expressed in percentages which must add up to 100%.

The tree as a whole depicts the outline composition of the operational value of the item and portrays the relative worth of each component of that value.

Developing Value Trees

Unfortunately, the process involved in developing value trees and assigning percentages is too complicated to be discussed in detail here but, fortunately, a wealth of information exists elsewhere. Annex A to this chapter has a reading list which will direct those who are interested to the relevant books. The subject is known generally as public policy analysis and value tree analysis is called multi-attribute evaluation. These procedures can be used for a host of other activities and were developed first for the civilian rather than the military market.

The Uses of the Value Tree

Having decided on the tree and assigned values to each element, our hypothetical family will want to know how it will help them to select a new car.

More particularly, what is the role of value trees in the process by which new armoured fighting vehicles should be selected and procured?

The value tree allows the members of our family to evaluate each car as they make their selection. To do this, they must apply the logic of the tree to each contender. In other words, the tree is the basis on which they should eventually be able to answer the question—is this the car that best fits my requirement? They could, of course, drive each car and select the winner on that basis, but that is simply substituting a different value tree. Alternatively, they could do both. The ideal selection process would be:

Determination of the value tree
Selection of all possible cars that could meet the requirement
Assessment of all contenders against the value tree
Reduction to 3 possibles
Full trial
Final selection

Value Tree for an Armoured Fighting Vehicle

A moment's reflection will indicate that there is nothing inherently new in using a value tree. We use it instinctively as we pursue our daily lives; we each conduct multi-attribute evaluations when we purchase meals, books or clothing or make decisions. The value tree merely formalises the process and expands it to cover the greater number of variables. These procedures can be used in evaluating armoured fighting vehicles against the SOR although the process is more complex because the value trees are much more complex than one for a family automobile. Because of the greater complexity, the books listed at Annex A should be consulted and technical assistance from experts should be sought before a value tree for an armoured vehicle is drawn up. However, some general points can be made;

The process of determining the requirement for a new armoured vehicle requires not only that the attributes of the ideal vehicle be set out, but also that the relative importance attached to each be stipulated. Thus, the value tree is an integral part of the SOR; indeed it is the framework that relates each characteristic of the requirement to the others and determines its relative importance.

Technical procedures for determining the relative importance of vehicle characteristics are available. They should be used.

Having produced a value tree incorporatng the SOR, it must be used as an aspect of the assessment process for each contender.

The actual process of evaluation must be made clear to each manufacturer to avoid allegations of favouritism (or incompetence) in selecting the vehicle that best meets the requirement.

Examples of Value Trees

The followng figures give examples of possible value trees for the vehicles indicated:

Value Tree for a Tank-Destroyer

INITIAL CAPABILITIES—55%
- Firepower—33%
  - Engagement time
  - Weapon system performance
  - Sustainability
  - Availability
- Survivability—21%
  - In action
  - Out of action
  - Availability
- Mobility—15%
  - Battlefield mobility
  - Tactical mobility
  - Strategic mobility
  - Availability
- Fightability—20%
  - Battlefield surveillance and awareness
  - Crew system interfaces
  - Crew conditions
- Training Requirements—11%
  - Firepower systems
  - Survivability systems
  - Mobility systems
  - RAM-D systems
  - Fighting systems

GROWTH POTENTIAL—45%
- Firepower—35%
- Survivability—22%
- Mobility—15%
- Fightability—20%
- Training systems—8%

FIG. 12.2 A value tree for a tank-destroyer.

Value Tree for a Mechanised Infantry Combat Vehicle

INITIAL CAPABILITIES—60%
- Firepower—24%
  - Against personnel
  - Against light armoured vehicles
- Mobility—21%
  - Strategic
  - Tactical
  - Manoeuvre
- Survivability—18%
  - Indirect attack
  - Direct attack
- Capacity—15%
  - Personnel
  - Stores
  - Combat supplies
- Availability—13%
  - System availability
  - System durability
  - System reliability
  - System maintainability
- Ergonomics—9%
  - Capacity

Mobility systems
Survivability systems
Firepower systems
GROWTH POTENTIAL—40%
Firepower—24%
Mobility—20%
Survivability—19%
Capacity—15%
Availability—13%
Ergonomics—9%

FIG. 12.3 A value tree for a mechanised infantry combat vehicle.

Value Tree for a Main Battle Tank

INITIAL CAPABILITIES—60%
Firepower—28%
Engagement time
Weapon system performance
Sustainability
Survivability—21%
In action
Out of action
Mobility—18%
Battlefield mobility
Tactical mobility
Strategic mobility
RAM-D—11%
The order of letters in the RAM-D acronym is predicated on what sensibly be pronounced rather than an order of priority. The following order is preferred:
System availability
System durability
System maintainability
System repairability
Fightability—14%
Battlefield surveillance and awareness
Crew system interfaces
Crew workload
Crew conditions
Training Requirements—8%
Firepower systems
Survivability systems
Mobility systems
RAM-D systems
Fighting systems
GROWTH POTENTIAL—40%
Firepower
Survivability
Mobility
RAM-D
Fightability
Training systems

FIG. 12.4 A value tree for a main battle tank.

The above value trees are illustrative only. They have not been used as part of an SOR for any known vehicle and serve only as a guide to the operational requirements staff developing their own. The need to include training systems and growth potential in the value tree has been indicated.

Ways to State Performance

There are three ways in which performance of a vehicle can be stated—the direct, indirect and relative approaches.

Direct Method

In the direct method, the requirement is stated as it is determined by the requirements staff: if the infantry section comprises 8 men, the section vehicle must be able to carry those men and their weapons, kit and supplies. The stipulation of this aspect of carriage capacity is straightforward. Another example would be the top speed of the vehicle on a hard surface—so many kilometres per hour.

The direct approach should be used when all the parameters can be detailed in a technical specification. For example, it is possible to be precise when defining engagement times as follows:

> *Time Start:* gun laid off target requiring a 540 mil (30 degree) line switch for the commander to lay gunner onto target. Power controls to be used
> Gunner carries out fine lay
> *Time Finish:* shot exit

The direct method is in every case the preferred option. It stipulates the requirement as it can be seen by the ultimate user of the equipment and is testable in the field as specified.

Agility, that is a vehicle's ability to dart about the battlefield from cover to cover so as to minimise chances of detection and engagement, is a characteristic that should be stated directly; but to do so is not easy. How much agility is enough? How is it to be measured? Is it adequate just to state a time from moving from one fire position to another? How are the extraneous factors, such as the state of the ground, to be specified and the reproducibility of the test guaranteed. An alternative method is needed.

Indirect Method

The second approach involves the idea that if a particular capability, such as a given level of protection against a particular type of attack, is required, it may be more appropriate to specify it indirectly. In other words one way to specify survivability is to make it difficult for a weapon to hit the vehicle in the first place. Agility, referred to above, can also be used as part of the indirect approach in specifying protection. Furthermore, this method has the advantage that it is possible to link one vehicle characteristic to another. A heavy vehicle, while providing good protection, is unlikely to be agile unless the engine produces very high power and a first rate suspension system has been fitted. It is all too easy to treat each vehicle characteristic of firepower, survivability and protection as independent only to find the design ascending the Design Spiral (Figure 4.12). By specifying a degree of agility, it may be possible to achieve part of the survivability requirement, but with a smaller engine, using less fuel, having a lower heat signature while still meeting the SOR.

Relative Method

The relative method of specification takes as a base line the demonstrable performance of a known vehicle and then demands an improvement. This improvement is usually expressed as a percentage. Take, for instance, the requirement in some armies for tanks and APCs to operate on the northern flank of NATO. They must not be immobilised by a few centimetres of snow and the operational requirements staff must be able to write a specification for through-snow mobility. However, snow has a very complex structure and its condition is determined by its immediate history of freezing and thawing. In these circumstances, specifying the snow through which the vehicle most operate is virtually impossible and laying down a mobility specification is equally difficult. The only alternative is to state a requirement in terms of the mobilty of a vehicle whose performance in snow is well known and can be demonstrated. By detailing mobility requirements in terms relative to the performance of a known vehicle, the characteristics its successor can be specified.

We must not overlook the fact that this approach suffers from one significant limitation. It is the least satisfactory method of specification as it provides little scope for specifying improvements. Perhaps the best example of this type of specification is a vehicle mid-life upgrade. Here the established parameters of the vehicle are known and only certain aspects of it are to be improved. It would be reasonable to specify an engagement time for a new fire control system, for instance, in terms of a percentage improvement over the old system. The operational staff officer should realise the limitations of this method and only use it when no other means of stating the specification exists.

Substantiating the SOR

It is far simpler to state a particular performance level in an SOR than it is to have to justify it technically. Nevertheless, all performance levels must be fully justified as any attempt to give an ambiguous answer or worse, to guess, will inevitably lead to misunderstanding and possibly nugatory expense. The user who will ultimately go into battle in the vehicle deserves an explanation as to why it provides a specific level of performance and not higher, especially if it is likely to have a bearing on the rate at which he is expected to take casualties. Financial managers at all levels will want to be assured that the performance is adequate for the task, there is no evidence of 'gold plating' and that the taxpayer is getting value for money.

Having prepared a document that justifies the levels of performance demanded, some formal arrangements need to be established for reviewing it so as to provide answers to the following questions:

Are the performance levels demanded for each characteristic at a level that ensures the SOR remains in balance?
Will the combat effectiveness of the troops to whom the equipment will eventually issued be enhanced?
Does this combat enhancement represent good value for money?
Can the performance levels demanded be obtained at reduced cost but without reducing the vehicle's combat effectiveness?
Are there any recent technological advances which could increase the level of combat effectiveness but without an inordinate increase in costs?
Have all the relevant performance characteristics been specified? Have any unnecesary characteristics been included?
Have all the performance characteristics been stated in ways that permit subsequent evaluation both in the field and in engineering tests?

Conclusion

The statement of requirement for a new item of equipment is a fundamentally important document. It must set out the characteristics of the weapon system in sufficient detail so that the designer is not constrained in putting forward options but it must not recommend a particular design. The preparation of the SOR therefore, deserves the best efforts of those involved in its production. The time and effort required at this vital first stage in an equipment's life is seldom wasted. The soldiers who use the equipment in war deserve the very best efforts of technical staff officers in peace.

Annex A to Chaper 12

FURTHER READING

Multi-attribute Evaluation

An excellent introduction is given by Ward Edwards and J. Robert Newman in their book *Multi-attribute Evaluation*. The book is published by Sage Publications, Beverly Hill, London and New Delhi. This 96 page book explains the requirement for, and uses of, value trees and provides simple processes for evaluating the sensitivity of the process itself. If only one book were to be recommended, this would be it.

A Primer for Policy Analysis

This is a more general introduction to the wider field of technical decision processes. It is written by Edith Stokely and Richard Zeckhauser and published by W. W. Norton Inc. of New York in 1978.

The Analytic Hierarchy Process Planning, Priority Setting and Resource Allocation

Written by Thomas L. Saaty, this book is for the strong-minded. Published by McGraw-Hill in New York in 1980, it provides a mind-expanding discourse on how to determine a consensus on the elements of a value tree. Not for the technically timid.

The Logic of Priorities-Applications in Business, Energy, Health and Transportation

Fortunately, Saaty, with a collaborator Luis G. Vargas, has written a more digestible book which is published by Kluwer-Nijhoff of Boston, The Hague and London. It provides a simpler explanation of the technique and gives many more examples of its use.

Decision Making for Leaders

Again written by Saaty but published by Lifetime Learning of Belmont, California, is another book with many examples of this process.

Annex B to Chapter 12

ASSIGNING NUMERICAL VALUES TO THE ELEMENTS OF A VALUE TREE

Assigning numerical values to the elements of a value tree is necessary to determine the relative importance of each element. There are at least two ways by which it may be accomplished. We will describe a simple and not entirely satisfactory method first and a second, more complex method which overcomes the inadequacies of the first.

Method A

First, to simplify matters, we will take the hypothetical tree, Figure 12.2 developed for the family car, remove the arbitrary assigned values and compress it down to only its first level of attributes as shown in Figure 12B.1 below.

Colour
Style
Cost
Performance

FIG. 12B.1 Car value toll analysis compressed to one level.

Our problem is to assign numbers to these various elements in a way that reflected a consensus of the family members. As originally discussed, the values were arrived at by discussion, a potentially interminable procedure if those involved held strong views.

One way to assign numbers to these values in this situation is to have each member of the family rank the attributes in this truncated tree in order of importance. Suppose that this has been done and that the various members of the family assigned values as given in Figure 12B.2 below. It is then a simple procedure to add up the total column (which equates to the ranking of the attributes) and from it determine a final priority in the right hand column—the lower the sum, the higher the importance the family assigns to the attribute.

This procedure is simple and straightforward and produces an order of precedence for the attributes. It doe not, however, provide an indication of the extent of the preference for one attribute over that of the next lower in the hierarchy. For this reason the more complicated version is preferred.

Method B

Our requirement can be met if we invoke the procedure suggested by Saaty in his book Analytic Hierarchy Process (listed in Annex A). We arrange that each member of the family rate each attribute in a one-to-one comparison with each other attribute; subsequent analysis then indicates the extent of the preference of the family as a whole for each attribute with repect to every other.

This procedure requires a little preparation—a scoring sheet on the lines of Figure 12B.3 would be required. Assuming that our family have this sheet, each member could then rate each attribute against each of the others by indicating a preference. To do so the member would make only one grading per line and would select the relationship which best describes his or her perception and fills in the solid line with the 'score' shown in parenthesis above that line. When all have completed the rating, the scores for each attribute assigned by each member could then be written into a matrix format as shown in Figure 12B.4 below where the father's hypothetical values have been recorded. These values correspond roughly with the values shown for him in Figure 12B.2 above in which he ranked the attributes in the same order but we can now see the extent of his preferences of one attribute vis-a-vis each of the others.

It is now necessary to check the responses of each family member to confirm that each has assigned consistent values for each preference. Two aspects of consistency which need to be borne in mind:

Consistency of Logic

If attribute A is preferred to B and B is preferred to C, then A must unavoidably be preferred to C. if this preference is not recorded, then the responses must be reviewed and corrected accordingly.

Consistency of Values

If attribute A is vastly preferred to B and B vastly preferred to C, then A must be vastly preferred to C. Any lower level of preference is not consistent and will have to be corrected.

Checking and correcting for consistency must be completed before any signifi-

Attributes	*Father*	*Mother*	*Son*	*Daughter*	*Total Ranks*	*Order*
Colour	4	3	4	2	13	4
Style	3	1	2	3	9	2
Cost	1	2	3	1	7	1
Performance	2	4	1	4	11	3

FIG. 12B.2 Ranks assigned to attributes by family members.

cance can be attached to the result. We can assume that the hypothetical values in Figure 12B.4 have met this requirement.

When all family members have filled in the form correctly, ideally this data would be fed into a computer programmed to produce the consensus of the family on the relative importance of these attributes implicit in their assigned preferences. In the absence of such a programme the average of their scores for each cell can be approximated by taking the geometric, not the arithmetical, mean of those scores.

When all the cells have been filled in with these geometric means, the geometric means of the rows are then calculated as shown in Figure 12B.5. The figures are then added and the sum in each row is normalised as indicated. A detailed explanation of this is given in Saaty but space precludes it being done here. The resulting figures are an approximation (as no computer programme has been used) of the consensus of the relative importance assigned by members of the family to the attributes listed in the value tree. Again the rank order of the attributes has not changed from that indicated at Figure 12B.2 (although it could have done as a result of the more careful consideration achieved by this method). Furthermore, we now can see the extent of the preference of the family for each attribute with respect to each of the others.

A similar procedure can be undertaken for each of the attributes in any limb. In this way the whole value tree can be completed. Figure 12B.6 shows the completed value tree for the car of our hypothetical family which might have emerged if the Saaty Technique had been applied to the complete tree and not just to its first level. Having determined the relative importance of the elements in the tree relative to each other, it is essential to do some simple multiplication to determine the absolute importance of each element in the tree. This is accomplished by multiplying the values at a particular level by the value of the node from which it is descended. Figure 12B.7 shows the new calculations, based on the details from Figure 12B.6.

Some comments should be noted:

The total of the figures for the immediate descendants of any first level attribute equals its percentage.

Since the total of the percentages of the first level themselves equal 1, the total of all percentages equals 2. We have, in effect, added the totals of the first level which equals 1 to the total of the second level which also equals 1.

The attributes in the second level can now be compared to each other; several are clearly not important at all.

At this stage the whole tree should be reviewed to confirm that each value is of sufficient significance to warrant its retention in the tree. If it is decided to

	Vastly More Important (7)	*Much More Important (5)*	*Somewhat More Important (3)*	*Just As Important (1)*	*Somewhat Less Important (0.333)*	*Much Less Important (0.2)*	*Vastly Less Important (0.143)*	
Attributes								Attributes
Colour	____	____	____	____	____	____	____	Style
Colour	____	____	____	____	____	____	____	Cost
Colour	____	____	____	____	____	____	____	Performance
Style	____	____	____	____	____	____	____	Cost
Style	____	____	____	____	____	____	____	Performance
Cost	____	____	____	____	____	____	____	Performance

FIG. 12B.3 Form to achieve consensus-related information.

	Colour	*Style*	*Cost*	*Performance*	*Geometric Mean*	*Normalised Mean*
Colour	1	0.333	0.143	0.2	0.312	0.06
Style	3	1	0.2	0.333	0.669	0.12
Cost	7	5	1	3	3.2	0.56
Performance	5	3	0.333	1	1.495	0.26
TOTAL					5.676	1

FIG. 12B.4 Father's hypothetical values for relative importance of the attributes.

	Colour	*Style*	*Cost*	*Performance*	*Geometric Mean*	*Normalised Mean*
Colour	1	0.386	0.2697	0.809	0.539	0.131
Style	1.968	1	0.775	0.714	1.022	0.248
Cost	3.71	1.291	1	2.14	1.789	0.433
Performance	1.236	1.401	0.209	1	0.776	0.188
TOTAL					4.126	1

FIG. 12B.5 Development of parameters indicating the relative importance of attributes.

Colour—13.1%
- Exterior—78%
- Interior—22%

Style—24.8%
- Saloon—56%
- Hatch-back—17%
- Station wagon or shooting brake—27%

Cost—43.3%
- Initial price—49%
- Cost of loan—22%
- Cost of maintenance—29%

Performance—18.8%
- Reliability—39%
- Power—11%
- Transmission—13%
- Ride—20%
- Handling—17%

FIG. 12B.6 Value tree with new figures inserted.

remove an attribute, the process would then have to be repeated for the new, amended tree. The use of a computer speeds up this process.

The value tree as shown in Figure 12B.7 is in the form in which we would want a tree included in the SOR for an armoured fighting vehicle. The tree would, of course, be considerably more complicated.

For the interested reader, the recommended reading list in Annex A should be consulted.

Colour—13.1%
Exterior—10.2%
Interior—2.9%
Style—24.8%
Saloon—13.9%
Hatch-back—4.2%
Station wagon or shooting brake—6.7%
Cost—43.3%
Initial price—21.2%
Cost of loan—9.5%
Cost of maintenance—12.6%
Performance—18.8%
Reliability—7.3%
Power—2.1%
Transmission—2.4%
Ride—3.8%
Handing—3.2%

FIG. 12B.7 Value tree with values multiplied through to the second level.

Annex C to Chapter 12

USING THE VALUE TREE IN THE SELECTION PROCESS

The value tree comes into its own during the process by which the contending vehicles are evaluated against the Statement of the Requirement (SOR) and its associated technical specification.

There are a number of ways by which this selection process can be carried out. The one described here is that which represents the approach suggested in the book *Multi-attribute Evaluation* (listed in the reading list in Annex A). It has been selected because it represents an orderly and defensible method. The process is straightforward in principle. Each contending vehicle is evaluated against the criteria in the value tree associated with the SOR. The judges express their judgments by indicating the extent to which a certain option meets a particular characteristic as a percentage of the 100% available. Each option is therefore being compared with all the others and is given a score which reflects the judge; opinion as to the extent it meets a particular requirement. The total score indicates in an absolute sense how a particular option fared in the evaluation; however, it is necessary to weight these scores on the basis of their individual importance in the value tree. To do this the corresponding elements in the two trees are multiplied together and the resulting figures are added up. That sum is the 'utility' of the particular option measured against the requirement. The vehicle having the highest score clearly comes closest to meeting the requirement and, subject to any other test that may be carried out, should be selected.

Figure 12C.1. contains the hypothetical scores that might have arisen if a family had used the simplifed tree in Figure 12B.8 to evaluate three different cars. It can be seen that Car A most closely meets the criteria although it was not the best in all the categories. Because of the weighting factors, certain features of the vehicle are more significant than others. This is implied in the value tree and reflects the nature of the SOR. The score assigned to each item can be varied for each option vehicle to determine the sensitivity of the outcome to these changes. This exercise is worth carrying out as a sensitivity test of the validity of the initial value tree and

SOR Value Tree	*Tree Car A*	*Score Car A*	*Tree Car B*	*Score Car B*	*Tree Car C*	*Score Car C*
Colour						
Exterior—10%	33.3	339.66	33.3	339.66	33.3	339.66
Interior—2.9%	33.3	96.57	33.3	96.57	33.3	96.57
Style						
Saloon—13.9%	33.3	462.87	33.3	462.87	33.3	462.87
Hatch back—4.2%	50	210	0	0	50	210
Station wagon—6.7%	50	35	50	335	0	0
Cost						
Initial price—21.2%	25	530	45	949.5	30	633
Cost of loan—9.5%	30	285	40	380	30	285
Cost of maintenance—12.6%	40	504	23	289.8	36	453.6
Performance						
Reliability—7.3%	65	473.5	25	182.5	10	73
Power—2.1%	39	81.9	34	71.4	27	56.7
Transmission—2.4%	33.3	79.92	33.3	79.92	33.3	79.92
Ride—3.8%	22	83.6	41	155.8	37	140.6
Handling—3.2%	31	9.2	29	92.8	40	128
Totals 100%		3582.22		3425.82	2958.92	
Ranking		First		Second		Third

FIG. 12C.1 Value trees and scores for hypothetical cars showing the final outcome.

of the scores assigned by the judges. Clearly if a change in one variable causes a change in the result, the judges will want to be sure that the figures used in the value tree and the judgments themselves are correct and defensible.

Making the judgements by which the vehicles are evaluated and scored is not an easy task. It is of little use to insert features into an SOR if it then proves impossible to make objective decisions regarding that feature on the various options. An SOR is only as good as the evaluation process in which it will be used; if the process will not produce repeatable, defensible results, the SOR itself may be at fault. It follows that while the criteria in the SOR are being developed, the processes for the evaluation of the options must also be going through the same process. The two processes are interdependent; they should not be undertaken independently.

Glossary

Terms

AFV. Armoured fighting vehicle.
Ackerman geometry. Arrangement of the steering linkage of a wheeled vehicle to ensure that both near and off-side wheels roll tangentially when cornering.
Ackerman steer angle. The mean angle at which a pair of steered wheels needs to be set for the vehicle to follow a given path at low speed.
Active suspension. Suspension which, using a source of power, responds to counter the irregularities in the surface over which the vehicle is travelling. The aim is to reduce as far as possible the perturbations of the wheels or tracks being transmitted to the hull.
Active system. An active observation or target ranging system (such as an infra-red sight or a ranging machine-gun) producing an output which can be detected by the enemy. See passive system.
Aiming mark. The mark on a sight graticule which the operator lays on the target.
Aim-off. The angular displacement of a gun in azimuth when it moves to its firing position.
Airborne infantry. A special type of light infantry deployable by aircraft and parachute.
All burnt position. The location of a shell in the barrel when all the propellant has been burnt.
Ambient light level. The naturally occurring level of light.
Angle of gun. The angle of a gun from the horizontal, when laid onto a target.
Armoured infantry. Infantry organised, equipped and trained to operate integrally with, and in support of, tanks.
Armour Piercing Discarding Sabot (APDS). A type of kinetic energy ammunition where a sub-calibre penetrator of heavy material is surrounded by a light weight 'pot' or sabot which supports the penetrator in the barrel. The use of the sabot ensures that the largest possible base area is presented to the propellant gases over which pressure can be exerted. The sabot falls to the ground a few hundred metres from the barrel, leaving the sub-calibre penetrator to continue to the target.
Aspect ratio. The ratio of the section height/overall width of a pneumatic tyre.
Attentuation. The reduction in strength of a light beam or some other signal as it passes through the atmosphere.
Autoloader. A mechanical system to load the main armament and so eliminate one member (loader) from the tank crew.

Availability. Normally expressed as a percentage to indicate the time an equipment is ready to carry out its task without any reduction in its capability. Availability includes basic reliability but is also a function of logistic support policy, the amount of spares provision and other policy decisions.

Azimuth. The horizontal plane.

Ballistic dispersion. Minor differences in each round of ammunition produce marginally different trajectories. Thus, if a number of rounds are fired at the same aiming point, there will be variations in the fall of shot and this is referred to as ballistic dispersion.

Barrel bend. Distortion of the barrel caused by uneven heating or cooling when in use.

Barrel wear. Wear of the barrel bore caused by the hot gases created during gun firing.

Basic characteristics. The basic characteristics of an armoured vehicle are the prime factors in its capabilities.

Battlefield mobility. Battlefield mobility is the ability to manoeuvre in order to win the encounter battle.

Beam axle. Non-independent suspension where the wheels are carried at either end of a transverse beam.

Beam splitter. An optical device, such as a half-silvered mirror, which diverts a proportion of an incoming light beam and allows the remainder to pass through, thus creating two beams.

Binocular sight. An optical system with an independent channel for both eyes. Each channel has its own objective lens and eyepiece, so that the images presented to the eyes are slightly different.

Biocular sight. An optical system with one objective lens and two eyepieces, in which the same image is presented to each eye.

Body force. Force arising due to the mass of the vehicle i.e. either due to gravity or acceleration.

Bogey. A suspension with wheels grouped in sets of two or more and so linked that the load on each set (bogey) is shared equally between them.

Brinell. Measure of the hardness of metal.

Bulk loaded liquid propellant gun. A liquid propellant gun in which all the propellant used for a single charge is loaded into the chamber before ignition.

Bump stop. A stiff spring or rubber block to cushion the hull from impact when the total suspension bump travel is exceeded.

Bush (track). A component of the track link between the pin and link body usually made of strong rubber.

Bustle. The rear of the turret which usually overhangs the engine decks, and is often used to stow ammunition. See bustle autoloader.

Bustle autoloader. A type of autoloader in which the ammunition is stowed in the turret bustle i.e. in the rear overhang of the turret.

Camber angle. The angle that a wheel leans away from the vertical.

Cambrai. The Battle of Cambrai on 20 November 1917, was the first occasion the tank was used in significant numbers and on suitable ground. It was to be a crucial battle in that it proved conclusively the value of the new weapon system.

Carburettor. A device for premixing air and fuel in the required proportions before ingestion into the cylinder(s) of a petrol engine.
Carcass. The structure of a pneumatic tyre built up from successive layers or piles.
Carousel autoloader. A type of autoloader in which the ammunition is stowed in a circular magazine in the hull, below the turret ring.
Castor. The angle by which the steering swivel axis is inclined backwards from the vertical.
Change-speed gearbox. A device fitted between the engine and the driven road wheels or sprockets of a land vehicle, to change the speed ratio between them.
Charge coupled device. An array of electrodes, under which information can be stored in the form of discrete electrical packets. The charge packet can be induced electrically or optically, as when the CCD is used in a television camera.
Chemical energy ammunition. A nature of ammunition where the penetrative power is generated by chemical (explosive) energy rather than by kinetic energy.
Christie suspension. A type of suspension named after its American designer. It achieves large suspension travel, with each wheel sprung independently through a bell-crank and a coil spring.
Chrome plating. Chrome plating is the plating of the inside of both smooth and rifled bore barrels to reduce wear and increase durability.
Cleft turret. A type of turret where the gun is set between the two turret crewmen, one either side. See Figures 6.2 and 6.3.
Closed down. A tank is operating 'closed down' when all the hatches are shut and the crew are relying on their vision devices to fight the vehicle.
Coaxially mounted machine gun. A machine gun, usually of small arms calibre (7.62–12.7 mm), mounted alongside the main armament and used against suitable targets in order to save main armament ammunition. The main armament gun controls are used to aim the coaxially mounted machine gun or 'coax', as it is often called.
Cohesive soil. A type of soil characterised by traction proportional to the area under shear. Clay is cohesive soil.
Coil spring. A spring formed from a steel rod wound into the form of a helix.
Cold finger. The cold part of a thermal imaging cooler, upon which the detector material is located.
Collimation. The accurate adjustment of a line of sight.
Combustion chamber. A space suitably contrived for the burning of fuel and air.
Compensated linkage. A sight linkage which changes in length to compensate for system variations, in order to maintain alignment accuracy.
Composite armour. If the type of armour is known, it is possible to optimise tank protection to give the highest value against a specific attack. Composite armour is a term used to describe armour which uses a number of different techniques to defeat the anti-armour threat e.g. rolled homogenous armour, explosive reactive armour, spaced armour.
Compressor. A machine for increasing the pressure and density of a gas (such as air) while reducing its volume, e.g. a tyre pump.
Coulomb friction. A friction force proportional to the normal load.

Coupling. A device for connecting or disconnecting the engine from the drive line and hence from the road wheels or sprockets.
Cross-ply tyre. A tyre whose piles have cords which cross the circumference at an angle of substantially less than 90 degrees.
Cryogenic. Relating to very low temperatures.
Cycle. The sequence of operations that the working gas undergoes inside an engine.
Cylinder head. The closing piece which seals up one end of the cylinder(s) within which the piston(s) of a piston engine move. The cylinder head usually incorporates the valves and a spark-plug.
Damper. A suspension component designed to attenuate oscillation of the vehicle mass on its springs by dissipating energy.
Dark adaption. Dark adaption occurs at night, when the iris in the eye opens to make better use of the available light. A sudden burst of bright light blinds the eye and temporarily destroys the dark adaption.
Dark current. The naturally occurring current in a semiconductor material. See Signal to noise ratio.
Data bus. A single wire capable of carrying multiple signals, structured as a serial stream of data.
Dead ground. From a tank some areas (particularly those close to the tank) cannot be seen through the vision devices. This is referred to as dead ground. So too are areas obscured to the tank commander by topography e.g. the reverse slope of a hill.
Defensive Aids Suite (DAS). DAS is the acronym given to studies designed to give better protection to the tank against the increasing threat. This will include protection against top attack, laser damage weapons, fire-and-forget guided weapons and the like.
Depression. Normally applied to the gun. It is the amount, measured in degrees or mils, of the ability of the gun to be depressed to its maximum. It is a crucial parameter in tank design. See Chapter 4.
De-rotation optics. In a panoramic sight, the de-rotation optics keep the image the right way up as the sight head is traversed through 180 degrees.
Digibus. A form of digital data transmission used in the French aircraft industry and also used in the fire control system in the French Leclerc tank.
Direct Fire Weapon Effect Simulator. A tank-mounted training equipment, which realistically simulates (usually by means of a laser) the engagement of targets by the main armament.
Direct stress. Stress which is normal to the section of the component (tensile or compressive).
Dog clutch. A clutch having interlocking male/female teeth on its two members rather than frictional material between them.
Doping. The introduction of additional elements into a semi-conductor material in order to change its performance characteristics.
Directional Probability Variation (DPV). Usually entitled Whittaker's DPV after Lt Col Whittaker who analysed many thousands of attack profiles of anti-tank guns engaging tanks based on information gained in the Second World War. It is used to determine the most probable direction of attack so that the armour can be placed on a tank to cover the most likely direction.

Drift. The tendency of a spin-stabilised round to move in azimuth away from the direction in which it was fired.

Drive-line (transmission. The complete system for modifying the power developed by the engine and transmitting it to the road wheels or sprockets.

Dry pin. A type of track pin that is mounted directly in the body of the link and not in a rubber bush.

Electromagnetic Gun—EM gun. See Chapter 2. Electromagnetic propulsion is a technique employing electrical energy instead of chemical to propel a kinetic energy projectile. Speeds of 10–15 kms per second are possible.

Enfilade fire. Enfilade fire is fire directed at an enemy from a flank.

Equivalent thickness. Sloping armour plate on the front and sides of a tank both reduces weight and increases protection by ensuring the penetrator has to travel a longer path length. To give a measure of comparison, the thickness of armour is normally expressed as Equivalent Thickness. A full description, including the formula used to calculate it, is given in Chapter 5.

Error budget. A listing which sums all the electrical, mechanical, human and environmental factors which contribute to weapon system error, in order to calculate the overall hit probability of a gun system.

Explosive Reactive Armour (ERA). A form of armour in which explosive is sandwiched between two thin armour plates. The force of the penetrator hitting the front armour plate causes the explosive to detonate, reducing penetration. ERA is more effective against HEAT attack.

External gun tank. An unconventional tank in which the gun is mounted in a separate mini-turret above the hull. The crew, usually three, in order to accommodate an autoloader, is located in the hull and hence all surveillance and target acquisition have to be accomplished by the use of remote viewing devices.

Family concept. A series of vehicles based on a common chassis, usually including an armoured personnel carrier, engineer variant, SP gun etc.

Female tank. See Male tank.

Field of view. The limits of vision through a sight, usually defined by a horizontal angle and a vertical angle.

Fightability. Fightability, or more properly ergonomics, is a new term which has been coined to cover the man–machine interface.

Fin stabilised. The full title is armour piercing fin stabilised discarding sabot—APFSDS. The principle of using the discarding sabot (see APDS) is the same but in this case the penetrator used is the long rod where the length/diameter ratio is usually more than 7:1.

Fire control system. Those elements of the weapon system used to calculate the correct fire position for the gun.

Firepower or F Kill. This definition covers the occasion when the main armament cannot be operated either because it is damaged or because the crew are no longer capable of operating it.

Firing ports. Firing ports are apertures fitted into the sides of an armoured personnel carrier to enable the troops inside to fire small arms before they dismount.

Frictional. A soil type characterised by traction proportional to the vertical loading. Sand is a frictional soil.

Graticule. A pattern of marks in a sight field of view, used for gun laying, system calibration (see Muzzle Bore Sight) or the estimation of range (see Stadiametric ranging).

Governor. A device for limiting or controlling automatically the speed of an engine.

Grouser. A projection on the underside of a track link in order to provide grip in cohesive soils or snow.

Handling. The motion of the vehicle associated with yaw and lateral accelarations.

Heat shimmer. Distortion of the target image caused by localised heating of the air between the firing tank and the target. Also called Jitter.

High Explosive Squash Head (HESH) or High Explosive Plastic (HEP). This type of anti-tank ammunition is not velocity dependent as it relies on chemical energy to achieve its effect. The explosive is contained in a thin-walled projectile which deforms on contact with the target, allowing the explosive to spread. A base fuse then detonates the explosive which sends shock waves through the armour. The shock waves are reflected from the internal face of the armour and when they meet the next incoming wave, the resulting wave front causes the armour to fracture.

High explosive. See chemical energy.

High Explosive Anti-Tank (HEAT) or Hollow Charge Warhead. The HEAT warhead is not velocity dependent. In order to achieve penetration, the limited amount of explosive is shaped into an inverted, rearward-facing cone lined with a metal such as copper or some other ductile material. When the charge is detonated by a nose fuze, a jet of high energy gas and vaporised metal is projected forward at speeds, typically, of 6,000 m per second. This plasma jet acts like a cutting torch.

Hit probability. The probability that a round will hit a target, usually expressed as a percentage or a decimal value between zero and one.

Horn. A projection from the top of the track link to engage the sides of the road wheels.

Horstman suspension. See bogey.

Hull down position. A fire position for a tank where the barrel and upper part of the turret is visible from the front i.e. everything from the 'hull down' is protected behind cover.

Hydrogas. A type of suspension unit in which the force from the wheel is transmitted by hydraulic pressure to compress a gas and so provide suspension springing.

Hydrokinetic (pump or motor). A device pumping or driven by an incompressible fluid (oil) wherein the pressure changes are small and the flow rate is large.

Hydrostatic (pump or motor). A device pumping or driven by high pressure incompressible fluid (oil) wherein the pressure changes are large and the flow rate is small.

Hyperbar. A form of advanced turbocharging in which the turbo is also coupled mechanically to the engine.

Hypergolic bipropellant. A type of liquid propellant used in a liquid propellant gun, consisting of a fuel and an oxidiser which ignite spontaneously when mixed.

Idler wheel. A single wheel, one for each track, at the opposite end of the vehicle to the sprocket, over which the track is guided. The idler wheel does not transmit power to the track. See also sprocket.

Image enhancement. The use of a computer to improve the definition of an electronically generated image.

Image intensification. A technique to achieve vision at night in which low levels of available light are amplified electronically to give an image.

Infra-red. Infra-red radiation lies just beyond the visible spectrum and is invisible to the naked eye.

Jitter. See HEAT shimmer.

Joule-Thompson minicooler. A cryogenic device, in which air from an external supply is expanded through an orifice to produce a refrigerating medium.

Jump. Jump is the small vertical movement of a gun muzzle, which occurs when a gun is fired. See Throw off.

Kinetic energy ammunition. A nature of ammunition where the penetrative power is generated by mass (M) and velocity (V) according to the formula ($\frac{1}{2}MV^2$).

Knocked out or K Kill. The term 'knocked out' is used to describe a tank which is no longer functional in any respect. The ideal is to achieve a K Kill with the first round.

L/C ratio. The steering ratio or L/C ratio is the relationship between the length of track in contact with the ground, L, and the distance between the track centres, C. For a tracked vehicle, the ratio should be kept as near as possible and certainly no higher than 1.8. If lower than 1.5, the tracked vehicle will be unstable in the turns and if over 1.8. will be difficult to turn.

Laser. A device which produces an intensely bright narrow beam of coherent light which can be used to establish target range.

Laser Sensor Damage Weapons. A laser used to knock out the sensors on a tank, including the human eye.

Length/diameter ratio or L/D ratio. The ratio of length to diameter, sometimes called the 'slenderness' ratio. It applies both to spin and fin stabilised ammunition but is usually used to describe the length to diameter ratio of a long rod penetrator. A ratio over about 20:1 is classified as a long rod and must be fin, not spin stabilised. It is difficult to spin stabilise penetrators with an L/D ratio over about 7:1.

Light infantry. Infantry lightly equipped and trained for mountainous or jungle operations or for special tasks such as rear area security. Can also be used to reinforce armoured or mechanised infantry.

Light transmission. The percentage of incoming light which passes through an optical sight to the operator's eyes.

Line of sight. An imaginary line from the aiming mark of a sight to the target.

Liquid propellant gun. See Chapter 2. A conventional chemical gun employing a liquid propellant instead of the more common solid propellant.

Live axle. A beam axle containing the driveshafts and differential.

Low recoil. A type of recoil mechanism which enables a high velocity gun to be fitted to a relatively lightweight vehicle.

Lug (track). A projection of the tyre tread to provide traction in cohesive soils.

Lux. Lumens per square metre (a measure of light).

Male tank. First World War Mark 1 tank fitted with two 6-pounder guns. The term had no significance other than to distinguish this tank from a Female, a Mark 1 fitted with machine guns only.

Mantlet. The area around the gun aperture in the front of a tank turret.

MBT. Main battle tank.

Mean point of impact (MPI). When a number of rounds are fired at a target they will form a pattern. The centre of the pattern, calculated arithmetically, is the MPI.

Mechanised infantry. In the main, mechanised infantry are heavy infantry equipped, trained and organised to operate with both tanks and on their own.

Metadyne. An electro-mechanical amplifier, consisting of a coupled motor and generator.

Metalled (road). A road surface prepared for use by typical wheeled vehicles (concrete or tarmac).

Micron. A measurement of length, equal to one millionth of a metre.

Mil. An angular measurement, equal to one 6400th of a circumference. One degree = 17.777 mils.

Mission reliability. The probability of completing a mission, a sortie or an operation without disruption stemming from a failure within the system.

Miznay Schardin effect. An anti-armour technique using chemical energy to project a self-forming fragment at the target. Not particularly useful in guns but has been used in mines and more recently in a sub-munition for top attack.

Military Load Classification (MLC). A NATO agreed measurement of a vehicle's weight, to assess it's suitability to cross bridges. MLC is calculated from a number of parameters including track length, ground pressure and is not solely a function of the weight of a vehicle.

Mobility or M Kill. An M kill is achieved if a tank is incapable of exercising controlled movement on the battlefield.

Monocular sight. An optical system with a single objective lens and a single eyepiece.

Muzzle Bore Sight. An optical device which fits in the muzzle of a gun and is used initially to align the bore of the barrel to the tank sighting system.

Muzzle Reference System. An on-board alignment system to check and adjust gun to sight alignment during vehicle operations.

Nano Second. $\frac{1}{1,000,000,000}$ of a second.

Nominal Ground Pressure (NGP). NGP is found by dividing the all-up weight of the vehicle by the area of track in contact with the ground. It is a measure of a vehicle's ability to negotiate different types of going (ground conditions). In general terms the lower the NGP, the better a given vehicle's ability to negotiate soft going. For example, a tracked vehicle which is required to perform in snow has to have very low ground pressure.

Ninety-five percentile man. Dimensions which encompass 95% of the adult male population. The details need to be known by the tank designer so that he can determine what internal space is needed for the crew.

Non-hypergolic bipropellant. Two separate liquids used in a liquid propellant gun. One liquid is the fuel and the other is the oxidiser, but being non-hypergolic they need an igniter to initiate combustion.

Non-hypergolic monopropellant. A type of fuel used in a liquid propellant gun

which contains its own fuel and oxidiser in the same liquid but needs an igniter to initiate combustion.
Nuclear hard. Optical and electronic components which are resistant to the effects of nuclear radiation are described as 'nuclear hard'.
Objective lens. The lens through which light enters a sight.
Optronics. A description of the technology used when both optical and electronics are used in one equipment, for example, in modern day and all-weather sights.
Oscillating turret. The oscillating turret is a two-piece turret where the bottom half allows a 6400 mils rotation on a conventional turret ring but the upper half is mounted on trunnions at either side. The gun is fixed in the upper part of the turret and gun elevation and depression is obtained by tilting the whole of the upper part of the turret. See Fig. 6.4.
Overhead top attack. A method of attack in which sub-munitions are fired against the top of the tank from an overflying missile or aircraft.
Overmatch. In order to be successfully defeated, a target must be penetrated with a high degree of overmatch i.e. the penetrator must be capable of defeating more, and preferably far more, than the thickest armour of the tank.
Over/under steer. Over or under steer occurs when a vehicle corners with a greater or smaller slip angle at the rear tyres than at the front.
Pad. Hard rubber insert on the underside of a track fitted in order to protect the road surfaces. As a general rule, rubber track pads give worse performance across country when compared to the all-steel track.
Panoramic sight. A panoramic sight can be rotated to enable an operator to observe the scene throughout an azimuth angle of 6400 mils.
Parallax error. A gun-to-sight error which arises from the physical separation of the gun bore and the line of sight. Modern computer systems can compensate for this permanent offset.
Passenger or P Kill. P Kill applies to armoured personnel carriers when at least 40% of the personnel inside have been rendered incapable of performing their role.
Passive suspension. A passive suspension is composed of components whose characteristics remain fixed.
Passive system. A passive observation or target ranging system (such as an II sight or an optical rangefinder) operates without producing an output detectable by the enemy.
Periscope. A sight in which the objective lens is at a different height to the eyepiece(s), usually above. See also Telescope.
Phosphor. A material which produces photons of light when struck by electrons.
Photocathode. A sensitive material which produces electrons when struck by photons of light.
Photodiode. A light sensitive semiconductor material which conducts a varying electrical current according to the amount of light falling on it.
Photon. A quantity of light energy.
Piles. Layers of the carcass of a pneumatic tyres composed of uni-directional cords in a rubber matrix.
Power train. The complete installation, with its auxiliaries, for propelling a land vehicle.

Profile (tyre). See also aspect ratio.
Pyrophoric. Pyrophoric material emits sparks when struck.
Radial ply. A tyre whose full width piles cross the circumference at an angle substantially equal to 90 degrees. Belting piles are added around the circumference.
Rail gauge. See TZ gauge.
Railgun. A colloquial expression used to refer to the type of gun employing electromagnetic propulsion instead of chemical.
Range. It is always difficult to be specific about long, medium or short ranges but as a rough guide for tank engagements, short is defined as 0-1000 m, medium as 1000–2000 m and 2000–4000 m as long range.
Range table. A table giving gun elevation angles for different sets of conditions, such as target range, air temperature, etc.
Ranging machine-gun. A machine-gun, mounted coaxially with the main armament and used to establish the range to a target.
Raster scan. An electronic method of building up an image by scanning across it in parallel sweeps.
Regenerative liquid propellant gun. The principle of operation is that the pressure generated by the combustion process acts on a piston which has a number of injectors. More propellant is fed into the chamber as combustion is in process.
Resolution. The ability of an optical system to distinguish the detail of an image.
Resonance. This occurs when the frequency of excitation from the ground coincides with the natural frequency of the vehicle on its springs.
Reverse Stirling-cycle engine. A closed cycle cooling device which operates by compressing air and then allowing it to expand to create a refrigerating medium.
Reversionary mode. A back-up method of operation, brought into use when the primary mode fails.
Ride. The motion of the vehicle associated with the pitch and bounce accelerations.
Road wheels. The wheels bearing the weight of a land vehicle onto the ground or its own tracks.
Rolled Homogeneous Armour (RHA). In order to achieve the best possible strength, it is essential to have armour plate with the same hardness and structure throughout. The production of armour plate involves a rolling process to bring it to the correct thickness and to induce some desirable metallurgical properties. The expression RHA is used as a measure of the ability of a penetrator to defeat armour. Usually measured in millimetres, RHA can be used to assess one type of armour against another i.e. spaced armour and monoblock (solid) armour.
Run-flat. A pneumatic tyre capable of continuing to function despite the release of air pressure following a puncture.
Scavenge blower. A device for pushing air or air-fuel mixture into a two-stroke engine. A two-stroke engine does not have a separate induction stroke, as does a four-stroke.
Secondary weapons. A tank needs a weapon of smaller calibre in order to conserve main armament ammunition. Usually machine guns of about 7.62 mm or 12.7 mm (0.5 in) are fitted either coaxially (alongside the main gun) or at the commander's station.

Self-entrenching device. A small dozer blade attached to the front of an armoured vehicle to enable the vehicle to dig itself in, in order to give better protection.

Sensor. Any device which measures the value of a parameter, as an input to a system.

Shear stress. Stress, tending to cause adjacent layers of material to slide over each other.

Shillelagh missile. A American 152 mm calibre HEAT missile fired from the Sheridan reconnaissance vehicle. The vehicle is now no longer in service.

Shock absorber. A damper, acting in response to an impulse, which reduces severe bump to lessen the chance of bump-stop contact.

Shock action. The ability of armour to concentrate firepower by the use of mobility and so achieve success through surprise.

Shot peening. Surface treatment for torsion, whereby impact of small steel balls induces compressive stress in the metal.

Sight offsets. The horizontal and vertical distances between the axis of the main armament and the line of sight.

Sight picture. This is the image retained by the gunner in his mind's eye of the fall of shot on the ground in relation to the sight. By retaining the correct sight picture, a gunner is able to carry out a correction to adjust fire from the fall of shot.

Signal to noise ratio. The ratio between the signal of interest and any naturally occurring signal in the system.

Silent watch. In silent watch, a vehicle will operate on batteries only, so that no tell-tale engine or generator noise will give away it's location.

Single Shot Kill Probability (SSKP). The chance of defeating a tank with one shot depends not only on the chance of hitting it but of penetrating the armour. By multiplying accuracy and penetration together, a figure called SSKP is obtained.

Slip angle. The angle between the plane of the tyre and the direction it is moving over the road.

Slip ring (pneumatic). A sealed chamber to allow the transfer of air from a fixed axle to a rotating wheel.

Soft skinned. A general description applied to any unarmoured vehicle.

Specially Equipped Version (SEV). An SEV is a standard vehicle, such as the infantry section carrier, which is fitted with a kit to allow it to perform a special function such as an ambulance, command post etc. See also Variant.

Sprocket. A simple wheel, one for each track, which transmits power from the transmission to the track.

Stabilisation. The ability of the fire control system to keep the barrel level irrespective of the ground conditions or whether the tank is turning. Gun stabilisation does NOT keep the gun locked onto the target and therefore the gunner has to use his controls to feed a demand (left, right, up and down) into the fire control system.

Stadiametric ranging. A method of ranging in which markings in the field of view are compared with an assumed standard dimension of the target—for example vehicle height.

Stand-off distance. A HEAT warhead must be initiated at the correct distance from the armour to be penetrated. If not, then penetration will be reduced.

Staring array. An array of thermal imaging detectors which observes a scene without the need for scanning.

Stealth technology. A term used to describe any technique which reduces the signature (radar, thermal, acoustic and visual) of an equipment.

Stiction. The force between two static objects which opposes their relative movement.

Strategic mobility. Strategic mobility is the ability to move forces to a theatre of operations.

Stretch potential. The ability of an equipment to be upgraded in service with new technology.

Strut suspension. Independent suspension with the wheel carried at the lower end of a telescopic strut, whose top is pivoted on the hull and which is located transversely by a single link.

Subtense. The size of a target can be expressed as the angle it presents at the gun. This angle is called target subtense.

Swept volume. The volume of the cylinder traversed by the piston as it moves from one end of its travel (stroke) to the other. In multi-cylinder engines, the swept volume is the sum of the separate volumes of the individual cylinders.

Suspension. A group of components locating and transmitting force between road-wheel and hull.

Tactical mobility. Tactical mobility is the ability to move within a theatre of operations.

Tangent elevation. The angular displacement of a gun in elevation when it moves to its firing position.

Telescope. A sight in which the objective lens and the eyepiece are, approximately, at the same height. See also Periscope.

Test bed. An installation for assessing the performance of a complete vehicle or of its individual automotive components e.g. its engine and gearbox.

Thermal blanket. An insulating blanket placed around a gun barrel to prevent it distorting as a result of uneven heating or cooling.

Thermal imaging. The use of infra-red technology to produce a picture of the heat signature of an object against its background.

Thermo-electric cooling. A method of cooling thermal imaging detectors using the Peltier Effect, in which current flowing through two junctions made of dissimilar metals causes one junction to cool and one to heat up.

Throw-off. Throw-off is the small azimuth movement of a gun muzzle, which occurs when a gun is fired. See also Jump.

Toe-in/out. The relative setting of the two wheels on either side of a vehicle such that they are no longer parallel to one another.

Top attack. A form of attack against the more vulnerable top of an armoured vehicle.

Top mirror. The upper element of a periscopic sight. In stabilised sights it is this component which is connected to the gyroscopes and which can be directed independently of the sight body.

Top roller. A small wheel supporting the top run of the track.

Torsion bar/tube. A solid or hollow steel bar whose twist in response to torque provides springing.

Tracks. The continuous, flexible or hinged path which a track laying vehicle lays down on the ground in front of itself to spread its weight and to secure adhesion, and picks up again behind itself.
Track up. A tank in a position where it presents a full sized target to attacking fire is everything from the 'track up' is visible.
Transmission. See drive line.
Trunnion tilt. The angle of the gun trunnions when the turret is on a side slope.
Turbine. A machine for expanding high pressure gas and extracting power from it.
Turret down position. A position of observation for a tank where only the commander's sight is above the direct line of sight is everything else is 'turret down'.
TZ gauge. The rail loading gauge used on the Continent. To move without limitation on most rail lines in Europe, a tank must come within the limits of the TZ Gauge.
Ultra Light Armoured Vehicles (ULAV). Though there is no NATO or industrial standard, for the purposes of this book ULAVs are defined as vehicles under 5 tonnes.
Unity vision. Vision through a sight having $\times 1$ magnification.
Unsprung mass. Part of a vehicle not carried by suspension spring.
Value tree. A Value Tree is a depiction of the relative value that is attached to the various capabilities of a particular vehicle.
Valve timing. The four points in the cycle of a four-stroke engine at which the valves start to open and finish closing.
Variant. A variant is a vehicle whose characteristics are so different from those of the basic vehicle on which its design is based that the chassis is itself different.
Virtual image. The reflected image seen in a mirror.
Wave length. The distance between successive crests on undulating ground.
Weapon system. This collective name encompasses the components used to acquire the target, establish the correct gun firing position and bring the gun to that position.
Wheel hop. The resonant bounce of a wheel on its tyre.
Wheel travel. The vertical movement of a wheel between rebound and bump positions.
Wishbone suspension. Independent suspension with wheel located by two transverse links (often resembling the breastbone of a bird).

Acronyms

AFV	Armoured Fighting Vehicle
AMRS	Automatic Muzzle Reference System
APC	Armoured Personnel Carrier
APDS	Armour Piercing Discarding Sabot
APFSDS	Armour Piercing Fin Stabilised Discarding Sabot
ATDT	Automatic Target Detection and Tracking
ATGW	Anti-Tank Guided Weapon
BITE	Built-In Test Equipment

BMS	Battlefield Management System
CCD	Charged-Couple Device
CCIR	Closed Circuit Infra-Red
CE	Chemical Energy
CET	Combat Engineer Tractor
CI	Compression Ignition
CMT	Cadmium Mercury Telluride
CO2	Carbon Dioxide
CR	Compression Ratio
CVR(T)	Combat Vehicle Reconnaissance (Tracked)
CVT	Continuously Variable Transmission
CW	Continuous Wave
DAS	Defensive Aids Suite
DC	Direct Current
EM	Electromagnetic
ERA	Explosive Reactive Armour
ESR	Electroslag Refined
'F'	Firepower (Kill)
FDP	Fatique Decreased Proficiency
FOV	Field of View
HE	High Explosive
HEAT	High Explosive Anti-Tank
HEP	High Explosive Plastic (US term for HESH)
HESH	High Explosive Squash Head
HOL	High Order Language
HTP	High Test Peroxode
II	Image Intensifier
IR	Infra-Red
JT	Joule-Thompson
'K'	Knocked Out (Kill)
KE	Kinetic Energy
L/D	Length/Diameter ratio
Laser	Light Amplification by Stimulated Emission of Radiation
LAUV	Light Armoured Utility Vehicle
LAV	Light Armoured Vehicle
LLTV	Low Light Television
LOS	Line of Sight
LP	Liquid Propellant
LRU	Line Replacement Unit
'M'	Mobility (Kill)
MBS	Muzzle Bore Sight
MBT	Main Battle Tank
MMP	Mean Maximum Pressure
MPI	Mean Point of Impact
MRS	Muzzle Reference System
NBC	Nuclear, Biological and Chemical
Nd YAG	Neodymium Yttrium Aluminium Garnet

NGP	Nominal Ground Pressure
OTA	Overhead Top Attack
'P'	Passenger (Kill)
PROMS	Programmable Read Only
RAM-D	Reliability, Availability, Maintainability and Durability
RAMS	Random Access Memory
RARDE	Royal Armament Research and Development Establishment
RF	Run-Flat
RHA	Rolled Homogeneous Armour
RMG	Ranging Machine Gun
ROC	Required Operational Capability
RTC	Required Technical Characteristics
SD	Standard Deviation
SEV	Specially Equipped Version
SI	Spark Ignition
SOR	Statement of Requirement
SP	Self-Propelled
SPRITE	Signal Processing in the Element
SSKP	Single Shot Kill Probability
SSPA	Solid State Power Amplifier
TE	Tangent Elevation
TI	Thermal Image
TOGS	Thermal Observation and Gunnery System
TS	Technical Specification
ULAV	Ultra-Light Armoured Vehicle

Index

TABLE 1 *Mass, Weight and Power*

Vehicle	Mass (*t*)	Weight (kN)	(kPa)	NGP (lb/sq in)	Engine (kW)	Power (bhp)
Tanks						
Centurion Mk 13	51.8	508	91.6	13.3	485	690
Chieftain Mk 2	52.0	510	88.2	12.8	485	650
Chieftain Mk 5	55.0	539	93.5	13.6	537	720
Challenger	62	605	98.0	14.2	895	1200
Vickers Mk 3	38.4	379	87.0	12.4	485	676
M1 A1	56.0	548	90.4	13.1	1120	1500
M60 A1	48	471	76.5	11.1	560	750
M60 A2	51.0	500	74.4	10.8	560	750
Leopard 1	40.1	393	84.0	12.2	610	818
Leopard 2	55.0	540	83.0	12.1	1100	1475
T 55	36.6	359	79.0	11.5	433	580
T 62	37.0	363	79.0	11.5	433	580
T 72	41.0	404	87.0	12.6	582	780
T 10M	50.8	489	69.0	10.0	522	700
AMX 30	36.0	353	76.0	11.2	537	720
Leclerc	54(?)	530(?)	—	—	1120	1500
Merkava	56.0	548	—	—	671	900
S tank	37.6	369	88.0	12.8	K60:179 Tur:365	240 490
Reconnaissance Vehicles						
Scorpion	7.9	77	34.5	5.0	145	195
Sheridan	15.8	155	47.2	6.8	224	300
M 2 (Cav)						
PT 76	14.0	137	47.0	6.8	179	240
Infantry Armoured Vehicles						
FV 432	15.0	147	77.0	11.2	179	240
M 113	11.0	107	51.6	7.5	160	215
M 2						
Marder (FGR)	28.7	281	78.0	11.3	441	590
BMP	14.0	137	50.0	7.1	210	280
PBV 302 (Sweden)	13.5	132	58.0	8.4	202	270
Warrior	25.4	268	71.0	10.4	410	550